OECD/G20 Base Erosion and Profit Shifting Project

Making Dispute Resolution Mechanisms More Effective – Consolidated Information on Mutual Agreement Procedures 2023

OECD

BETTER POLICIES FOR BETTER LIVES

Please cite this publication as:
OECD (2023), *Making Dispute Resolution Mechanisms More Effective – Consolidated Information on Mutual Agreement Procedures 2023*, OECD/G20 Base Erosion and Profit Shifting Project, OECD Publishing, Paris, https://doi.org/10.1787/69b789e7-en.

ISBN 978-92-64-64100-6 (print)
ISBN 978-92-64-84089-8 (PDF)
ISBN 978-92-64-91081-2 (HTML)
ISBN 978-92-64-87683-5 (epub)

OECD/G20 Base Erosion and Profit Shifting Project
ISSN 2313-2604 (print)
ISSN 2313-2612 (online)

Photo credits: Cover © sdecoret/Shutterstock.com.

Corrigenda to OECD publications may be found at: https://www.oecd.org/en/publications/support/corrigenda.html.

Foreword

Digitalisation and globalisation have had a profound impact on economies and the lives of people around the world, and this impact has only accelerated in the 21st century. These changes have brought with them challenges to the rules for taxing international business income, which have prevailed for more than a hundred years and created opportunities for base erosion and profit shifting (BEPS), requiring bold moves by policy makers to restore confidence in the system and ensure that profits are taxed where economic activities take place and value is created.

In 2013, the OECD ramped up efforts to address these challenges in response to growing public and political concerns about tax avoidance by large multinationals. The OECD and G20 countries joined forces and developed an Action Plan to address BEPS in September 2013. The Action Plan identified 15 actions aimed at introducing coherence in the domestic rules that affect cross-border activities, reinforcing substance requirements in the existing international standards, and improving transparency as well as certainty.

After two years of work, measures in response to the 15 actions, including those published in an interim form in 2014, were consolidated into a comprehensive package and delivered to G20 Leaders in November 2015. The BEPS package represents the first substantial renovation of the international tax rules in almost a century. As the BEPS measures are implemented, it is expected that profits will be reported where the economic activities that generate them are carried out and where value is created. BEPS planning strategies that rely on outdated rules or on poorly co-ordinated domestic measures will be rendered ineffective.

OECD and G20 countries also agreed to continue to work together to ensure a consistent and coordinated implementation of the BEPS recommendations and to make the project more inclusive. As a result, they created the OECD/G20 Inclusive Framework on BEPS (Inclusive Framework), bringing all interested and committed countries and jurisdictions on an equal footing in the Committee on Fiscal Affairs and its subsidiary bodies. With over 140 members, the Inclusive Framework monitors and peer reviews the implementation of the minimum standards and is completing the work on standard setting to address BEPS issues. In addition to its members, other international organisations and regional tax bodies are involved in the work of the Inclusive Framework, which also consults business and the civil society on its different work streams.

Although implementation of the BEPS package is dramatically changing the international tax landscape and improving the fairness of tax systems, one of the key outstanding BEPS issues – to address the tax challenges arising from the digitalisation of the economy – remained unresolved. In a major step forward on 8 October 2021, over 135 Inclusive Framework members, representing more than 95% of global GDP, joined a two-pillar solution to reform the international taxation rules and ensure that multinational enterprises pay a fair share of tax wherever they operate and generate profits in today's digitalised and globalised world economy.

Acknowledgements

The Making Dispute Resolution Mechanisms More Effective – Consolidated Information on Mutual Agreement Procedures (CIM) has been produced by the Organisation for Economic Co-operation and Development (OECD)'s Centre for Tax Policy and Administration (CTPA) under the auspices of the Forum on Tax Administration's Mutual Agreement Procedure Forum of the Committee on Fiscal Affairs.

The report was prepared by Mr Pierre-Louis Chenu, Mr Jonathan Fraser, Mr Sriram Govind, and Ms Aya Okimoto, all part of the Tax Certainty Unit, under the supervision of Ms Sandra Knaepen, Co-Head of the Tax Certainty Unit and Acting Head of Tax Administration and VAT (TAV) Division within CTPA.

The authors would like to thank colleagues in the OECD for their invaluable comments and practical support in finalising the publication, including Ms Sonia Nicolas, Ms Zoe Wellenkamp, Ms Madeleine Kotfitzki, and Mr Alasdair Baker of the TAV, as well as the CTPA Communications team. The authors would also like to thank the FTA MAP Forum delegates for their contributions to the collected information.

Table of contents

Abbreviations and Acronyms

BEPS	Base Erosion and Profit Shifting
DTT	
FTA	Forum on Tax Administration
FTE	
MAP	Mutual Agreement Procedure
MLI	Multilateral Instrument
OECD	Organisation for Economic Co-operation and Development

Executive Summary

Recognising that the actions to counter Base Erosion and Profit Shifting ("**BEPS**") must be complemented with actions that ensure certainty for taxpayers, BEPS Action 14 calls for effective dispute resolution mechanisms. The report on Action 14: Making Dispute Resolution Mechanisms More Effective[1] (OECD, 2015) includes a minimum standard that all members of the Inclusive Framework on BEPS ("**Inclusive Framework Members**") have committed to implement, which ensures that these Inclusive Framework Members resolve treaty-related disputes in a timely, effective and efficient manner, particularly through the Mutual Agreement Procedure ("**MAP**").

Pursuant to implementing the Action 14 minimum standard, Inclusive Framework Members have now published an unprecedented amount of information on their MAP programmes. This includes: (i) rules, guidelines and procedures to access and use MAP, made available to taxpayers usually through the website of their ministry of finance or tax administration ; (ii) a country MAP profile pursuant to an agreed template on a shared public platform available on the OECD website, ; (iii) MAP statistics, pursuant to an agreed reporting framework[2], available on the OECD website; and (iv) peer review reports under the Action 14 minimum standard that provide information on how the Inclusive Framework Member has implemented the Action 14 minimum standard , also available on the OECD website. However, previously this information was only available in different places, so taxpayers and MAP competent authorities had to seek out this information for each Inclusive Framework Member separately.

To make this information more accessible to all stakeholders, the FTA MAP Forum agreed in December 2022 to summarise and consolidate published information concerning MAP for all Inclusive Framework Members in a single publication, titled Consolidated Information on Mutual Agreement Procedures ("**Report**"). The objective behind the Report is to give a concise picture of each Inclusive Framework Member's MAP programme, to further highlight the ongoing efforts in the FTA MAP Forum to make the MAP more timely, effective and efficient.

This Report sets out for each Inclusive Framework Member: (i) recent developments concerning MAP; (ii) a brief overview of its MAP programme, including its tax treaty network, the organisation of its competent authority, and links to its MAP guidance and MAP profile; and (iii) a summary of its MAP Statistics, with the exception of jurisdictions that do not have tax treaties that are in force containing any provisions on the allocation of taxing rights.[3] Where information in any category has not been provided by the jurisdiction concerned, this is noted in the relevant section. The overview of each jurisdiction's MAP Statistics contained in this Report presents the data that was submitted by that jurisdiction for publication on the OECD website each year and does not take into account any adjustments made in the course of the peer reviews under Action 14 or otherwise following publication of that year's MAP Statistics

---

1 Available at www.oecd.org/tax/making-dispute-resolution-mechanisms-more-effective-action-14-2015-final-report9789264241633-en.htm.

2 Available at https://www.oecd.org/tax/beps/beps-action-14-on-more-effective-dispute-resolution-peer-review-documents.pdf

3 Please note that this report only includes information and developments until 15 August 2023 with respect to each jurisdiction.

1 Individual country reports

Albania

Recent developments relating to MAP in Albania prior to 15 August 2023

Developments relating to MAP in the tax treaty network

- Albania did not provide the relevant information.

Other developments relating to MAP

- Albania did not provide the relevant information.

Latest Action 14 Peer Review report

Albania is yet to be peer reviewed under Action 14.

Tax treaty network of Albania

- 46 treaties, applicable to 46 jurisdictions (covering all treaties signed, although not necessarily in force)
- status of MLI: in force.

Table 1. State of play of Albania's tax treaty network

Treaties in line with the Action 14 Minimum Standard following MLI impact	Treaties where actions are ongoing to make them in line with the Action 14 Minimum Standard	Following impact/actions, remaining treaties that are not in line with Action 14 Minimum Standard
43	No information	No information

Source: OECD

Albania's MAP programme

Organisation of competent authority function

- three persons:
  - one head of unit
  - two persons working on MAP cases.
- contact persons for MAP requests:
  - General Directory of Taxation
    Street; "Gjin Bue Shpata", Tirana, Albania
    www.tatime.gov.al
    e-mail; ilda.koja@tatime.gov.al
    phone: +355693012113.

Figure 1. Competent Authority Organisational Structure

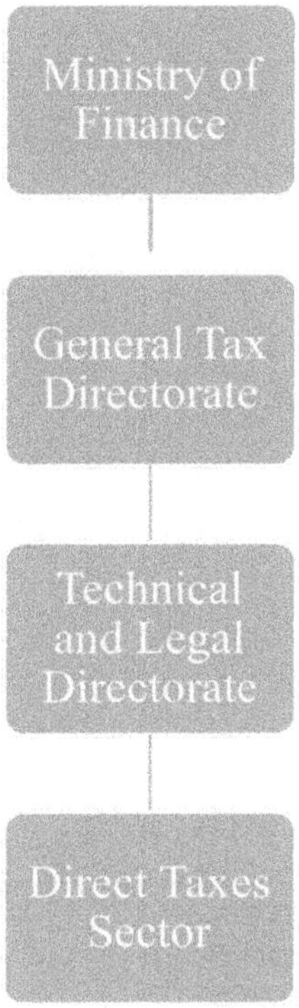

Table 2. Guidance on the MAP process

MAP guidance	No MAP guidance published	
MAP profile	23 May 2023	https://www.oecd.org/tax/dispute/albania-dispute-resolution-profile.pdf

Overview of Albania's MAP Statistics for 2022

Please refer to https://www.oecd.org/tax/dispute/map-statistics-albania.pdf for details with respect to Albania's MAP Statistics.

Cases closed in 2022

No MAP cases were closed by Albania in 2022.

Figure 2. Evolution of Albania's MAP caseload (2019-22)

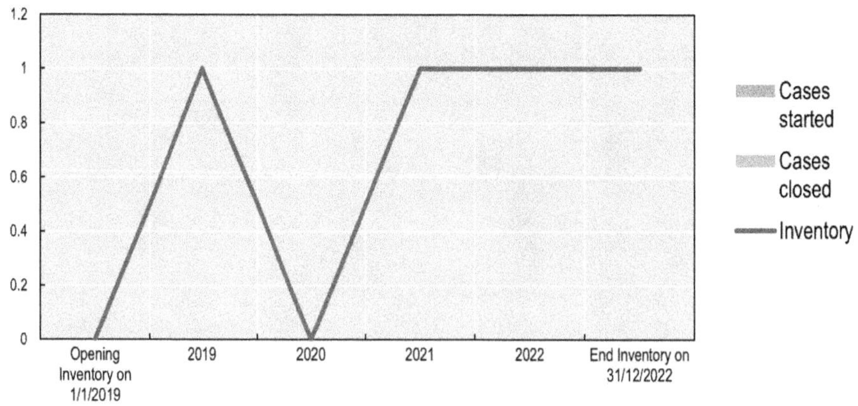

Source: OECD

Table 3. Overview of Albania's MAP caseload for 2022

Inventory for year 2022	Opening Inventory 1/1/2022	Cases started	Cases Closed	End Inventory 31/12/2022
Attribution/allocation cases	0	0	0	0
Other cases	1	0	0	1
Total	1	0	0	1

Source: OECD

Table 4. Albania's average time to resolve MAP cases in 2022

Cases resolved in year 2022	Pre-2019 cases		Post-2018 cases		All	
	Number of cases	**Average time**	**Number of cases**	**Average time** **Start to End**	**Number of cases**	**Average time**
Attribution / Allocation cases	0	N/A	0	N/A	0	N/A
Other cases	0	N/A	0	N/A	0	N/A
All cases	0	N/A	0	N/A	0	N/A

Source: OECD

Andorra

Recent developments relating to MAP in Andorra prior to 15 August 2023

Developments relating to MAP in the tax treaty network

- Andorra did not provide the relevant information.

Other developments relating to MAP

- Andorra did not provide the relevant information.

Latest Action 14 Peer Review report

14 April 2022 - https://doi.org/10.1787/dc816eb2-en

Tax treaty network of Andorra

- 13 treaties, applicable to 13 jurisdictions (covering all treaties signed, although not necessarily in force)
- status of MLI: in force.

Table 1. State of play of Andorra's tax treaty network

Treaties in line with the Action 14 Minimum Standard following MLI impact	Treaties where actions are ongoing to make them in line with the Action 14 Minimum Standard	Following impact/actions, remaining treaties that are not in line with Action 14 Minimum Standard
13	0	0

Source: OECD

Andorra's MAP programme

Organisation of competent authority function

- five persons
- contact persons for MAP requests:
  - Marc Ballestà Alias, Secretary of State for International Financial Matters

    Phone: (+376) 875 606 |E-mail: marcballesta@govern.ad

    Carlos FERREIRA GONZÁLEZ, General director of the tax administration

    Phone: (+376) 879 900|E-mail: carlos_ferreiragonzalez@govern.ad

    Address: C. Prat de la Creu, 62-64 - Edif. Administratiu | AD500 Andorra la Vella (Principality of Andorra) |Fax (+376) 875 695.

Figure 1. Competent Authority Organisational Structure

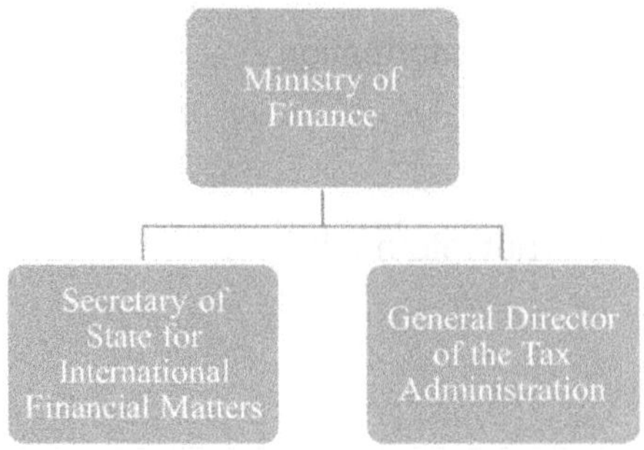

Source: OECD

Table 2. Guidance on the MAP process

MAP guidance	Guidance under development	
MAP profile	17 June 2022	https://www.oecd.org/tax/dispute/andorra-dispute-resolution-profile.pdf

Overview of Andorra's MAP Statistics for 2022

Please refer to https://www.oecd.org/tax/dispute/map-statistics-andorra.pdf for details with respect to Andorra's MAP Statistics.

Cases closed in 2022

No MAP cases were closed by Andorra in 2022.

Figure 2. Evolution of Andorra's MAP caseload (2016-22)

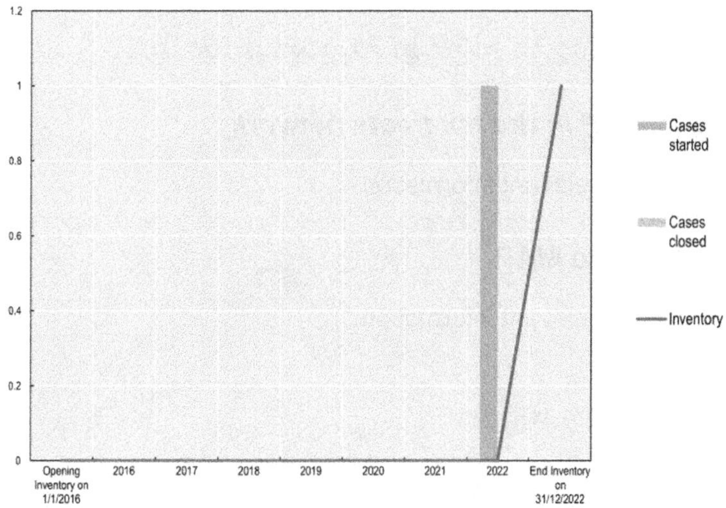

Source: OECD

Table 3. Overview of Andorra's MAP caseload for 2022

Inventory for year 2022	Opening Inventory 1/1/2022	Cases started	Cases Closed	End Inventory 31/12/2022
Attribution/allocation cases	0	1	0	1
Other cases	0	0	0	0
Total	0	1	0	1

Source: OECD

Table 4. Andorra's average time to resolve MAP cases in 2022

Cases resolved in year 2022	Pre-2016 cases		Post-2015 cases		All	
	Number of cases	**Average time**	**Number of cases**	**Average time** **Start to End**	**Number of cases**	**Average time**
Attribution / Allocation cases	0	N/A	0	N/A	0	N/A
Other cases	0	N/A	0	N/A	0	N/A
All cases	0	N/A	0	N/A	0	N/A

Source: OECD

Angola

Recent developments relating to MAP in Angola prior to 15 August 2023

Developments relating to MAP in the tax treaty network

- Angola did not provide the relevant information.

Other developments relating to MAP

- Angola did not provide the relevant information.

Latest Action 14 Peer Review report

- Angola is yet to be peer reviewed under Action 14.

Tax treaty network of Angola

- six treaties, applicable to six jurisdictions (covering all treaties signed, although not necessarily in force).
- status of MLI: not signed.

Table 1. State of play of Angola's tax treaty network

Treaties in line with the Action 14 Minimum Standard following MLI impact	Treaties where actions are ongoing to make them in line with the Action 14 Minimum Standard	Following impact/actions, remaining treaties that are not in line with Action 14 Minimum Standard
4	No information	No information

Source: OECD

Angola's MAP programme

Organisation of competent authority function

- Angola did not provide the relevant information.

Table 2. Guidance on the MAP process

MAP guidance	Angola did not provide the relevant information	
MAP profile	No MAP profile published	

Overview of Angola's MAP Statistics for 2022

Angola did not report any MAP cases in its 2022 MAP Statistics.

Please refer to https://www.oecd.org/tax/dispute/map-statistics-angola.pdf for details with respect to Angola's MAP Statistics.

Anguilla

Recent developments relating to MAP in Anguilla prior to 15 August 2023

Developments relating to MAP in the tax treaty network

- Anguilla did not provide the relevant information.

Other developments relating to MAP

- Anguilla did not provide the relevant information.

Latest Action 14 Peer Review report

Anguilla is yet to be peer reviewed under Action 14.

Tax treaty network of Anguilla

- one treaty, applicable to one jurisdiction (covering all treaties signed, although not necessarily in force)
- status of MLI: not signed.

Table 1. State of play of Anguilla's tax treaty network

Treaties in line with the Action 14 Minimum Standard following MLI impact	Treaties where actions are ongoing to make them in line with the Action 14 Minimum Standard	Following impact/actions, remaining treaties that are not in line with Action 14 Minimum Standard
0	No information	No information

Source: OECD

Anguilla's MAP programme

Organisation of competent authority function

- Anguilla did not provide the relevant information.

Table 2. Guidance on the MAP process

MAP guidance	Anguilla did not provide the relevant information	
MAP profile	No MAP profile published	

Overview of Anguilla's MAP Statistics for 2022

Anguilla did not report any MAP cases in its 2022 MAP Statistics.

Please refer to https://www.oecd.org/tax/dispute/map-statistics-anguilla.pdf for details with respect to Anguilla's MAP Statistics.

Antigua and Barbuda

Recent developments relating to MAP in Antigua and Barbuda prior to 15 August 2023

Developments relating to MAP in the tax treaty network

- No developments were reported

Other developments relating to MAP

- No developments were reported

Latest Action 14 Peer Review report

The stage 1 Simplified Peer Review report of Antigua and Barbuda is expected to be published early 2024

Tax treaty network of Antigua and Barbuda

- four treaties, applicable to 12 jurisdictions (covering all treaties signed, although not necessarily in force
- status of MLI: not signed.

Table 1. State of play of Antigua and Barbuda's tax treaty network

Treaties in line with the Action 14 Minimum Standard following MLI impact	Treaties where actions are ongoing to make them in line with the Action 14 Minimum Standard	Following impact/actions, remaining treaties that are not in line with Action 14 Minimum Standard
1	0	3

Source: OECD

Antigua and Barbuda's MAP programme

Organisation of competent authority function

- four persons working on MAP (all of which work on other tasks as well)
- contact persons for MAP requests:
  - Antigua and Barbuda did not provide the relevant information.

Figure 1. Competent Authority Organisational Structure

Source: OECD

Table 2. Guidance on the MAP process

MAP guidance	No MAP guidance published
MAP profile	No MAP profile published

Source: OECD

Overview of Antigua and Barbuda's MAP Statistics for 2022

Antigua and Barbuda did not report any MAP cases in its 2022 MAP Statistics.

Please refer to https://www.oecd.org/tax/dispute/map-statistics-Antigua_and_Barbuda.pdf for details with respect to Antigua and Barbuda's MAP Statistics.

Argentina

Recent developments relating to MAP in Argentina prior to 15 August 2023

Developments relating to MAP in the tax treaty network

- Argentina did not provide the relevant information.

Other developments relating to MAP

- Argentina did not provide the relevant information.

Latest Action 14 Peer Review report

26 July 2021 - https://doi.org/10.1787/ad982afd-en

Tax treaty network of Argentina

- 26 treaties, applicable to 26 jurisdictions (covering all treaties signed, although not necessarily in force)
- status of MLI: signed.

Table 1. State of play of Argentina's tax treaty network

Treaties in line with the Action 14 Minimum Standard following MLI impact	Treaties where actions are ongoing to make them in line with the Action 14 Minimum Standard	Following impact/actions, remaining treaties that are not in line with Action 14 Minimum Standard
20	No information	No information

Source: OECD

Argentina's MAP programme

Organisation of competent authority function

- three persons
- contact persons for MAP requests:
  - Secretaría de Hacienda, Ministerio de Economía
    Hipólito Yrigoyen 250, of. 921, Buenos Aires, Argentina
    Tel: +54 11 4349 6901.

Figure 1. Competent Authority Organisational Structure

Source: OECD

Table 2. Guidance on the MAP process

MAP guidance	Argentina did not provide the relevant information.	
MAP profile	12 November 2020	https://www.oecd.org/tax/dispute/argentina-dispute-resolution-profile.pdf

Overview of Argentina's MAP Statistics for 2022

Please refer to https://www.oecd.org/tax/dispute/map-statistics-argentina.pdf for details with respect to Argentina's MAP Statistics.

Figure 2. Cases closed in 2022

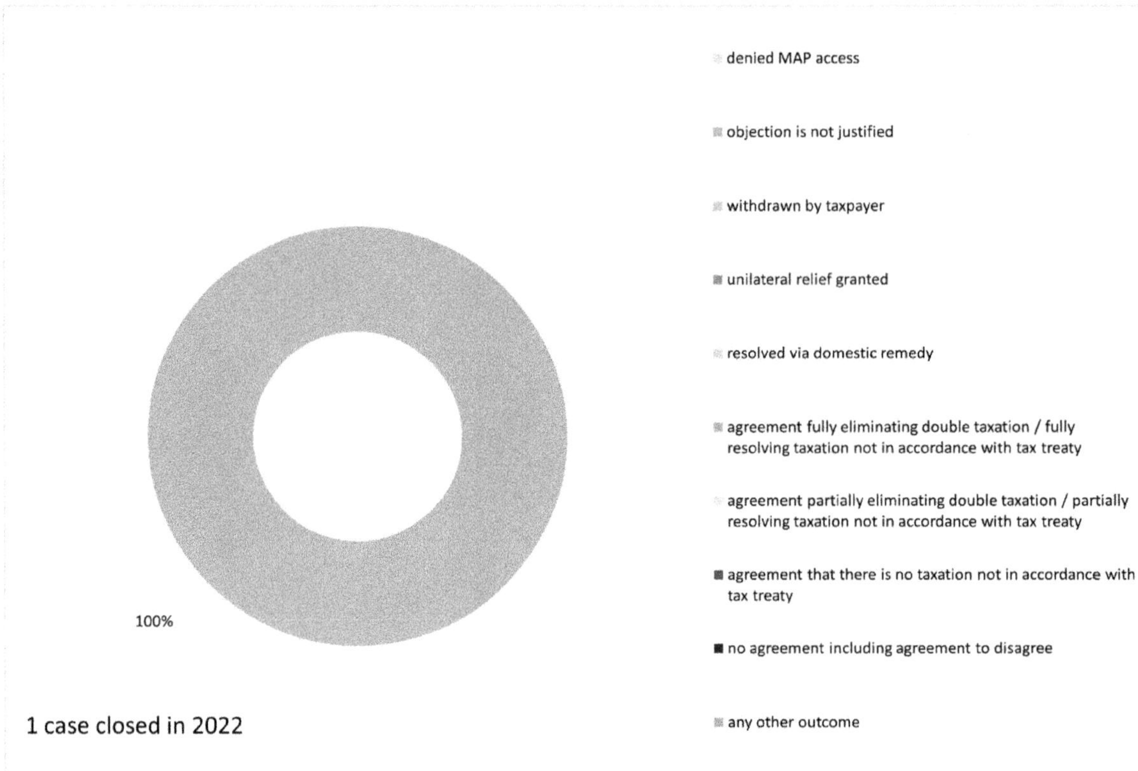

Source: OECD

Figure 3. Evolution of Argentina's MAP caseload (2016-22)

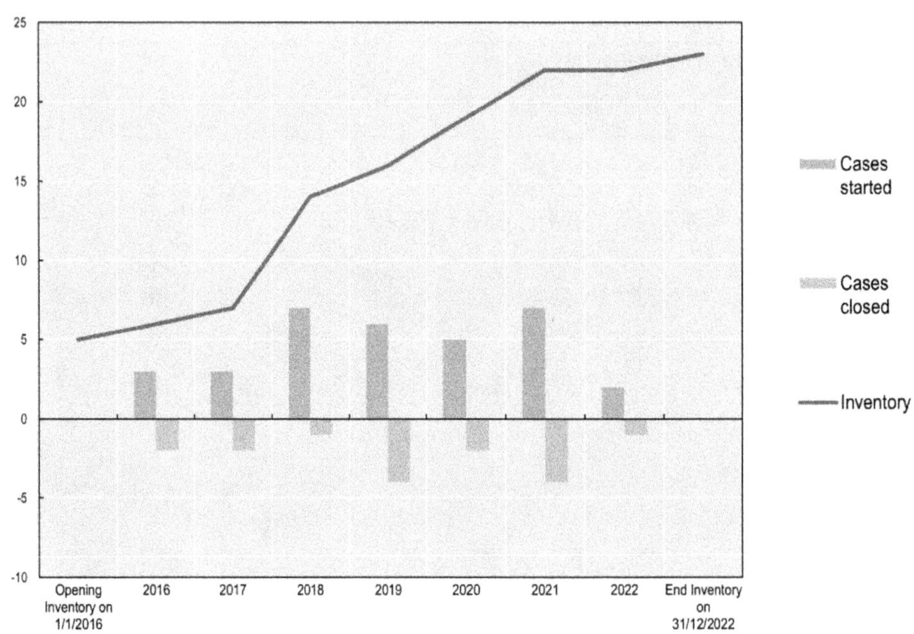

Source: OECD

Table 3. Overview of Argentina's MAP caseload for 2022

Inventory for year 2022	Opening Inventory 1/1/2022	Cases started	Cases Closed	End Inventory 31/12/2022
Attribution/allocation cases	12	0	0	12
Other cases	10	2	1	11
Total	22	2	1	23

Source: OECD

Table 4. Argentina's average time to resolve MAP cases in 2022

Cases resolved in year 2022	Pre-2016 cases		Post-2015 cases		All	
	Number of cases	**Average time**	**Number of cases**	**Average time** **Start to End**	**Number of cases**	**Average time**
Attribution / Allocation cases	0	N/A	0	N/A	0	N/A
Other cases	0	N/A	1	35.90	1	35.90
All cases	0	N/A	1	35.90	1	35.90

Source: OECD

Armenia

Recent developments relating to MAP in Armenia prior to 15 August 2023

Developments relating to MAP in the tax treaty network

- The MLI position of Armenia is in the process of ratification. Regarding its tax treaty network, the double tax treaty with Kyrgyzstan became effective starting from 1 January 2023.

Other developments relating to MAP

- Working on amendments of Government decree No. 1727-N of 10 November 2022 “On establishing the procedure for and terms of settling the disputes on tax issues through the mutual agreement procedure” in order to make it in line with BEPS Action 14 Minimum Standard.

Latest Action 14 Peer Review report

- Armenia is yet to be peer reviewed under Action 14.

Tax treaty network of Armenia

- 51 treaties, applicable to 51 jurisdictions (covering all treaties signed, although not necessarily in force)
- status of MLI: signed, pending ratification.

Table 1. State of play of Armenia's tax treaty network

Treaties in line with the Action 14 Minimum Standard following MLI impact	Treaties where actions are ongoing to make them in line with the Action 14 Minimum Standard	Following impact/actions, remaining treaties that are not in line with Action 14 Minimum Standard
45	6	0

Source: OECD

Armenia's MAP programme

Organisation of competent authority function

- three persons:
  - one head of unit
  - two persons working on MAP (all of which work on other tasks as well).
- contact persons for MAP requests: Armenia did not provide the relevant information.

Figure 1. Competent Authority Organisational Structure

Source: OECD

Table 2. Guidance on the MAP process

MAP guidance	*Government Decree No. 1727-N*, 10 November 2022	http://www.irtek.am/views/act.aspx?aid=118615 The link is in Armenian only.
MAP profile	No MAP profile published	-

Overview of Armenia's MAP Statistics for 2022

Armenia did not report any MAP cases in its 2022 MAP Statistics.

Please refer to https://www.oecd.org/tax/dispute/map-statistics-armenia.pdf for details with respect to Armenia's MAP Statistics.

Aruba

Recent developments relating to MAP in Aruba prior to 15 August 2023

Developments relating to MAP in the tax treaty network

- No developments were reported

Other developments relating to MAP

- No developments were reported

Latest Action 14 Peer Review report

13 September 2022 - https://doi.org/10.1787/ed55fc1a-en

Tax treaty network of Aruba

- six treaties, applicable to nine jurisdictions (covering all treaties signed, although not necessarily in force)
- status of MLI: not signed.

Table 1. State of play of Aruba's tax treaty network

Treaties in line with the Action 14 Minimum Standard following MLI impact	Treaties where actions are ongoing to make them in line with the Action 14 Minimum Standard	Following impact/actions, remaining treaties that are not in line with Action 14 Minimum Standard
1	0	5

Source: OECD

Aruba's MAP programme

Organisation of competent authority function

- Aruba's competent authority currently has no staff.
- contact persons for MAP requests:
  - Coördinatie Bureau Fiscale Zaken (CBFZ),
    Camacuri 2, Oranjestad, Aruba
    telephone number: +297 5227423 ext. 752, 599 and 467
    fax number: +297 5227429
    e-mail address: caa@impuesto.aw.

Figure 1. Competent Authority Organisational Structure

Source: OECD

Table 2. Guidance on the MAP process

MAP guidance	*Mutual Agreement Procedure (MAP)*, May 2020	https://www.impuesto.aw/_flysystem/media/policy_mutual_agreement_procedure_final_08-06-2020.pdf (Section 3 to be referred to for form and content of a MAP request, including information requirements)
MAP profile	27 January 2022	https://www.oecd.org/tax/dispute/aruba-dispute-resolution-profile.pdf

Source: OECD

Overview of Aruba's MAP Statistics for 2022

Aruba did not report any MAP cases in its 2022 MAP Statistics.

Please refer to https://www.oecd.org/tax/dispute/map-statistics-aruba.pdf for details with respect to Aruba's MAP Statistics.

Australia

Recent developments relating to MAP in Australia prior to 15 August 2023

Developments relating to MAP in the tax treaty network

- Australia is conducting ongoing bilateral negotiations with Latvia, Colombia, Slovenia, Estonia, Lithuania, Greece, Luxembourg and Portugal. None of these countries had previously agreed a tax treaty with Australia.
- Australia signed a tax treaty with Iceland in October 2022, which is fully compliant with BEPS Action 14.

Other developments relating to MAP

- Nothing to add currently in terms of updating MAP articles.
- Updated MAP guidance in August 2022.

Latest Action 14 Peer Review report

15 April 2021 - https://doi.org/10.1787/da7fc990-en

Tax treaty network of Australia

- 53 treaties, applicable to 53 jurisdictions (covering all treaties signed, although not necessarily in force)
- status of MLI: in force

Table 1. State of play of Australia's tax treaty network

Treaties in line with the Action 14 Minimum Standard following MLI impact	Treaties where actions are ongoing to make them in line with the Action 14 Minimum Standard	Following impact/actions, remaining treaties that are not in line with Action 14 Minimum Standard
21	0	20

Source: OECD

Australia's MAP programme

Organisation of competent authority function

- 12 persons:
  - one head of unit
  - 12 persons working on MAP cases (all of which work on other tasks as well):
    - of which 10 persons work on attribution/allocation cases and two persons work on other cases.

- contact persons for MAP requests:
  - for attribution/allocation cases: internationalsgatekeeper@ato.gov.au
  - for other cases: internationalsgatekeeper@ato.gov.au.

Figure 1. Competent Authority Organisational Structure

Source: OECD

Table 2. Guidance on the MAP process

MAP guidance	Mutual agreement procedure, 25 August 2022	https://www.ato.gov.au/Business/International-tax-for-business/In-detail/Mutual-agreement-procedure/ (Section "How to request a MAP" to be referred to for form and content of a MAP request, including information requirements)
MAP profile	21 June 2019	https://www.oecd.org/ctp/dispute/australia-dispute-resolution-profile.pdf

Overview of Australia's MAP Statistics for 2022

Please refer to https://www.oecd.org/tax/dispute/map-statistics-australia.pdf for details with respect to Australia's MAP Statistics.

Figure 2. Cases closed in 2022

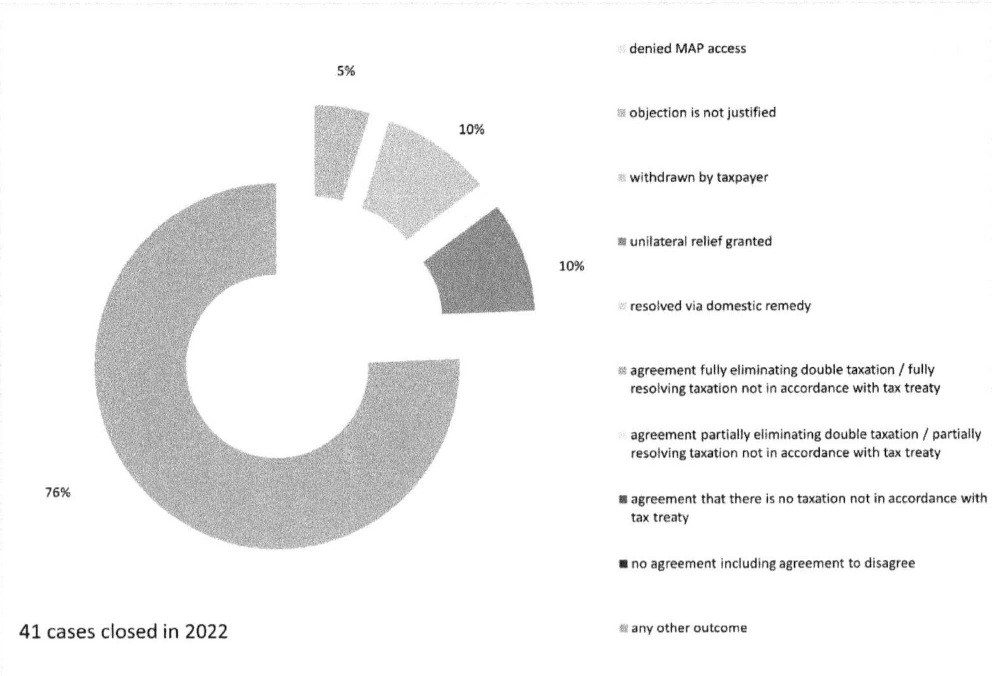

Source: OECD

Figure 3. Evolution of Australia's MAP caseload (2016-22)

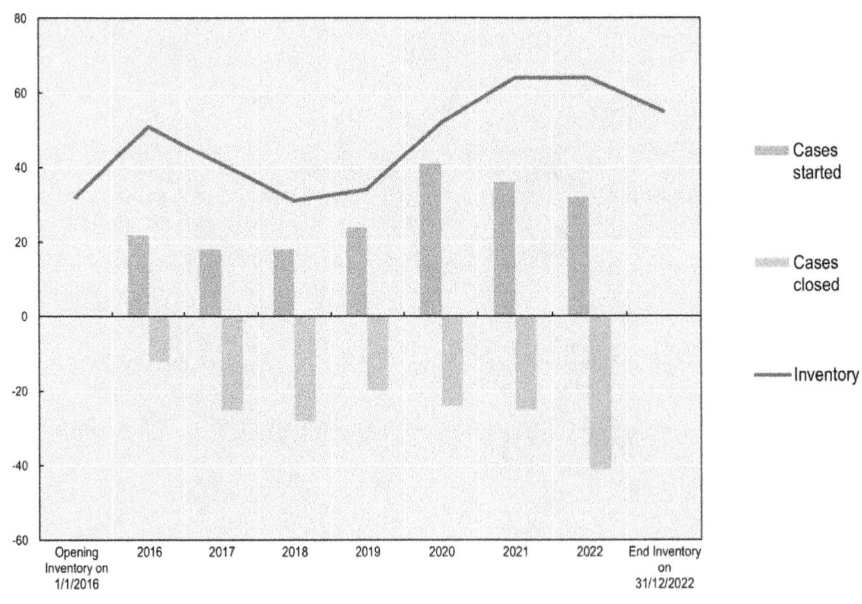

Source: OECD

Table 3. Overview of Australia's MAP caseload for 2022

Inventory for year 2022	Opening Inventory 1/1/2022	Cases started	Cases Closed	End Inventory 31/12/2022
Attribution/allocation cases	33	13	10	36
Other cases	31	19	31	19
Total	64	32	41	55

Source: OECD

Table 4. Australia's average time to resolve MAP cases in 2022

Cases resolved in year 2022	Pre-2016 cases		Post-2015 cases		All	
	Number of cases	**Average time**	**Number of cases**	**Average time** **Start to End**	**Number of cases**	**Average time**
Attribution / Allocation cases	1	173.06	9	19.39	10	34.76
Other cases	0	N/A	31	14.28	31	14.28
All cases	1	173.06	40	15.43	41	19.27

Source: OECD

Austria

Recent developments relating to MAP in Austria prior to 15 August 2023

Developments relating to MAP in the tax treaty network

- New reservations and notifications to the MLI have been approved by the Austrian Parliament.

Other developments relating to MAP

- Update of Austria's MAP guidance in 2023.

Latest Action 14 Peer Review report

9 April 2020: https://doi.org/10.1787/40c9f1b5-en

Tax treaty network of Austria

- 91 treaties, applicable to 91 jurisdictions (covering all treaties signed, although not necessarily in force)
- status of MLI: in force.

Table 1. State of play of Austria's tax treaty network

Treaties in line with the Action 14 Minimum Standard following MLI impact	Treaties where actions are ongoing to make them in line with the Action 14 Minimum Standard	Following impact/actions, remaining treaties that are not in line with Action 14 Minimum Standard
83	8	0

Source: OECD

Austria's MAP programme

Organisation of competent authority function

- seven persons:
  - one head of unit
  - six persons working on MAP cases (three persons on attribution/allocation cases and three persons on other cases).
- contact person(s) for MAP requests:
  - Mr. Harald PÖLZL
    Head of MAP/APA Team
    Tax Authority for Large Traders
    Address: Post office box 251, 1000 AUSTRIA
    Phone: +43 (0)1 502 33 556451

E-mail: Post.FAG-Verstaendigungsverfahren@bmf.gv.at.

Figure 1. Competent Authority Organisational Structure

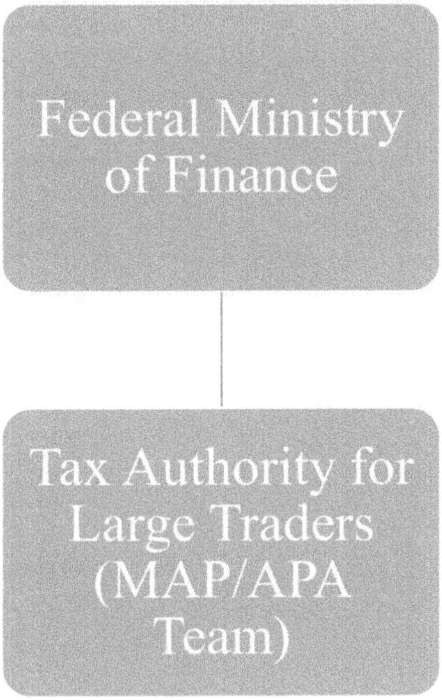

Source: OECD

Table 2. Guidance on the MAP process

MAP guidance	BMF-Info zu Verständigungs- und Schiedsverfahren, 5 May 2022	https://findok.bmf.gv.at/findok?execution=e100000s1&segmentId=86584be8-e4a4-4572-91cd-a772a524a4ee (Section B.1 to be referred to for form and content of a MAP request, including information requirements) https://www.bmf.gv.at/en/topics/taxation/double-taxation-agreements/Mutual-Agreement-Procedures-(MAPs).html (unofficial translation into English)
	Web page	https://www.bmf.gv.at/themen/steuern/internationales-steuerrecht/verstaendigungsverfahren.html
MAP profile	26 February 2020	https://www.oecd.org/tax/dispute/austria-dispute-resolution-profile.pdf

Overview of Austria's MAP Statistics for 2022

Please refer to https://www.oecd.org/tax/dispute/map-statistics-austria.pdf for details with respect to Austria's MAP Statistics.

Figure 2. Cases closed in 2022

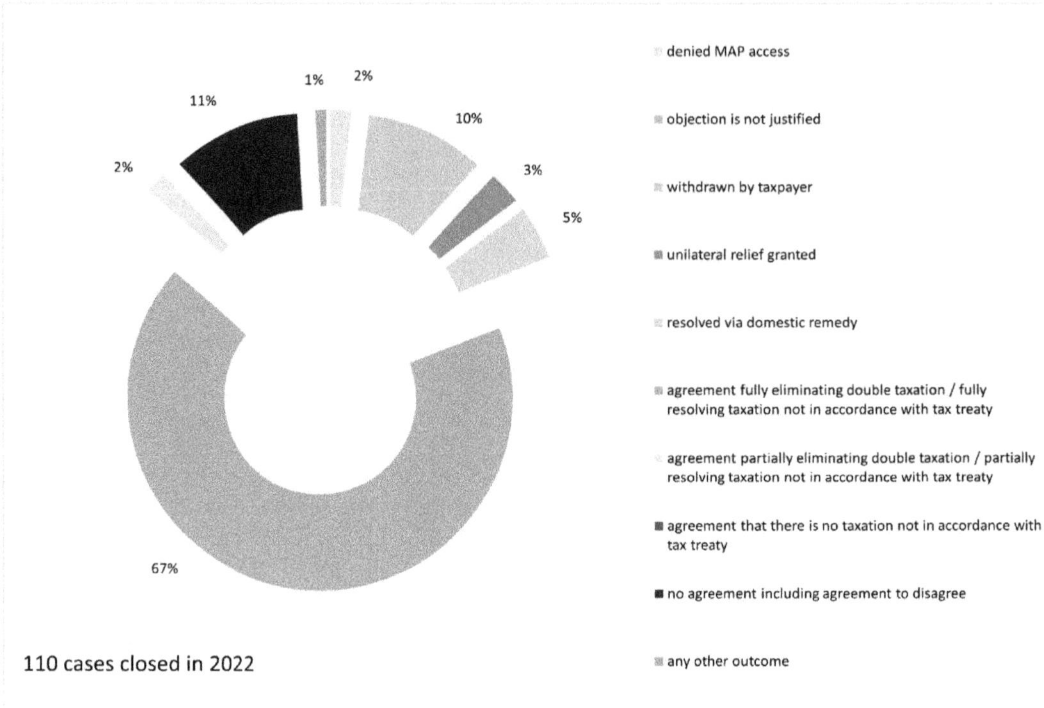

Source: OECD

Figure 3. Evolution of Austria's MAP caseload (2016-22)

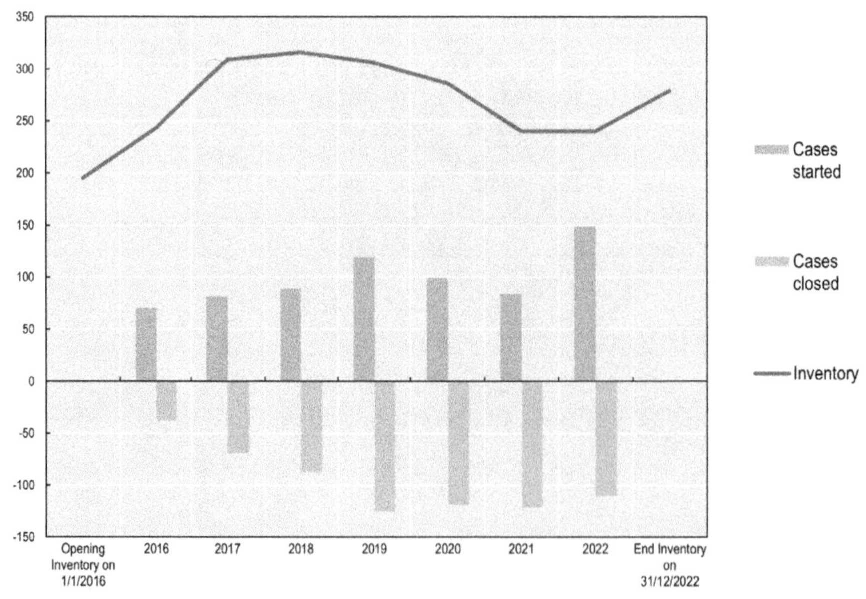

Source: OECD

Table 3. Overview of Austria's MAP caseload for 2022

Inventory for year 2022	Opening Inventory 1/1/2022	Cases started	Cases Closed	End Inventory 31/12/2022
Attribution/allocation cases	95	74	40	129
Other cases	145	75	70	150
Total	240	149	110	279

Source: OECD

Table 4. Austria's average time to resolve MAP cases in 2022

Cases resolved in year 2022	Pre-2016 cases		Post-2015 cases		All	
	Number of cases	**Average time**	**Number of cases**	**Average time** **Start to End**	**Number of cases**	**Average time**
Attribution / Allocation cases	2	94.09	38	27.11	40	30.46
Other cases	8	105.83	62	16.38	70	26.61
All cases	10	103.48	100	20.46	110	28.01

Source: OECD

Azerbaijan

Recent developments relating to MAP in Azerbaijan prior to 15 August 2023

Developments relating to MAP in the tax treaty network

- Azerbaijan is in the process of signing the MLI. The ratification process will ensue.
- Signature of the tax treaty with Japan on 27 December 2022.
- Signature of the tax treaty with Slovakia on 7 June 2023.

Other developments relating to MAP

- A draft MAP guidance is under works.

Latest Action 14 Peer Review report

Azerbaijan is yet to be peer reviewed under Action 14.

Tax treaty network of Azerbaijan

- 56 treaties, applicable to 54 jurisdictions (covering all treaties signed, although not necessarily in force)
- status of MLI: not signed.

Table 1. State of play of Azerbaijan's tax treaty network

Treaties in line with the Action 14 Minimum Standard following MLI impact	Treaties where actions are ongoing to make them in line with the Action 14 Minimum Standard	Following impact/actions, remaining treaties that are not in line with Action 14 Minimum Standard
39	4	1

Source: OECD

Azerbaijan's MAP programme

Organisation of competent authority function

- four persons:
  - four persons working on MAP cases
    - two persons work on attribution/allocation cases and two persons work on other cases.
- contact persons for MAP requests:
  - for attribution / allocation cases: Orkhan Musayev,
    Head of the International taxation and tax monitoring department,
    State Tax Service under the Ministry of the Economy, Orxan.Musayev@taxes.gov.az

Jeyhun Ismayilov,

Deputy-head of the International taxation and tax monitoring department, State Tax Service under the Ministry of the Economy, Ceyhun.Ismayilov@taxes.gov.az.

- for other cases: Elkin Mammadov,

  Head of the International taxation division,

  State Tax Service under the Ministry of the Economy, Elkin.Memmedov@taxes.gov.az.

Figure 1. Competent Authority Organisational Structure

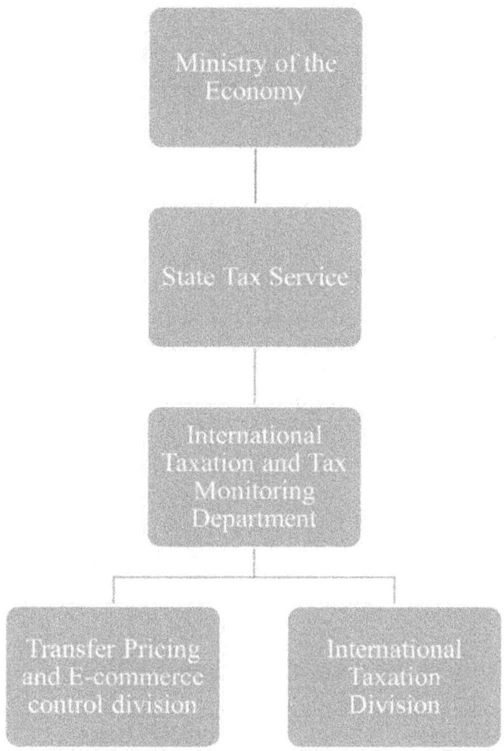

Source: OECD

Table 2. Guidance on the MAP process

MAP guidance	In draft stage	
MAP profile	4 April 2023	https://www.oecd.org/tax/dispute/azerbaijan-dispute-resolution-profile.pdf

Overview of Azerbaijan's MAP Statistics for 2022

Please refer to https://www.oecd.org/tax/dispute/map-statistics-azerbaijan.pdf for details with respect to Azerbaijan's MAP Statistics.

Cases closed in 2022

No MAP cases were closed by Azerbaijan in 2022.

Figure 2. Evolution of Azerbaijan's MAP caseload (2022)

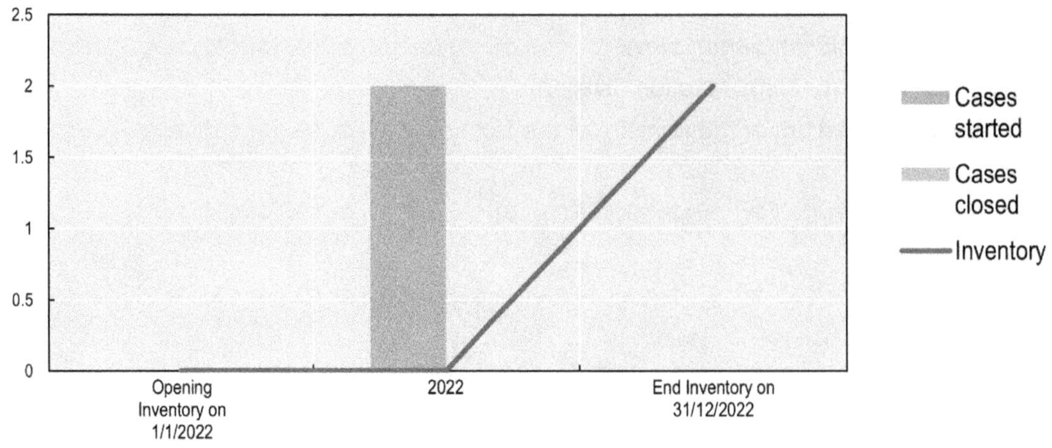

Source: OECD

Table 3. Overview of Azerbaijan's MAP caseload for 2022

Inventory for year 2022	Opening Inventory 1/1/2022	Cases started	Cases Closed	End Inventory 31/12/2022
Attribution/allocation cases	0	1	0	1
Other cases	0	1	0	1
Total	0	2	0	2

Source: OECD

Table 4. Azerbaijan's average time to resolve MAP cases in 2022

Cases resolved in year 2022	Pre-2022 cases		Post-2021 cases		All	
	Number of cases	**Average time**	**Number of cases**	**Average time** **Start to End**	**Number of cases**	**Average time**
Attribution / Allocation cases	0	N/A	0	N/A	0	N/A
Other cases	0	N/A	0	N/A	0	N/A
All cases	0	N/A	0	N/A	0	N/A

Source: OECD

The Bahamas

Recent developments relating to MAP in The Bahamas prior to 15 August 2023

Developments relating to MAP in the tax treaty network

- No developments were reported

Other developments relating to MAP

- No developments were reported

Latest Action 14 Peer Review report

14 April 2022 - https://doi.org/10.1787/3e3d34d5-en

Tax treaty network of The Bahamas

- one treaty, applicable to one jurisdiction (covering all treaties signed, although not necessarily in force)
- status of MLI: not signed.

Table 1. State of play of The Bahamas' tax treaty network

Treaties in line with the Action 14 Minimum Standard following MLI impact	Treaties where actions are ongoing to make them in line with the Action 14 Minimum Standard	Following impact/actions, remaining treaties that are not in line with Action 14 Minimum Standard
0	0	1

Source: OECD

The Bahamas' MAP programme

Organisation of competent authority function

- The Bahamas did not provide the relevant information.

Figure 1. Competent Authority Organisational Structure

Source: OECD

Table 2. Guidance on the MAP process

MAP guidance	No MAP guidance published	-
MAP profile	13 July 2021	https://www.oecd.org/tax/dispute/the-bahamas-dispute-resolution-profile.pdf

Overview of The Bahamas' MAP Statistics for 2022

The Bahamas did not report any MAP cases in its 2022 MAP Statistics.

Please refer to https://www.oecd.org/tax/dispute/map-statistics-bahamas.pdf for details with respect to the Bahamas' MAP Statistics.

Bahrain

Recent developments relating to MAP in Bahrain prior to 15 August 2023

Developments relating to MAP in the tax treaty network

- Bahrain did not provide the relevant information.

Other developments relating to MAP

- Bahrain did not provide the relevant information.

Latest Action 14 Peer Review report

13 September 2022 - https://doi.org/10.1787/0f90e048-en

Tax treaty network of Bahrain

- 45 treaties, applicable to 45 jurisdictions (covering all treaties signed, although not necessarily in force)
- status of MLI: in force.

Table 1. State of play of Bahrain's tax treaty network

Treaties in line with the Action 14 Minimum Standard following MLI impact	Treaties where actions are ongoing to make them in line with the Action 14 Minimum Standard	Following impact/actions, remaining treaties that are not in line with Action 14 Minimum Standard
35	No information	No information

Source: OECD

Bahrain's MAP programme

Organisation of competent authority function

- one head of unit
- contact persons for MAP requests:
  - Foreign Tax Relations Directorate
    National Bureau for Revenue
    Bahrain World Trade Centre, West Tower
    P.O. Box 17555 Manama Kingdom of Bahrain
    Tel No: +973 17502322
    e-Fax No: +973 17910098
    E-mail: Competent.Authority@nbr.gov.bh.

Figure 1. Competent Authority Organisational Structure

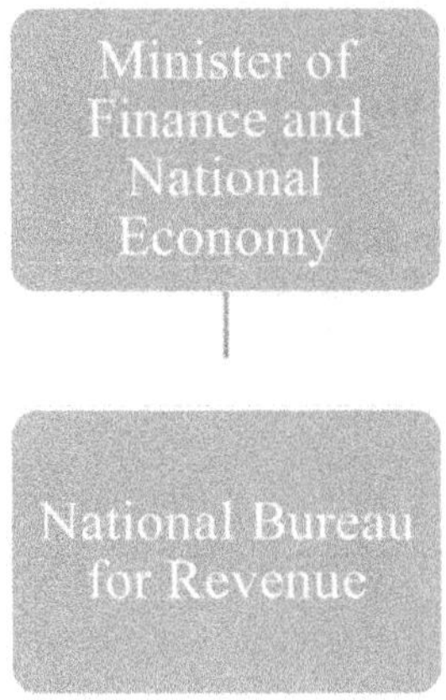

Source: OECD

Table 2. Guidance on the MAP process

MAP guidance	*Guidance on Mutual Agreement Procedure (MAP)*, September 2021	https://www.nbr.gov.bh/publications/view/Bahrains_Mutual_Agreement_Procedure_MAP_Guidance (Sections "How does it work?" and "Minimum requirements for a MAP request" to be referred to for form and content of a MAP request, including information requirements)
MAP profile	27 October 2021	https://www.oecd.org/tax/dispute/bahrain-dispute-resolution-profile.pdf

Overview of Bahrain's MAP Statistics for 2022

Bahrain did not report any MAP cases in its 2022 MAP Statistics.

Please refer to https://www.oecd.org/tax/dispute/map-statistics-bahrain.pdf for details with respect to Bahrain's MAP Statistics.

Barbados

Recent developments relating to MAP in Barbados prior to 15 August 2023

Developments relating to MAP in the tax treaty network

- Barbados did not provide the relevant information.

Other developments relating to MAP

- Barbados did not provide the relevant information.

Latest Action 14 Peer Review report

13 September 2022 - https://doi.org/10.1787/352eebcd-en

Tax treaty network of Barbados

- 35 treaties, applicable to 44 jurisdictions (covering all treaties signed, although not necessarily in force)
- status of MLI: in force.

Table 1. State of play of Barbados' tax treaty network

Treaties in line with the Action 14 Minimum Standard following MLI impact	Treaties where actions are ongoing to make them in line with the Action 14 Minimum Standard	Following impact/actions, remaining treaties that are not in line with Action 14 Minimum Standard
32	No information	No information

Source: OECD

Barbados' MAP programme

Organisation of competent authority function

- three persons
- contact persons for MAP requests:
  - Graeme O Stoute
    International Relations Unit Barbados Revenue Authority
    4th Floor, Weymouth Corporate Centre Roebuck Street Bridgetown St. Michael Barbados W.I
    Phone: (246) 535-8369 Email: graeme.stoute@bra.gov.bb.

Figure 1. Competent Authority Organisational Structure

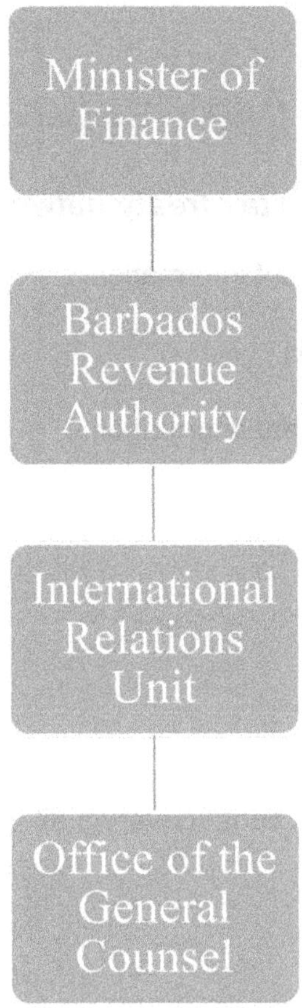

Source: OECD

Table 2. Guidance on the MAP process

MAP guidance	Guidance on Mutual Agreement Procedures, March 2021	https://bra.gov.bb/About/Exchange-of-Information/Mutual-Agreement-Procedures-MAP.aspx (Section "Making a MAP request" to be referred to for form and content of a MAP request, including information requirements)
MAP profile	14 April 2022	https://www.oecd.org/tax/dispute/barbados-dispute-resolution-profile.pdf

Overview of Barbados' MAP Statistics for 2022

Please refer to https://www.oecd.org/tax/dispute/map-statistics-barbados.pdf for details with respect to Barbados' MAP Statistics.

Cases closed in 2022

No MAP cases were closed by Barbados in 2022.

Figure 2. Evolution of Barbados' MAP caseload (2017-22)

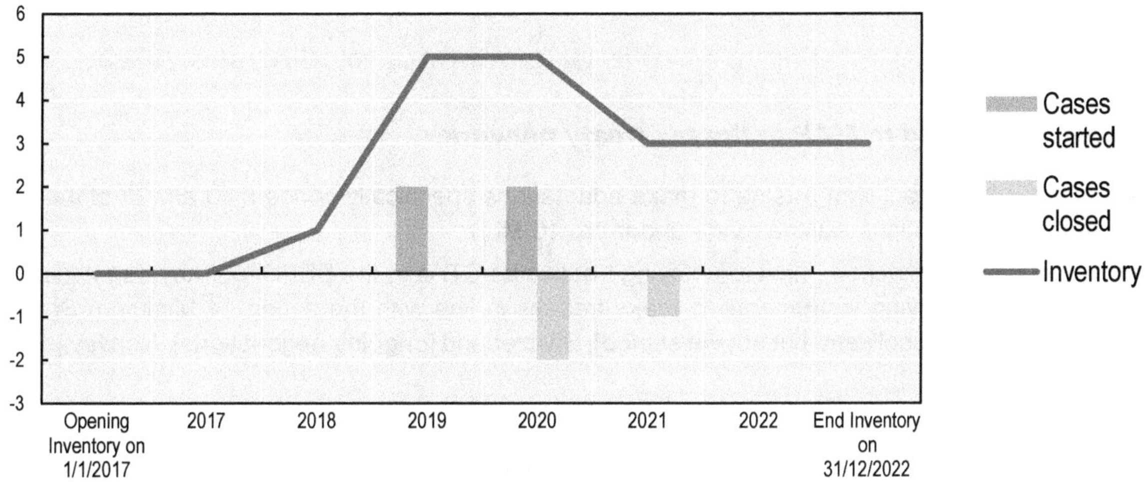

Source: OECD

Table 3. Overview of Barbados' MAP caseload for 2022

Inventory for year 2022	Opening Inventory 1/1/2022	Cases started	Cases Closed	End Inventory 31/12/2022
Attribution/allocation cases	1	0	0	1
Other cases	2	0	0	2
Total	3	0	0	3

Source: OECD

Table 4. Barbados' average time to resolve MAP cases in 2022

Cases resolved in year 2022	Pre-2017 cases		Post-2016 cases		All	
	Number of cases	**Average time**	**Number of cases**	**Average time** **Start to End**	**Number of cases**	**Average time**
Attribution / Allocation cases	0	N/A	0	N/A	0	N/A
Other cases	0	N/A	0	N/A	0	N/A
All cases	0	N/A	0	N/A	0	N/A

Source: OECD

Belgium

Recent developments relating to MAP in Belgium prior to 15 August 2023

Developments relating to MAP in the tax treaty network

- Belgium is in contact with Austria to make adaptations specifically concerning art. 25 of the treaty (given the reservations Austria made under art. 16 MLI).
- Belgium has taken action - next to notifying treaties as CTAs to the BEPS MLI - by negotiating and concluding complying instruments to make treaties in line with the action 14 Minimum Standard (e.g. Algeria [protocol sent, but not yet signed], Switzerland [ongoing negotiations], Norway [signed, but not yet in force]).
- Negotiations for a new DTA are ongoing with Germany.
- New DTA signed with France on 09.11.2021, but not entered into force yet.
- New DTA signed with The Netherlands on 21.06.2023, but not entered into force yet.

Other developments relating to MAP

- EU directive 2017/1852 transposed in Belgian Law.

Latest Action 14 Peer Review report

13 August 2019 - https://doi.org/10.1787/734c25f4-en

Tax treaty network of Belgium

- 95 treaties in force (the treaty with Taipei is included, the treaties with USSR and ex-Yugoslavia are not counted as additional treaties).
- status of MLI: in force.

Table 1. State of play of Belgium's tax treaty network

Treaties in line with the Action 14 Minimum Standard following MLI impact	Treaties where actions are ongoing to make them in line with the Action 14 Minimum Standard	Following impact/actions, remaining treaties that are not in line with Action 14 Minimum Standard
57	22	16

Source: OECD

Belgium's MAP programme

Organisation of competent authority function

- 17 persons:
  - one head of unit

- 15 persons working on MAP cases (among which eight persons work on other tasks as well):
  - of which four persons work on attribution/allocation cases and eleven persons work on other cases.
- one person working on administrative duties.
- contact persons for MAP requests:
  - Federal Public Service Finance, Belgium
    North Galaxy A24, Koning Albert II laan 33 bus 515, 1030
    Brussel Email: map.apa@minfin.fed.be.

Figure 1. Competent Authority Organisational Structure

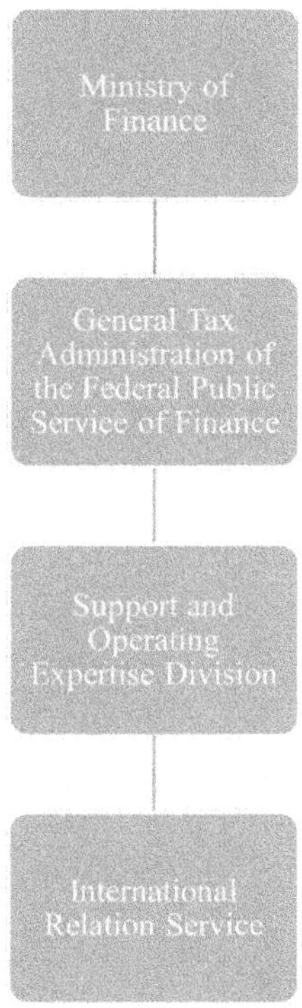

Source: OECD

Table 2. Guidance on the MAP process

MAP guidance	Circular 2018/C/27, 07 March 2018	https://eservices.minfin.fgov.be/myminfin-web/pages/public/fisconet/document/78e7a318-5f00-4a08-ade2-cd4a9fbbe92e (Section 2.4 to be referred to for form and content of a MAP request, including information requirements)
	FAQ	https://finance.belgium.be/sites/default/files/downloads/126-mutual-agreement-apa-faq-20210312.pdf
MAP profile	27 June 2022	https://www.oecd.org/tax/dispute/belgium-dispute-resolution-profile.pdf

Overview of Belgium's MAP Statistics for 2022

Please refer to https://www.oecd.org/tax/dispute/map-statistics-belgium.pdf for details with respect to Belgium's MAP Statistics.

Figure 2. Cases closed in 2022

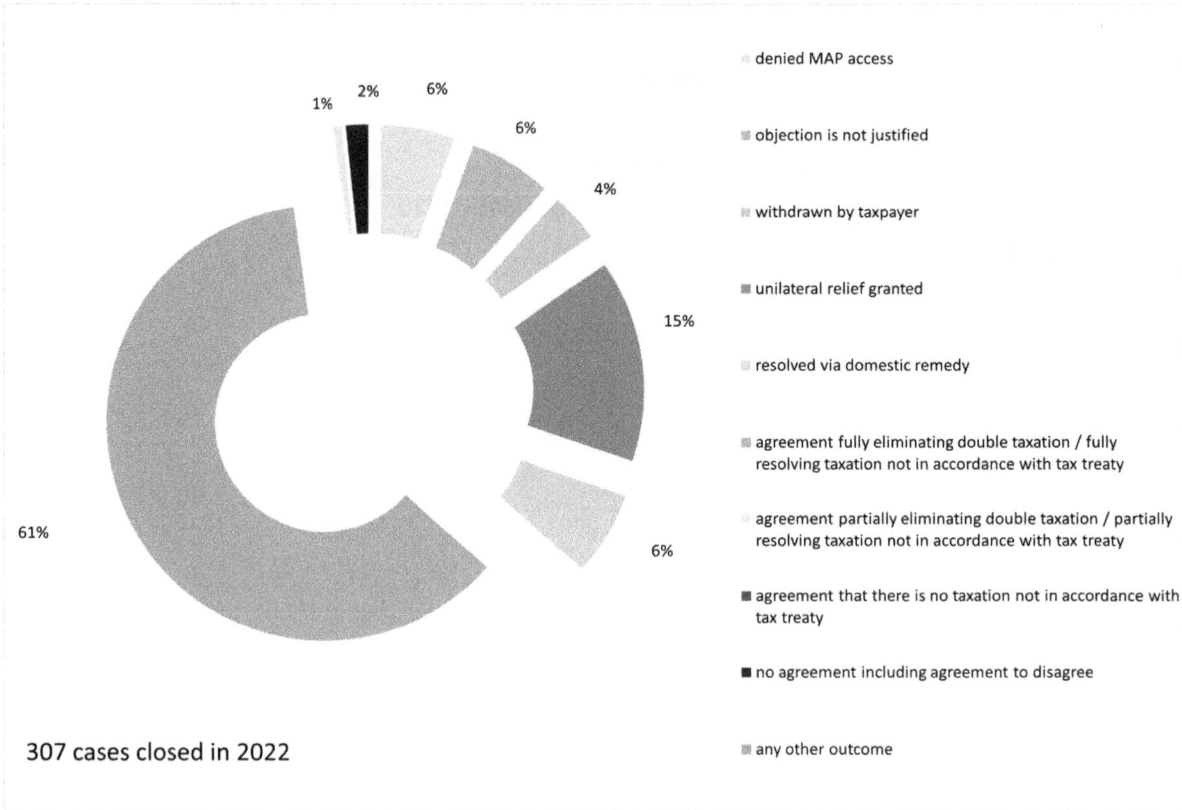

Source: OECD

Figure 3. Evolution of Belgium's MAP caseload (2016-22)

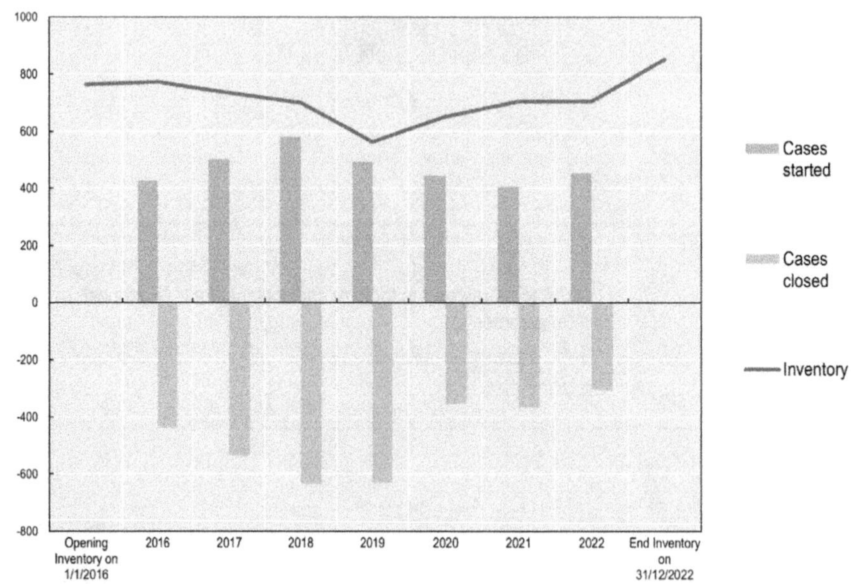

Source: OECD

Table 3. Overview of Belgium's MAP caseload for 2022

Inventory for year 2022	Opening Inventory 1/1/2022	Cases started	Cases Closed	End Inventory 31/12/2022
Attribution/allocation cases	132	61	36	157
Other cases	573	392	271	694
Total	705	453	307	851

Source: OECD

Table 4. Belgium's average time to resolve MAP cases in 2022

Cases resolved in year 2022	Pre-2016 cases		Post-2015 cases		All	
	Number of cases	**Average time**	**Number of cases**	**Average time** **Start to End**	**Number of cases**	**Average time**
Attribution / Allocation cases	1	137.69	35	23.40	36	26.58
Other cases	6	104.93	265	14.91	271	16.91
All cases	7	109.61	300	15.90	307	18.04

Source: OECD

Belize

Recent developments relating to MAP in Belize prior to 15 August 2023

Developments relating to MAP in the tax treaty network

- Belize did not provide the relevant information.

Other developments relating to MAP

- Belize did not provide the relevant information.

Latest Action 14 Peer Review report

- Belize is yet to be peer reviewed under Action 14.

Tax treaty network of Belize

- five treaties, applicable to 14 jurisdictions (covering all treaties signed, although not necessarily in force)
- status of MLI: in force.

Table 1. State of play of Belize's tax treaty network

Treaties in line with the Action 14 Minimum Standard following MLI impact	Treaties where actions are ongoing to make them in line with the Action 14 Minimum Standard	Following impact/actions, remaining treaties that are not in line with Action 14 Minimum Standard
3	No information	No information

Source: OECD

Belize's MAP programme

Organisation of competent authority function

- six persons:
  - one Head of Unit
  - five persons working on MAP (who also work on other tasks).
- contact persons for MAP requests: Belize did not provide the relevant information.

Figure 1. Competent Authority Organisational Structure

Source: OECD

Table 2. Guidance on the MAP process

MAP guidance	No MAP Guidance published	-
MAP profile	No MAP Profile published	-

Overview of Belize's MAP Statistics for 2022

Belize did not report any MAP cases in its 2022 MAP Statistics.

Please refer to https://www.oecd.org/tax/dispute/map-statistics-belize.pdf for details with respect to Belize's MAP Statistics.

Benin

Recent developments relating to MAP in Benin prior to 15 August 2023

Developments relating to MAP in the tax treaty network

- Entry into force of a tax treaty with Morocco in 2022.
- Signing of a tax treaty with Rwanda in 2023.

Other developments relating to MAP

- No developments were reported

Latest Action 14 Peer Review report

Benin is yet to be peer reviewed under Action 14.

Tax treaty network of Benin

- seven treaties, applicable to 14 jurisdictions (covering all treaties signed, although not necessarily in force)
- status of MLI: not signed.

Table 1. State of play of Benin's tax treaty network

Treaties in line with the Action 14 Minimum Standard following MLI impact	Treaties where actions are ongoing to make them in line with the Action 14 Minimum Standard	Following impact/actions, remaining treaties that are not in line with Action 14 Minimum Standard
5	No information	No information

Source: OECD

Benin's MAP programme

Organisation of competent authority function

- seven persons:
  - one head of unit
  - seven persons working on MAP cases (all of which work on other tasks as well).
- contact persons for MAP requests:
  - Monsieur Romuald WADAGNI
    Ministre de l'Economie et des Finances du Bénin
    Tel : +22921301247, +229 97970101, +229 94491111
    RWADAGNI@FINANCES.BJ
    Boîte Postale : 01-302 COTONOU-BENIN.

Figure 1. Competent Authority Organisational Structure

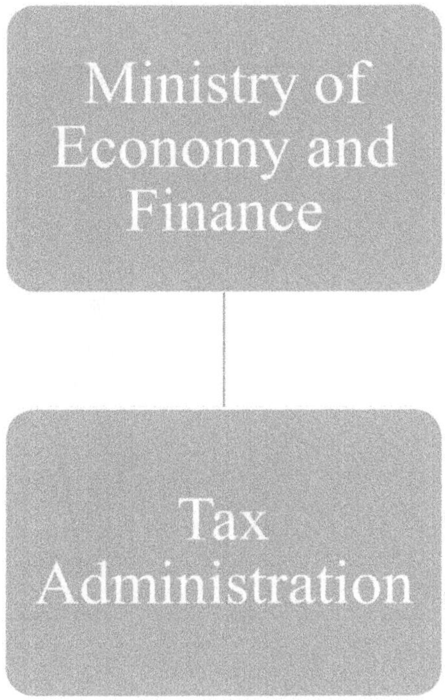

Source: OECD

Table 2. Guidance on the MAP process

MAP guidance	Benin did not provide the relevant information.	
MAP profile	12 January 2018	https://www.oecd.org/tax/dispute/Benin-Dispute-Resolution-Profile.pdf

Overview of Benin's MAP Statistics for 2022

Please refer to https://www.oecd.org/tax/dispute/map-statistics-benin.pdf for details with respect to Benin's MAP Statistics.

Cases closed in 2022

No MAP cases were closed by Benin in 2022.

Figure 2. Evolution of Benin's MAP caseload (2016-22)

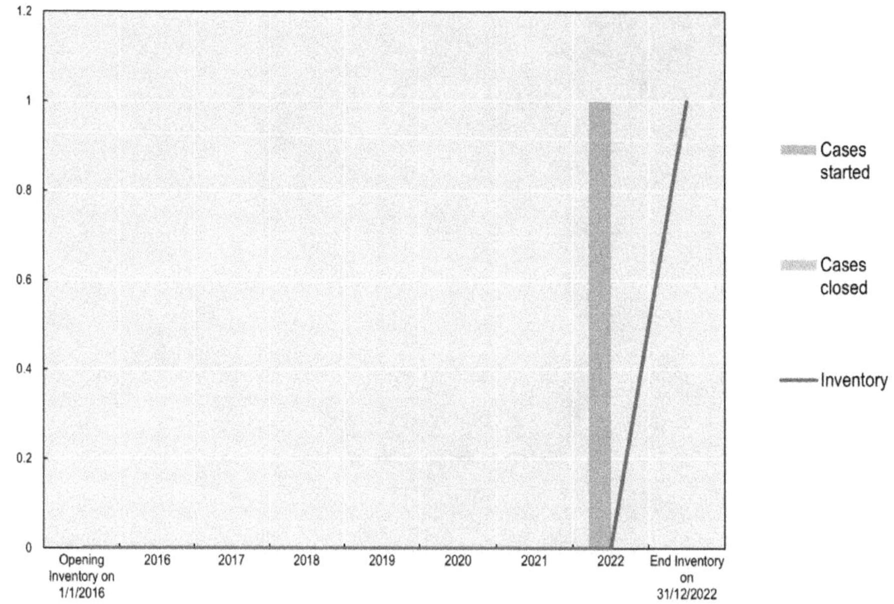

Source: OECD

Table 3. Overview of Benin's MAP caseload for 2022

Inventory for year 2022	Opening Inventory 1/1/2022	Cases started	Cases Closed	End Inventory 31/12/2022
Attribution/allocation cases	0	1	0	1
Other cases	0	0	0	0
Total	0	1	0	1

Source: OECD

Table 4. Benin's average time to resolve MAP cases in 2022

Cases resolved in year 2022	Pre-2016 cases		Post-2015 cases		All	
	Number of cases	**Average time**	**Number of cases**	**Average time**	**Number of cases**	**Average time**
				Start to End		
Attribution / Allocation cases	0	N/A	0	N/A	0	N/A
Other cases	0	N/A	0	N/A	0	N/A
All cases	0	N/A	0	N/A	0	N/A

Source: OECD

Bermuda

Recent developments relating to MAP in Bermuda prior to 15 August 2023

Developments relating to MAP in the tax treaty network

- Bermuda did not provide the relevant information.

Other developments relating to MAP

- Bermuda did not provide the relevant information.

Latest Action 14 Peer Review report

14 April 2022 - https://doi.org/10.1787/45f1b476-en

Tax treaty network of Bermuda

- 13 treaties, applicable to 13 jurisdictions (covering all treaties signed, although not necessarily in force)
- status of MLI: not signed.

Table 1. State of play of Bermuda's tax treaty network

Treaties in line with the Action 14 Minimum Standard following MLI impact	Treaties where actions are ongoing to make them in line with the Action 14 Minimum Standard	Following impact/actions, remaining treaties that are not in line with Action 14 Minimum Standard
3	No information	No information

Source: OECD

Bermuda's MAP programme

Organisation of competent authority function

- one person:
- contact persons for MAP requests:
    - Ministry of Finance, Bermuda with cc to treaty@gov.bm
    - Wayne L. Brown ACII, CBII Assistant Financial Secretary, <wlbrown@gov.bm> Telephone: office +14412955151 extension 1281 | Mobile +14415052780
    - OR Arisha Flood Senior Exchange of Information Officer <anflood@gov.bm> Telephone: office +14412955151 extension 3307| Telephone +1441 294 9227.

Figure 1. Competent Authority Organisational Structure

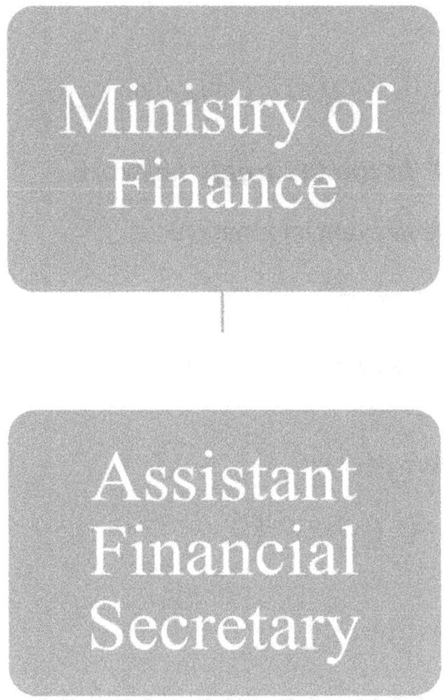

Source: OECD

Table 2. Guidance on the MAP process

MAP guidance	*Guidelines for requesting Mutual Agreement Procedure ("MAP") assistance in Bermuda,* 11 February 2020	https://www.gov.bm/sites/default/files/Guidelines-for-requesting-Mutual-Agreement-Procedure-Feb-2020.pdf (Section "Making a MAP request" to be referred to for form and content of a MAP request, including information requirements)
MAP profile	30 June 2021	https://www.oecd.org/tax/dispute/bermuda-dispute-resolution-profile.pdf

Source: OECD

Overview of Bermuda's MAP Statistics for 2022

Bermuda did not report any MAP cases in its 2022 MAP Statistics.

Please refer to https://www.oecd.org/tax/dispute/map-statistics-bermuda.pdf for details with respect to Bermuda's MAP Statistics.

Bosnia and Herzegovina

Recent developments relating to MAP in Bosnia and Herzegovina prior to 15 August 2023

Developments relating to MAP in the tax treaty network

- No developments were reported

Other developments relating to MAP

- For the Republic of Srpska: the Ministry of Finance of the Republic of Srpska plans to work on a draft MAP guidance in 2023.

Latest Action 14 Peer Review report

- Bosnia and Herzegovina is yet to be peer reviewed under Action 14.

Tax treaty network of Bosnia and Herzegovina

- 37 treaties, applicable to 38 jurisdictions (covering all treaties signed, although not necessarily in force)
- status of MLI: signed/ratified/in force.

Table 1. State of play of Bosnia and Herzegovina's tax treaty network

Treaties in line with the Action 14 Minimum Standard following MLI impact	Treaties where actions are ongoing to make them in line with the Action 14 Minimum Standard	Following impact/actions, remaining treaties that are not in line with Action 14 Minimum Standard
30	7	0

Source: OECD

Bosnia and Herzegovina's MAP programme

Organisation of competent authority function

- personnel working on MAP cases:
  - Federation of Bosnia and Herzegovina, four staff who deal with other tasks as well
  - Brčko District, three staff who deal with other tasks as well
  - Republic of Srpska, three to four staff who deal with other tasks as well.
- contact persons for MAP requests:
  - Competent authority for the territory of Federation of Bosnia and Herzegovina:

    The Federal Ministry of Finance – Department for tax policy, public revenue and game of chance – Tax policy division

Address: Mehmeda Spahe 5, 71000 Sarajevo, Bosnia and Herzegovina

Tel: +387 33 253 400 Generic email: eoi.fbih@fmf.gov.ba

Ms Medina Dudo, Assistant Ministry for Department for tax policy, public revenue and game of chance

Tel: +387 33 442 880 Individual Email: medina.dudo@fmf.gov.ba

- Competent authority for the territory of Republic of Srpska:

  Ministry of Finance of Republic of Srpska - Fiscal Division

  Address: Trg Republike Srpske 1, 78 000 Banja Luka, Repubic of Srpska, BIH

  Tel:+387 51 339 177 Fax: +387 51 339 655

  Ms. Slobodanka Popović, Assistant Minister, Fiscal Division Ministry of finance RS

  Tel: +387 51 339 177 Fax: +387 51 339 655 Individual Email: s.popovic@mf.vladars.net

- The competent authority for the territory of Brčko District:

  Brčko District Finance Directorate

  Address: Miroslava Krleže 1, 76100 Brčko District of Bosnia and Herzegovina

  Mr. Daniel Šolaja, Head of Director's Office

  Tel:+387 49 220 890 Individual mail: daniel.solaja@df.bdcentral.net.

Figure 1. Competent Authority Organisational Structure

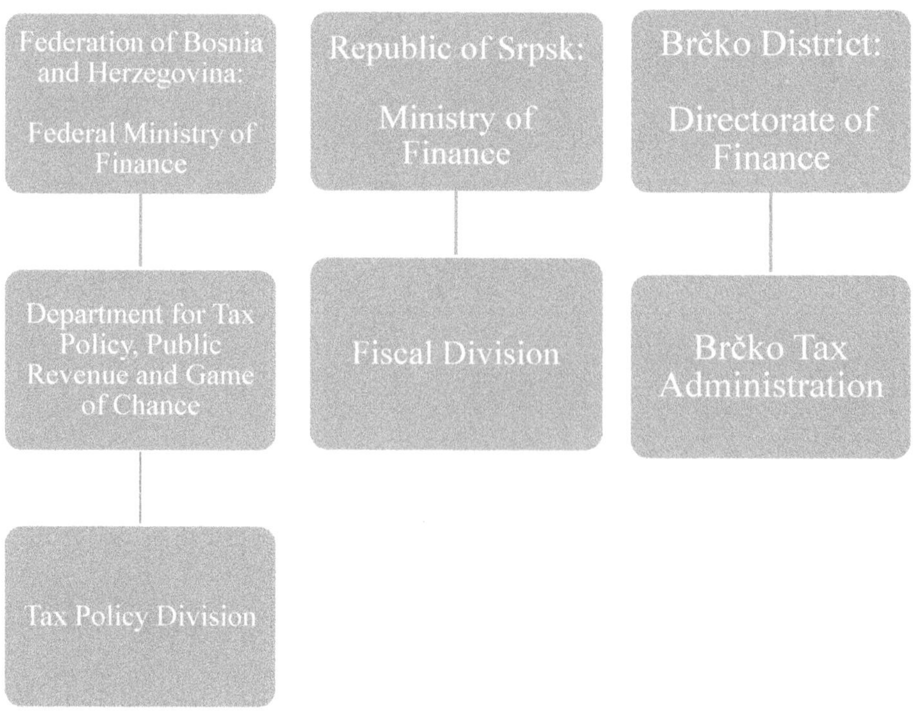

Source: OECD

Table 2. Guidance on the MAP process

MAP guidance	Bosnia and Herzegovina did not provide the relevant information	
MAP profile	No MAP profile published	

Overview of Bosnia and Herzegovina's MAP Statistics for 2022

Bosnia and Herzegovina did not report any MAP cases in its 2022 MAP Statistics.

Please refer to https://www.oecd.org/tax/dispute/map-statistics-bosnia-and-herzegovina.pdf for details with respect to Bosnia and Herzegovina's MAP Statistics.

Botswana

Recent developments relating to MAP in Botswana prior to 15 August 2023

Developments relating to MAP in the tax treaty network

- Botswana did not provide the relevant information.

Other developments relating to MAP

- Botswana did not provide the relevant information.

Latest Action 14 Peer Review report

The stage 1 Simplified Peer Review report of Botswana is expected to be published early 2024.

Tax treaty network of Botswana

- 24 treaties, applicable to 24 jurisdictions (covering all treaties signed, although not necessarily in force)
- status of MLI: not signed.

Table 1. State of play of Botswana's tax treaty network

Treaties in line with the Action 14 Minimum Standard following MLI impact	Treaties where actions are ongoing to make them in line with the Action 14 Minimum Standard	Following impact/actions, remaining treaties that are not in line with Action 14 Minimum Standard
22	No information	No information

Source: OECD

Botswana's MAP programme

Organisation of competent authority function

- three persons
- contact persons for MAP requests:
    - Botswana did not provide the relevant information.

Figure 1. Competent Authority Organisational Structure

Source: OECD

Table 2. Guidance on the MAP process

MAP guidance	Botswana did not provide the relevant information.	
MAP profile	No MAP profile published	

Overview of Botswana's MAP Statistics for 2022

Please refer to https://www.oecd.org/tax/dispute/map-statistics-botswana.pdf for details with respect to Botswana's MAP Statistics.

Figure 2. Cases closed in 2022

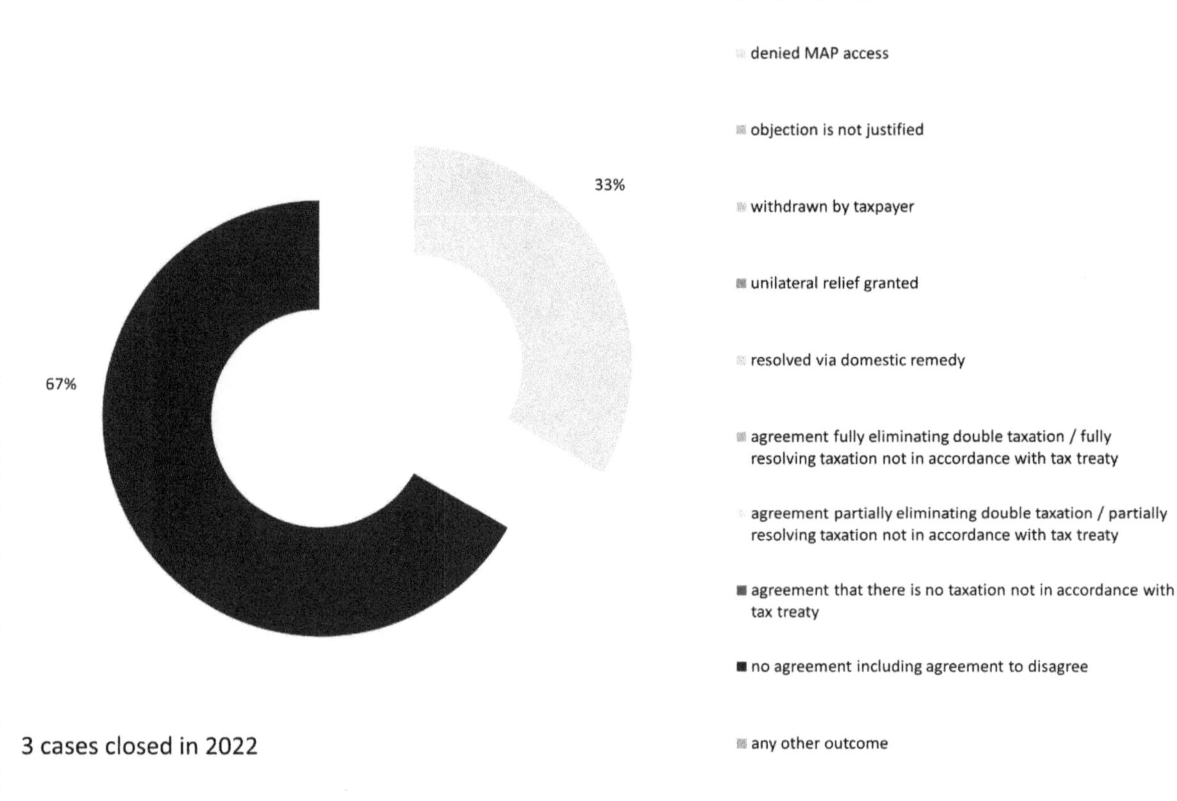

Source: OECD

Figure 3. Evolution of Botswana's MAP caseload (2017-22)

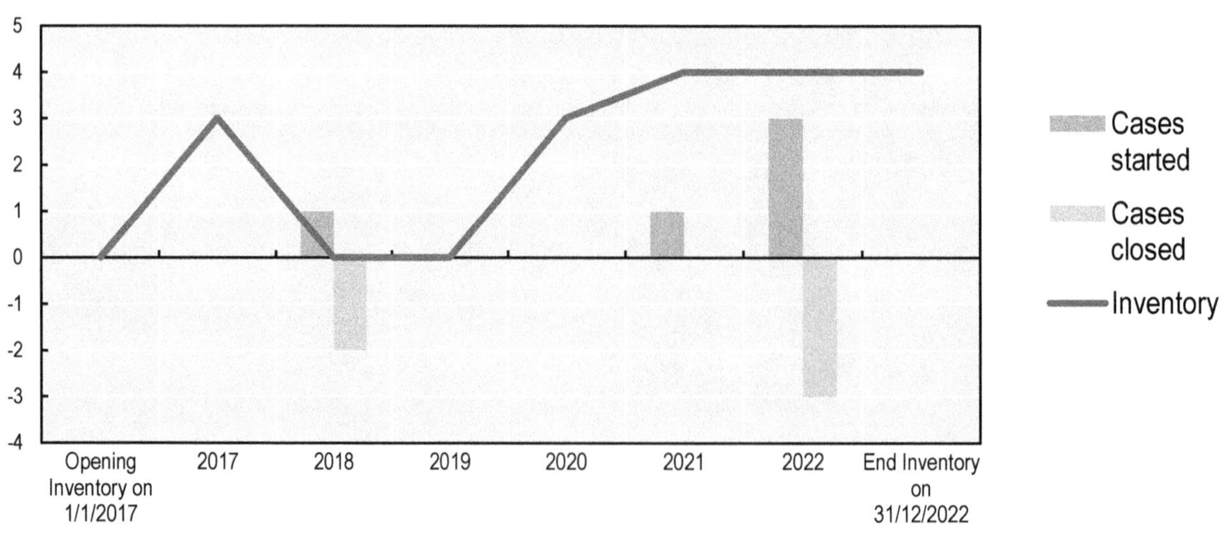

Source: OECD

Table 3. Overview of Botswana's MAP caseload for 2022

Inventory for year 2022	Opening Inventory 1/1/2022	Cases started	Cases Closed	End Inventory 31/12/2022
Attribution/allocation cases	0	1	0	1
Other cases	4	2	3	3
Total	4	3	3	4

Source: OECD

Table 4. Botswana's average time to resolve MAP cases in 2022

Cases resolved in year 2022	Pre-2017 cases		Post-2016 cases		All	
	Number of cases	**Average time**	**Number of cases**	**Average time** **Start to End**	**Number of cases**	**Average time**
Attribution / Allocation cases	0	N/A	0	N/A	0	N/A
Other cases	0	N/A	3	37.93	3	37.93
All cases	0	N/A	3	37.93	3	37.93

Source: OECD

Brazil

Recent developments relating to MAP in Brazil prior to 15 August 2023

Developments relating to MAP in the tax treaty network

- In 2022, new treaties were signed with Colombia, Norway, Poland and the United Kingdom in line with the Action 14 Minimum Standard. Furthermore, amending protocols were signed with China, Chile and India implementing the Action 14 Minimum Standard in those treaties.

Other developments relating to MAP

- No developments were reported

Latest Action 14 Peer Review report

18 October 2021 - https://doi.org/10.1787/30e8a050-en

Tax treaty network of Brazil

- 39 treaties, applicable to 40 jurisdictions (covering all treaties signed, although not necessarily in force)
- status of MLI: not signed.

Table 1. State of play of Brazil's tax treaty network

Treaties in line with the Action 14 Minimum Standard following MLI impact	Treaties where actions are ongoing to make them in line with the Action 14 Minimum Standard	Following impact/actions, remaining treaties that are not in line with Action 14 Minimum Standard
12	25	1

Source: OECD

Brazil's MAP programme

Organisation of competent authority function

- nine persons:
    - two heads of unit
    - seven persons working on MAP cases (all of which work on other tasks as well).
- contact persons for MAP requests:
    - Special Secretary of Federal Revenue of Brazil (competent authority of Brazil)

      Point of contact: International Relations Office (Asain)

      Address: Setor de Autarquias Sul, Quadra 3, Bloco "O", Sala 805 CEP: 70.079-900 – Brasília/DF

Email asain@rfb.gov.br.

Figure 1. Competent Authority Organisational Structure

Source: OECD

Table 2. Guidance on the MAP process

MAP guidance	Manual Mutual Agreement Procedure, December 2018	https://www.gov.br/receitafederal/pt-br/acesso-a-informacao/legislacao/acordos-internacionais/map/manual-map_en.pdf (Section "How to initiate a MAP" to be referred to for form and content of a MAP request, including information requirements)
MAP profile	13 February 2019	https://www.oecd.org/tax/dispute/brazil-dispute-resolution-profile.pdf

Overview of Brazil's MAP Statistics for 2022

Please refer to https://www.oecd.org/tax/dispute/map-statistics-brazil.pdf for details with respect to Brazil's MAP Statistics.

Figure 2. Cases closed in 2022

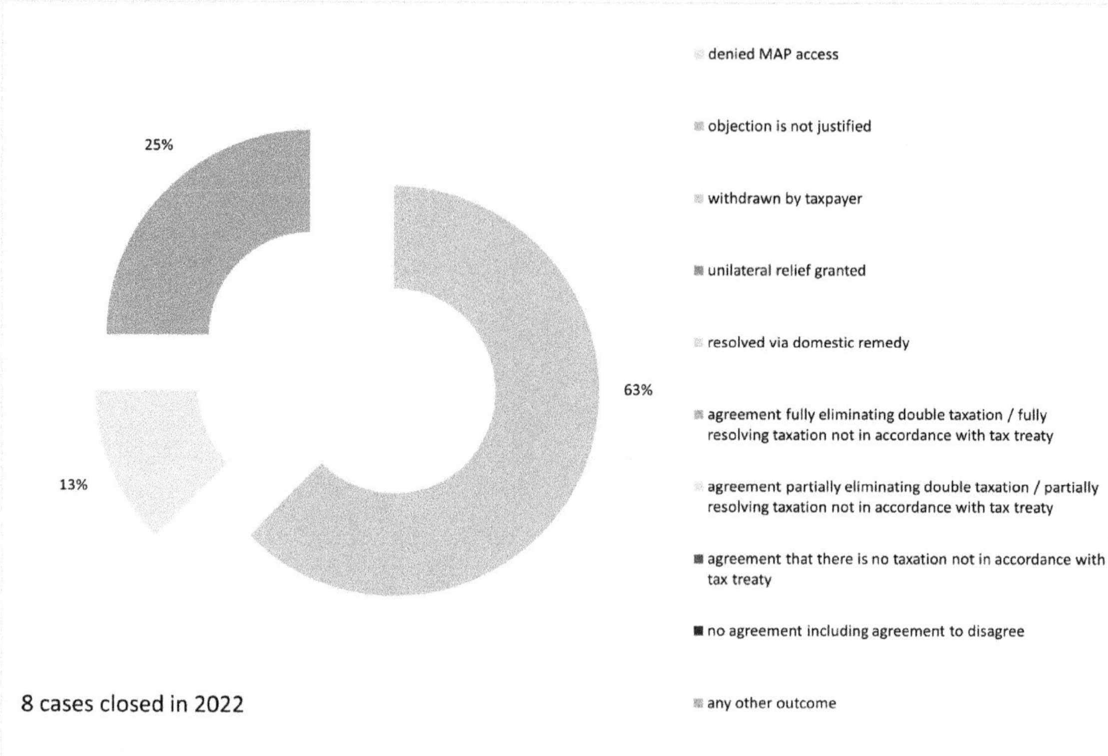

Source: OECD

Figure 3. Evolution of Brazil's MAP caseload (2016-22)

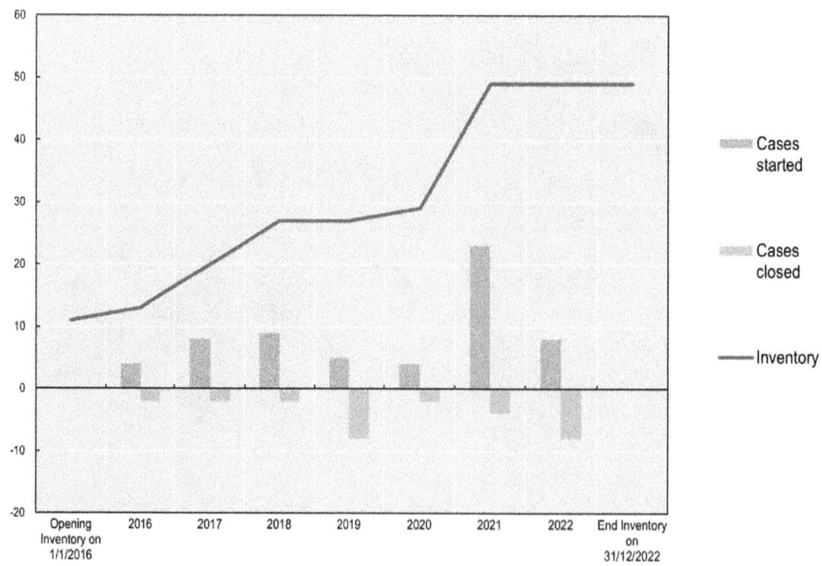

Source: OECD

Table 3. Overview of Brazil's MAP caseload for 2022

Inventory for year 2022	Opening Inventory 1/1/2022	Cases started	Cases Closed	End Inventory 31/12/2022
Attribution/allocation cases	42	7	7	42
Other cases	7	1	1	7
Total	49	8	8	49

Source: OECD

Table 4. Brazil's average time to resolve MAP cases in 2022

Cases resolved in year 2022	Pre-2016 cases		Post-2015 cases		All	
	Number of cases	**Average time**	**Number of cases**	**Average time** **Start to End**	**Number of cases**	**Average time**
Attribution / Allocation cases	0	N/A	7	37.57	7	37.57
Other cases	0	N/A	1	46.75	1	46.75
All cases	0	N/A	8	38.72	8	38.72

Source: OECD

British Virgin Islands

Recent developments relating to MAP in British Virgin Islands prior to 15 August 2023

Developments relating to MAP in the tax treaty network

- British Virgin Islands did not provide the relevant information.

Other developments relating to MAP

- British Virgin Islands did not provide the relevant information.

Latest Action 14 Peer Review report

14 April 2022 - https://doi.org/10.1787/36402208-en

Tax treaty network of British Virgin Islands

- 11 treaties, applicable to 11 jurisdictions (covering all treaties signed, although not necessarily in force)
- status of MLI: not signed.

Table 1. State of play of British Virgin Islands' tax treaty network

Treaties in line with the Action 14 Minimum Standard following MLI impact	Treaties where actions are ongoing to make them in line with the Action 14 Minimum Standard	Following impact/actions, remaining treaties that are not in line with Action 14 Minimum Standard
0	No information	No information

Source: OECD

British Virgin Islands' MAP programme

Organisation of competent authority function

- contact persons for MAP requests:
  - La Toya James Director International Tax Authority Peace House, Pickering Drive Road Town, Tortola British Virgin Islands Telephone: (284) 394-4415.

Figure 1. Competent Authority Organisational Structure

Source: OECD

Table 2. Guidance on the MAP process

MAP guidance	British Virgin Islands did not provide the relevant information.	
MAP profile	31 May 2021	https://www.oecd.org/tax/dispute/british-virgin-islands-dispute-resolution-profile.pdf

Overview of British Virgin Islands' MAP Statistics for 2022

British Virgin Islands did not report any MAP cases in its 2022 MAP Statistics.

Please refer to https://www.oecd.org/tax/dispute/map-statistics-british-virgin-islands.pdf for details with respect to British Virgin Islands' MAP Statistics.

Brunei Darussalam

Recent developments relating to MAP in Brunei Darussalam prior to 15 August 2023

Developments relating to MAP in the tax treaty network

- Brunei Darussalam did not provide the relevant information.

Other developments relating to MAP

- Brunei Darussalam did not provide the relevant information.

Latest Action 14 Peer Review report

24 January 2022 - https://doi.org/10.1787/83469e1b-en

Tax treaty network of Brunei Darussalam

- 19 treaties, applicable to 19 jurisdictions (covering all treaties signed, although not necessarily in force)
- status of MLI: not signed.

Table 1. State of play of Brunei Darussalam's tax treaty network

Treaties in line with the Action 14 Minimum Standard following MLI impact	Treaties where actions are ongoing to make them in line with the Action 14 Minimum Standard	Following impact/actions, remaining treaties that are not in line with Action 14 Minimum Standard
14	No information	No information

Source: OECD

Brunei Darussalam's MAP programme

Organisation of competent authority function

- three persons
- contact persons for MAP requests:
  - Director
    Revenue Division, Ministry of Finance and Economy
    Ministry of Finance and Economy Building,
    Commonwealth Drive Bandar Seri Begawan BB3910, Brunei Darussalam
    international.revenue@mofe.gov.bn.

Figure 1. Competent Authority Organisational Structure

Source: OECD

Table 2. Guidance on the MAP process

MAP guidance	Mutual Agreement Procedure Guidelines, December 2020	https://www.mofe.gov.bn/SiteAssets/divisions/avoidance-of-double-taxation-adta/MOFE%20MAP%20Guidelines.pdf (Sections 6 and 7 to be referred to for form and content of a MAP request, including information requirements)
MAP profile	19 May 2021	https://www.oecd.org/tax/dispute/brunei-dispute-resolution-profile.pdf

Overview of Brunei Darussalam's MAP Statistics for 2022

Brunei Darussalam did not report any MAP cases in its 2022 MAP Statistics.

Please refer to https://www.oecd.org/tax/dispute/map-statistics-brunei-darussalam.pdf for details with respect to Brunei Darussalam's MAP Statistics

Bulgaria

Recent developments relating to MAP in Bulgaria prior to 15 August 2023

Developments relating to MAP in the tax treaty network

- Entry into force of the MLI for Bulgaria's tax treaties in 2023.
- Ongoing bilateral negotiations with Malta and Switzerland. Bulgaria has proposed to start negotiations for a new treaty to be considered by Italy.

Other developments relating to MAP

- No developments were reported

Latest Action 14 Peer Review report

18 October 2021 - https://doi.org/10.1787/8e7b2363-en

Tax treaty network of Bulgaria

- 70 treaties, applicable to 71 jurisdictions (covering all treaties signed, although not necessarily in force)
- status of MLI: in force.

Table 1. State of play of Bulgaria's tax treaty network

Treaties in line with the Action 14 Minimum Standard following MLI impact	Treaties where actions are ongoing to make them in line with the Action 14 Minimum Standard	Following impact/actions, remaining treaties that are not in line with Action 14 Minimum Standard
65	3	2

Source: OECD

Bulgaria's MAP programme

Organisation of competent authority function

- 14 persons:
  - one head of unit
  - 11 persons working on MAP cases (all of them work on other tasks as well):
    - all of the 11 employees work on other cases and three of these 11 also work on attribution/allocation cases.
- contact persons for MAP requests:
  - Director, Tax Treaties Directorate
    National Revenue Agency

52 Dondukov Blvd. 1000 Sofia, Bulgaria
Tel: + 359 2 9859 3061 Email: bg-eoi@nra.bg.

Figure 1. Competent Authority Organisational Structure

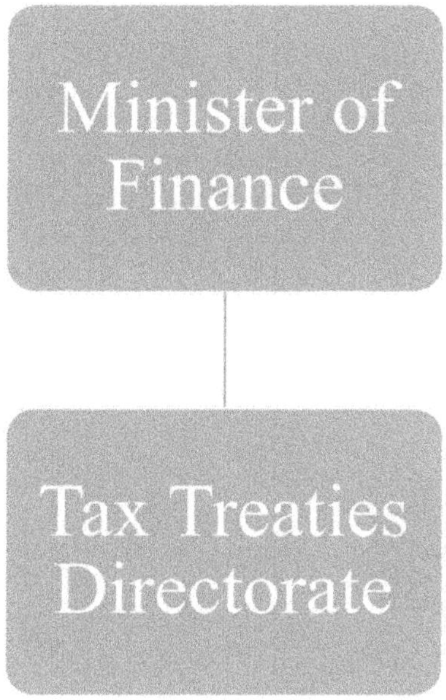

Source: OECD

Table 2. Guidance on the MAP process

MAP guidance	Guidance, March 2019	https://old.nra.bg/en/page?id=711 (Section V to be referred to for form and content of a MAP request, including information requirements)
MAP profile	2 February 2021	https://www.oecd.org/tax/dispute/bulgaria-dispute-resolution-profile.pdf

Overview of Bulgaria's MAP Statistics for 2022

Please refer to https://www.oecd.org/tax/dispute/map-statistics-bulgaria.pdf for details with respect to Bulgaria's MAP Statistics.

Figure 2. Cases closed in 2022

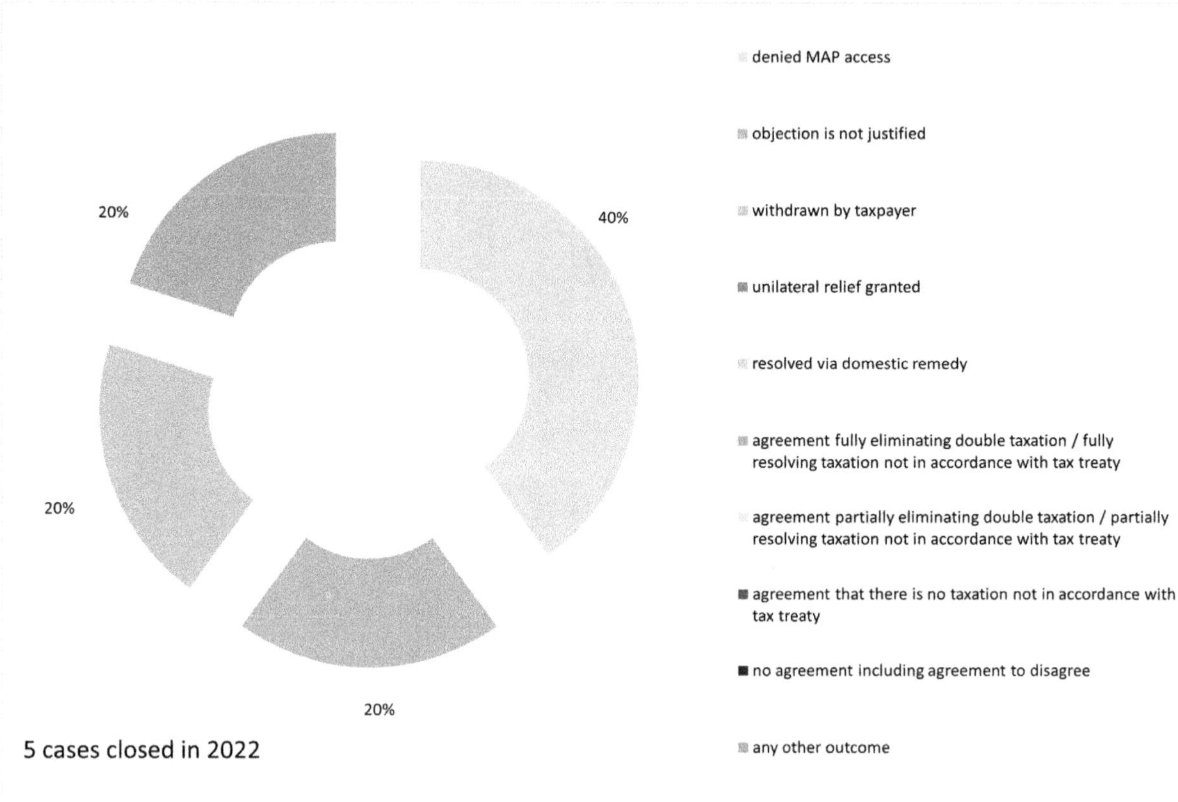

Source: OECD

Figure 3. Evolution of Bulgaria's MAP caseload (2016-22)

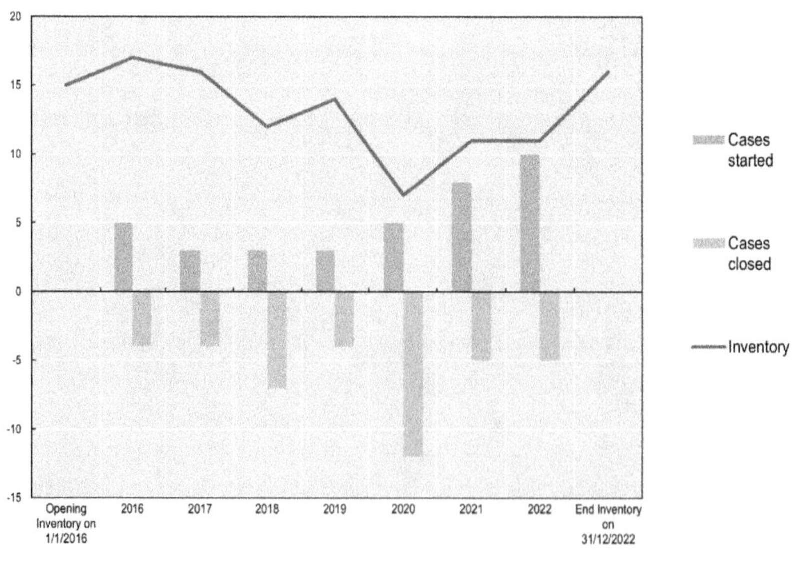

Source: OECD

Table 3. Overview of Bulgaria's MAP caseload for 2022

Inventory for year 2022	Opening Inventory 1/1/2022	Cases started	Cases Closed	End Inventory 31/12/2022
Attribution/allocation cases	3	6	1	8
Other cases	8	4	4	8
Total	11	10	5	16

Source: OECD

Table 4. Bulgaria's average time to resolve MAP cases in 2022

Cases resolved in year 2022	Pre-2016 cases		Post-2015 cases		All	
	Number of cases	**Average time**	**Number of cases**	**Average time** **Start to End**	**Number of cases**	**Average time**
Attribution / Allocation cases	0	N/A	1	6.44	1	6.44
Other cases	0	N/A	4	27.88	4	27.88
All cases	0	N/A	5	23.59	5	23.59

Source: OECD

Burkina Faso

Recent developments relating to MAP in Burkina Faso prior to 15 August 2023

Developments relating to MAP in the tax treaty network

- Burkina Faso did not provide the relevant information.

Other developments relating to MAP

- Burkina Faso did not provide the relevant information.

Latest Action 14 Peer Review report

Burkina Faso is yet to be peer reviewed under Action14.

Tax treaty network of Burkina Faso

- five treaties, applicable to 11 jurisdictions (covering all treaties signed, although not necessarily in force)
- status of MLI: signed.

Table 1. State of play of Burkina Faso's tax treaty network

Treaties in line with the Action 14 Minimum Standard following MLI impact	Treaties where actions are ongoing to make them in line with the Action 14 Minimum Standard	Following impact/actions, remaining treaties that are not in line with Action 14 Minimum Standard
3	No information	No information

Source: OECD

Burkina Faso's MAP programme

Organisation of competent authority function

- contact persons for MAP requests:
  - Le Directeur général des impôts
Avenue du général Sangoulé Lamizana
Ouagadougou – Burkina Faso.

Competent Authority Organisational Structure

Burkina Faso did not provide the relevant information.

Table 2. Guidance on the MAP process

MAP guidance	Burkina Faso did not provide the relevant information	-
MAP profile	12 October 2022	https://www.oecd.org/tax/dispute/burkina-faso-dispute-resolution-profile.pdf

Overview of Burkina Faso's MAP Statistics for 2022

Burkina Faso did not report any MAP cases in its 2022 MAP Statistics.

Please refer to https://www.oecd.org/tax/dispute/map-statistics-burkina-faso.pdf for details with respect to Burkina Faso's MAP Statistics.

Cabo Verde

Recent developments relating to MAP in Cabo Verde prior to 15 August 2023

Developments relating to MAP in the tax treaty network

- Cabo Verde did not provide the relevant information.

Other developments relating to MAP

- Cabo Verde did not provide the relevant information.

Latest Action 14 Peer Review report

Cabo Verde is yet to be peer reviewed under Action 14.

Tax treaty network of Cabo Verde

- 11 treaties, applicable to 11 jurisdictions (covering all treaties signed, although not necessarily in force)
- status of MLI: not signed.

Table 1. State of play of Cabo Verde's tax treaty network

Treaties in line with the Action 14 Minimum Standard following MLI impact	Treaties where actions are ongoing to make them in line with the Action 14 Minimum Standard	Following impact/actions, remaining treaties that are not in line with Action 14 Minimum Standard
6	No information	No information

Source: OECD

Cabo Verde's MAP programme

Organisation of competent authority function

- Cabo Verde did not provide the relevant information.

Table 2. Guidance on the MAP process

MAP guidance	Cabo Verde did not provide the relevant information.	
MAP profile	No MAP profile published	

Overview of Cabo Verde's MAP Statistics for 2022

Cabo Verde did not report any MAP cases in its 2022 MAP Statistics.

Please refer to https://www.oecd.org/tax/dispute/map-statistics-cabo-verde.pdf for details with respect to Cabo Verde's MAP Statistics.

Cameroon

Recent developments relating to MAP in Cameroon prior to 15 August 2023

Developments relating to MAP in the tax treaty network

- Cameroon did not provide the relevant information.

Other developments relating to MAP

- Cameroon did not provide the relevant information.

Latest Action 14 Peer Review report

Cameroon is yet to be peer reviewed under Action14.

Tax treaty network of Cameroon

- six treaties, applicable to six jurisdictions (covering all treaties signed, although not necessarily in force)
- status of MLI: in force.

Table 1. State of play of Cameroon's tax treaty network

Treaties in line with the Action 14 Minimum Standard following MLI impact	Treaties where actions are ongoing to make them in line with the Action 14 Minimum Standard	Following impact/actions, remaining treaties that are not in line with Action 14 Minimum Standard
4	No information	No information

Source: OECD

Cameroon's MAP programme

Organisation of competent authority function

- contact persons for MAP requests:
  - Competent authority : Le Ministre des Finances : Monsieur Alamine Ousmane MEY
    Téléphone : 00 (237) 222224702 alamine_ousmane_mey@hotmail.com
    Delegated competent authority : Le Directeur Général des Impôts
    Téléphone : 00 (237) 222222315 mopa75@yahoo.fr.

Competent Authority Organisational Structure

Cameroon did not provide the relevant information.

Table 2. Guidance on the MAP process

MAP guidance	Cameroon did not provide the relevant information.
MAP profile	No MAP profile published.

Overview of Cameroon's MAP Statistics for 2022

Cameroon did not report any MAP cases in its 2022 MAP Statistics.

Please refer to https://www.oecd.org/tax/dispute/map-statistics-cameroon.pdf for details with respect to Cameroon's MAP Statistics.

Canada

Recent developments relating to MAP in Canada prior to 15 August 2023

Developments relating to MAP in the tax treaty network

- Since the last peer review period, Canada completed the ratification process for the MLI, which entered into force for Canada on 1 December 2019. Canada also completed the ratification process for its treaty with Madagascar, which entered into force on 3 June 2020. Canada remains committed to the BEPS minimum standards and continues to be engaged in bilateral negotiations to bring its treaties in line with this standard, in accordance with the plan outlined in Canada's stage 2 peer review report.

Other developments relating to MAP

- Canada has completed the update to its MAP guidance on 1 June 2021 to reflect the implementation of the BEPS minimum standards and the ratification of the MLI.
- Canada has also completed changes to its inventory management system to ensure an accurate reporting of MAP statistics and changes to standard correspondence templates.

Latest Action 14 Peer Review report

13 August 2019 - https://doi.org/10.1787/67dba2bb-en

Tax treaty network of Canada

- 96 treaties, applicable to 96 jurisdictions (covering all treaties signed, although not necessarily in force)
- status of MLI: in force.

Table 1. State of play of Canada's tax treaty network

Treaties in line with the Action 14 Minimum Standard following MLI impact	Treaties where actions are ongoing to make them in line with the Action 14 Minimum Standard	Following impact/actions, remaining treaties that are not in line with Action 14 Minimum Standard
40	4	52

Source: OECD

Canada's MAP programme

Organisation of competent authority function

- Competent Authority Services Division (CASD):
  - 46 persons:
    - one head of unit (Director)

    - 45 persons working on MAP cases:
        - 30 [Transfer pricing MAP/APA sections, exclusively attribution/allocation cases]
        - nine [MAP technical section, exclusively Other cases]
  - contact persons for MAP requests:

    Director, Competent Authority Services Division

    344 Slater Street, Canada Bldg., 18th Floor, Ottawa, Ontario K1A 0L5

    email: CPMAPAPAG@cra-arc.gc.ca
  - Requests can also be made electronically using the Canada Revenue Agency E-Services – see following link for more information: https://www.canada.ca/en/revenue-agency/services/e-services.html.
- Competent Authority Policy and Treaty Advisory Section:
  - eight persons:
    - one head of unit (Director)
    - seven persons working on treaty negotiations, developing treaty policy and resolving interpretative issues with respect to tax treaties (among which six persons work on other tasks as well).
  - contact persons for requests concerning general application or interpretation of Double Tax Treaties (DTT):
    - Director General, Legislative Policy Directorate, Competent Authority Policy and Treaty Advisory Section

      320 Queen St., Place de Ville Tower A, 6th Floor, Ottawa, Ontario K1A 0L5.

Figure 1. Competent Authority Organisational Structure

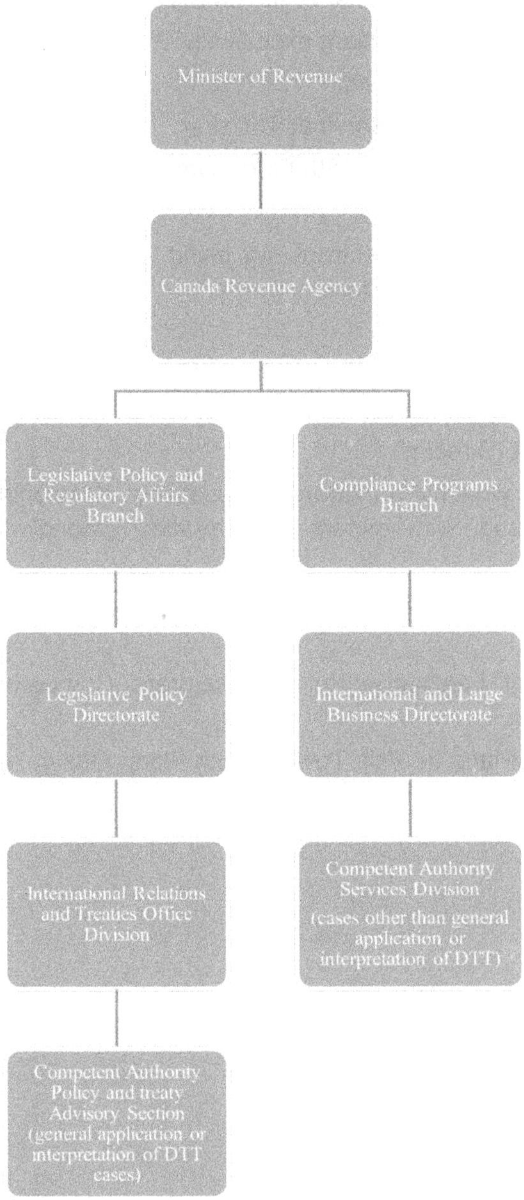

Source: OECD

Table 2. Guidance on the MAP process

MAP guidance	IC71-17R6 Competent Authority Assistance under Canada's Tax Conventions, 1 June 2021	https://www.canada.ca/en/revenue-agency/services/forms-publications/publications/ic71-17.html (Section "Making a request" to be referred to for form and content of a MAP request, including information requirements)
MAP profile	26 July 2022	https://www.oecd.org/tax/dispute/canada-dispute-resolution-profile.pdf

Overview of Canada's MAP Statistics for 2022

Please refer to https://www.oecd.org/tax/dispute/map-statistics-canada.pdf for details with respect to Canada's MAP Statistics.

Figure 2. Cases closed in 2022

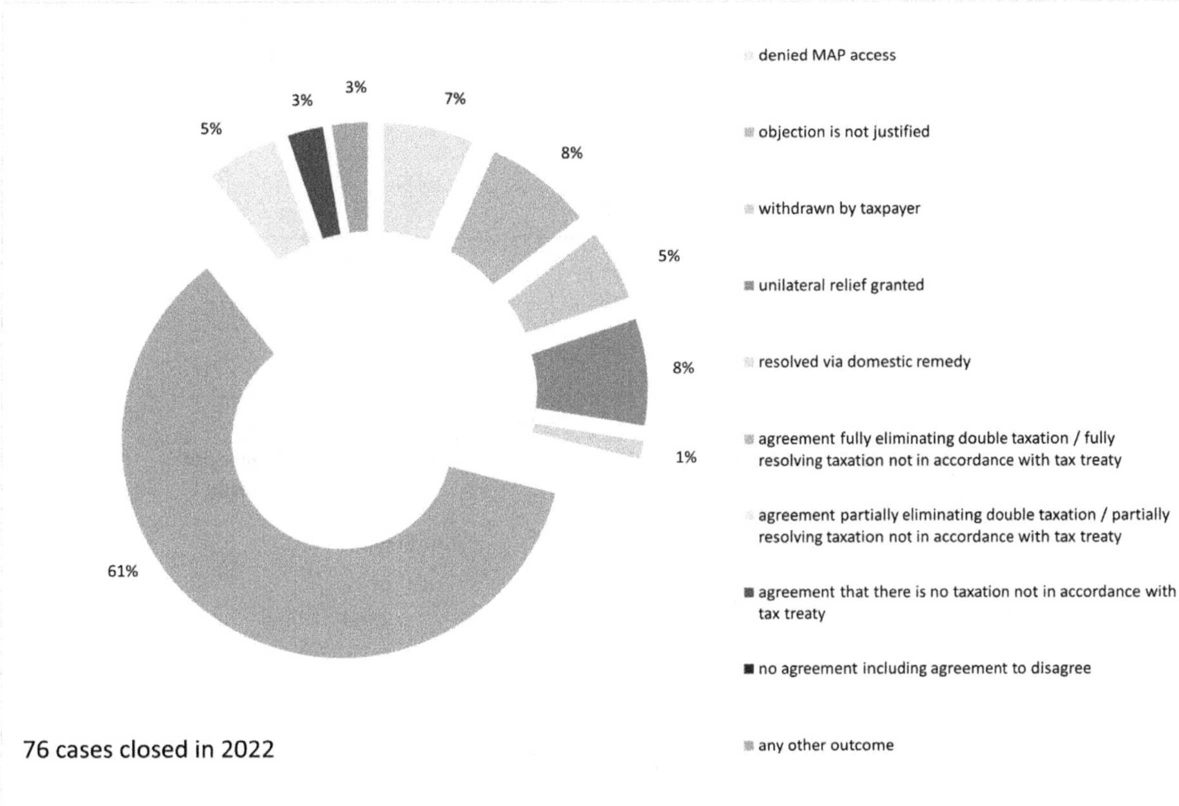

Source: OECD

Figure 3. Evolution of Canada's MAP caseload (2016-22)

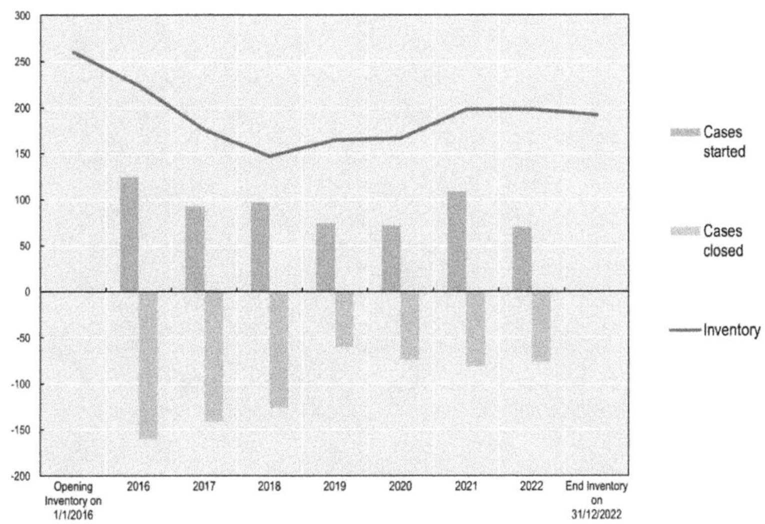

Source: OECD

Table 3. Overview of Canada's MAP caseload for 2022

Inventory for year 2022	Opening Inventory 1/1/2022	Cases started	Cases Closed	End Inventory 31/12/2022
Attribution/allocation cases	134	34	42	126
Other cases	64	36	34	66
Total	198	70	76	192

Source: OECD

Table 4. Canada's average time to resolve MAP cases in 2022

Cases resolved in year 2022	Pre-2016 cases		Post-2015 cases		All	
	Number of cases	**Average time**	**Number of cases**	**Average time** **Start to End**	**Number of cases**	**Average time**
Attribution / Allocation cases	0	N/A	42	23.53	42	23.53
Other cases	2	72.61	32	11.53	34	15.12
All cases	2	72.61	74	18.34	76	19.77

Source: OECD

Cayman Islands

Recent developments relating to MAP in Cayman Islands prior to 15 August 2023

Developments relating to MAP in the tax treaty network

- Cayman Islands did not provide the relevant information.

Other developments relating to MAP

- Cayman Islands did not provide the relevant information.

Latest Action 14 Peer Review report

14 April 2022 - https://doi.org/10.1787/6ef52ae4-en

Tax treaty network of Cayman Islands

- 10 treaties, applicable to 10 jurisdictions (covering all treaties signed, although not necessarily in force)
- status of MLI: not signed.

Table 1. State of play of Cayman Islands' tax treaty network

Treaties in line with the Action 14 Minimum Standard following MLI impact	Treaties where actions are ongoing to make them in line with the Action 14 Minimum Standard	Following impact/actions, remaining treaties that are not in line with Action 14 Minimum Standard
1	No information	No information

Source: OECD

Cayman Islands' MAP programme

Organisation of competent authority function

- six persons:
- contact persons for MAP requests:
    - Tax Information Authority
      Department for International Tax Cooperation | Cayman Islands Government
      Government Administration Building, Box 135
      133 Elgin Avenue |George Town | Grand Cayman KY1 9000 | Cayman Islands
      Direct: +1 (345) 244-2215 Email: TIA@gov.ky.

Figure 1. Competent Authority Organisational Structure

Source: OECD

Table 2. Guidance on the MAP process

MAP guidance	Cayman Islands did not provide the relevant information.	
MAP profile	18 October 2019	https://www.oecd.org/tax/dispute/Cayman-Islands-Dispute-Resolution-Profile.pdf

Source: OECD

Overview of Cayman Islands' MAP Statistics for 2022

Cayman Islands did not report any MAP cases in its 2022 MAP Statistics.

Please refer to https://www.oecd.org/tax/dispute/map-statistics-cayman-islands.pdf for details with respect to Cayman Islands' MAP Statistics.

Chile

Recent developments relating to MAP in Chile prior to 15 August 2023

Developments relating to MAP in the tax treaty network

- Entry into force in 2023 of tax treaties with India, the Netherlands and United Arab Emirates.

Other developments relating to MAP

- Protocols amending tax treaties in force with Brazil and the Netherlands have been signed in 2022 to meet Action 14 minimum standard. They are currently awaiting compliance with the internal procedures required by each country's legislation for their entry into force.
- Circular that gives instructions regarding the provisions on the MAP established in the tax treaties signed by Chile has been published in 2022 and 2023.

Latest Action 14 Peer Review report

26 July 2021 - https://doi.org/10.1787/1c650976-en

Tax treaty network of Chile

- 37 treaties, applicable to 37 jurisdictions (covering all treaties signed, although not necessarily in force)
- status of MLI: in force.

Table 1. State of play of Chile's tax treaty network

Treaties in line with the Action 14 Minimum Standard following MLI impact	Treaties where actions are ongoing to make them in line with the Action 14 Minimum Standard	Following impact/actions, remaining treaties that are not in line with Action 14 Minimum Standard
4	33	0

Source: OECD

Chile's MAP programme

Organisation of competent authority function

- 13 persons:
  - two heads of unit
  - 11 persons working on MAP cases:
    - of which, six persons work on attribution/allocation cases and five persons work on other cases.
- contact persons for MAP requests:

- Mr. Hernan Frigolet, Director
  Servicio de Impuestos Internos
  Teatinos 120, Piso 6, Santiago, Chile
  Tel: +56 2 223951600 Email: director.sii@sii.cl.

Figure 1. Competent Authority Organisational Structure

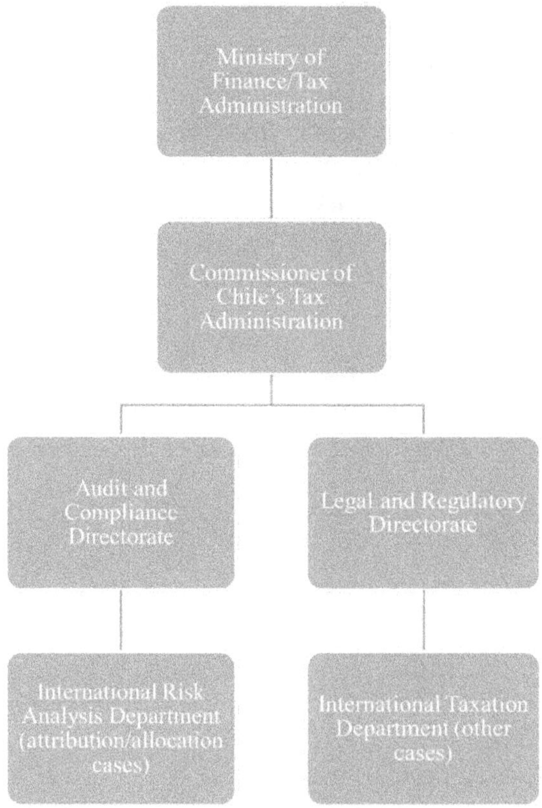

Source: OECD

Table 2. Guidance on the MAP process

MAP guidance	Circulars N°13/2022, March 2022 and N° 19/2023, April 2023	https://www.sii.cl/normativa_legislacion/circulares/2022/circu13.pdf https://www.sii.cl/normativa_legislacion/circulares/2023/circu19.pdf
MAP profile	31 July 2023	https://www.oecd.org/tax/dispute/chile-dispute-resolution-profile.pdf

Overview of Chile's MAP Statistics for 2022

Please refer to https://www.oecd.org/tax/dispute/map-statistics-chile.pdf for details with respect to Chile's MAP Statistics.

Figure 2. Cases closed in 2022

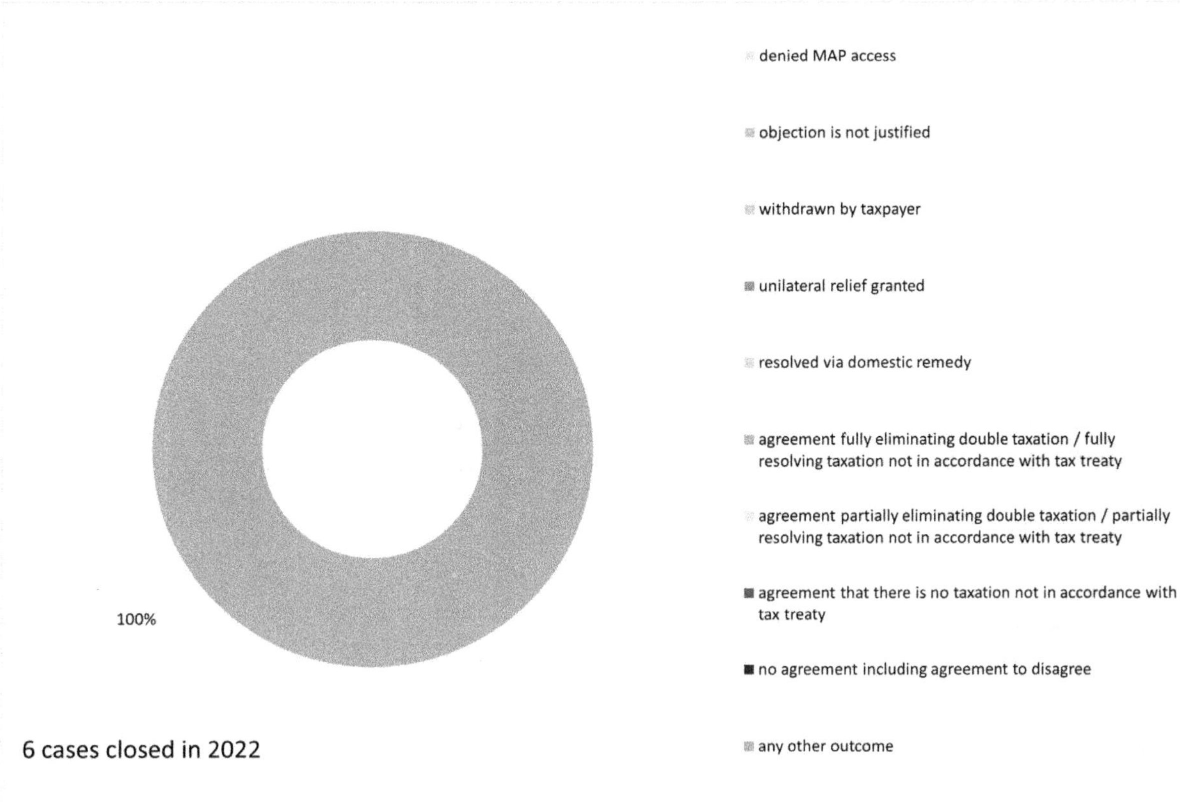

Source: OECD

Figure 3. Evolution of Chile's MAP caseload (2016-22)

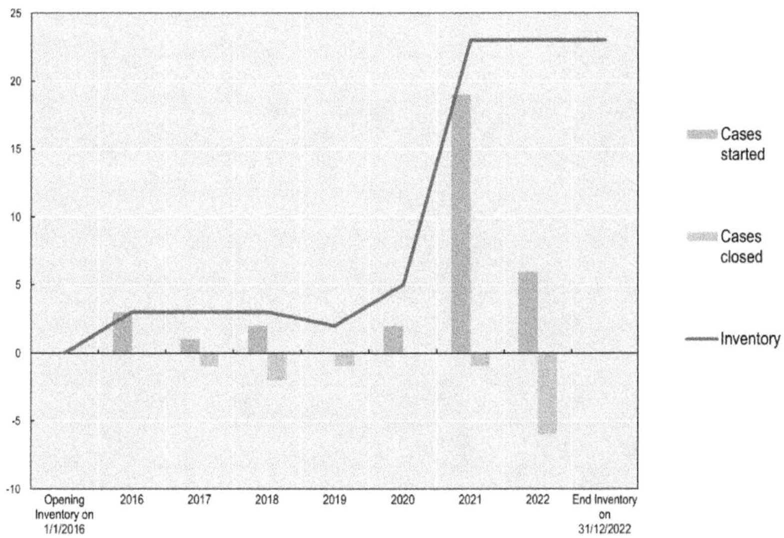

Source: OECD

Table 3. Overview of Chile's MAP caseload for 2022

Inventory for year 2022	Opening Inventory 1/1/2022	Cases started	Cases Closed	End Inventory 31/12/2022
Attribution/allocation cases	21	3	6	18
Other cases	2	3	0	5
Total	23	6	6	23

Source: OECD

Table 4. Chile's average time to resolve MAP cases in 2022

Cases resolved in year 2022	Pre-2016 cases		Post-2015 cases		All	
	Number of cases	**Average time**	**Number of cases**	**Average time** **Start to End**	**Number of cases**	**Average time**
Attribution / Allocation cases	0	N/A	6	17.96	6	17.96
Other cases	0	N/A	0	N/A	0	N/A
All cases	0	N/A	6	17.96	6	17.96

Source: OECD

China (People's Republic of)

Recent developments relating to MAP in China prior to 15 August 2023

Developments relating to MAP in the tax treaty network

- Entry into force of the tax treaty with Rwanda occurred in 2023.

Other developments relating to MAP

- No developments were reported

Latest Action 14 Peer Review report

18 October 2021 - https://doi.org/10.1787/2819971c-en

Tax treaty network of China

- 107 treaties, applicable to 108 jurisdictions (covering all treaties signed, although not necessarily in force)
- status of MLI: in force.

Table 1. State of play of China's tax treaty network

Treaties in line with the Action 14 Minimum Standard following MLI impact	Treaties where actions are ongoing to make them in line with the Action 14 Minimum Standard	Following impact/actions, remaining treaties that are not in line with Action 14 Minimum Standard
105	3	0

Source: OECD

China's MAP programme

Organisation of competent authority function

- 31 persons:
  - four heads of unit
  - 31 persons working on MAP cases:
    - 23 persons work on attribution/allocation cases and eight persons work on other cases.
- contact persons for MAP requests:
  - For attribution / allocation cases: the taxpayer should make the MAP request directly to the STA headquarters, with the "Application for Initiating Mutual Agreement Procedures Concerning Special Tax Adjustments" and relevant information related to the special tax adjustments within the time period specified in the tax treaty.

- For other cases: Chinese resident (national) should make the MAP request to the relevant Provincial Tax Authority, and the Provincial Tax Authority will forward the file to State Taxation Administration (STA) after collecting all necessary information.

Figure 1. Competent Authority Organisational Structure

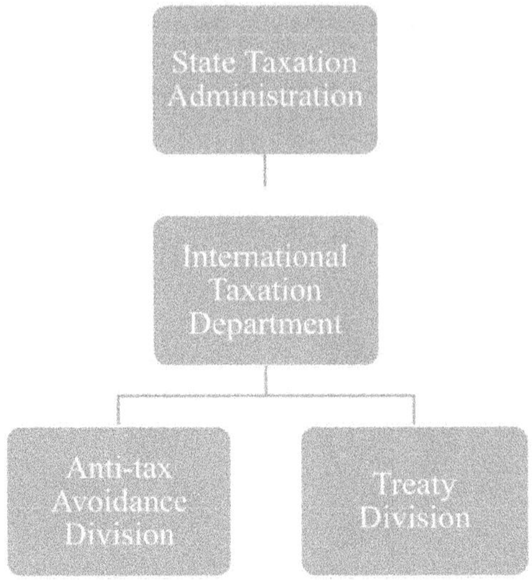

Source: OECD

Table 2. Guidance on the MAP process

MAP guidance	For non-TP cases: *STA Public Notice [2013] No. 56*, 24 September 2013	http://www.chinatax.gov.cn/n810341/n810755/c3523242/content.html (Section XX to be referred to for form and content of a MAP request, including information requirements)
	For TP cases: *STA Public Notice [2017] No. 6*, 17 March 2017	http://www.chinatax.gov.cn/n810341/n810755/c2538695/content.html
MAP profile	28 January 2019	https://www.oecd.org/tax/dispute/china-dispute-resolution-profile.pdf

Overview of China's MAP Statistics for 2022

Please refer to https://www.oecd.org/tax/dispute/map-statistics-china.pdf for details with respect to China (People's Republic of)'s MAP Statistics.

Figure 2. Cases closed in 2022

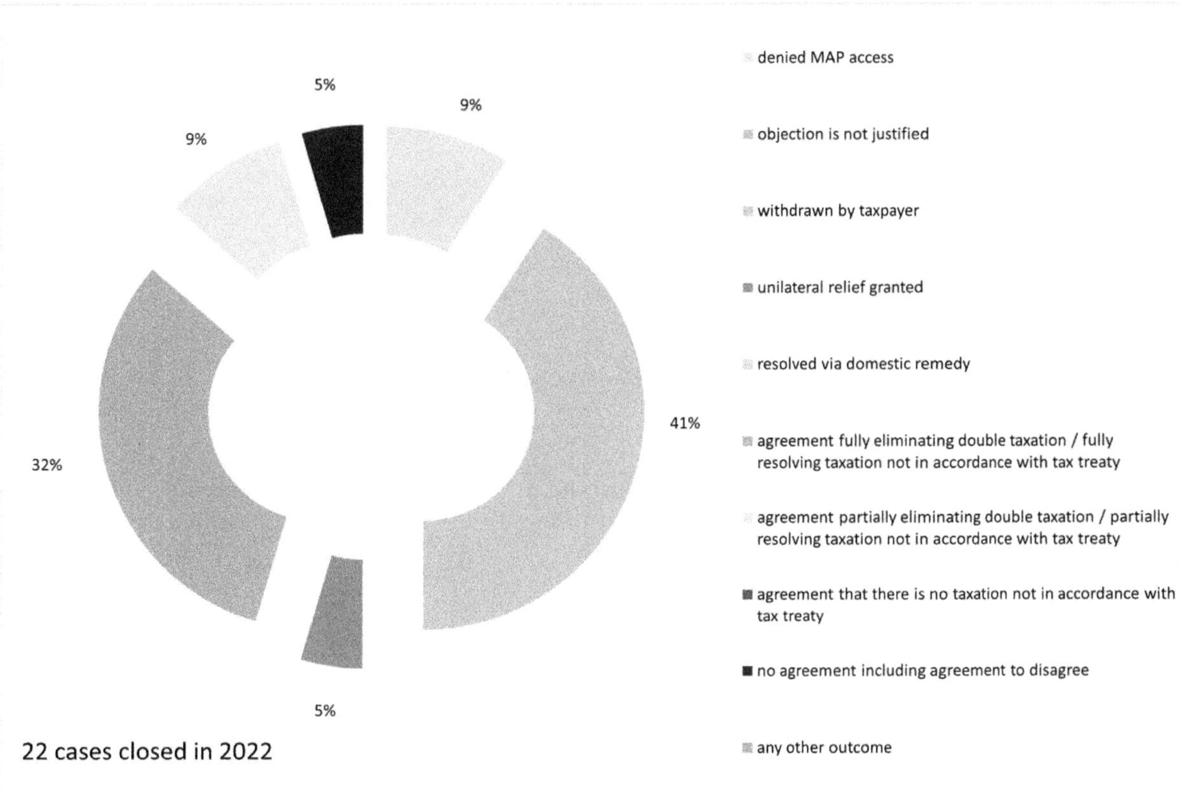

Source: OECD

Figure 3. Evolution of China's MAP caseload (2016-22)

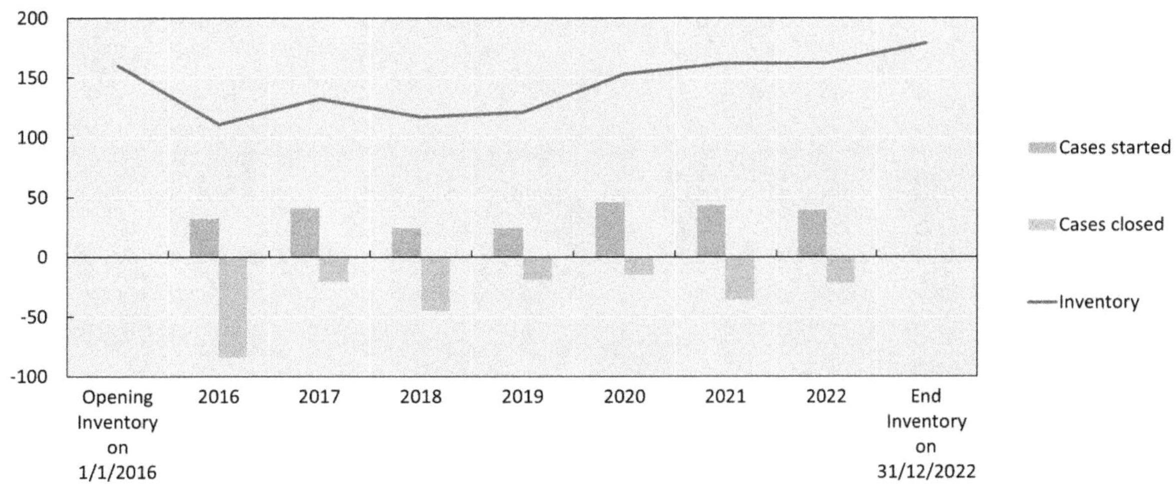

Source: OECD

Table 3. Overview of China's MAP caseload for 2022

Inventory for year 2022	Opening Inventory 1/1/2022	Cases started	Cases Closed	End Inventory 31/12/2022
Attribution/allocation cases	64	16	12	68
Other cases	98	23	10	111
Total	162	39	22	179

Source: OECD

Table 4. China's average time to resolve MAP cases in 2022

Cases resolved in year 2022	Pre-2016 cases		Post-2015 cases		All	
	Number of cases	**Average time**	**Number of cases**	**Average time** **Start to End**	**Number of cases**	**Average time**
Attribution / Allocation cases	1	102.41	11	33.44	12	39.19
Other cases	1	160.96	9	28.84	10	42.05
All cases	2	131.69	20	31.37	22	40.49

Source: OECD

Colombia

Recent developments relating to MAP in Colombia prior to 15 August 2023

Developments relating to MAP in the tax treaty network

- All treaty negotiations include MAP provisions in line with Action 14 Minimum Standard.

Other developments relating to MAP

- Update of the MAP profile on 25 September 2023.

Latest Action 14 Peer Review report

26 July 2021 - https://doi.org/10.1787/01c36574-en

Tax treaty network of Colombia

- 19 treaties, applicable to 21 jurisdictions (covering all treaties signed, although not necessarily in force)
- status of MLI: signed.

Table 1. State of play of Colombia's tax treaty network

Treaties in line with the Action 14 Minimum Standard following MLI impact	Treaties where actions are ongoing to make them in line with the Action 14 Minimum Standard	Following impact/actions, remaining treaties that are not in line with Action 14 Minimum Standard
16	3	0

Source: OECD

Colombia's MAP programme

Organisation of competent authority function

- four persons:
  - one head of unit
  - three persons working on MAP cases.
- contact persons for MAP requests:
  - General Commissioner Dirección de Impuestos y Aduanas Nacionales - DIAN
    dirgen_map@dian.gov.co
    Tel:6079999
    ext 901060 Carrera 8 No. 6C-38 piso 6, Bogotá – Colombia.

Figure 1. Competent Authority Organisational Structure

Source: OECD

Table 2. Guidance on the MAP process

MAP guidance	*Resolution No. 000085*, 21 August 2020	https://www.dian.gov.co/normatividad/Normatividad/Resoluci%C3%B3n%20000085%20de%2021-08-2020.pdf (Article 14 to be referred to for form and content of a MAP request, including information requirements)
MAP profile	19 July 2023	https://www.oecd.org/tax/dispute/colombia-dispute-resolution-profile.pdf

Overview of Colombia's MAP Statistics for 2022

Please refer to https://www.oecd.org/tax/dispute/map-statistics-colombia.pdf for details with respect to Colombia's MAP Statistics.

Cases closed in 2022

No MAP cases were closed by Colombia in 2022.

Figure 2. Evolution of Colombia's MAP caseload (2016-22)

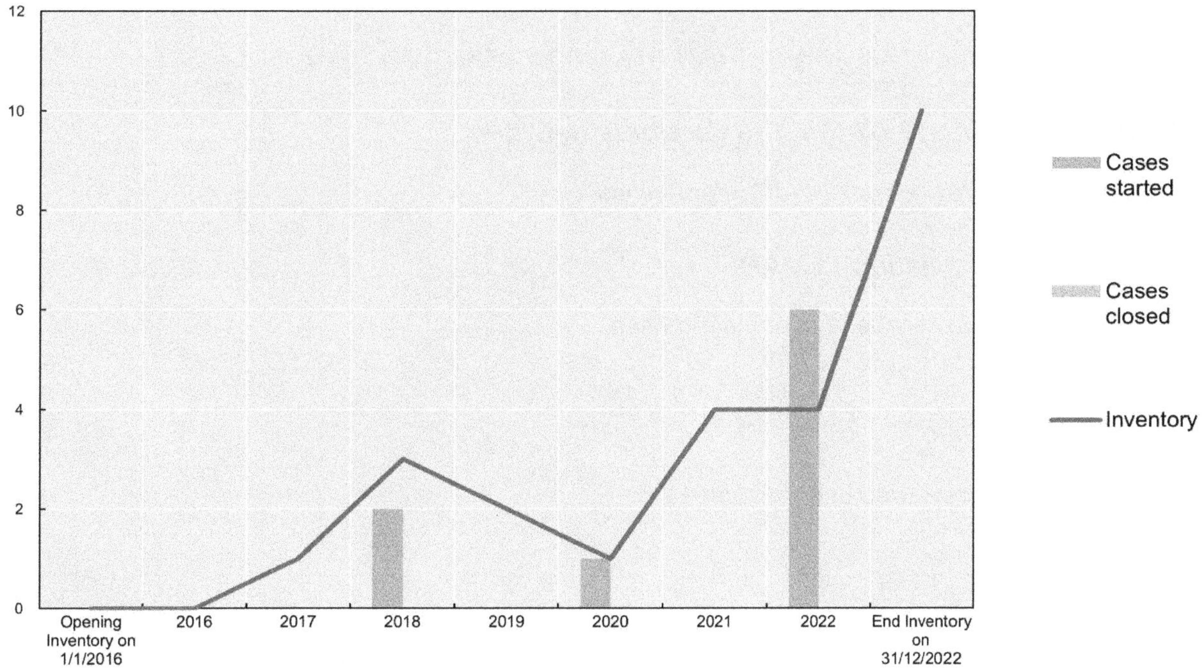

Source: OECD

Table 3. Overview of Colombia's MAP caseload for 2022

Inventory for year 2022	Opening Inventory 1/1/2022	Cases started	Cases Closed	End Inventory 31/12/2022
Attribution/allocation cases	1	5	0	6
Other cases	3	1	0	4
Total	4	6	0	10

Source: OECD

Table 4. Colombia's average time to resolve MAP cases in 2022

Cases resolved in year 2022	Pre-2016 cases		Post-2015 cases		All	
	Number of cases	**Average time**	**Number of cases**	**Average time** **Start to End**	**Number of cases**	**Average time**
Attribution / Allocation cases	0	N/A	0	N/A	0	N/A
Other cases	0	N/A	0	N/A	0	N/A
All cases	0	N/A	0	N/A	0	N/A

Source: OECD

Congo (Republic of the)

Recent developments relating to MAP in Congo prior to 15 August 2023

Developments relating to MAP in the tax treaty network

- Congo did not provide the relevant information.

Other developments relating to MAP

- Congo did not provide the relevant information.

Latest Action 14 Peer Review report

Congo is yet to be peer reviewed under Action 14.

Tax treaty network of Congo

- eight treaties, applicable to eight jurisdictions (covering all treaties signed, although not necessarily in force)
- status of MLI: not signed.

Table 1. State of play of Congo's tax treaty network

Treaties in line with the Action 14 Minimum Standard following MLI impact	Treaties where actions are ongoing to make them in line with the Action 14 Minimum Standard	Following impact/actions, remaining treaties that are not in line with Action 14 Minimum Standard
3	No information	No information

Source: OECD

Republic of the Congo's MAP programme

Organisation of competent authority function

- Congo did not provide the relevant information.

Table 2. Guidance on the MAP process

MAP guidance	Congo did not provide the relevant information.	
MAP profile	No MAP profile published	

Overview of Republic of the Congo's MAP Statistics for 2022

Republic of the Congo did not declare its MAP Statistics for 2022

Cook Islands

Recent developments relating to MAP in Cook Islands prior to 15 August 2023

Developments relating to MAP in the tax treaty network

- Cook Islands did not provide the relevant information.

Other developments relating to MAP

- Cook Islands did not provide the relevant information.

Latest Action 14 Peer Review report

- The stage 1 Simplified Peer Review report of Cook Islands is expected to be published early 2024.

Tax treaty network of Cook Islands

- two treaties, applicable to two jurisdictions (covering all treaties signed, although not necessarily in force)
- status of MLI: not signed.

Table 1. State of play of Cook Islands' tax treaty network

Treaties in line with the Action 14 Minimum Standard following MLI impact	Treaties where actions are ongoing to make them in line with the Action 14 Minimum Standard	Following impact/actions, remaining treaties that are not in line with Action 14 Minimum Standard
0	1	1

Source: OECD

Cook Islands' MAP programme

Organisation of competent authority function

- competent authority has no resources currently available.
- contact persons for MAP requests:
  - Xavier Mitchell | Collector, Comptroller and Director Revenue Management Division
    Ministry of Finance and Economic Management
    Rarotonga, , Cook Islands | PO Box 120
    phone: 29365 ext 8210, web: www.mfem.gov.ck, email: xavier.mitchell@cookislands.gov.ck.

Figure 1. Competent Authority Organisational Structure

Source: OECD

Table 2. Guidance on the MAP process

MAP guidance	No MAP guidance published	-
MAP profile	1 March 2023	https://www.oecd.org/tax/dispute/cook-islands-dispute-resolution-profile.pdf

Overview of Cook Islands' MAP Statistics for 2022

Cook Islands did not report any MAP cases in its 2022 MAP Statistics.

Please refer to https://www.oecd.org/tax/dispute/map-statistics-cook-islands.pdf for details with respect to Cook Islands' MAP Statistics.

Costa Rica

Recent developments relating to MAP in Costa Rica prior to 15 August 2023

Developments relating to MAP in the tax treaty network

- Costa Rica did not provide the relevant information.

Other developments relating to MAP

- Costa Rica did not provide the relevant information.

Latest Action 14 Peer Review report

- The stage 1 Simplified Peer Review report of Costa Rica is expected to be published early 2024.

Tax treaty network of Costa Rica

- four treaties, applicable to four jurisdictions (covering all treaties signed, although not necessarily in force)
- status of MLI: in force.

Table 1. State of play of Costa Rica's tax treaty network

Treaties in line with the Action 14 Minimum Standard following MLI impact	Treaties where actions are ongoing to make them in line with the Action 14 Minimum Standard	Following impact/actions, remaining treaties that are not in line with Action 14 Minimum Standard
4	No information	No information

Source: OECD

Costa Rica's MAP programme

Organisation of competent authority function

- two persons working on MAP cases (among which one person works on other tasks as well)
- contact persons for MAP requests:
  - Mr. Mario Ramos-Martínez, Director of the Tax Administration.
    San José-Costa Rica. Central and 1° Avenue 5° Streets. La Llacuna Building, 14th floor.
    Telephone: (506)2539-6517 Email: direcciongeneral-dgt@hacienda.go.cr
    Please also, mark in copy: tributacioninter@hacienda.go.cr.

Figure 1. Competent Authority Organisational Structure

Source: OECD

Table 2. Guidance on the MAP process

MAP guidance	*Resolution N° DGT-R-12-201, art. 99 of the General Tax Code*, December 2017	http://www.pgrweb.go.cr/scij/Busqueda/Normativa/Normas/nrm_texto_completo.aspx?param1=NRTC&nValor1=1&nValor2=84749&nValor3=109464&strTipM=TC%20 (Section XX to be referred to for form and content of a MAP request, including information requirements)
MAP profile	23 December 2022	https://www.oecd.org/tax/dispute/costa-rica-dispute-resolution-profile.pdf

Overview of Costa Rica's MAP Statistics for 2022

Please refer to https://www.oecd.org/tax/dispute/map-statistics-costa-rica.pdf for details with respect to Costa Rica's MAP Statistics.

Cases closed in 2022

No MAP cases were closed by Costa Rica in 2022.

Figure 2. Evolution of Costa Rica's MAP caseload (2016-22)

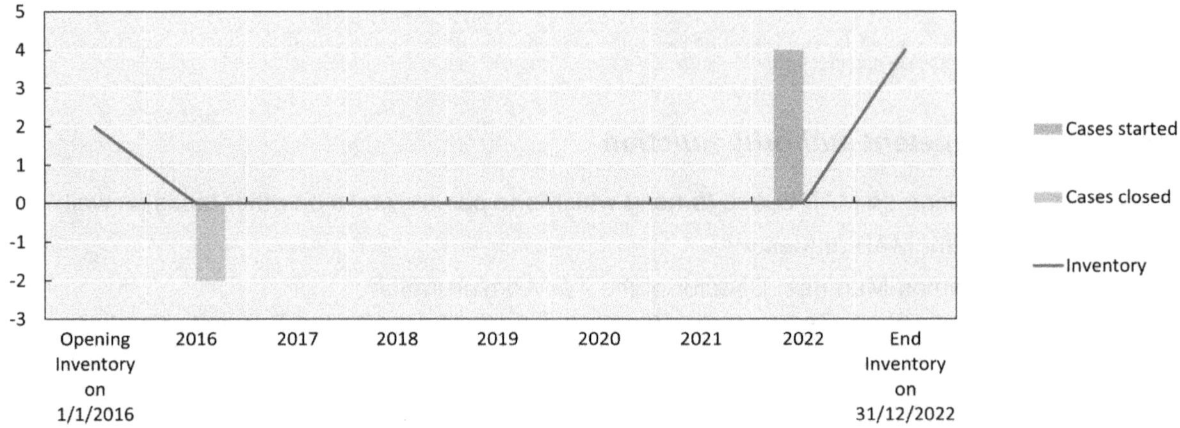

Source: OECD

Table 3. Overview of Costa Rica's MAP caseload for 2022

Inventory for year 2022	Opening Inventory 1/1/2022	Cases started	Cases Closed	End Inventory 31/12/2022
Attribution/allocation cases	0	4	0	4
Other cases	0	0	0	0
Total	0	4	0	4

Source: OECD

Table 4. Costa Rica's average time to resolve MAP cases in 2022

Cases resolved in year 2022	Pre-2016 cases		Post-2015 cases		All	
	Number of cases	**Average time**	**Number of cases**	**Average time** **Start to End**	**Number of cases**	**Average time**
Attribution / Allocation cases	0	N/A	0	N/A	0	N/A
Other cases	0	N/A	0	N/A	0	N/A
All cases	0	N/A	0	N/A	0	N/A

Source: OECD

Côte d'Ivoire

Recent developments relating to MAP in Côte d'Ivoire prior to 15 August 2023

Developments relating to MAP in the tax treaty network

- Côte d'Ivoire did not provide the relevant information.

Other developments relating to MAP

- Côte d'Ivoire did not provide the relevant information.

Latest Action 14 Peer Review report

Côte d'Ivoire is yet to be peer-reviewed under Action 14.

Tax treaty network of Côte d'Ivoire

- 14 treaties, applicable to 20 jurisdictions (covering all treaties signed, although not necessarily in force)
- status of MLI: signed.

Table 1. State of play of Côte d'Ivoire's tax treaty network

Treaties in line with the Action 14 Minimum Standard following MLI impact	Treaties where actions are ongoing to make them in line with the Action 14 Minimum Standard	Following impact/actions, remaining treaties that are not in line with Action 14 Minimum Standard
6	No information	No information

Source: OECD

Côte d'Ivoire's MAP programme

Organisation of competent authority function

- contact persons for MAP requests:
  - M. OUATTARA Sié Abou, Directeur général des Impôts
    BP V103 Abidjan Cité administrative Plateau-Abidjan, Tour E 10ème étage
    Tél : (+225) 20 21 70 15 | Fax : (+225) 20 22 87 86 | Email : infodgi@dgi.gouv.ci

Competent Authority Organisational Structure

Côte d'Ivoire did not provide the relevant information.

Table 2. Guidance on the MAP process

MAP guidance	No MAP guidance published	-
MAP profile	20 June 2017	https://www.oecd.org/tax/dispute/cote-divoire-dispute-resolution-profile.pdf

Overview of Côte d'Ivoire's MAP Statistics for 2022

Côte d'Ivoire did not report any MAP cases in its 2022 MAP Statistics.

Please refer to https://www.oecd.org/tax/dispute/map-statistics-cote-d-ivoire.pdf for details with respect to Côte d'Ivoire's MAP Statistics.

Croatia

Recent developments relating to MAP in Croatia prior to 15 August 2023

Developments relating to MAP in the tax treaty network

- Croatia updated its MAP guidelines and introduced a documented bilateral notification process. Accordingly, Croatia applies its notification process for future cases in which its competent authority considered the objection raised in a MAP request not to be justified and when the tax treaty concerned does not contain Article 25(1) of the OECD Model Tax Convention as amended by the Action 14 final report. Accordingly, Croatia is introducing, in its newly negotiated treaties, an alternative provision on bilateral notification process.

Other developments relating to MAP

- Croatia updated its MAP guidelines in 2022.

Latest Action 14 Peer Review report

26 July 2021 - https://doi.org/10.1787/7a89e6e4-en

Tax treaty network of Croatia

- 65 treaties, applicable to 66 jurisdictions (covering all treaties signed, although not necessarily in force)
- status of MLI: in force.

Table 1. State of play of Croatia's tax treaty network

Treaties in line with the Action 14 Minimum Standard following MLI impact	Treaties where actions are ongoing to make them in line with the Action 14 Minimum Standard	Following impact/actions, remaining treaties that are not in line with Action 14 Minimum Standard
60	3	2

Source: OECD

Croatia's MAP programme

Organisation of competent authority function

- two persons working on MAP cases
  - One head of unit
  - Two persons working on MAP cases (all of which work on other tasks as well)
  - One person works on attribution/allocation cases and one person works on other cases
- contact persons for MAP requests:

- Republic of Croatia, Ministry of Finance, Croatian Tax Administration, Central office, Boskoviceva 5, 10 000 Zagreb, Croatia Phone: +385 1 4809 000 / Fax: +385 1 4809 129 / Email: su_pis@porezna-uprava.hr.

Figure 1. Competent Authority Organisational Structure

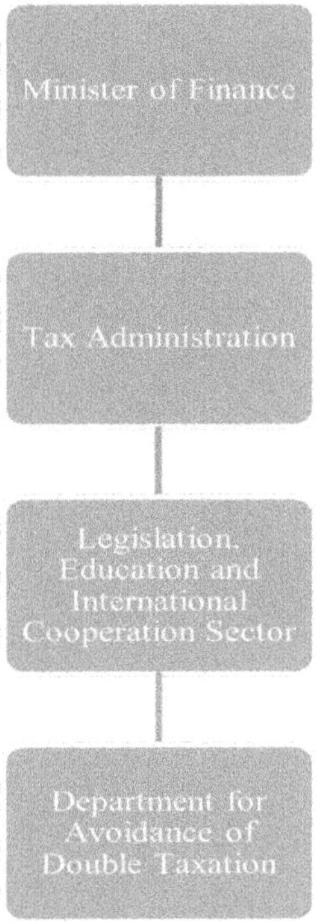

Source: OECD

Table 2. Guidance on the MAP process

MAP guidance	*Smjernice za postupak zajedničkog dogovaranja, ažurirano 2022. (Guidelines for MAP, updated 2022)*	https://www.porezna-uprava.hr/Dokumenti%20vijesti/Postupak%20zajedni%C4%8Dkog%20dogovaranja%20.pdf (Section 4.1.2. to be referred to for form and content of a MAP request, including information requirements)
MAP profile	15 September 2023	https://www.oecd.org/tax/dispute/croatia-dispute-resolution-profile.pdf

Overview of Croatia's MAP Statistics for 2022

Please refer to https://www.oecd.org/tax/dispute/map-statistics-croatia.pdf for details with respect to Croatia's MAP Statistics.

Figure 2. Cases closed in 2022

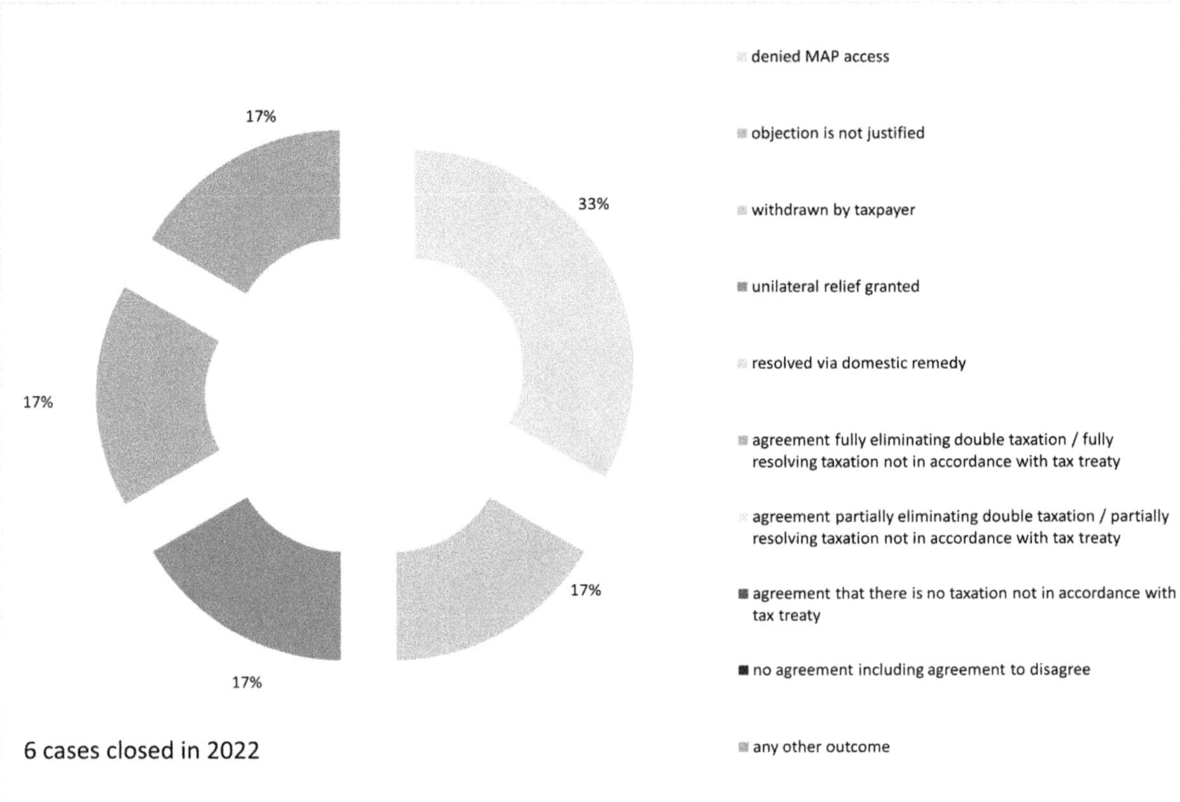

Source: OECD

Figure 3. Evolution of Croatia's MAP caseload (2016-22)

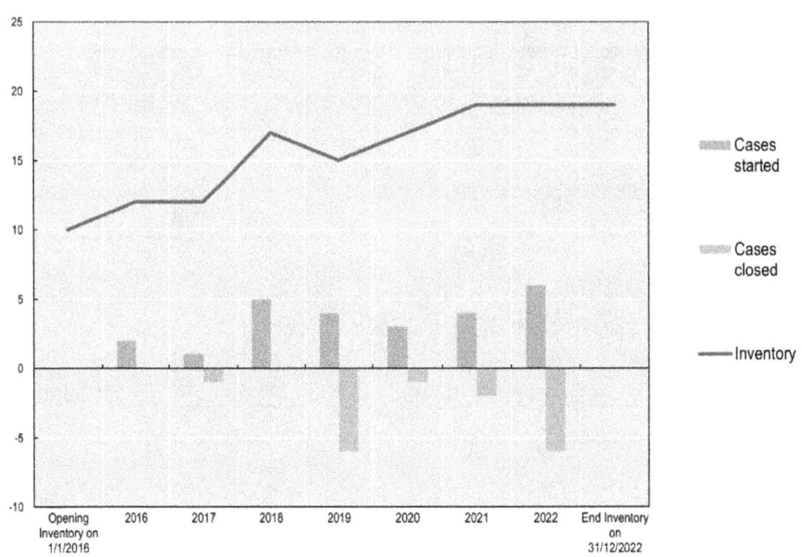

Source: OECD

Table 3. Overview of Croatia's MAP caseload for 2022

Inventory for year 2022	Opening Inventory 1/1/2022	Cases started	Cases Closed	End Inventory 31/12/2022
Attribution/allocation cases	6	4	2	8
Other cases	13	2	4	11
Total	19	6	6	19

Source: OECD

Table 4. Croatia's average time to resolve MAP cases in 2022

Cases resolved in year 2022	Pre-2016 cases		Post-2015 cases		All	
	Number of cases	**Average time**	**Number of cases**	**Average time** **Start to End**	**Number of cases**	**Average time**
Attribution / Allocation cases	0	N/A	2	23.61	2	23.61
Other cases	1	53.00	3	16.07	4	25.30
All cases	1	53.00	5	19.08	6	24.74

Source: OECD

Curaçao

Recent developments relating to MAP in Curaçao prior to 15 August 2023

Developments relating to MAP in the tax treaty network

- The treaties to promote economic relations with Denmark and Finland have been abolished as per June 1, 2021.

Other developments relating to MAP

- No developments were reported

Latest Action 14 Peer Review report

24 January 2022 - https://doi.org/10.1787/29b97fc3-en

Tax treaty network of Curaçao

- six treaties, applicable to seven jurisdictions (covering all treaties signed, although not necessarily in force)
- status of MLI: in force.

Table 1. State of play of Curaçao's tax treaty network

Treaties in line with the Action 14 Minimum Standard following MLI impact	Treaties where actions are ongoing to make them in line with the Action 14 Minimum Standard	Following impact/actions, remaining treaties that are not in line with Action 14 Minimum Standard
4	Not applicable, the treaty with Denmark and Finland have been abolished.	Not applicable as these remaining treaties are to promote economic relations. Curaçao will comply with the Action 14 Minimum Standard when concluding all of its future tax treaties.

Source: OECD

Curaçao's MAP programme

Organisation of competent authority function

- two persons:
  - one head of unit (Director of Fiscal Affairs)
  - one person working on MAP cases (this person works on other tasks as well):
    - these 2 persons work on attribution/allocation cases and on other cases. We refer to section C.3 of Curaçao's latest Action 14 Peer Review report. There is no change in the number of MAP cases and therefore this is still applicable.

- contact persons for MAP requests:
  - Attn. Mrs. R Sillé, LL.M. Director of Fiscal Affairs, Ministry of Finance, E-mail: runela.sille@gobiernu.cw
  - For MAP requests relating to the residence of taxpayers for corporate tiebreaker procedures: Attn. Mrs. J. Isenia, LL.M. Inspectorate of Taxes, Curaçao Regentesselaan z/n Curaçao, E-mail: jamila.isenia@gobiernu.cw.

Figure 1. Competent Authority Organisational Structure

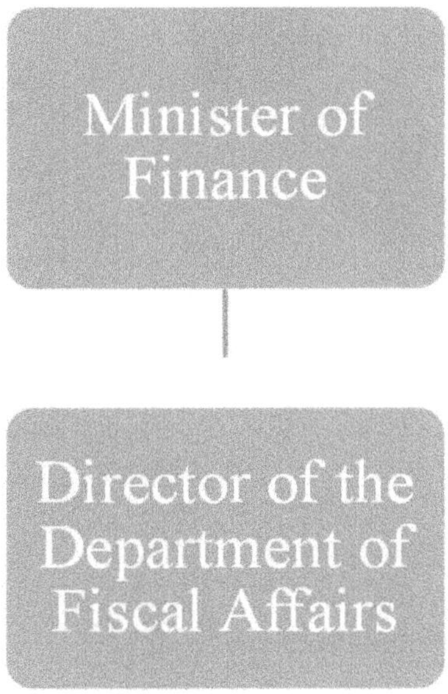

Source: OECD

Table 2. Guidance on the MAP process

MAP guidance	*The International Mutual Agreement Procedure (MAP)*, June 2021	https://minfin.cw/wp-content/uploads/2021/07/MAP-guidelines_updated-in-June-2021.pdf (Sections 6 and 14 to be referred to for form and content of a MAP request, including information requirements)
MAP profile	20 July 2021	https://www.oecd.org/tax/dispute/curacao-dispute-resolution-profile.pdf

Overview of Curaçao's MAP Statistics for 2022

Please refer to https://www.oecd.org/tax/dispute/map-statistics-curaçao.pdf for details with respect to Curaçao's MAP Statistics.

Figure 2. Cases closed in 2022

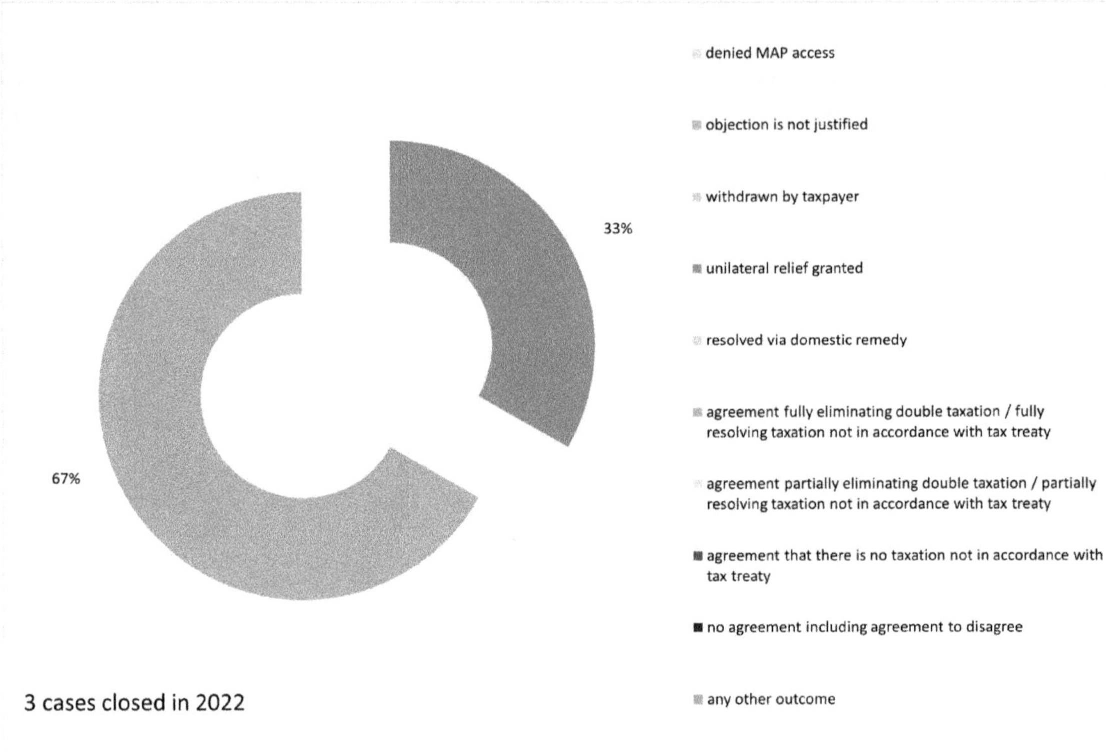

Source: OECD

Figure 3. Evolution of Curaçao's MAP caseload (2016-22)

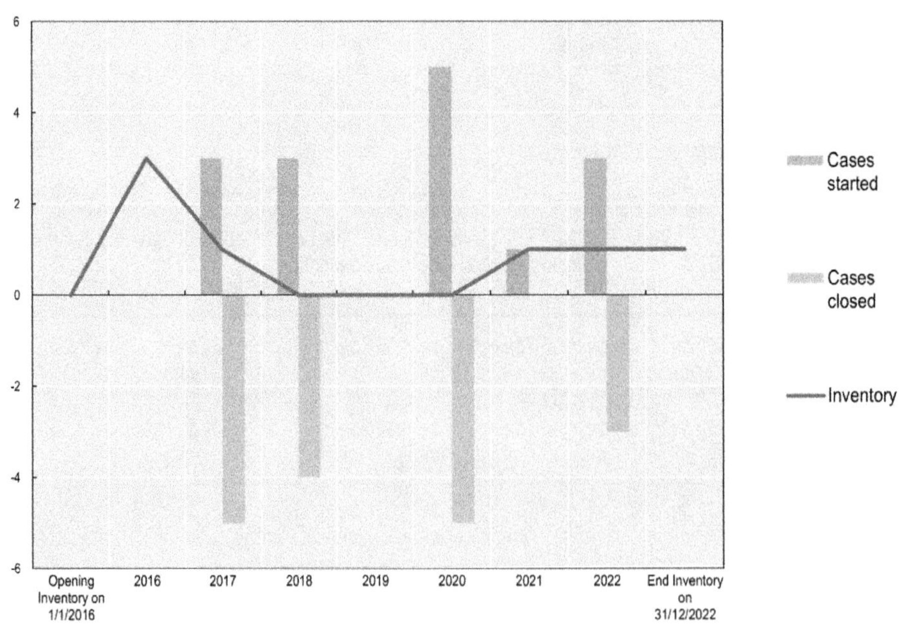

Source: OECD

Table 3. Overview of Curaçao's MAP caseload for 2022

Inventory for year 2022	Opening Inventory 1/1/2022	Cases started	Cases Closed	End Inventory 31/12/2022
Attribution/allocation cases	0	0	0	0
Other cases	1	3	3	1
Total	1	3	3	1

Source: OECD

Table 4. Curaçao's average time to resolve MAP cases in 2022

Cases resolved in year 2022	Pre-2016 cases		Post-2015 cases		All	
	Number of cases	**Average time**	**Number of cases**	**Average time** **Start to End**	**Number of cases**	**Average time**
Attribution / Allocation cases	0	N/A	0	N/A	0	N/A
Other cases	0	N/A	3	6.05	3	6.05
All cases	0	N/A	3	6.05	3	6.05

Source: OECD

Czechia

Recent developments relating to MAP in Czechia prior to 15 August 2023

Developments relating to MAP in the tax treaty network

- On July 24, 2023, DTT with Kosovo came into force; on May 24, 2023, new DTT with UAE was signed, on May 2, 2023, DTT with Rwanda was signed.
- On February 7, 2023, DTT with Cameroon was signed; on February 3, 2023, new DTT with Sri Lanka was signed.

Other developments relating to MAP

- MAP guidance in the process of preparation

Latest Action 14 Peer Review report

22 October 2020 - https://doi.org/10.1787/b8ee5001-en

Tax treaty network of Czechia

- 96 treaties, applicable to 97 jurisdictions
- status of MLI: in force.

Table 1. State of play of Czechia's tax treaty network

Treaties in line with the Action 14 Minimum Standard following MLI impact	Treaties where actions are ongoing to make them in line with the Action 14 Minimum Standard	Following impact/actions, remaining treaties that are not in line with Action 14 Minimum Standard
89	2	5

Source: OECD

Czechia's MAP programme

Organisation of competent authority function

- 15 persons:
  - two head(s) of unit
  - 13 persons working on MAP cases (all of which work on other tasks as well):
    - nine persons work on attribution/allocation cases and four persons work on other cases.
- contact persons for MAP requests:
  - for other MAP cases: Václav Zíka, Head of the Division of International Taxation, Ministry of Finance, Letenská 15, 118 10 Prague 1, the Czechia / Tel: +420257043197 / Email: vaclav.zika@mfcr.cz

- for attribution/allocation cases: Vítězslav Kapoun, Director of the Income Taxes Department II, General Financial Directorate Lazarská 7, 117 22 Prague 1, the Czechia / Tel: +420296851751 / Fax: +420296853047 / Email: vitezslav.kapoun@fs.mfcr.cz.

Figure 1. Competent Authority Organisational Structure

Source: OECD

Table 2. Guidance on the MAP process

MAP guidance	MAP guidance in the process of being prepared	-
MAP profile	02 October 2023	https://www.oecd.org/tax/dispute/czech-republic-dispute-resolution-profile.pdf

Overview of Czechia's MAP Statistics for 2022

Please refer to https://www.oecd.org/tax/dispute/map-statistics-czech-republic.pdf for details with respect to Czechia's MAP Statistics.

Figure 2. Cases closed in 2022

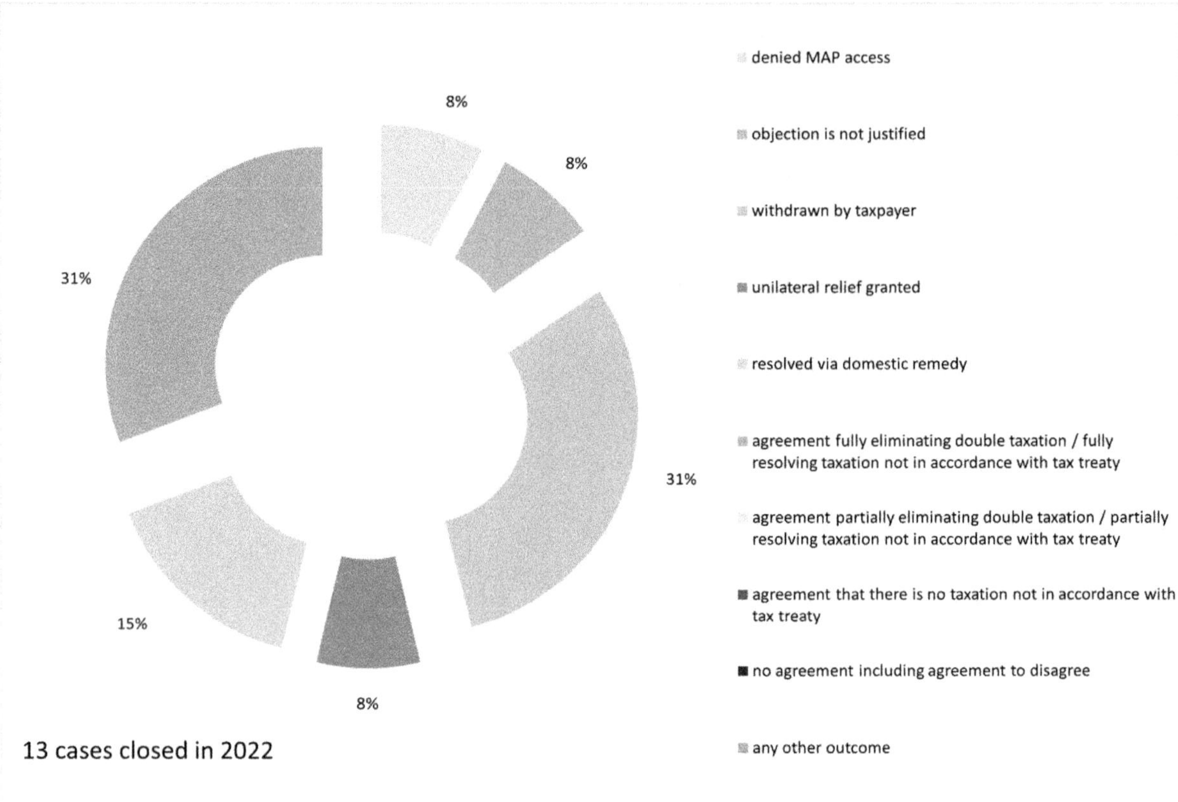

Source: OECD

Figure 3. Evolution of Czechia's MAP caseload (2016-22)

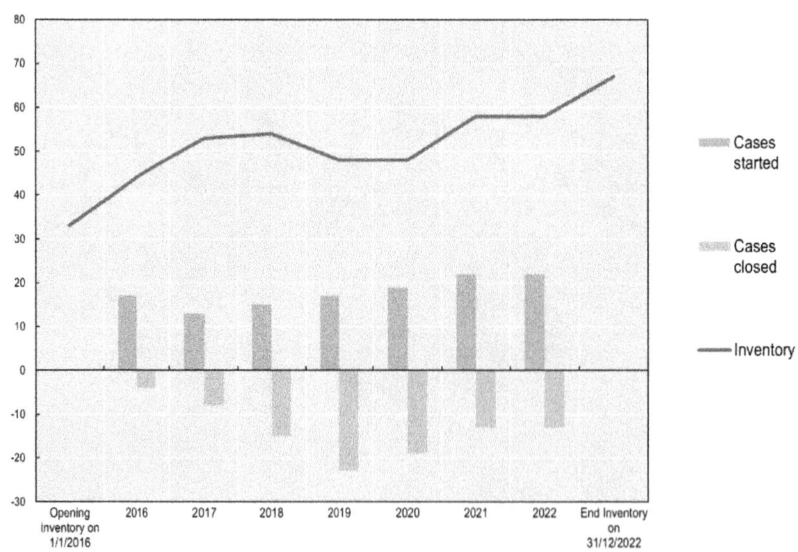

Source: OECD

Table 3. Overview of Czechia's MAP caseload for 2022

Inventory for year 2022	Opening Inventory 1/1/2022	Cases started	Cases Closed	End Inventory 31/12/2022
Attribution/allocation cases	30	14	6	38
Other cases	28	8	7	29
Total	58	22	13	67

Source: OECD

Table 4. Czechia's average time to resolve MAP cases in 2022

Cases resolved in year 2022	Pre-2016 cases		Post-2015 cases		All	
	Number of cases	**Average time**	**Number of cases**	**Average time** **Start to End**	**Number of cases**	**Average time**
Attribution / Allocation cases	1	111.95	5	13.45	6	29.87
Other cases	0	N/A	7	10.42	7	10.42
All cases	1	111.95	12	11.68	13	19.40

Source: OECD

Democratic Republic of the Congo

Recent developments relating to MAP in Democratic Republic of the Congo prior to 15 August 2023

Developments relating to MAP in the tax treaty network

- Democratic Republic of the Congo did not provide the relevant information.

Other developments relating to MAP

- Democratic Republic of the Congo did not provide the relevant information.

Latest Action 14 Peer Review report

Democratic Republic of the Congo is yet to be peer reviewed under Action 14.

Tax treaty network of Democratic Republic of the Congo

- seven treaties, applicable to seven jurisdictions (covering all treaties signed, although not necessarily in force)
- status of MLI: not signed.

Table 1. State of play of Democratic Republic of the Congo's tax treaty network

Treaties in line with the Action 14 Minimum Standard following MLI impact	Treaties where actions are ongoing to make them in line with the Action 14 Minimum Standard	Following impact/actions, remaining treaties that are not in line with Action 14 Minimum Standard
5	No information	No information

Source: OECD

Democratic Republic of the Congo's MAP programme

Organisation of competent authority function

- Democratic Republic of the Congo did not provide the relevant information.

Table 2. Guidance on the MAP process

MAP guidance	MAP guidance not published	-
MAP profile	9 March 2017	https://www.oecd.org/tax/dispute/drc-dispute-resolution-profile.pdf

Overview of Democratic Republic of the Congo's MAP Statistics for 2022

Democratic Republic of the Congo did not report any MAP cases in its 2022 MAP Statistics.

Please refer to https://www.oecd.org/tax/dispute/map-statistics-dem-rep-congo.pdf for details with respect to Democratic Republic of the Congo's MAP Statistics.

Denmark

Recent developments relating to MAP in Denmark prior to 15 August 2023

Developments relating to MAP in the tax treaty network

- No developments were reported

Other developments relating to MAP

- No developments were reported

Latest Action 14 Peer Review report

- 22 October 2020 - https://doi.org/10.1787/bd0276f1-en

Tax treaty network of Denmark

- 72 treaties, applicable to 77 jurisdictions (covering all treaties signed, although not necessarily in force)
- status of MLI: in force.

Table 1. State of play of Denmark's tax treaty network

Treaties in line with the Action 14 Minimum Standard following MLI impact	Treaties where actions are ongoing to make them in line with the Action 14 Minimum Standard	Following impact/actions, remaining treaties that are not in line with Action 14 Minimum Standard
68	2	2

Source: OECD

Denmark's MAP programme

Organisation of competent authority function

- 15 persons:
  - two head(s) of unit
  - 13 persons working on MAP cases (among which four persons work on other tasks as well):
    - nine persons work on attribution/allocation cases and four persons work on other cases.
- contact persons for MAP requests:

  For attribution / allocation cases: Mr. Bo Darling Larsen, Large Companies – Competent Authority, Skattestyrelsen/Danish Tax Agency, Hannemanns Allé 25, DK-2300 Copenhagen S, Denmark or by email to store-selskaber-sikker-post@sktst.dk

  For other cases: Mr. Jesper Leth Vestergaard, Law Department – Competent Authority

Skattestyrelsen/Danish Tax Agency, Hannemanns Allé 25, DK-2300 Copenhagen S, Denmark or by email to HovedpostkasseJura@SKTST.dk.

Figure 1. Competent Authority Organisational Structure

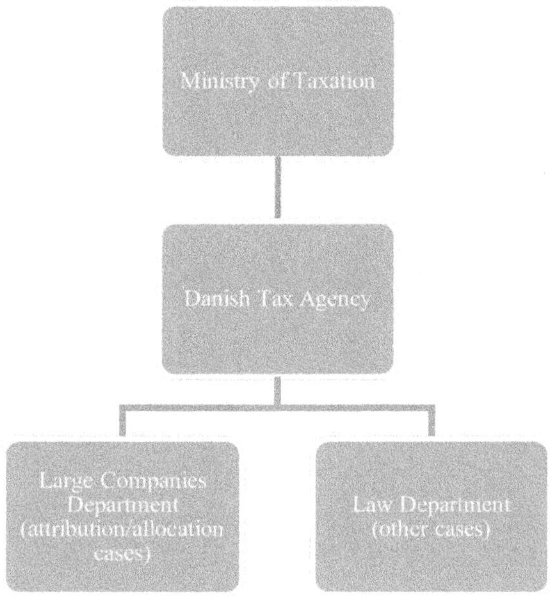

Source: OECD

Table 2. Guidance on the MAP process

MAP guidance	*C.F.8.2.2.25.2 The taxpayer's request for MAP*	https://info.skat.dk/data.aspx?oid=16280 (Section "Minimum requirements of a request" to be referred to for form and content of a MAP request, including information requirements)
MAP profile	*11 February 2020*	https://www.oecd.org/tax/dispute/denmark-dispute-resolution-profile.pdf

Overview of Denmark's MAP Statistics for 2022

Please refer to https://www.oecd.org/tax/dispute/map-statistics-denmark.pdf for details with respect to Denmark's MAP Statistics.

Figure 2. Cases closed in 2022

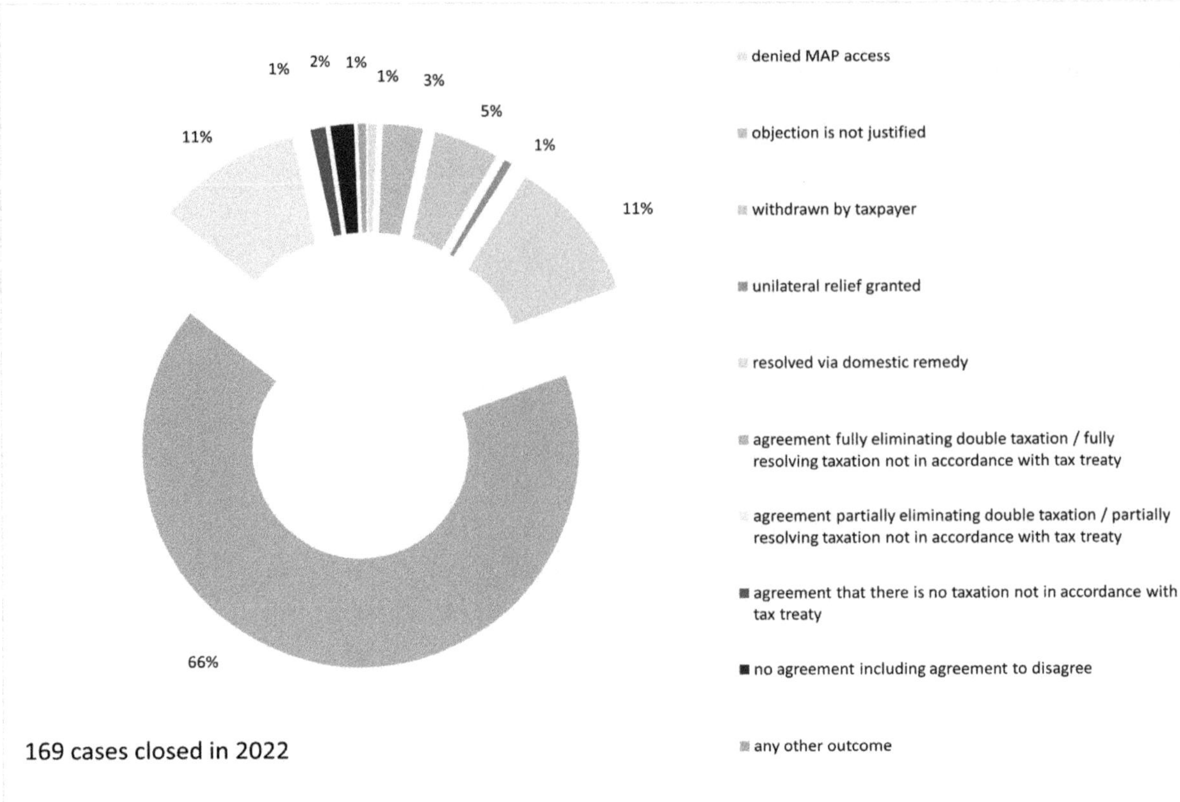

Source: OECD

Figure 3. Evolution of Denmark's MAP caseload (2016-22)

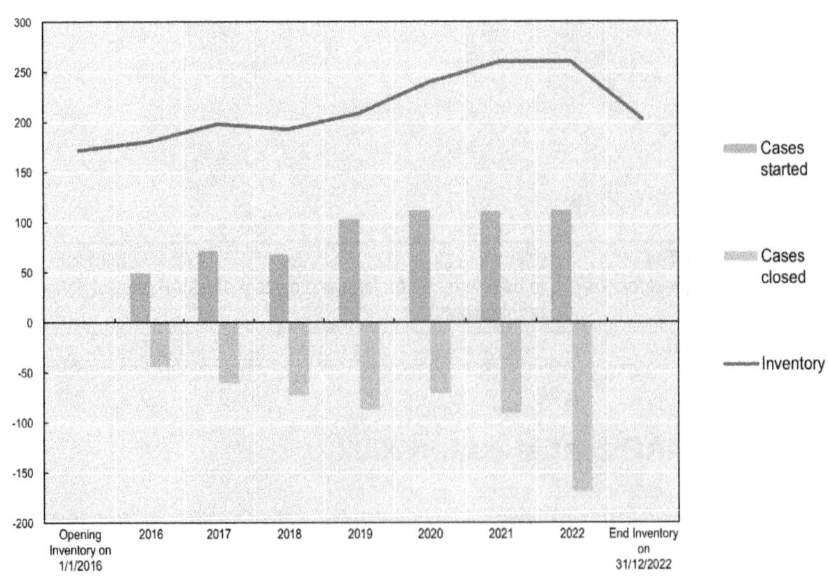

Source: OECD

Table 3. Overview of Denmark's MAP caseload for 2022

Inventory for year 2022	Opening Inventory 1/1/2022	Cases started	Cases Closed	End Inventory 31/12/2022
Attribution/allocation cases	194	61	143	112
Other cases	66	51	26	91
Total	260	112	169	203

Source: OECD

Table 4. Denmark's average time to resolve MAP cases in 2022

Cases resolved in year 2022	Pre-2016 cases		Post-2015 cases		All	
	Number of cases	**Average time**	**Number of cases**	**Average time** **Start to End**	**Number of cases**	**Average time**
Attribution / Allocation cases	12	43.65	131	20.05	143	22.03
Other cases	2	104.56	24	20.47	26	26.94
All cases	14	52.35	155	20.12	169	22.79

Source: OECD

Djibouti

Recent developments relating to MAP in Djibouti prior to 15 August 2023

Developments relating to MAP in the tax treaty network

- Djibouti did not provide the relevant information.

Other developments relating to MAP

- Djibouti did not provide the relevant information.

Latest Action 14 Peer Review report

Djibouti is yet to be peer reviewed under Action 14.

Tax treaty network of Djibouti

- one treaty, applicable to one jurisdiction (covering all treaties signed, although not necessarily in force)
- status of MLI: not signed.

Table 1. State of play of Djibouti's tax treaty network

Treaties in line with the Action 14 Minimum Standard following MLI impact	Treaties where actions are ongoing to make them in line with the Action 14 Minimum Standard	Following impact/actions, remaining treaties that are not in line with Action 14 Minimum Standard
No information	No information	No information

Source: OECD

Djibouti's MAP programme

Organisation of competent authority function

- Djibouti did not provide the relevant information.

Table 2. Guidance on the MAP process

MAP guidance	Djibouti did not provide the relevant information.	-
MAP profile	No MAP profile published	-

Overview of Djibouti's MAP Statistics for 2022

Djibouti did not report any MAP cases in its 2022 MAP Statistics.

Please refer to https://www.oecd.org/tax/dispute/map-statistics-djibouti.pdf for details with respect to Djibouti's MAP Statistics.

Dominica

Recent developments relating to MAP in Dominica prior to 15 August 2023

Developments relating to MAP in the tax treaty network

- No developments were reported

Other developments relating to MAP

- No developments were reported

Latest Action 14 Peer Review report

- Dominica is yet to be peer reviewed under Action 14.

Tax treaty network of Dominica

- two treaties, applicable to 12 jurisdictions (covering all treaties signed, although not necessarily in force)
- status of MLI: not signed.

Table 1. State of play of Dominica's tax treaty network

Treaties in line with the Action 14 Minimum Standard following MLI impact	Treaties where actions are ongoing to make them in line with the Action 14 Minimum Standard	Following impact/actions, remaining treaties that are not in line with Action 14 Minimum Standard
0	0	2

Source: OECD

Dominica's MAP programme

Organisation of competent authority function

- five persons:
  - Competent Authority (Comptroller of IRD):
    - one head of unit
    - three persons working on MAP cases (all of which work on other tasks as well).
- contact persons for MAP requests:
  - Sylma Lloyd
    Comptroller (Ag) -Inland Revenue Division - High Street, Roseau Dominica
    Email.: scotlandlloyds@dominica.gov.dm Tel #: 767-2663635(W); Cell.: 767-2776.

Figure 1. Competent Authority Organisational Structure

Source: OECD

Table 2. Guidance on the MAP process

MAP guidance	No MAP guidance published	-
MAP profile	No MAP profile published	-

Overview of Dominica's MAP Statistics for 2022

Dominica did not report any MAP cases in its 2022 MAP Statistics.

Please refer to https://www.oecd.org/tax/dispute/map-statistics-dominica.pdf for details with respect to Dominica's MAP Statistics

Dominican Republic

Recent developments relating to MAP in Dominican Republic prior to 15 August 2023

Developments relating to MAP in the tax treaty network

- No developments were reported

Other developments relating to MAP

- No developments were reported

Latest Action 14 Peer Review report

- The stage 1 Simplified Peer Review report of Dominican Republic is expected to be published early 2024.

Tax treaty network of Dominican Republic

- Two treaties, applicable to two jurisdictions (covering all treaties signed, although not necessarily in force)
- Status of MLI: not signed

Table 1. State of play of Dominican Republic's tax treaty network

Treaties in line with the Action 14 Minimum Standard following MLI impact	Treaties where actions are ongoing to make them in line with the Action 14 Minimum Standard	Following impact/actions, remaining treaties that are not in line with Action 14 Minimum Standard
0	0	2

Source: OECD

Dominican Republic's MAP programme

Organisation of competent authority function

- Two persons (all of whom work on other tasks as well)
- Contact persons for MAP requests:
  - Mrs. Ricela Spraus Deputy Director of Compliance Management DGII Dirección General de Impuestos Internos Telf. 809-689-2181, ext:2828 / Email: rspraus@dgii.gov.do
  - Atte: Mrs. Chaly Cruz International Taxation Department Chief Dirección General de Impuestos Internos –- DGII Telf. 809-689-2181, ext:2267 / Email: Cncruz@dgii.gov.do
  - Atte: Mr. Luis Madera International Taxation Department Dirección General de Impuestos Internos – DGII Telf. 809-689-2181, ext:2914 / Email: Lmadera@dgii.gov.do

- Mrs. Marlene Tapia Tax cooperation and international taxation Department Chief Ministry of Finance Telf. 809-687-5131 ext:2255 / Email: matapia@hacienda.gov.do
- Address: Ave. México No.48 International Taxation Agreements Section Santo Domingo, Dominican Republic (10204)

Figure 1. Competent Authority Organisational Structure

Source: OECD

Table 2. Guidance on the MAP process

MAP guidance	NORMA GENERAL NÚM. 10-2022, *August 2022*	https://dgii.gov.do/legislacion/normasGenerales/Documents/ (Section II to be referred to for form and content of a MAP request, including information requirements)
MAP profile	*9 March 2023*	https://www.oecd.org/tax/dispute/dominican-republic-dispute-resolution-profile.pdf

Overview of Dominican Republic's MAP Statistics for 2022

Please refer to https://www.oecd.org/tax/dispute/map-statistics-dominican-republic.pdf for details with respect to Dominican Republic's MAP Statistics.

Cases closed in 2022

No MAP cases were closed by Dominican Republic in 2022.

Figure 2. Evolution of Dominican Republic's MAP caseload (2016-22)

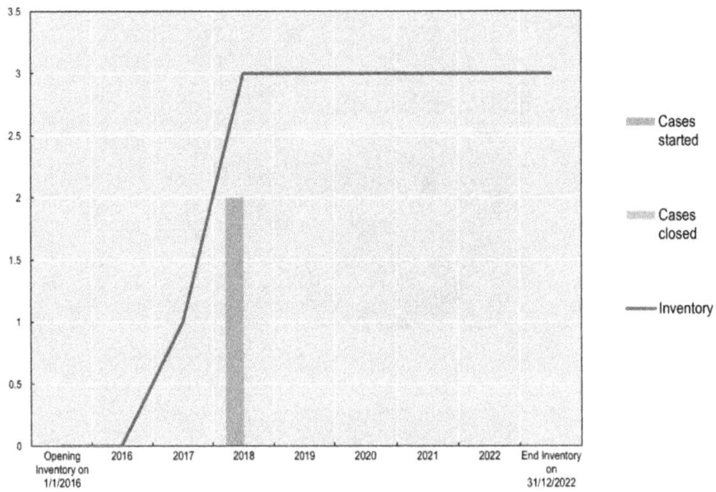

Source: OECD

Table 3. Overview of Dominican Republic's MAP caseload for 2022

Inventory for year 2022	Opening Inventory 1/1/2022	Cases started	Cases Closed	End Inventory 31/12/2022
Attribution/allocation cases	0	0	0	0
Other cases	3	0	0	3
Total	3	0	0	3

Source: OECD

Table 4. Dominican Republic's average time to resolve MAP cases in 2022

Cases resolved in year 2022	Pre-2016 cases		Post-2015 cases		All	
	Number of cases	**Average time**	**Number of cases**	**Average time** **Start to End**	**Number of cases**	**Average time**
Attribution / Allocation cases	0	N/A	0	N/A	0	N/A
Other cases	0	N/A	0	N/A	0	N/A
All cases	0	N/A	0	N/A	0	N/A

Source: OECD

Egypt

Recent developments relating to MAP in Egypt prior to 15 August 2023

Developments relating to MAP in the tax treaty network

- No developments were reported

Other developments relating to MAP

- No developments were reported

Latest Action 14 Peer Review report

- The stage 1 Simplified Peer Review report of Egypt is expected to be published early 2024.

Tax treaty network of Egypt

- 59 treaties, applicable to 59 jurisdictions (covering all treaties signed, although not necessarily in force)
- status of MLI: in force.

Table 1. State of play of Egypt's tax treaty network

Treaties in line with the Action 14 Minimum Standard following MLI impact	Treaties where actions are ongoing to make them in line with the Action 14 Minimum Standard	Following impact/actions, remaining treaties that are not in line with Action 14 Minimum Standard
40	No information	No information

Source: OECD

Egypt's MAP programme

Organisation of competent authority function

- eight persons (all of whom work on other tasks as well)
- contact persons for MAP requests:
  - Ms. Ramy Mohamed
    Deputy Minister of Finance for Tax Policy and Reforms - Ministry of Finance
    Email: r.mohamed@mof.gov.eg Office Number: +201 004885674
  - Ms. Afaf Ibrahim
    Head of International Tax Department - Egyptian Tax Authority
    Email: afaf.ebrahim@eta.gov.eg Mobile: +201223435133
  - Ms. Reem Abuzeid
    Head of the Exchange of Information Department and International Agreement - Egyptian

Tax Authority
Email: reem.abuzied@eta.gov.eg Mobile: +201277990064.

Figure 1. Competent Authority Organisational Structure

Source: OECD

Table 2. Guidance on the MAP process

MAP guidance	No MAP guidance published	-
MAP profile	5 April 2023	https://www.oecd.org/tax/dispute/egypt-dispute-resolution-profile.pdf

Overview of Egypt's MAP Statistics for 2022

Please refer to https://www.oecd.org/tax/dispute/map-statistics-egypt.pdf for details with respect to Egypt's MAP Statistics.

Cases closed in 2022

No MAP cases were closed by Egypt in 2022.

Figure 2. Evolution of Egypt's MAP caseload (2016-22)

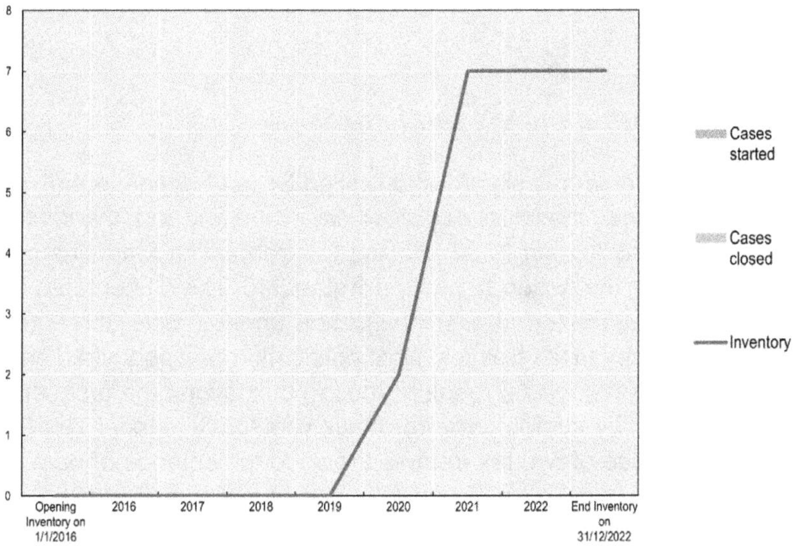

Source: OECD

Table 3. Overview of Egypt's MAP caseload for 2022

Inventory for year 2022	Opening Inventory 1/1/2022	Cases started	Cases Closed	End Inventory 31/12/2022
Attribution/allocation cases	6	0	0	6
Other cases	1	0	0	1
Total	7	0	0	7

Source: OECD

Table 4. Egypt's average time to resolve MAP cases in 2022

Cases resolved in year 2022	Pre-2016 cases		Post-2015 cases		All	
	Number of cases	**Average time**	**Number of cases**	**Average time** **Start to End**	**Number of cases**	**Average time**
Attribution / Allocation cases	0	N/A	0	N/A	0	N/A
Other cases	0	N/A	0	N/A	0	N/A
All cases	0	N/A	0	N/A	0	N/A

Source: OECD

Estonia

Recent developments relating to MAP in Estonia prior to 15 August 2023

Developments relating to MAP in the tax treaty network

- As of 15 August 2023, Estonia has signed and ratified 64 tax treaties, out of which 62 tax treaties have entered into force. Since the latest Action 14 peer review report, the tax treaty with Guernsey has entered into force on 6 August 2020 and the tax treaty with Mauritius on 12 October 2021. Both treaties are in line with the Action 14 minimum standard. The MLI entered into force for Estonia on 1 May 2021. Estonia submitted its first notification under Article 35 (7) (b) of the MLI on 25 November 2021 covering seven tax treaties. Next notification was submitted on 1 June 2022, which also covered seven tax treaties. As a result of these notifications the first sentence of paragraph 1of Article 25 was updated by the MLI in accordance with OECD Model Tax Convention (2017) in eight tax treaties and in case of two tax treaties the second sentence of paragraph 3 of Article 25 was added.

Other developments relating to MAP

- No developments were reported

Latest Action 14 Peer Review report

- **25 May 2021**, https://doi.org/10.1787/332796fc-en

Tax treaty network of Estonia

- 64 treaties, applicable to 64 jurisdictions (covering all treaties signed, although not necessarily in force)
- status of MLI: in force.

Table 1. State of play of Estonia's tax treaty network

Treaties in line with the Action 14 Minimum Standard following MLI impact	Treaties where actions are ongoing to make them in line with the Action 14 Minimum Standard	Following impact/actions, remaining treaties that are not in line with Action 14 Minimum Standard
61	3	0

Source: OECD

Estonia's MAP programme

Organisation of competent authority function

- six persons:
  - one head(s) of unit

    - five persons working on MAP cases (all of which work on other tasks as well).
- contact persons for MAP requests:
    - Mrs Merje Roomet, Chief expert of tax department, the Estonian Tax and Customs Board
      Lõõtsa 8 a, Tallinn, 15176
      phone + 372 676 2124
      map@emta.ee, www.emta.ee.

Figure 1. Competent Authority Organisational Structure

Source: OECD

Table 2. Guidance on the MAP process

MAP guidance	Resolution of disputes resulting from tax treaties, *1 June 2022*	https://www.emta.ee/en/private-client/e-resident-non-resident/non-residents/taxation-income-and-tax-treaties (Sections "Making a MAP request" and "Minimum information required to be in a valid MAP request" to be referred to for form and content of a MAP request, including information requirements)
MAP profile	*7 September 2023*	https://www.oecd.org/tax/dispute/Estonia-Dispute-Resolution-Profile.pdf

Overview of Estonia's MAP Statistics for 2022

Please refer to https://www.oecd.org/tax/dispute/map-statistics-estonia.pdf for details with respect to Estonia's MAP Statistics.

Figure 2. Cases closed in 2022

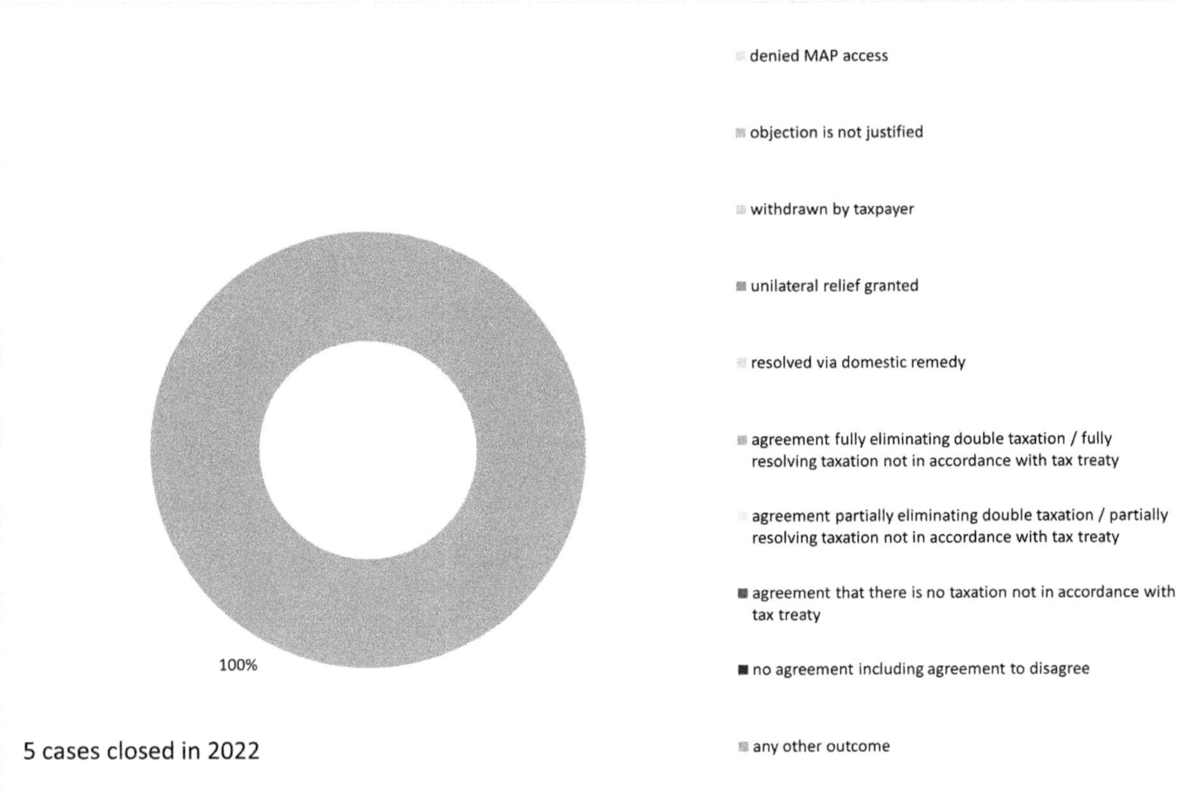

Source: OECD

Figure 3. Evolution of Estonia's MAP caseload (2016-22)

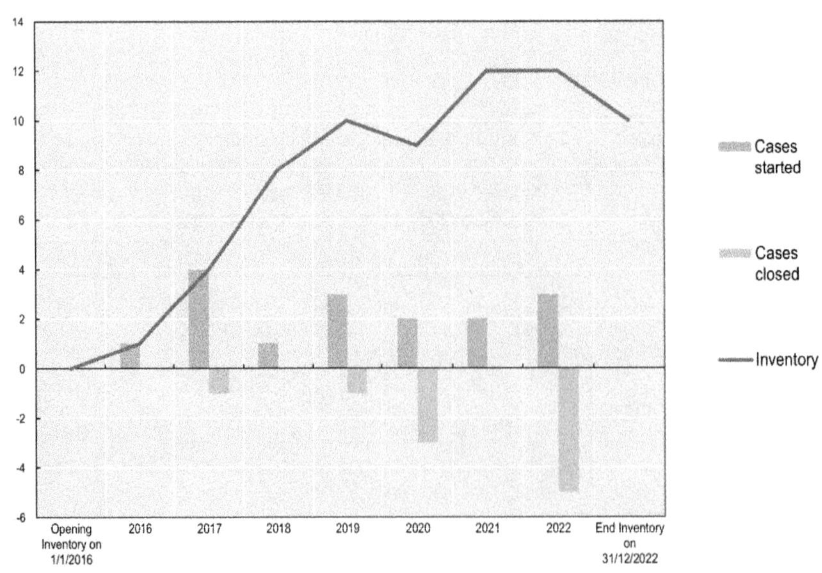

Source: OECD

Table 3. Overview of Estonia's MAP caseload for 2022

Inventory for year 2022	Opening Inventory 1/1/2022	Cases started	Cases Closed	End Inventory 31/12/2022
Attribution/allocation cases	1	0	1	0
Other cases	11	3	4	10
Total	12	3	5	10

Source: OECD

Table 4. Estonia's average time to resolve MAP cases in 2022

Cases resolved in year 2022	Pre-2016 cases		Post-2015 cases		All	
	Number of cases	**Average time**	**Number of cases**	**Average time** **Start to End**	**Number of cases**	**Average time**
Attribution / Allocation cases	0	N/A	1	9.37	1	9.37
Other cases	0	N/A	4	27.90	4	27.90
All cases	0	N/A	5	24.19	5	24.19

Source: OECD

Eswatini (Kingdom of)

Recent developments relating to MAP in Eswatini prior to 15 August 2023

Developments relating to MAP in the tax treaty network

- No developments were reported

Other developments relating to MAP

- No developments were reported

Latest Action 14 Peer Review report

Eswatini is yet to be peer reviewed under Action 14.

Tax treaty network of Eswatini

- seven treaties, applicable to seven jurisdictions (covering all treaties signed, although not necessarily in force)
- status of MLI: signed.

Table 1. State of play of Eswatini's tax treaty network

Treaties in line with the Action 14 Minimum Standard following MLI impact	Treaties where actions are ongoing to make them in line with the Action 14 Minimum Standard	Following impact/actions, remaining treaties that are not in line with Action 14 Minimum Standard
6	0	1

Source: OECD

Eswatini's MAP programme

Organisation of competent authority function

- four persons:
  - one head of unit
  - three persons working on MAP cases (all of which work on other tasks as well):
    - two persons work on attribution/allocation cases and one person works on other cases.
- contact persons for MAP requests:
  - Ms Nomcebo Marrengane
    Head of Legal Services
    Delegated Competent Authority
    Portion 419 of Farm 50, Along MR103, Ezulwini
    P.O. Box 5628 Mbabane, Eswatini

Tel: +268-24064000 | Direct: +268-24064018 | Mobile: +268-76063046 Fax: +268-24064001
E-mail: nmarrengane@ers.org.sz | Web: www.ers.org.sz.

Figure 1. Competent Authority Organisational Structure

Source: OECD

Table 2. Guidance on the MAP process

MAP guidance	No MAP guidance published	-
MAP profile	No MAP profile published	-

Overview of Eswatini's MAP Statistics for 2022

Eswatini did not report any MAP cases in its 2022 MAP Statistics.

Please refer to https://www.oecd.org/tax/dispute/map-statistics-eswatini.pdf for details with respect to Eswatini's MAP Statistics.

Faroe Islands

Recent developments relating to MAP in Faroe Islands prior to 15 August 2023

Developments relating to MAP in the tax treaty network

- No developments were reported

Other developments relating to MAP

- No developments were reported

Latest Action 14 Peer Review report

14 April 2022 - https://doi.org/10.1787/d91d70b1-en

Tax treaty network of Faroe Islands

- 11 treaties, applicable to 15 jurisdictions (covering all treaties signed, although not necessarily in force)
- status of MLI: in force.

Table 1. State of play of Faroe Islands's tax treaty network

Treaties in line with the Action 14 Minimum Standard following MLI impact	Treaties where actions are ongoing to make them in line with the Action 14 Minimum Standard	Following impact/actions, remaining treaties that are not in line with Action 14 Minimum Standard
3	0	8

Source: OECD

Faroe Islands's MAP programme

Organisation of competent authority function

- one person, Head of Unit (working on other tasks as well)
- contact persons for MAP requests:
  - Ms. Rúna F. Guttesen
    Director, Head of Division, Competent Authority, Mutual Agreement Procedure, Legal department, TAKS/Faroese Tax Authority
    PO Box 2151, Skálatrøð 20, FO-110 Tórshavn, Faroe Islands
    by email to taks@taks.fo or runa@taks.fo.

Figure 1. Competent Authority Organisational Structure

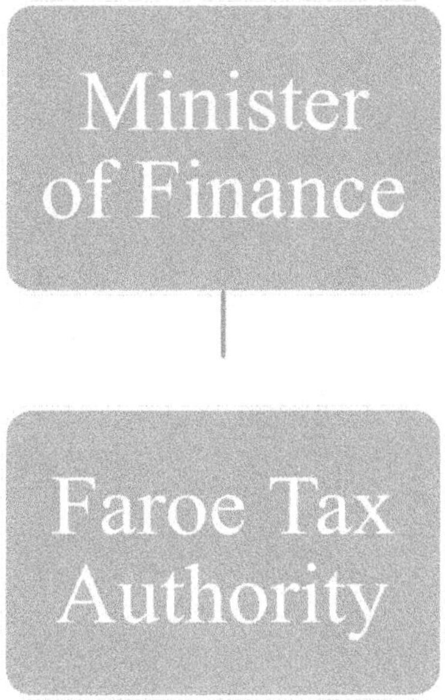

Source: OECD

Table 2. Guidance on the MAP process

MAP guidance	*Sínámillum avtalur sambært tvískattasáttmálum (Mutual Agreement Procedure, MAP)*, January 2020	https://www.taks.fo/fo/borgari/skattur/tviskatting/ (Section "Formlig krøv" to be referred to for form and content of a MAP request, including information requirements)
MAP profile	16 December 2019	https://www.oecd.org/tax/dispute/The-Faroe-Islands-Dispute-Resolution-Profile.pdf

Overview of Faroe Islands's MAP Statistics for 2022

Please refer to https://www.oecd.org/tax/dispute/map-statistics-faroe-islands.pdf for details with respect to Faroe Islands's MAP Statistics.

Figure 2. Cases closed in 2022

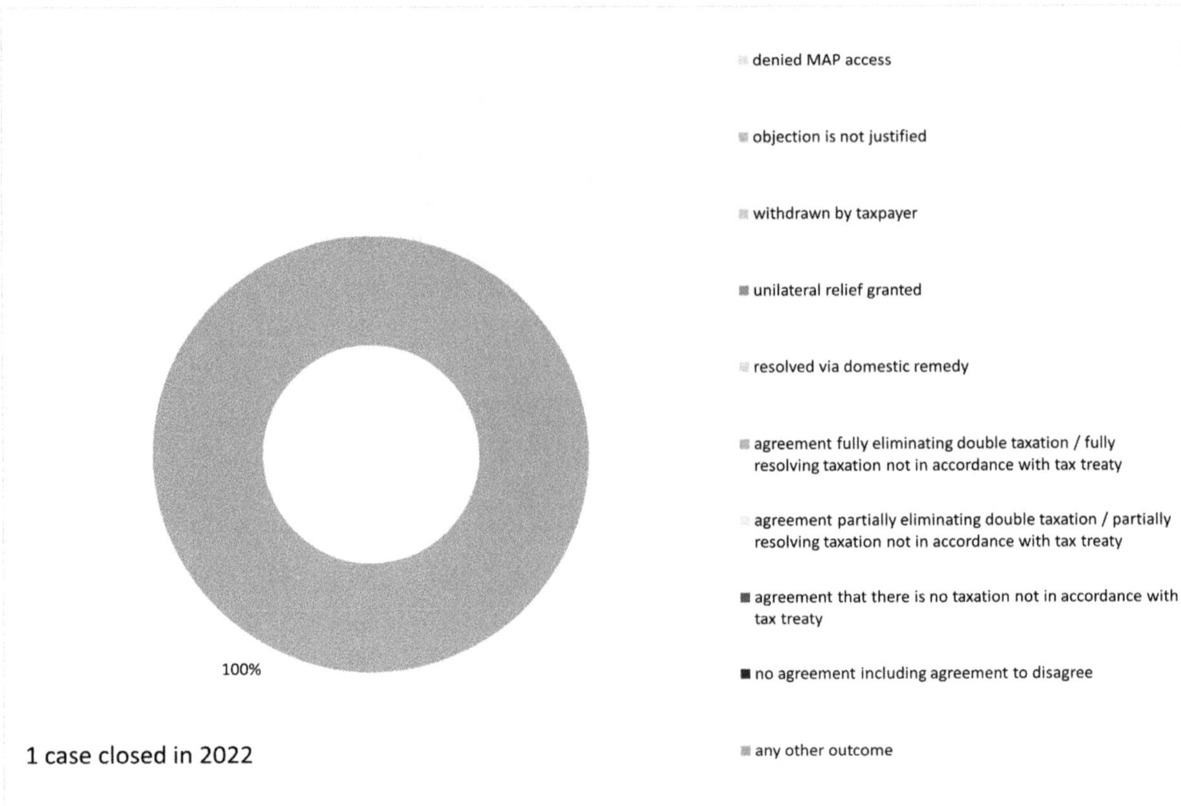

Source: OECD

Figure 3. Evolution of Faroe Island's MAP caseload (2016-22)

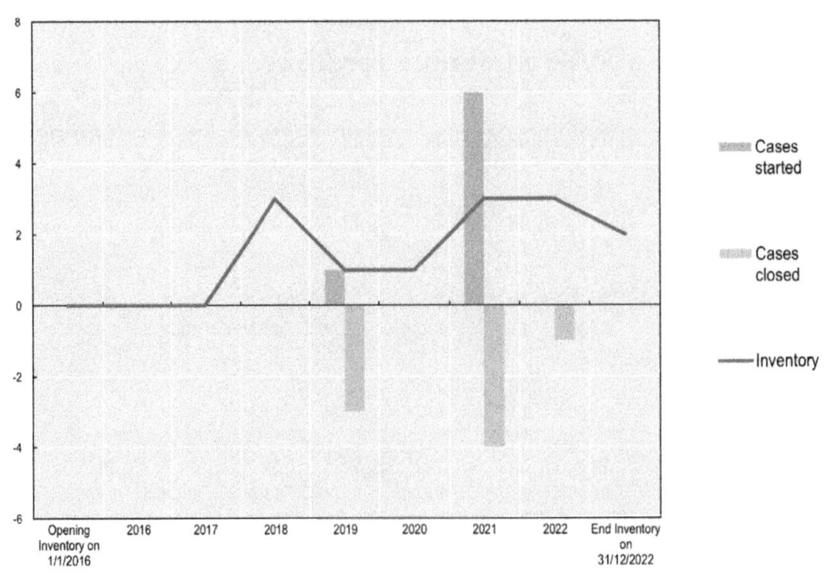

Source: OECD

Table 3. Overview of Faroe Islands' MAP caseload for 2022

Inventory for year 2022	Opening Inventory 1/1/2022	Cases started	Cases Closed	End Inventory 31/12/2022
Attribution/allocation cases	0	0	0	0
Other cases	3	0	1	2
Total	3	0	1	2

Source: OECD

Table 4. Faroe Islands' average time to resolve MAP cases in 2022

Cases resolved in year 2022	Pre-2016 cases		Post-2015 cases		All	
	Number of cases	**Average time**	**Number of cases**	**Average time** **Start to End**	**Number of cases**	**Average time**
Attribution / Allocation cases	0	N/A	0	N/A	0	N/A
Other cases	0	N/A	1	20.71	1	20.71
All cases	0	N/A	1	20.71	1	20.71

Source: OECD

Finland

Recent developments relating to MAP in Finland prior to 15 August 2023

Developments relating to MAP in the tax treaty network

- No developments were reported

Other developments relating to MAP

- No developments were reported

Latest Action 14 Peer Review report

22 October 2020 - https://doi.org/10.1787/64a87e14-en

Tax treaty network of Finland

- 81 treaties, applicable to 86 jurisdictions (covering all treaties signed, although not necessarily in force)
- status of MLI: in force.

Table 1. State of play of Finland's tax treaty network

Treaties in line with the Action 14 Minimum Standard following MLI impact	Treaties where actions are ongoing to make them in line with the Action 14 Minimum Standard	Following impact/actions, remaining treaties that are not in line with Action 14 Minimum Standard
74	7	0

Source: OECD

Finland's MAP programme

Organisation of competent authority function

- 20 persons:
  - of which, 14 persons work on attribution/allocation cases and six persons work on other cases.
- contact persons for MAP requests:
  - email address in all MAP requests is MAP@vero.fi
    The application should be sent as a secure email (instructions regarding secure email https://turvaposti.vero.fi)
  - for attribution / allocation cases and corporate cases: Finnish Tax Administration, Competent Authority
    P.O.Box 200, 00052 VERO, Finland

- for cases concerning individuals: Finnish Tax Administration, Competent Authority P.O. Box 700, 00052 VERO, Finland.

Figure 1. Competent Authority Organisational Structure

Source: OECD

Table 2. Guidance on the MAP process

MAP guidance	*International tax dispute resolution procedure*, 24 March 2022	https://www.vero.fi/en/detailed-guidance/guidance/77253/international-tax-dispute-resolution-procedure2/ (Section 3.1 to be referred to for form and content of a MAP request, including information requirements)
	Apply for a mutual agreement procedure	https://www.vero.fi/en/individuals/tax-cards-and-tax-returns/moving_away_from_finland/taxation-abroad-contrary-to-tax-treaty/application-for-mutual-agreement-procedure/
MAP profile	22 March 2022	https://www.oecd.org/tax/dispute/finland-dispute-resolution-profile.pdf

Overview of Finland's MAP Statistics for 2022

Please refer to https://www.oecd.org/tax/dispute/map-statistics-finland.pdf for details with respect to Finland's MAP Statistics.

Figure 2. Cases closed in 2022

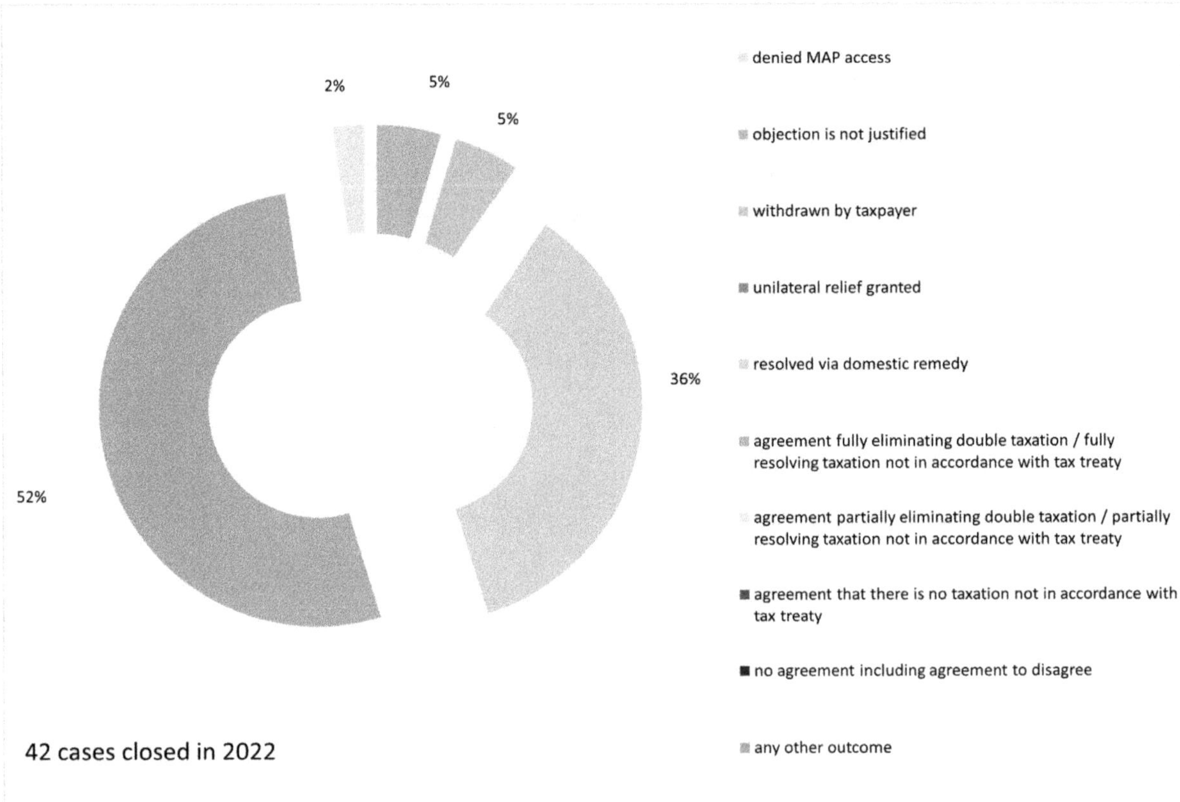

Source: OECD

Figure 3. Evolution of Finland's MAP caseload (2016-22)

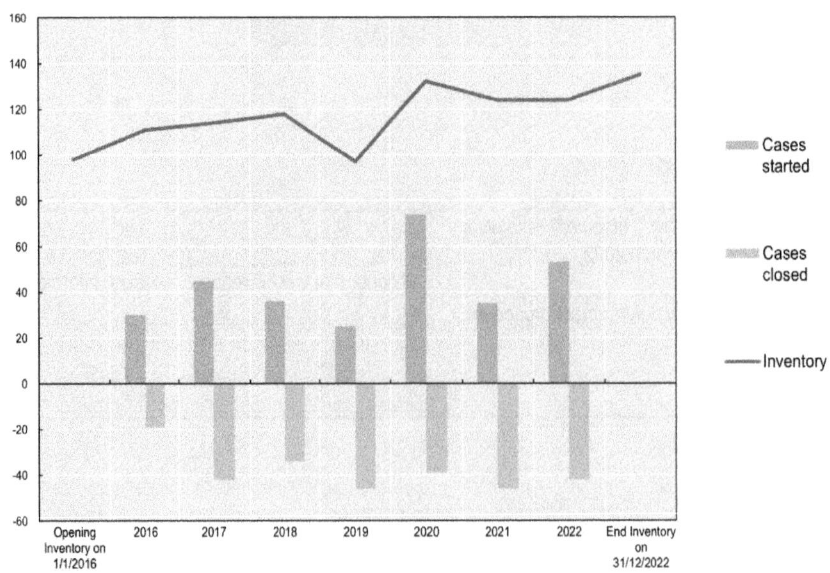

Source: OECD

Table 3. Overview of Finland's MAP caseload for 2022

Inventory for year 2022	Opening Inventory 1/1/2022	Cases started	Cases Closed	End Inventory 31/12/2022
Attribution/allocation cases	48	31	25	54
Other cases	76	22	17	81
Total	124	53	42	135

Source: OECD

Table 4. Finland's average time to resolve MAP cases in 2022

Cases resolved in year 2022	Pre-2016 cases		Post-2015 cases		All	
	Number of cases	**Average time**	**Number of cases**	**Average time** **Start to End**	**Number of cases**	**Average time**
Attribution / Allocation cases	1	81.96	24	24.81	25	27.09
Other cases	0	N/A	17	18.03	17	18.03
All cases	1	81.96	41	22.00	42	23.42

Source: OECD

France

Recent developments relating to MAP in France prior to 15 August 2023

Developments relating to MAP in the tax treaty network

- When negotiating or renegotiating double tax treaties, France systematically proposes the inclusion of Action 14 minimum Standard.
- Three new treaties (Moldova, Denmark, Rwanda) have been signed but not yet entered into force (awaiting ratification).

Other developments relating to MAP

- The French CA has been reinforced during the past few years, bringing the headcount to 19 FTE. Further reinforcement is planned between 2024 and 2027.

Latest Action 14 Peer Review report

9 April 2020 - https://doi.org/10.1787/a5d1cab8-en

Tax treaty network of France

- 128 treaties, applicable to 128 jurisdictions (covering all treaties signed, although not necessarily in force, including three awaiting ratification by the French Parliament)
- status of MLI: in force.

Table 1. State of play of France's tax treaty network

Treaties in line with the Action 14 Minimum Standard following MLI impact	Treaties where actions are ongoing to make them in line with the Action 14 Minimum Standard	Following impact/actions, remaining treaties that are not in line with Action 14 Minimum Standard
88	3	37

Source: OECD

France's MAP programme

Organisation of competent authority function

- 19 persons:
  - one head of unit and one deputy-head
  - three team managers
  - 13 persons working on MAP cases.
- contact persons for MAP requests:
  Direction générale des finances publiques (DGFiP)

Service de la sécurité juridique et du contrôle fiscal
Bureau SJCF 4B - Prévention et résolution des différends internationaux
64-70 allée de Bercy – Télédoc 849, 75574 Paris cedex 12, France
Tel : +33 (0)1 53 18 09 23

Figure 1. Competent Authority Organisational Structure

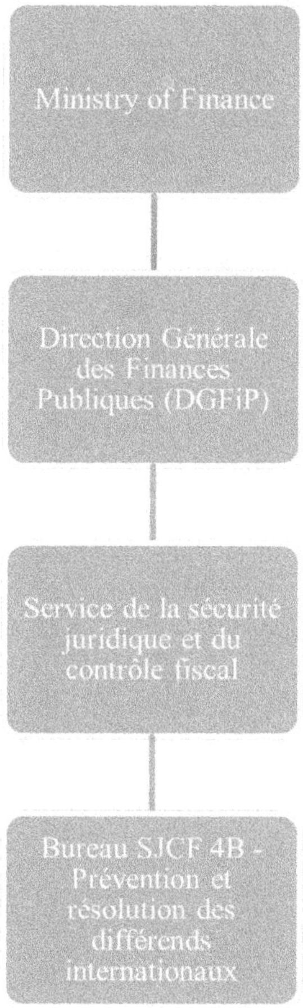

Source: OECD

Table 2. Guidance on the MAP process

MAP guidance	*BOI-INT-DG-20-30-10* *01 February 2017*	https://bofip.impots.gouv.fr/bofip/5344-PGP.html/identifiant=BOI-INT-DG-20-30-10-20170201 (Section II to be referred to for form and content of a MAP request, including information requirements)
	MAP webpage *16 February 2018*	https://www.impots.gouv.fr/international-particulier/mutual-agreement-procedure
MAP profile	*1 September 2021*	https://www.oecd.org/tax/dispute/france-dispute-resolution-profile.pdf

Overview of France's MAP Statistics for 2022

Please refer to https://www.oecd.org/tax/dispute/map-statistics-france.pdf for details with respect to France's MAP Statistics.

Figure 2. Cases closed in 2022

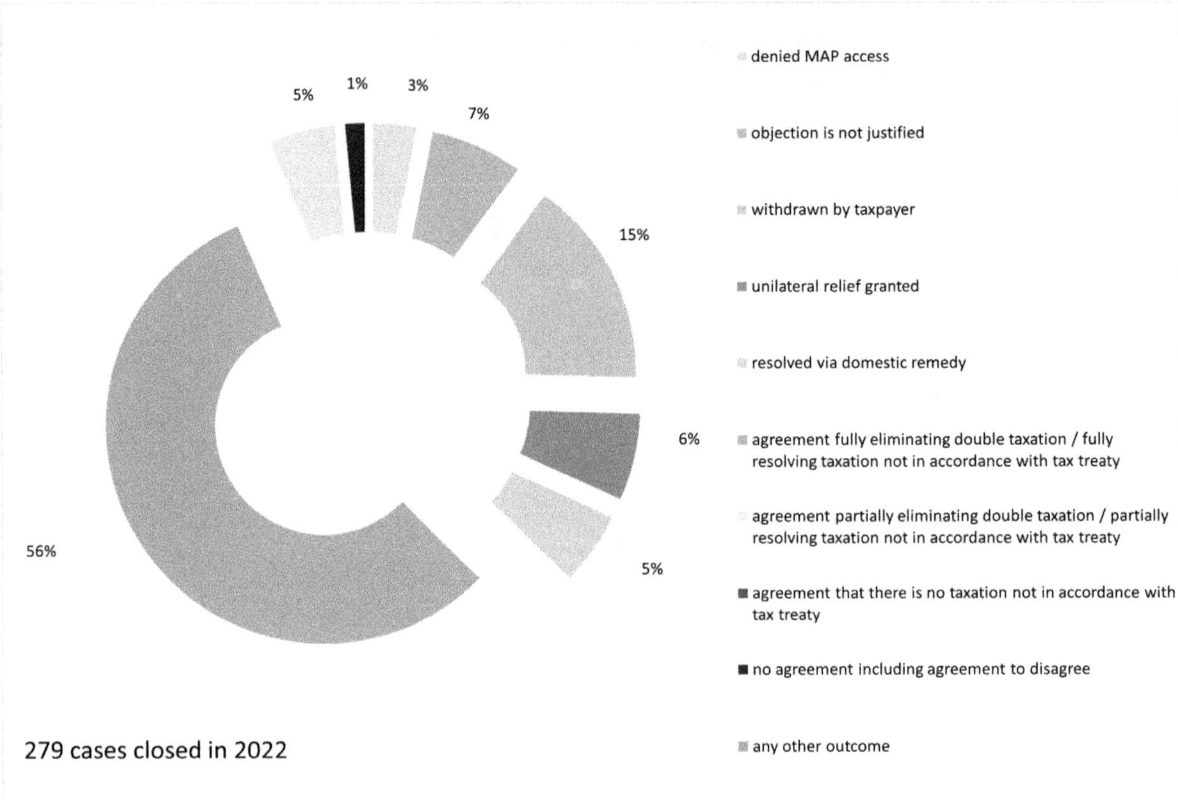

Source: OECD

Figure 3. Evolution of France's MAP caseload (2016-22)

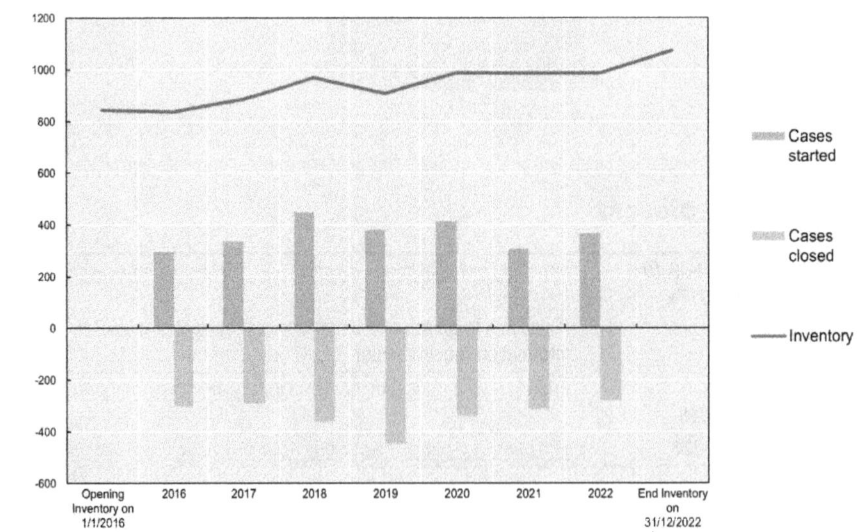

Source: OECD

Table 3. Overview of France's MAP caseload for 2022

Inventory for year 2022	Opening Inventory 1/1/2022	Cases started	Cases Closed	End Inventory 31/12/2022
Attribution/allocation cases	564	234	152	646
Other cases	422	133	127	428
Total	986	367	279	1074

Source: OECD

Table 4. France's average time to resolve MAP cases in 2022

Cases resolved in year 2022	Pre-2016 cases		Post-2015 cases		All	
	Number of cases	**Average time**	**Number of cases**	**Average time** **Start to End**	**Number of cases**	**Average time**
Attribution / Allocation cases	15	103.00	137	23.05	152	30.94
Other cases	9	96.00	118	21.02	127	26.34
All cases	24	100.38	255	22.11	279	28.84

Source: OECD

Gabon

Recent developments relating to MAP in Gabon prior to 15 August 2023

Developments relating to MAP in the tax treaty network

- Gabon did not provide the relevant information.

Other developments relating to MAP

- Gabon did not provide the relevant information.

Latest Action 14 Peer Review report

Gabon is yet to be peer reviewed under Action 14.

Tax treaty network of Gabon

- 14 treaties, applicable to 14 jurisdictions (covering all treaties signed, although not necessarily in force).
- status of MLI: signed.

Table 1. State of play of Gabon's tax treaty network

Treaties in line with the Action 14 Minimum Standard following MLI impact	Treaties where actions are ongoing to make them in line with the Action 14 Minimum Standard	Following impact/actions, remaining treaties that are not in line with Action 14 Minimum Standard
11	No information	No information

Source: OECD

Gabon's MAP programme

Organisation of competent authority function

- contact persons for MAP requests:
    - Monsieur OGOUMA Joël
      Directeur Général des Impôts BP 45, Libreville/Gabon ;
      Téléphone : (241) 07 94 74 53 ; e-mail : jogouma@yahoo.fr.

Competent Authority Organisational Structure

Gabon did not provide the relevant information.

Table 2. Guidance on the MAP process

MAP guidance	Gabon did not provide the relevant information	
MAP profile	28 July 2017	https://www.oecd.org/tax/dispute/Gabon-Dispute-Resolution-Profile.pdf

Overview of Gabon's MAP Statistics for 2022

Gabon did not declare its MAP Statistics for 2022.

Georgia

Recent developments relating to MAP in Georgia prior to 15 August 2023

Developments relating to MAP in the tax treaty network

- Entry into force of the tax treaty with Kyrgyzstan in May 2023.

Other developments relating to MAP

- Decree on Rule for the Mutual Agreement Procedure defined by the international agreement on the avoidance of double taxation and Rule for the Mutual Agreement Procedure defined by the international agreement on the avoidance of double taxation are in force from July 4, 2023.

Latest Action 14 Peer Review report

- Georgia is yet to be peer reviewed under Action 14.

Tax treaty network of Georgia

- 58 treaties, applicable to 58 jurisdictions (covering all treaties signed, although not necessarily in force)
- status of MLI: in force.

Table 1. State of play of Georgia's tax treaty network

Treaties in line with the Action 14 Minimum Standard following MLI impact	Treaties where actions are ongoing to make them in line with the Action 14 Minimum Standard	Following impact/actions, remaining treaties that are not in line with Action 14 Minimum Standard
38	20	0

Source: OECD

Georgia's MAP programme

Organisation of competent authority function

- 12 persons:
  - four heads of unit
  - six persons working on MAP cases (among which four persons work on other tasks as well):
    - of which, four persons work on attribution/allocation cases and two persons work on other cases.
- contact persons for MAP requests:

- Ms. Marine Khurtsidze, Head of Tax and Customs Policy Department, Ministry of Finance of Georgia, 16 Gorgasali st. 0105 Tbilisi, Georgia Phone: +995 32 2 262977; Cell: +995(595)342424 | E-mail: Mari.Khurtsidze@mof.ge
- Ms. Nini Nebieridze, Head of International Taxation Division, Tax and Customs Policy Department, Ministry of Finance of Georgia, 16 Gorgasali st. 0105 Tbilisi, Georgia Phone: +995 32 2 261543; Cell: +995(599)788050 | E-mail: NNebieridze@mof.ge
- Ms. Dinara Chubinidze, Head of Legal Department, Revenue Service of Georgia, 16 Gorgasali st. 0105 Tbilisi, Georgia Phone: +995 32 2 262471; Cell: +995(577)055202 | E-mail: d.chubinidze@rs.ge
- Mr. Lasha Koberidze, Deputy Head of Legal Department, Revenue Service of Georgia, 16 Gorgasali st. 0105 Tbilisi, Georgia Phone: +995 32 2 261248; Cell: +995(577)053775 | E-mail: l.koberidze@rs.ge.

Figure 1. Competent Authority Organisational Structure

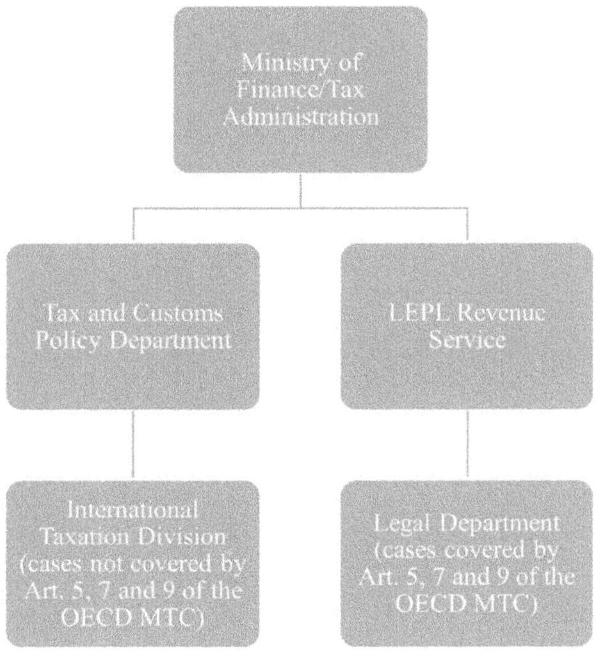

Source: OECD

Table 2. Guidance on the MAP process

MAP guidance	Rule for the Mutual Agreement Procedure defined by the international agreement on the avoidance of double taxation, 4 July 2023	https://www.mof.ge/en/5128
	Order № 258, on the approval of Rule for the Mutual Agreement Procedure defined by the international agreement on the avoidance of double taxation 4 July 2023	https://www.matsne.gov.ge/ka/document/view/5855596?publication=0
MAP profile	1 August 2023	https://www.oecd.org/tax/dispute/Georgia-Dispute-Resolution-Profile.pdf

Overview of Georgia's MAP Statistics for 2022

Georgia did not report any MAP cases in its 2022 MAP Statistics.

Please refer to https://www.oecd.org/tax/dispute/map-statistics-georgia.pdf for details with respect to Georgia's MAP Statistics.

Germany

Recent developments relating to MAP in Germany prior to 15 August 2023

Developments relating to MAP in the tax treaty network

- No developments were reported

Other developments relating to MAP

- Update of MAP guidance as of 21 August 2021.

Latest Action 14 Peer Review report

9 April 2020 - https://doi.org/10.1787/9d6c280c-en

Tax treaty network of Germany

- 96 treaties, applicable to 96 jurisdictions (covering all treaties signed, although not necessarily in force)
- status of MLI: in force.

Table 1. State of play of Germany's tax treaty network

Treaties in line with the Action 14 Minimum Standard following MLI impact	Treaties where actions are ongoing to make them in line with the Action 14 Minimum Standard	Following impact/actions, remaining treaties that are not in line with Action 14 Minimum Standard
72	14	10

Source: OECD

Germany's MAP programme

Organisation of competent authority function

- 70 persons:
  - four heads of unit, eight deputies
  - 58 persons working on MAP cases (among which seven persons work on other tasks as well):
    - 47 persons work on attribution/allocation cases and 11 persons work on other cases.
- contact persons for MAP requests:
  - Bundeszentralamt für Steuern // Federal Central Tax Office Referate S III 10 / S III 11 / S III 12 / S III 13 // Divisions S III 10 / S III 11 / S III 12 / S III 13 An der Küppe 1 53225 Bonn Germany
  - Tel.: +49-228-406-0 (central operator, please ask to be connected to Ms Meike Halfter (S III 10), Mr Arnim Hilse (S III 11), Dr Allit Lohbeck (S III 12), Mr Dominik Wichmann (S III 13), or one of their deputies) Fax.: +49-228-406-3118 EMail: vv_sv@bzst.bund.de.

Figure 1. Competent Authority Organisational Structure

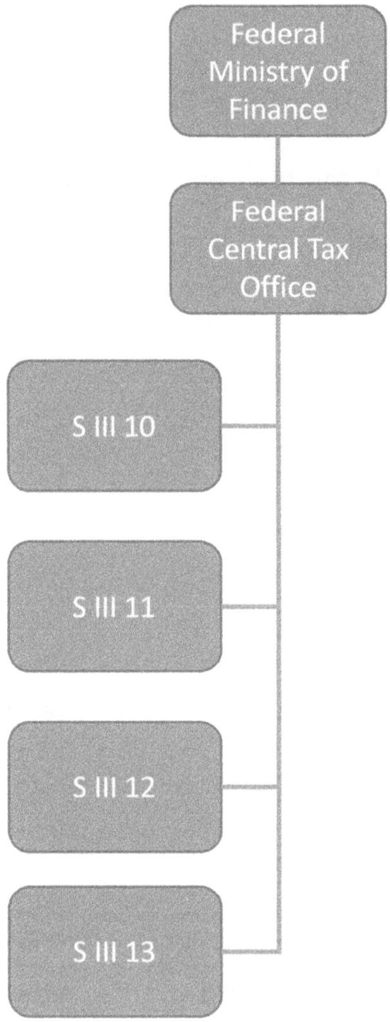

Source: OECD

Table 2. Guidance on the MAP process

MAP guidance	Federal Ministry of Finance circular on MAP (BStBl I 2021, 1495) (in German), 27 August 2021	https://www.bundesfinanzministerium.de/Content/DE/Downloads/BMF_Schreiben/Internationales_Steuerrecht/Allgemeine_Informationen/2021-08-27-merkblatt-zu-internationalen-verstaendigungs-und-schiedsverfahren-streitbeilegungsverfahren-auf-dem-gebiet-der-steuern-vom-einkommen-und-vom-vermoegen.html (Section 2.3 to be referred to for form and content of a MAP request, including information requirements)
	Overview of required information (in German)	https://www.bzst.de/SharedDocs/Downloads/DE/Merkblaetter/Merkblatt_Uebersicht_erforderliche_Angaben_Verstaendigungsverfahren.pdf
MAP profile	20 September 2022	https://www.oecd.org/tax/dispute/germany-dispute-resolution-profile.pdf

Overview of Germany's MAP Statistics for 2022

Please refer to https://www.oecd.org/tax/dispute/map-statistics-germany.pdf for details with respect to Germany's MAP Statistics.

Figure 2. Cases closed in 2022

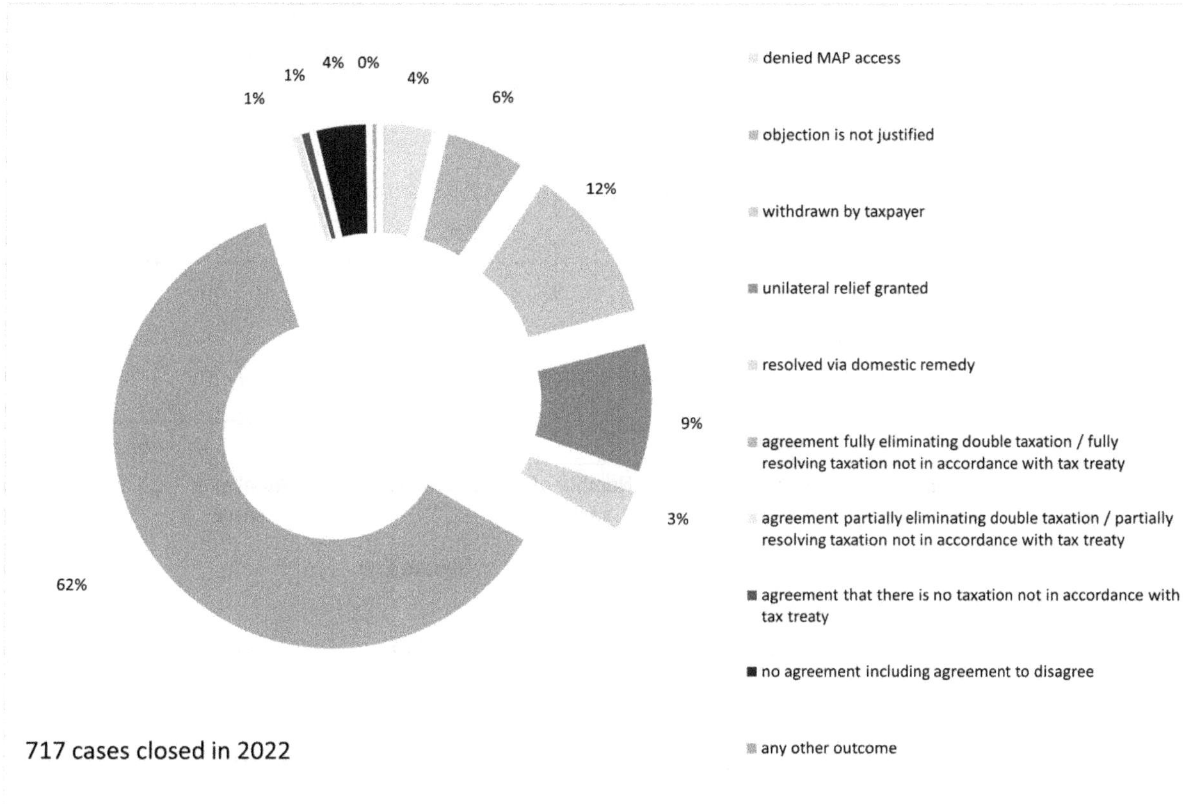

Source: OECD

Figure 3. Evolution of Germany's MAP caseload (2016-22)

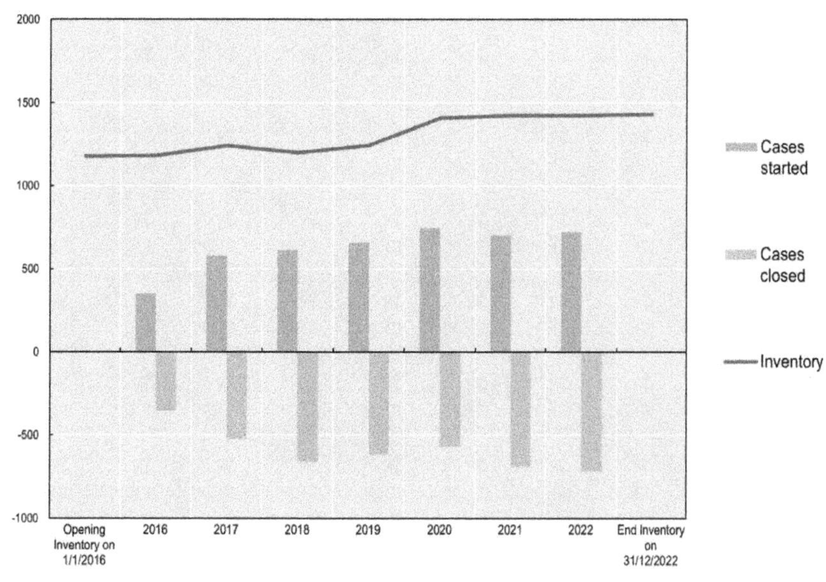

Source: OECD

Table 3. Overview of Germany's MAP caseload for 2022

Inventory for year 2022	Opening Inventory 1/1/2022	Cases started	Cases Closed	End Inventory 31/12/2022
Attribution/allocation cases	624	325	272	677
Other cases	800	399	445	754
Total	1424	724	717	1431

Source: OECD

Table 4. Germany's average time to resolve MAP cases in 2022

Cases resolved in year 2022	Pre-2016 cases		Post-2015 cases		All	
	Number of cases	**Average time**	**Number of cases**	**Average time** **Start to End**	**Number of cases**	**Average time**
Attribution / Allocation cases	11	100.00	261	22.23	272	25.37
Other cases	41	112.00	404	18.15	445	26.79
All cases	52	109.46	665	19.75	717	26.26

Source: OECD

Gibraltar

Recent developments relating to MAP in Gibraltar prior to 15 August 2023

Developments relating to MAP in the tax treaty network

- Gibraltar did not provide the relevant information.

Other developments relating to MAP

- Gibraltar did not provide the relevant information.

Latest Action 14 Peer Review report

13 September 2022 - https://doi.org/10.1787/f0cf72b8-en

Tax treaty network of Gibraltar

- one treaty, applicable to one jurisdiction (covering all treaties signed, although not necessarily in force)
- status of MLI: not signed.

Table 1. State of play of Gibraltar's tax treaty network

Treaties in line with the Action 14 Minimum Standard following MLI impact	Treaties where actions are ongoing to make them in line with the Action 14 Minimum Standard	Following impact/actions, remaining treaties that are not in line with the Action 14 Minimum Standard
1	0	0

Source: OECD

Gibraltar's MAP programme

Organisation of competent authority function

- Gibraltar did not provide the relevant information.
- contact persons for MAP requests:
  - Commissioner of Income Tax Competent Authority
    Ministry of Finance – H.M. Government of Gibraltar
    Income Tax Office
    St. Jago's Stone Block 331 Main Street GX11 1AA Gibraltar
    Email: competentauthority@gibraltar.gov.gi Telephone: +350 75260.

Figure 1. Competent Authority Organisational Structure

Source: OECD

Table 2. Guidance on the MAP process

MAP guidance	*Double taxation agreements, guidance on the mutual agreement procedure*, March 2020	https://www.gibraltar.gov.gi/uploads/Income%20Tax%20Office/Dispute-Resolution-Guidance-Double-Taxation/Gibraltar%20MAP%20Guidance.pdf (Sections 6.1 and 6.2 to be referred to for form and content of a MAP request, including information requirements)
MAP profile	14 October 2021	https://www.oecd.org/tax/dispute/gibraltar-dispute-resolution-profile.pdf

Overview of Gibraltar's MAP Statistics for 2022

Please refer to https://www.oecd.org/tax/dispute/map-statistics-gibraltar.pdf for details with respect to Gibraltar's MAP Statistics.

Figure 2. Cases closed in 2022

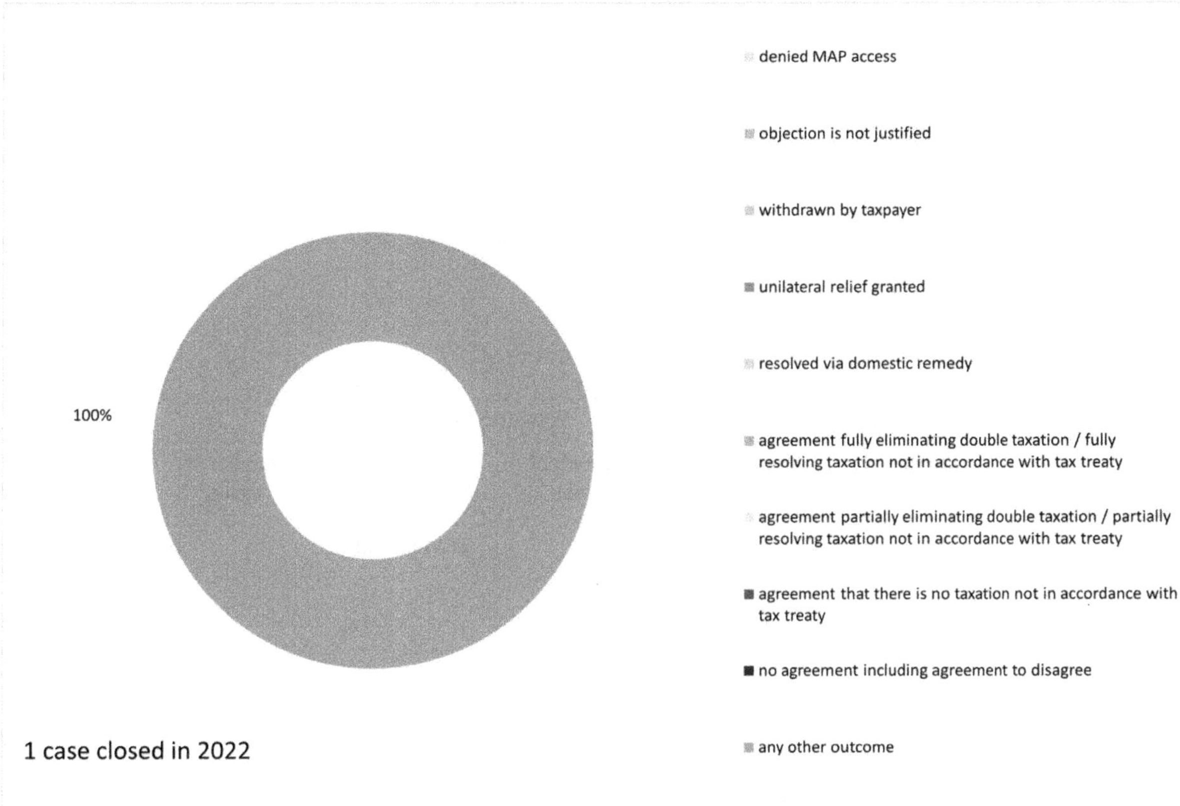

Source: OECD

Figure 3. Evolution of Gibraltar's MAP caseload (2019-22)

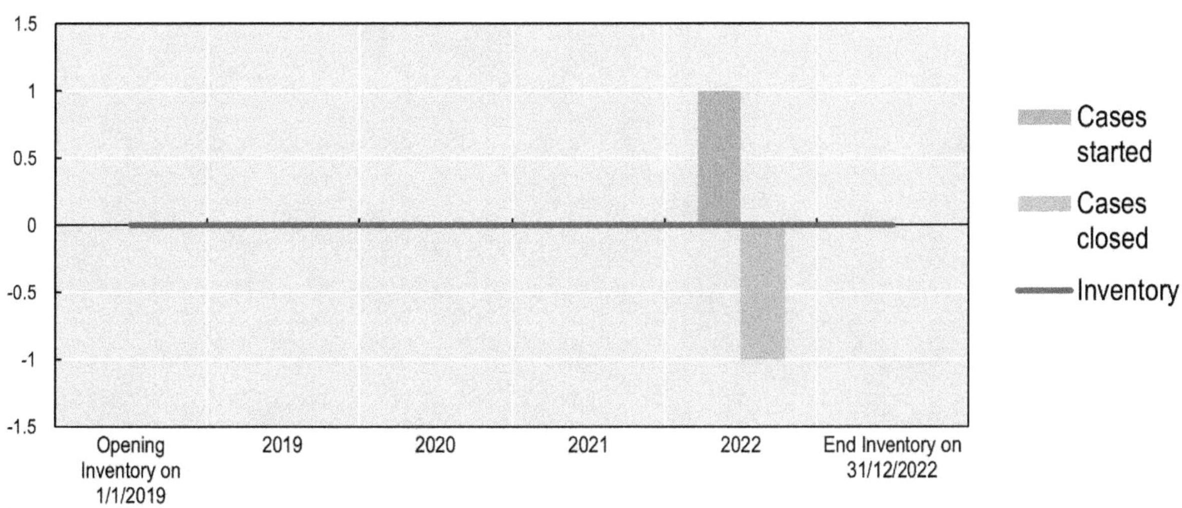

Source: OECD

Table 3. Overview of Gibraltar's MAP caseload for 2022

Inventory for year 2022	Opening Inventory 1/1/2022	Cases started	Cases Closed	End Inventory 31/12/2022
Attribution/allocation cases	0	0	0	0
Other cases	0	1	1	0
Total	0	1	1	0

Source: OECD

Table 4. Gibraltar's average time to resolve MAP cases in 2022

Cases resolved in year 2022	Pre-2019 cases		Post-2018 cases		All	
	Number of cases	**Average time**	**Number of cases**	**Average time** **Start to End**	**Number of cases**	**Average time**
Attribution / Allocation cases	0	n.a.	0	n.a.	0	n.a.
Other cases	0	n.a.	1	9.37	1	9.37
All cases	0	n.a.	1	9.37	1	9.37

Source: OECD

Greece

Recent developments relating to MAP in Greece prior to 15 August 2023

Developments relating to MAP in the tax treaty network

- New tax treaty with Republic of Singapore including article 25 of OECD Model in line with requirements of Action 14 (entry in force 01/01/2023).
- New tax treaty with Republic of France (replaced the older one) including article 25 of OECD Model in line with requirements of Action 14 (signed: 11/05/2022, ratified by Hellenic Parliament: 25/10/2022, entry in force is pending according to art. 29, par. 1 of the treaty).
- Termination of the tax treaty with the Kingdom of Sweden (not applicable since 01/01/2022).

Other developments relating to MAP

- Publication of the Decision no. 1226/2020 with subject: "Regulation of issues regarding the MAP in accordance with the bilateral Conventions for the Avoidance of Double Taxation on Income" in English language.
- Updated guidelines of MAP procedure and manual with "Frequently Questions and Answers" (in process- publication on Tax Administration's site after the conclusion of internal procedures).

Latest Action 14 Peer Review report

25 May 2021 - https://doi.org/10.1787/3bb76f22-en

Tax treaty network of Greece

- 57 treaties, applicable to 58 jurisdictions (covering all treaties signed, although not necessarily in force)
- status of MLI: in force.

Table 1. State of play of Greece's tax treaty network

Treaties in line with the Action 14 Minimum Standard following MLI impact	Treaties where actions are ongoing to make them in line with the Action 14 Minimum Standard	Following impact/actions, remaining treaties that are not in line with Action 14 Minimum Standard
55	0	2

Source: OECD

Greece's MAP programme

Organisation of competent authority function

- eight persons:
  - two heads of unit

- six persons working on MAP cases (all of which work on other tasks as well):
  - one person works on attribution/allocation cases and five persons work on other cases.
- contact persons for MAP requests:
  - for attribution / allocation cases: Independent Authority for Public Revenue
    - Directorate General for Tax Operations: Directorate for Audit Business Planning, Section D΄ Transfer Pricing-MLCs and Special Audits Department
    - Address:1, Chandri & Thessalonikis T.K. 183 46, Moschato, Greece
    - Tel. No: +30 210 4802688 Email: diesel04@aade.gr.
  - for other cases: Independent Authority for Public Revenue
    - Directorate General for Taxation: Directorate for International Tax Relations- International Tax Treaties and MAP's Department
    - Address: 8, Karageorgi Servias Str., 101 84, Athens, Greece
    - Tel. No: +30 210 3375580, Email: dos.a@aade.gr.

Figure 1. Competent Authority Organisational Structure

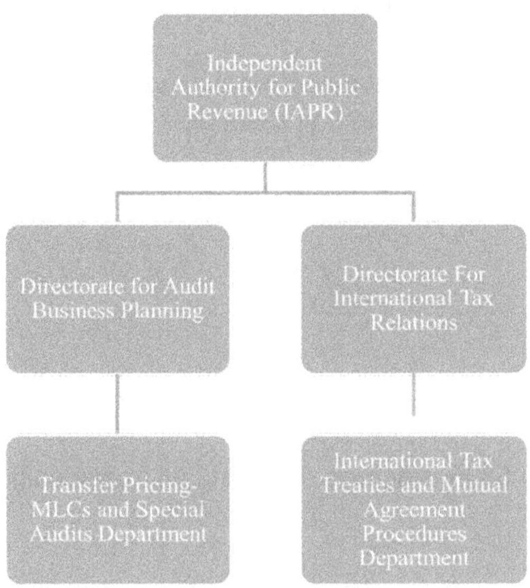

Source: OECD

Table 2. Guidance on the MAP process

MAP guidance	Mutual Agreement Procedure Handbook, January 2018	https://www.aade.gr/sites/default/files/2018-01/MAP%20HANDBOOK%20-%20ENGLISH%20VERSION.pdf (Sections "Filing a MAP request" and "Minimum information for a valid MAP request" to be referred to for form and content of a MAP request, including information requirements)
MAP profile	06 February 2018	https://www.oecd.org/tax/dispute/Greece-Dispute-Resolution-Profile.pdf

Overview of Greece's MAP Statistics for 2022

Please refer to https://www.oecd.org/tax/dispute/map-statistics-greece.pdf for details with respect to Greece's MAP Statistics.

Figure 2. Cases closed in 2022

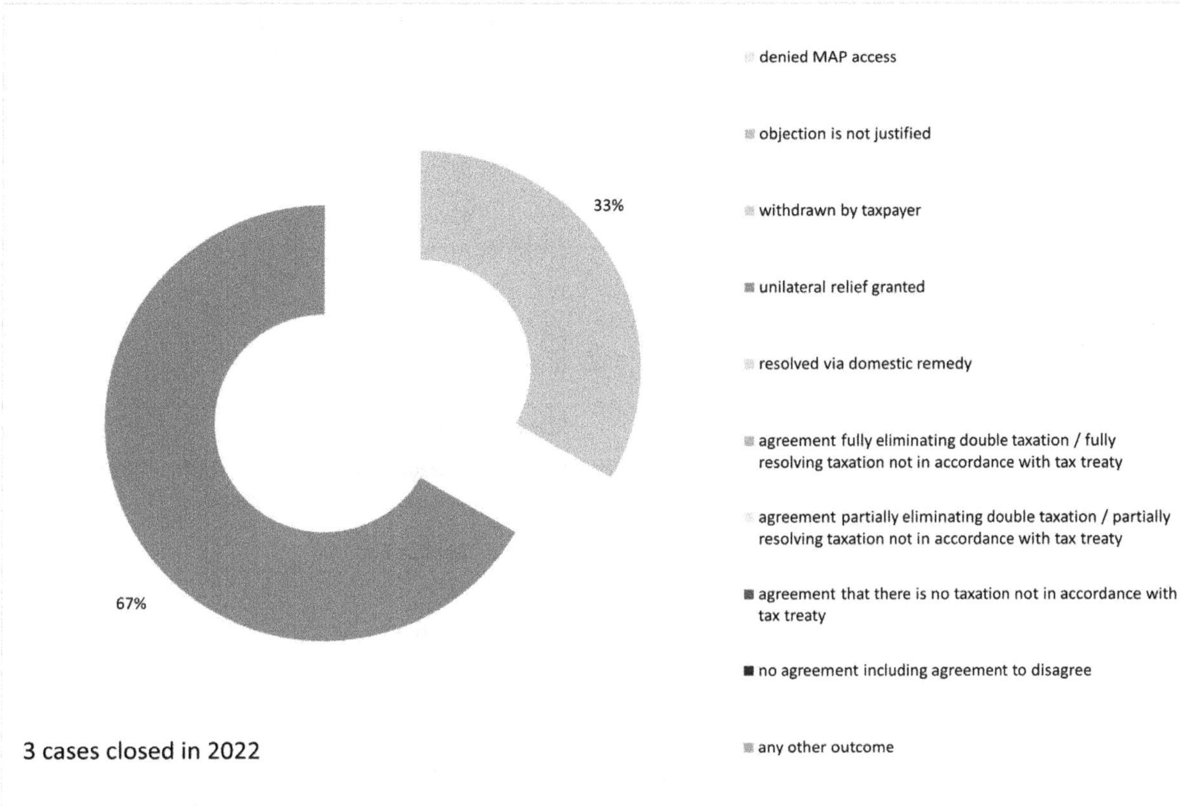

Source: OECD

Figure 3. Evolution of Greece's MAP caseload (2016-22)

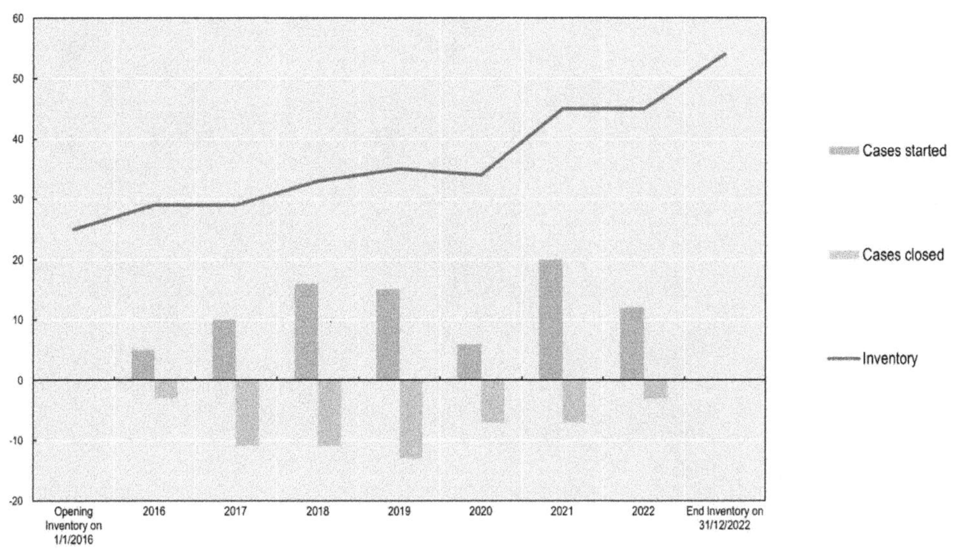

Source: OECD

Table 3. Overview of Greece's MAP caseload for 2022

Inventory for year 2022	Opening Inventory 1/1/2022	Cases started	Cases Closed	End Inventory 31/12/2022
Attribution/allocation cases	21	4	0	25
Other cases	24	0	3	29
Total	45	12	3	54

Source: OECD

Table 4. Greece's average time to resolve MAP cases in 2022

Cases resolved in year 2022	Pre-2016 cases		Post-2015 cases		All	
	Number of cases	**Average time**	**Number of cases**	**Average time** **Start to End**	**Number of cases**	**Average time**
Attribution / Allocation cases	0	N/A	0	N/A	0	N/A
Other cases	0	N/A	3	10.25	3	10.25
All cases	0	N/A	3	N/A	3	N/A

Source: OECD

Greenland

Recent developments relating to MAP in Greenland prior to 15 August 2023

Developments relating to MAP in the tax treaty network

- Greenland did not provide the relevant information.

Other developments relating to MAP

- Greenland did not provide the relevant information.

Latest Action 14 Peer Review report

13 September 2022 - https://doi.org/10.1787/b73a3abe-en

Tax treaty network of Greenland

- nine treaties, applicable to nine jurisdictions (covering all treaties signed, although not necessarily in force)
- status of MLI: not signed.

Table 1. State of play of Greenland's tax treaty network

Treaties in line with the Action 14 Minimum Standard following MLI impact	Treaties where actions are ongoing to make them in line with the Action 14 Minimum Standard	Following impact/actions, remaining treaties that are not in line with Action 14 Minimum Standard
0	No information	No information

Source: OECD

Greenland's MAP programme

Organisation of competent authority function

- two persons
- contact persons for MAP requests:
  - Anne-Marie Thorell Brandbyge, Government Official
    Organisation: The Greenlandic Tax Agency
    Contact e-mail: amtb@nanoq.gl, with CC to simog@nanoq.gl
    Contact phone: +299 34 65 59
    Contact mail: Intaleeqqap Aqqutaa nr. 1 | Postboks 1605 3900 Nuuk, Greenland.

Figure 1. Competent Authority Organisational Structure

Source: OECD

Table 2. Guidance on the MAP process

MAP guidance	No MAP guidance published	
MAP profile	18 March 2019	https://www.oecd.org/tax/dispute/Greenland-Dispute-Resolution-Profile.pdf

Overview of Greenland's MAP Statistics for 2022

Please refer to https://www.oecd.org/tax/dispute/map-statistics-greenland.pdf for details with respect to Greenland's MAP Statistics.

Figure 2. Cases closed in 2022

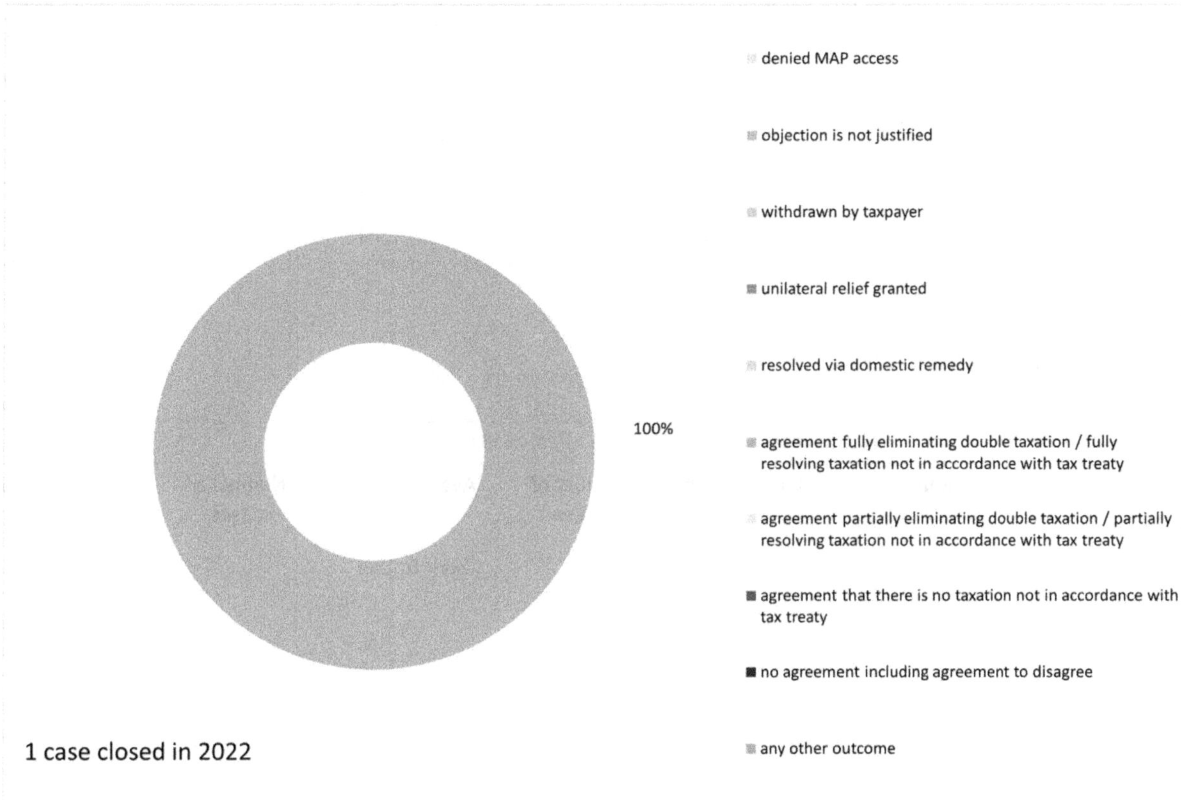

Source: OECD

Figure 3. Evolution of Greenland's MAP caseload (2019-22)

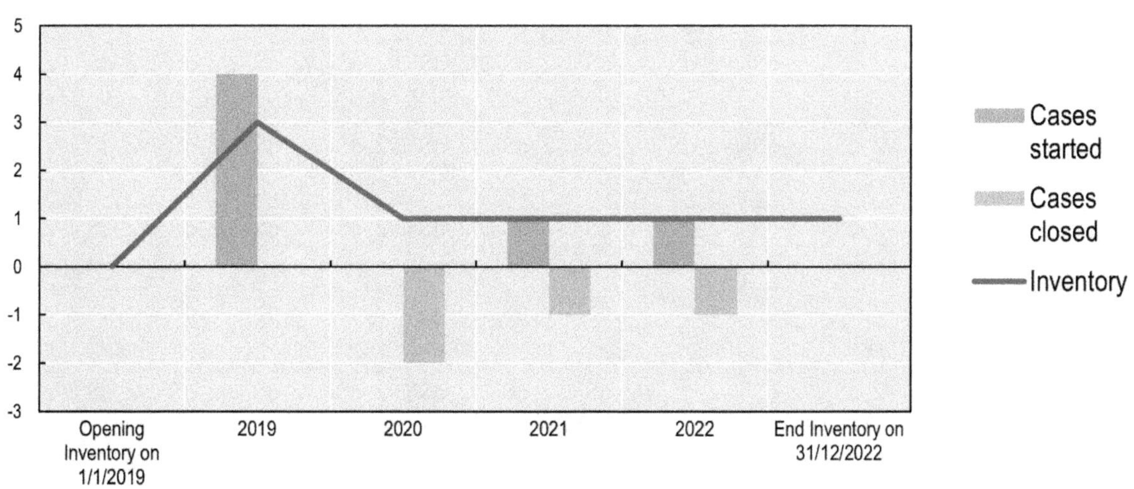

Source: OECD

Table 3. Overview of Greenland's MAP caseload for 2022

Inventory for year 2022	Opening Inventory 1/1/2022	Cases started	Cases Closed	End Inventory 31/12/2022
Attribution/allocation cases	1	0	0	1
Other cases	0	1	1	0
Total	1	1	1	1

Source: OECD

Table 4. Greenland's average time to resolve MAP cases in 2022

Cases resolved in year 2022	Pre-2019 cases		Post-2018 cases		All	
	Number of cases	**Average time**	**Number of cases**	**Average time** **Start to End**	**Number of cases**	**Average time**
Attribution / Allocation cases	0	N/A	0	N/A	0	N/A
Other cases	0	N/A	1	5.00	1	5.00
All cases	0	N/A	1	5.00	1	5.00

Source: OECD

Grenada

Recent developments relating to MAP in Grenada prior to 15 August 2023

Developments relating to MAP in the tax treaty network

- Grenada did not provide the relevant information.

Other developments relating to MAP

- Grenada did not provide the relevant information.

Latest Action 14 Peer Review report

Grenada is yet to be peer reviewed under Action 14.

Tax treaty network of Grenada

- four treaties, applicable to 14 jurisdictions (covering all treaties signed, although not necessarily in force)
- status of MLI: not signed.

Table 1. State of play of Grenada's tax treaty network

Treaties in line with the Action 14 Minimum Standard following MLI impact	Treaties where actions are ongoing to make them in line with the Action 14 Minimum Standard	Following impact/actions, remaining treaties that are not in line with Action 14 Minimum Standard
0	No information	No information

Source: OECD

Grenada's MAP programme

Organisation of competent authority function

- Grenada did not provide the relevant information.

Table 2. Guidance on the MAP process

MAP guidance	No MAP guidance published	
MAP profile	No MAP profile published	

Overview of Grenada's MAP Statistics for 2022

Grenada did not report any MAP cases in its 2022 MAP Statistics.

Please refer to https://www.oecd.org/tax/dispute/map-statistics-grenada.pdf for details with respect to Grenada's MAP Statistics.

Guernsey

Recent developments relating to MAP in Guernsey prior to 15 August 2023

Developments relating to MAP in the tax treaty network

- Protocol with Poland signed 19/5/22, ratified by Guernsey, still to enter into force as no notification of ratification yet received from Poland (Art 25(1) first sentence).
- Protocol with Qatar signed 19/5/22, entered into force 8/3/23 (Art 25(1) second sentence)
- Protocols previously signed with Finland (in 2020) entered into force 27/3/23 (Art 25(1) first sentence).
- Protocol previously signed with New Zealand (in 2019) entered into force 30/3/23 (Art 25(1) first sentence).
- Protocol signed with Ireland 8/12/21 entered into force 19/12/22 (Art 25(1) first sentence).
- Text of a Protocol with Jersey agreed at officer level and process for finalisation and seeking agreement to sign being implemented (Art 25(1) first sentence).
- No new treaties signed since 31/12/2020.

Other developments relating to MAP

- The MAP profile was updated in 2023.

Latest Action 14 Peer Review report

24 January 2022 - https://doi.org/10.1787/6933c16a-en

Tax treaty network of Guernsey

- 27 treaties, applicable to 27 jurisdictions (covering all treaties signed, although not necessarily in force)
- status of MLI: in force.

Table 1. State of play of Guernsey's tax treaty network

Treaties in line with the Action 14 Minimum Standard following MLI impact	Treaties where actions are ongoing to make them in line with the Action 14 Minimum Standard	Following impact/actions, remaining treaties that are not in line with Action 14 Minimum Standard
15	0	12

Source: OECD

Guernsey's MAP programme

Organisation of competent authority function

- five persons:
  - The Director of the Revenue Service has delegated Competent Authority functions to the Director of International Tax Policy, the Head of Policy, and two Technical Leads.
  - Three persons work on MAP cases (among which three persons work on other tasks as well). One additional officer (the Senior Technical Inspector) will assist in oversight of day to day MAP cases.
- contact persons for MAP requests:
  - Nig Garland, Head of Policy (Deputy Director) [Primary Point of Contact] States of Guernsey Revenue Service
    - PO Box 37, St Peter Port, GUERNSEY GY1 3AZ
    - Telephone: +44 (0) 1481 225700 | +44 (0) 7839 106304 | nig.garland@gov.gg.
  - Nicky Forshaw, Director of the Revenue Service States of Guernsey Revenue Service
    - PO Box 37, St Peter Port, GUERNSEY GY1 3AZ
    - Telephone: +44 (0) 1481 225700 | +44 (0) 1481 222243| nicky.forshaw@gov.gg.
  - Mandy Evans, Technical Head States of Guernsey Revenue Service
    - PO Box 37, St Peter Port, GUERNSEY GY1 3AZ
    - Telephone: +44 (0) 1481 225700 | +44 (0) 7839 700443| mandy.evans@gov.gg.

Figure 1. Competent Authority Organisational Structure

Source: OECD

Table 2. Guidance on the MAP process

MAP guidance	*Guidelines for requesting Mutual Agreement Procedure ("MAP") in Guernsey*, 28 February 2023	https://www.gov.gg/CHttpHandler.ashx?id=118907&p=0 (Sections 7.1 and 7.2 to be referred to for form and content of a MAP request, including information requirements)
MAP profile	7 September 2023	https://www.oecd.org/tax/dispute/Guernsey-Dispute-Resolution-Profile.pdf

Overview of Guernsey's MAP Statistics for 2022

Please refer to https://www.oecd.org/tax/dispute/map-statistics-guernsey.pdf for details with respect to Guernsey (Bailiwick of)'s MAP Statistics.

Figure 2. Cases closed in 2022

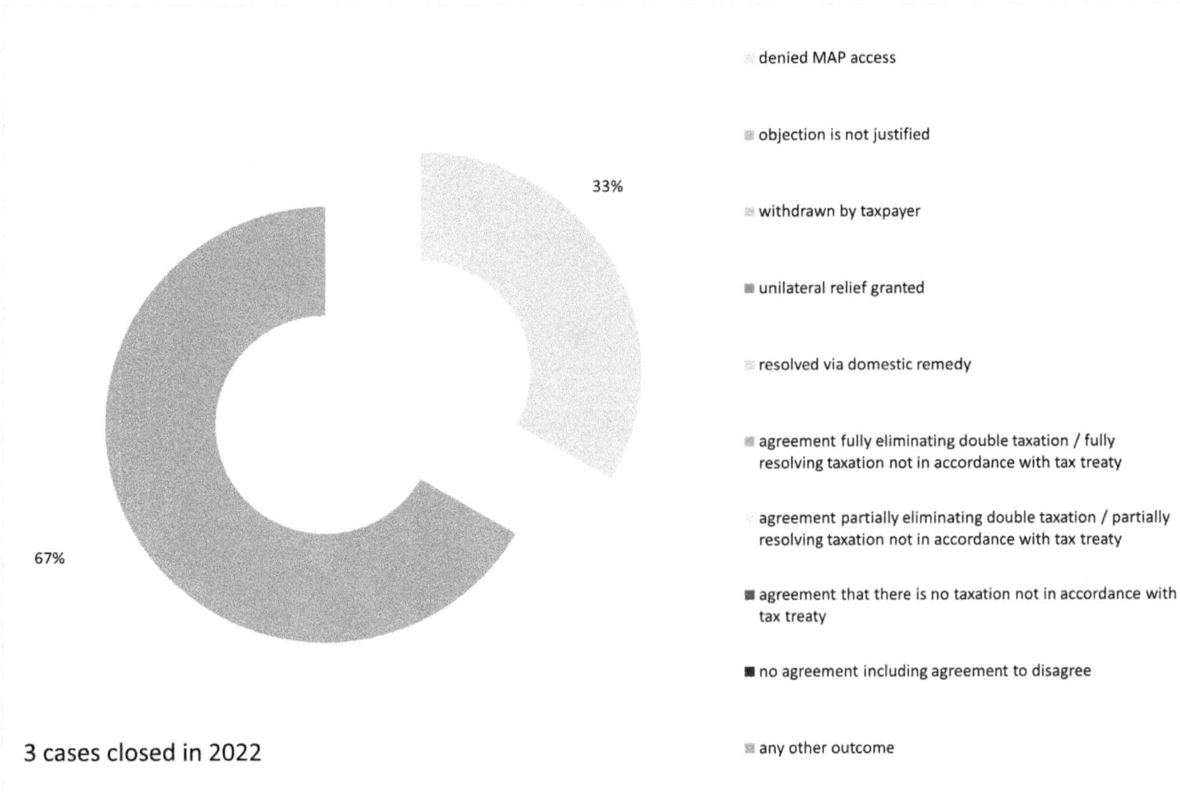

Source: OECD

Figure 3. Evolution of Guernsey's MAP caseload (2016-22)

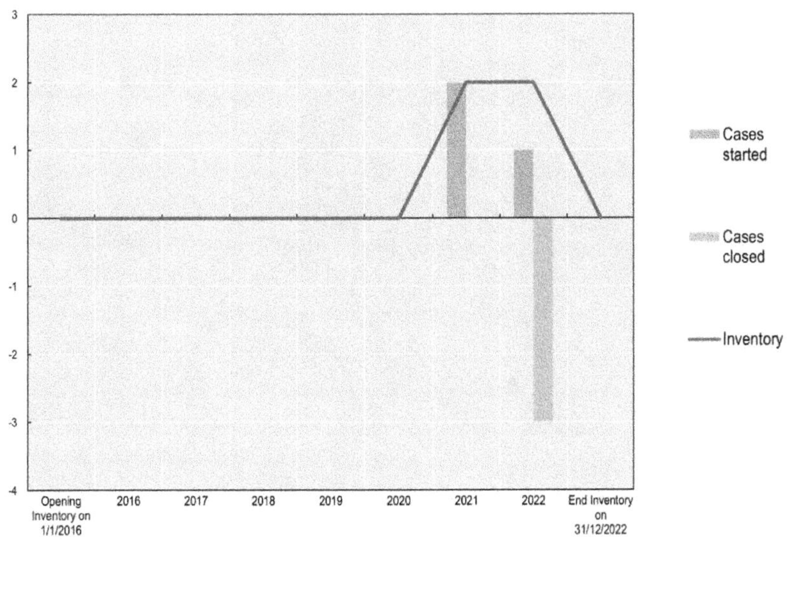

Source: OECD

Table 3. Overview of Guernsey's MAP caseload for 2022

Inventory for year 2022	Opening Inventory 1/1/2022	Cases started	Cases Closed	End Inventory 31/12/2022
Attribution/allocation cases	0	0	0	0
Other cases	2	1	3	0
Total	2	1	3	0

Source: OECD

Table 4. Guernsey's average time to resolve MAP cases in 2022

Cases resolved in year 2022	Pre-2016 cases		Post-2015 cases		All	
	Number of cases	**Average time**	**Number of cases**	**Average time** **Start to End**	**Number of cases**	**Average time**
Attribution / Allocation cases	0	N/A	0	N/A	0	N/A
Other cases	0	N/A	3	5.18	3	5.18
All cases	0	N/A	3	5.18	3	5.18

Source: OECD

Hong Kong, China

Recent developments relating to MAP in Hong Kong, China prior to 15 August 2023

Developments relating to MAP in the tax treaty network

- Entry into force of the tax treaty with Mauritius on 23 June 2023.

Other developments relating to MAP

- MAP guidance and MAP profile updated in 2023.

Latest Action 14 Peer Review report

18 October 2021 - https://doi.org/10.1787/a8bc6871-en

Tax treaty network of Hong Kong, China

- 44 treaties, applicable to 44 jurisdictions (covering all treaties signed, although not necessarily in force).
- status of MLI: in force.

Table 1. State of play of Hong Kong, China's tax treaty network

Treaties in line with the Action 14 Minimum Standard following MLI impact	Treaties where actions are ongoing to make them in line with the Action 14 Minimum Standard	Following impact/actions, remaining treaties that are not in line with Action 14 Minimum Standard
44	0	0

Source: OECD

Hong Kong, China's MAP programme

Organisation of competent authority function

- 35 professional officers of Tax Treaty Section:
  - Headed by two chief assessors
  - 33 professional officers working on MAP cases along with other treaty-related tasks
    - 12 professional officers working on APA and MAP cases involving transfer pricing and 21 professional officers working on other types of MAP cases.
- contact persons for MAP requests:
  - The Hong Kong Competent Authority
  - Tax Treaty Section Inland Revenue Department
  - GPO Box 10851, Hong Kong [Attn: Chief Assessor (Tax Treaty)]

- Tel: +852 2594 5402 Email: taxtt@ird.gov.hk.

Figure 1. Competent Authority Organisational Structure

Source: OECD

Table 2. Guidance on the MAP process

MAP guidance	Guidance on mutual agreement procedure, January 2023	https://www.ird.gov.hk/eng/pdf/2019/map_guidance.pdf (Section "Stage One" to be referred to for form and content of a MAP request, including information requirements)
	Web page	https://www.ird.gov.hk/eng/tax/dta_map.htm
MAP profile	9 January 2023	https://www.oecd.org/tax/dispute/hong-kong-dispute-resolution-profile.pdf

Overview of Hong Kong, China's MAP Statistics for 2022

Please refer to https://www.oecd.org/tax/dispute/map-statistics-hong-kong-china.pdf for details with respect to Hong Kong, China's MAP Statistics.

Figure 2. Cases closed in 2022

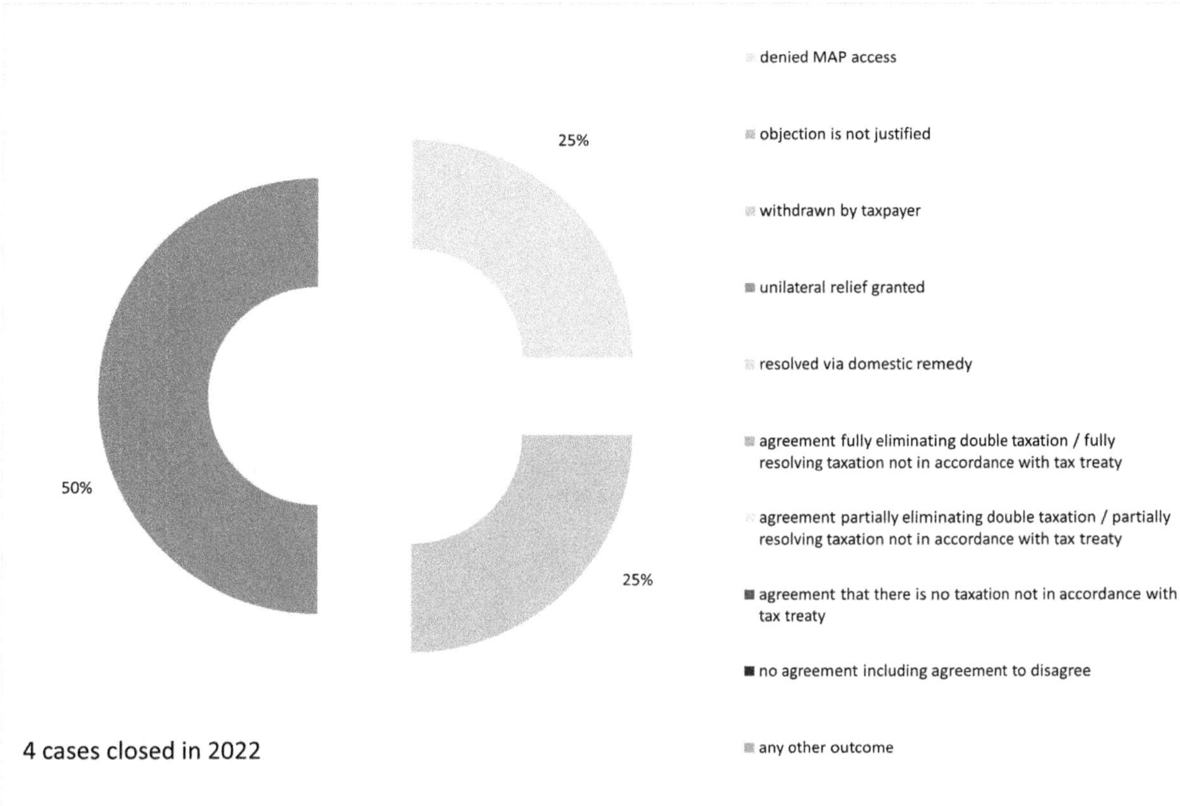

Source: OECD

Figure 3. Evolution of Hong Kong, China's MAP caseload (2016-22)

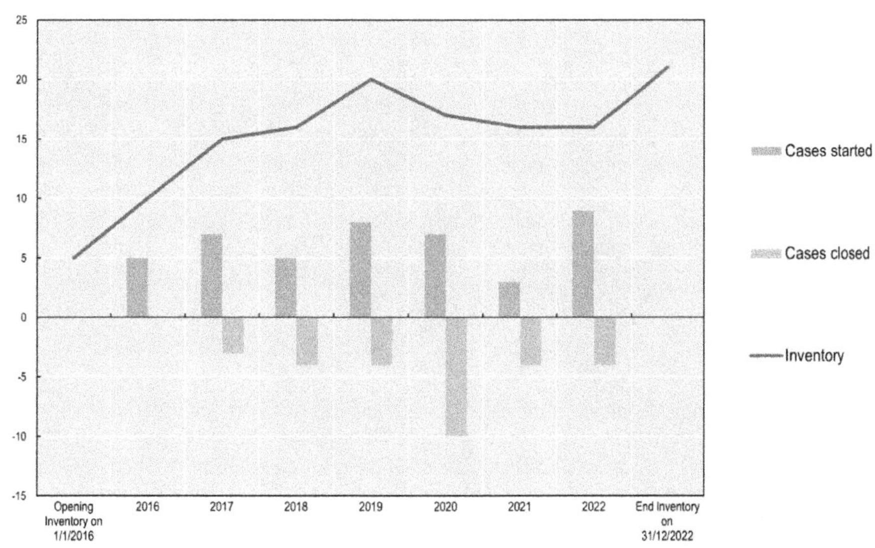

Source: OECD

Table 3. Overview of Hong Kong, China's MAP caseload for 2022

Inventory for year 2022	Opening Inventory 1/1/2022	Cases started	Cases Closed	End Inventory 31/12/2022
Attribution/allocation cases	6	7	2	11
Other cases	10	2	2	10
Total	16	9	4	21

Source: OECD

Table 4. Hong Kong, China's average time to resolve MAP cases in 2022

Cases resolved in year 2022	Pre-2016 cases		Post-2015 cases		All	
	Number of cases	**Average time**	**Number of cases**	**Average time** **Start to End**	**Number of cases**	**Average time**
Attribution / Allocation cases	0	N/A	2	19.96	2	19.96
Other cases	0	N/A	2	8.98	2	8.98
All cases	0	N/A	4	14.47	4	14.47

Source: OECD

Hungary

Recent developments relating to MAP in Hungary prior to 15 August 2023

Developments relating to MAP in the tax treaty network

- Entry into force of the tax treaty with Andorra in 2023

Other developments relating to MAP

- No developments were reported

Latest Action 14 Peer Review report

25 May 2021: https://doi.org/10.1787/da7fc990-en

Tax treaty network of Hungary

- 82 treaties, applicable to 83 jurisdictions (covering all treaties signed, although not necessarily in force)
- Status of MLI: in force

Table.1. State of play of Hungary's tax treaty network

Treaties in line with Action 14 Minimum Standard following MLI impact	Treaties where actions are ongoing to make them in line with the Action 14 Minimum Standard	Following impact/actions, remaining treaties that are not in line with Action 14 Minimum Standard
78	0	4

Source: OECD

Hungary's MAP programme

Organisation of competent authority function

- 15 persons:
  - Two heads of unit
  - 11 persons working on MAP cases
    - Where applicable, five persons work on attribution/allocation cases and six persons work on other cases
- Contact persons for MAP requests:
  - Róbert Csabai, Ministry of Finance
  - Department of International Taxation and Transfer Pricing, Head of Department
  - H-1051 Budapest, József nádor tér 2-4 / Email: robert.csabai@pm.gov.hu

Figure 1. Competent Authority Organisational Structure

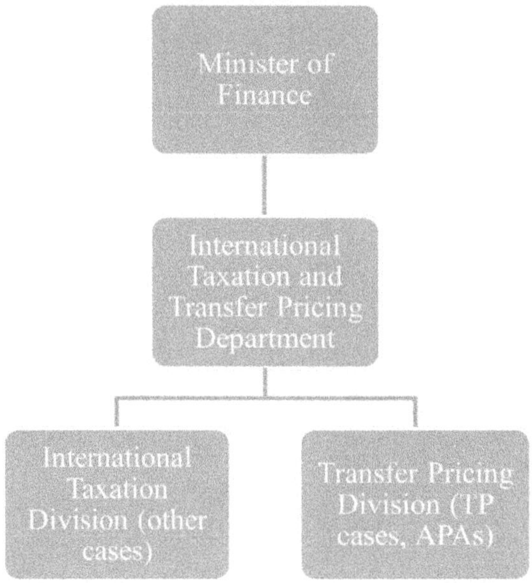

Source: OECD

Table 2. Guidance on the MAP process

MAP guidance	Information on the rules of the international tax dispute settlement procedure according to tax conventions, 21 September 2020	https://nav.gov.hu/ado/egyeb/map_tajekoztato
	Information about the European Union dispute resolution procedure initiated for the purpose of eliminating double taxation, 21 September 2020	https://nav.gov.hu/ado/egyeb/drd-map_tajekoztato
MAP profile	19 August 2022	https://www.oecd.org/tax/dispute/hungary-dispute-resolution-profile.pdf

Overview of Hungary's MAP Statistics for 2022

Please refer to https://www.oecd.org/tax/dispute/map-statistics-hungary.pdf for details with respect to Hungary's MAP Statistics.

Figure 2. Cases closed in 2022

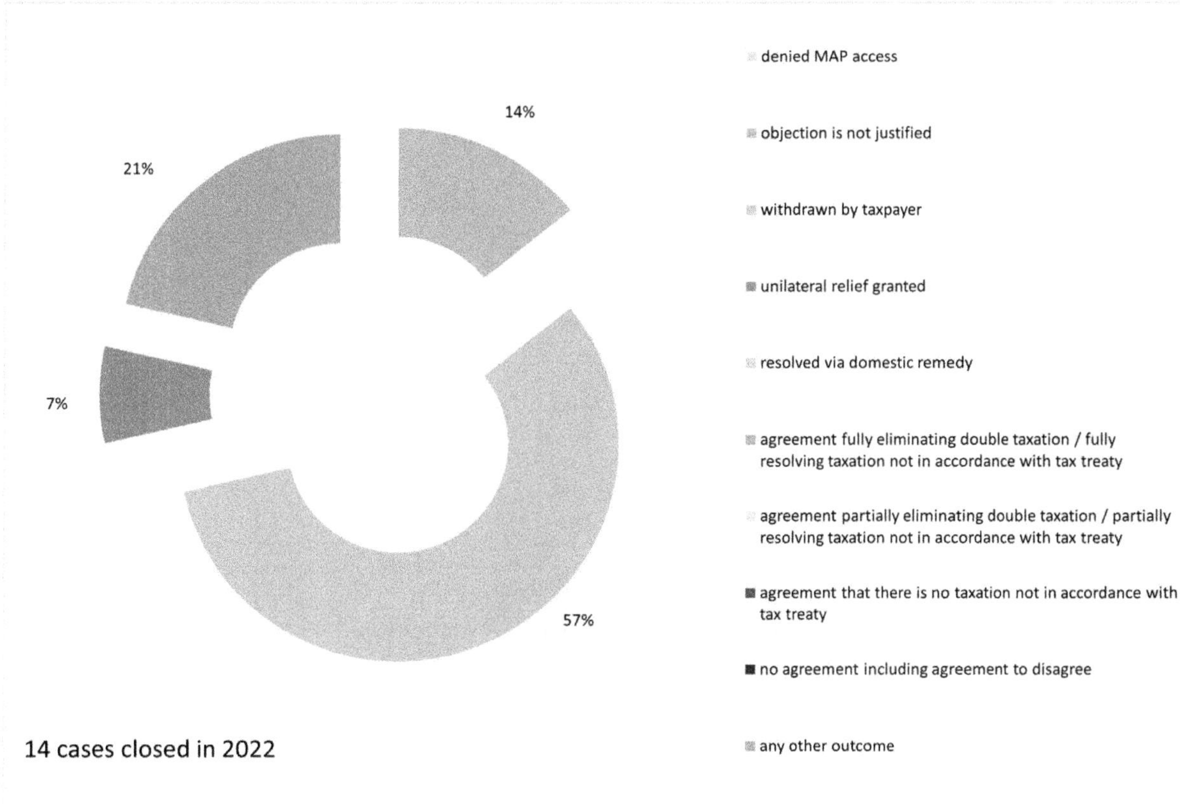

Source: OECD

Figure 3. Evolution of Hungary's MAP caseload (2016-2022)

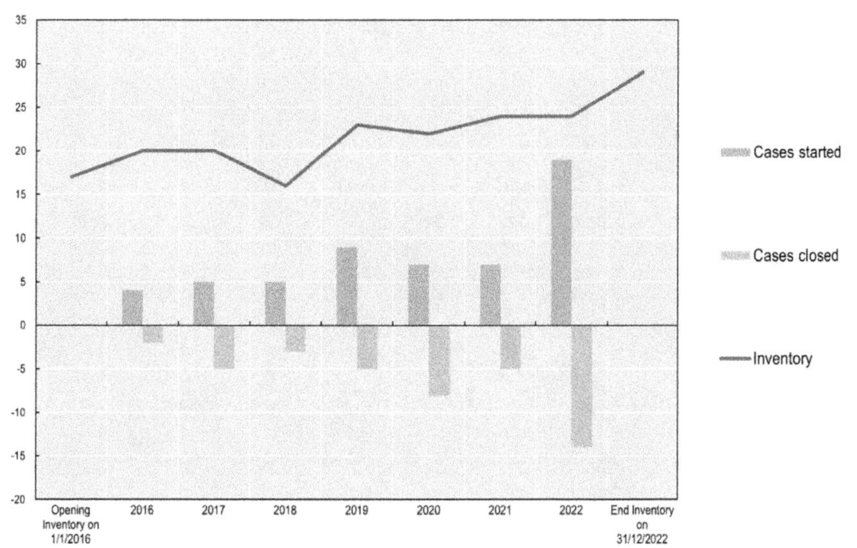

Source: OECD

Table 3. Overview of Hungary's MAP caseload for 2022

Inventory for year 2022	Opening Inventory 1/1/2022	Cases started	Cases Closed	End Inventory 31/12/2022
Attribution/allocation cases	12	17	14	15
Other cases	12	2	0	14
Total	24	19	14	29

Source: OECD

Table 4. Hungary's average time to resolve MAP cases in 2022

Cases resolved in year 2022	Pre-2016 cases		Post-2015 cases		All	
	Number of cases	**Average time**	**Number of cases**	**Average time** **Start to End**	**Number of cases**	**Average time**
Attribution / Allocation cases	0	N/A	14	11.95	14	11.95
Other cases	0	N/A	0	N/A	0	N/A
All cases	0	N/A	14	11.95	14	11.95

Source: OECD

Iceland

Recent developments relating to MAP in Iceland prior to 15 August 2023

Developments relating to MAP in the tax treaty network

- DTC was concluded with Japan and came into force on January 1, 2019. DTC's have also been signed with Australia in 2021 and Andorra in 2022. They have not been ratified by contracting states. Agreements have also been concluded with Saudi Arabia in 2022 and Brazil in June 2023. Both these agreements are waiting official signatures.

Other developments relating to MAP

- No developments were reported

Latest Action 14 Peer Review report

15 April 2021 - https://doi.org/10.1787/8b1deca3-en

Tax treaty network of Iceland

- 50 treaties, applicable to 56 jurisdictions (covering all treaties signed, although not necessarily in force)
- status of MLI: in force.

Table 1. State of play of Iceland's tax treaty network

Treaties in line with the Action 14 Minimum Standard following MLI impact	Treaties where actions are ongoing to make them in line with the Action 14 Minimum Standard	Following impact/actions, remaining treaties that are not in line with Action 14 Minimum Standard
42	5	3

Source: OECD

Iceland's MAP programme

Organisation of competent authority function

- one person:
    - one head of unit
    - one person working on MAP cases (that person works on other tasks as well):
        - the same person works on both attribution/allocation cases and other cases but can seek assistance from other units of the IRC if needed.
- contact persons for MAP requests:
    - Iceland Revenue and Customs

- att. Elin Margret Thrainsdottir
- Katrinartun 6
- 105 Reykjavik
- Iceland.

Figure 1. Competent Authority Organisational Structure

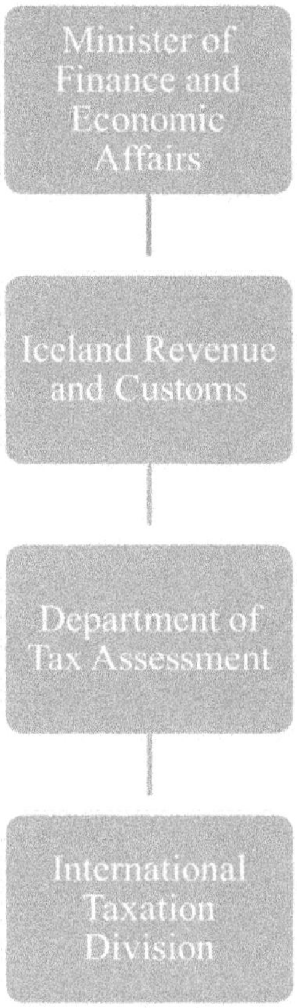

Source: OECD

Table 2. Guidance on the MAP process

MAP guidance	Gagnkvæmt samkomulag (MAP), October 2019	https://www.skatturinn.is/einstaklingar/skattskylda/tviskottunarsamningar/%23tab5 (Section "Hvernig skal óskað eftir gagnkvæmu samkomulagi?" to be referred to for form and content of a MAP request, including information requirements)
MAP profile	16 October 2019	https://www.oecd.org/tax/dispute/Iceland-Dispute-Resolution-Profile.pdf

Overview of Iceland's MAP Statistics for 2022

Please refer to https://www.oecd.org/tax/dispute/map-statistics-iceland.pdf for details with respect to Iceland's MAP Statistics.

Figure 2. Cases closed in 2022

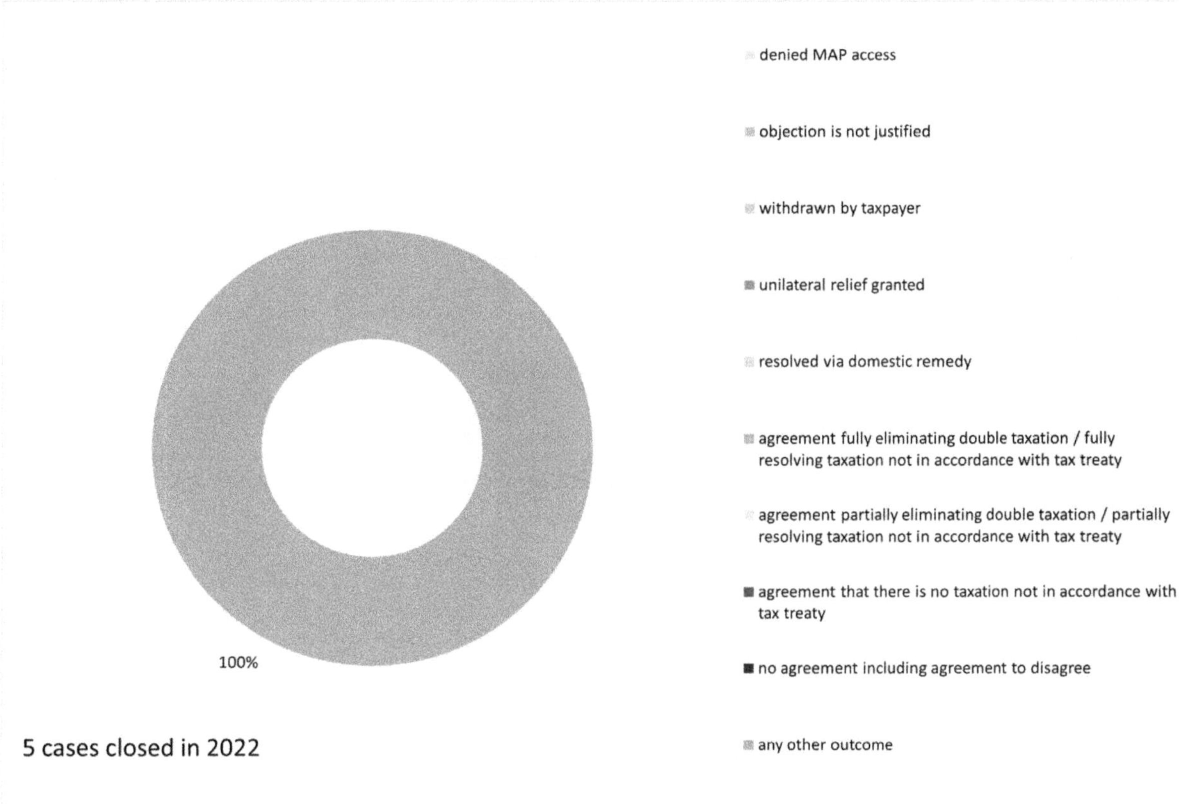

Source: OECD

Figure 3. Evolution of Iceland's MAP caseload (2016-22)

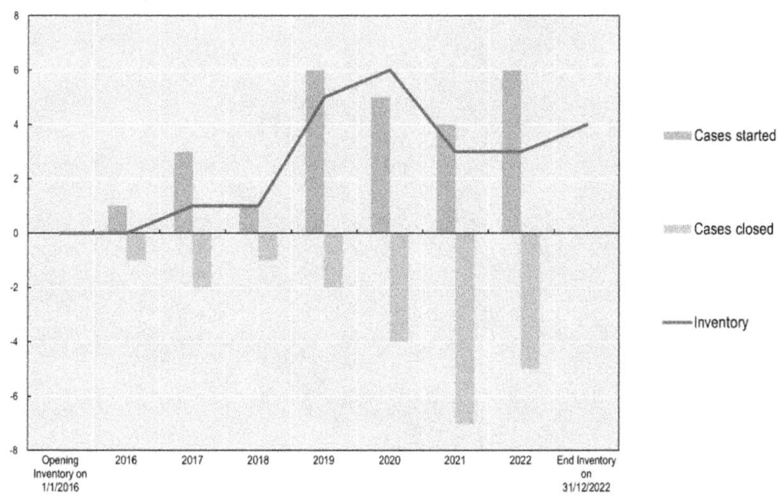

Source: OECD

Table 3. Overview of Iceland's MAP caseload for 2022

Inventory for year 2022	Opening Inventory 1/1/2022	Cases started	Cases Closed	End Inventory 31/12/2022
Attribution/allocation cases	1	0	0	1
Other cases	2	6	5	3
Total	3	6	5	4

Source: OECD

Table 4. Iceland's average time to resolve MAP cases in 2022

Cases resolved in year 2022	Pre-2016 cases		Post-2015 cases		All	
	Number of cases	**Average time**	**Number of cases**	**Average time** **Start to End**	**Number of cases**	**Average time**
Attribution / Allocation cases	0	N/A	0	N/A	0	N/A
Other cases	5	17.86	5	3.57	10	10.72
All cases	5	N/A	5	N/A	10	N/A

Source: OECD

India

Recent developments relating to MAP in India prior to 15 August 2023

Developments relating to MAP in the tax treaty network

- Entry into force in 2022 of the tax treaty with Chile.
- Entry into force in 2020 of the tax treaty with Iran.

Other developments relating to MAP

- No developments were reported

Latest Action 14 Peer Review report

26 July 2021 - https://doi.org/10.1787/cc6e7579-en

Tax treaty network of India

- 97 treaties, applicable to 97 jurisdictions (covering all treaties signed, although not necessarily in force)
- status of MLI: in force.

Table 1. State of play of India's tax treaty network

Treaties in line with the Action 14 Minimum Standard following MLI impact	Treaties where actions are ongoing to make them in line with the Action 14 Minimum Standard	Following impact/actions, remaining treaties that are not in line with Action 14 Minimum Standard
89	8	0

Source: OECD

India's MAP programme

Organisation of competent authority function

- 18 persons:
  - two Competent Authorities with five heads of unit:
    - 18 persons working on MAP cases (all of which work on other tasks as well).
- Contact persons for MAP requests:
  - for North America and Europe: Joint Secretary (Foreign Tax & Tax Research –I) and Competent Authority, Central Board of Direct Taxes, Department of Revenue, Ministry of Finance, Government of India Room No. 803, 8th Floor, C-Wing, HUDCO-Vishala Building, Bhikaji Cama Place, R.K. Puram New Delhi-110066, India Telephone – 011-26108402 | Fax – 011-26177990 | e-mail: jsfttr1@nic.in

- for countries not situated in North America or Europe: Joint Secretary (Foreign Tax & Tax Research –II) and Competent Authority, Central Board of Direct Taxes, Department of Revenue, Ministry of Finance, Government of India Room No. 804, 8th Floor, C-Wing, HUDCO-Vishala Building, BhikajiCama Place, R.K.Puram New Delhi-110066, India Telephone – 011-26104504, 26177527 | Fax – 011-26104504 | e-mail: jsfttr-2@gov.in.

Figure 1. Competent Authority Organisational Structure

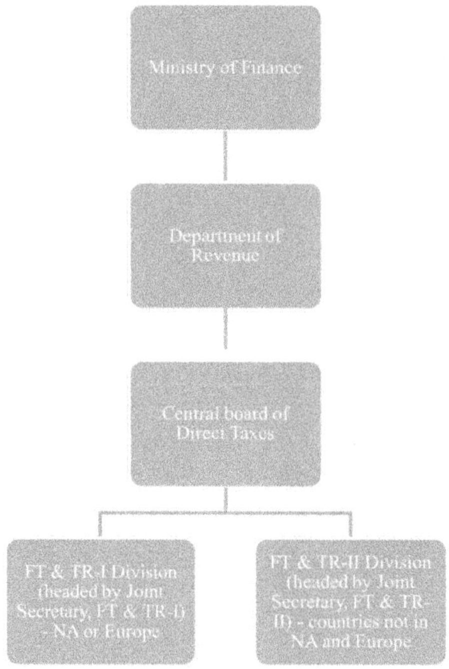

Source: OECD

Table 2. Guidance on the MAP process

MAP guidance	Mutual Agreement Procedure (MAP) Guidance, 10 June 2022	https://incometaxindia.gov.in/Documents/MAP-Guidance-2022.pdf (Section III to be referred to for form and content of a MAP request, including information requirements)
MAP profile	8 December 2020	https://www.oecd.org/tax/dispute/India-Dispute-Resolution-Profile.pdf

Overview of India's MAP Statistics for 2022

Please refer to https://www.oecd.org/tax/dispute/map-statistics-india.pdf for details with respect to India's MAP Statistics.

Figure 2. Cases closed in 2022

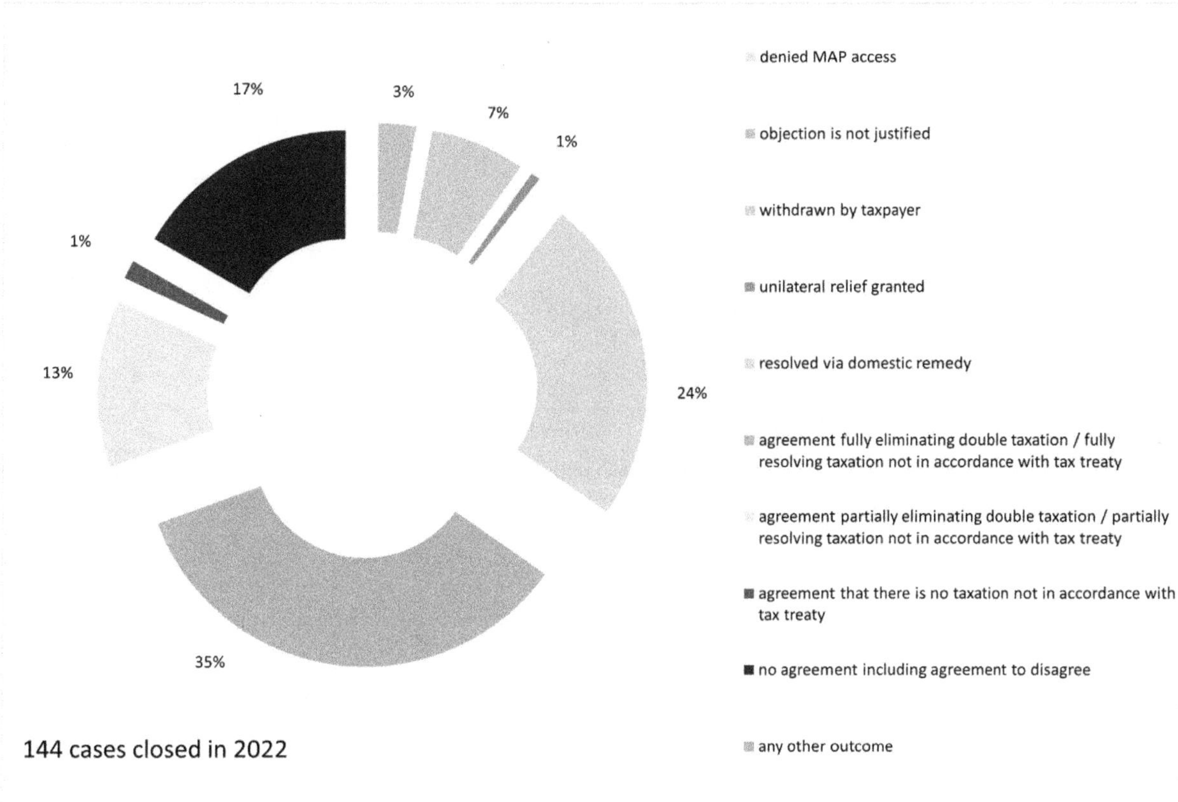

Source: OECD

Figure 3. Evolution of India's MAP caseload (2016-22)

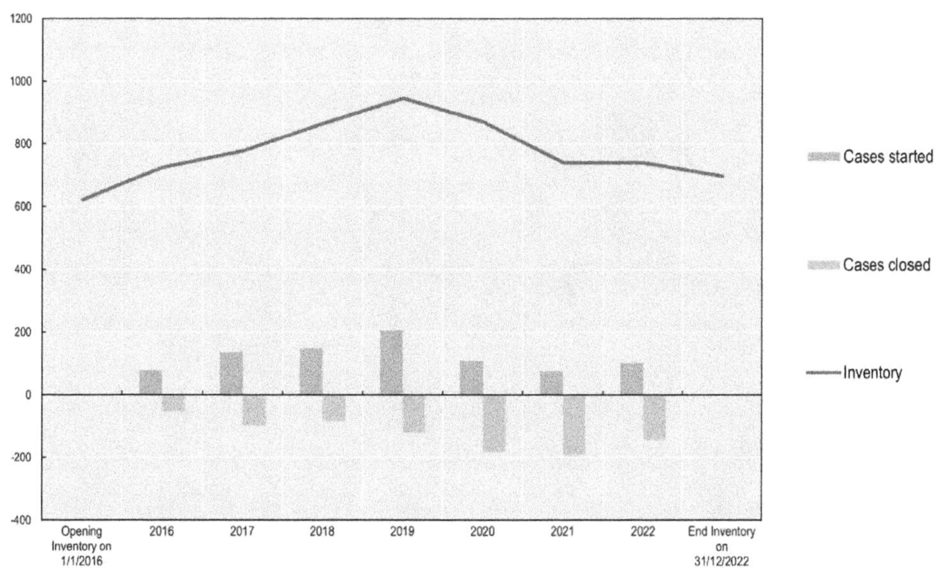

Source: OECD

Table 3. Overview of India's MAP caseload for 2022

Inventory for year 2022	Opening Inventory 1/1/2022	Cases started	Cases Closed	End Inventory 31/12/2022
Attribution/allocation cases	590	89	122	557
Other cases	150	12	22	140
Total	740	101	144	697

Source: OECD

Table 4. India's average time to resolve MAP cases in 2022

Cases resolved in year 2022	Pre-2016 cases		Post-2015 cases		All	
	Number of cases	**Average time**	**Number of cases**	**Average time** **Start to End**	**Number of cases**	**Average time**
Attribution / Allocation cases	19	127.17	103	34.54	122	48.97
Other cases	3	88.5	19	34.19	22	41.6
All cases	22	121.9	122	34.49	144	47.84

Source: OECD

Indonesia

Recent developments relating to MAP in Indonesia prior to 15 August 2023

Developments relating to MAP in the tax treaty network

- Modified by MLI, entry into effect in 2022 of the tax treaty with Hungary
- Modified by MLI, entry into effect in 2022 of the tax treaty with Croatia
- Modified by MLI, entry into effect in 2022 of the tax treaty with Malaysia
- Modified by MLI, entry into effect in 2022 of the tax treaty with Egypt
- Modified by MLI, entry into effect in 2022 of the tax treaty with Pakistan
- Modified by MLI, entry into effect in 2023 of the tax treaty with Seychelles
- Modified by MLI, entry into effect in 2023 of the tax treaty with Spain
- Modified by MLI, entry into effect in 2023 of the tax treaty with Thailand
- Modified by MLI, entry into effect in 2023 of the tax treaty with China (People's Republic of)

Other developments relating to MAP

- No developments were reported

Latest Action 14 Peer Review report

18 October 2021 - https://doi.org/10.1787/8095f743-en

Tax treaty network of Indonesia

- 72 treaties, applicable to 72 jurisdictions (covering all treaties signed, although not necessarily in force)
- status of MLI: in force.

Table 1. State of play of Indonesia's tax treaty network

Treaties in line with the Action 14 Minimum Standard following MLI impact	Treaties where actions are ongoing to make them in line with the Action 14 Minimum Standard	Following impact/actions, remaining treaties that are not in line with Action 14 Minimum Standard
39	31	2

Source: OECD

Indonesia's MAP programme

Organisation of competent authority function

- 38 persons:
  - One Director, one Deputy Director and four Head of Divisions

- 32 persons working on MAP cases (all of which work on other tasks as well)

- contact persons for MAP requests:
  - Director of International Taxation, Directorate General of Taxes
    - Jl. Jenderal Gatot Subroto Kav.40-42 Jakarta 12190
    - Phone +62 21 5250208, Fax +62 21 5732064 email: map@pajak.go.id.
  - Other than that, Tax Resident of Indonesia may submit the MAP request to the Tax Office in which the Taxpayer is registered.

Figure 1. Competent Authority Organisational Structure

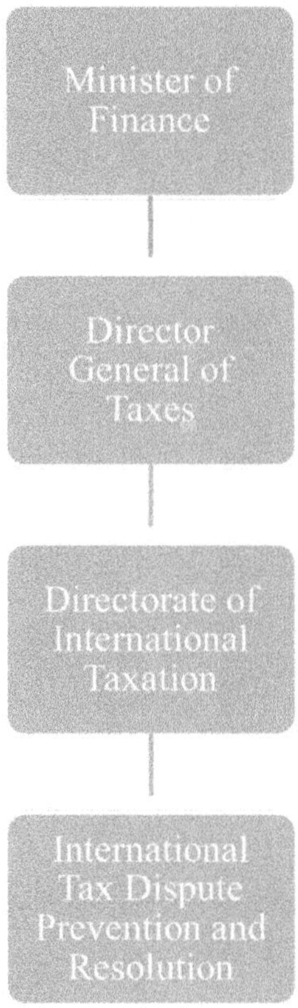

Source: OECD

Table 2. Guidance on the MAP process

MAP guidance	Mutual Agreement Procedure (MAP)	https://www.pajak.go.id/id/apa-map#MAP (Section "MAP Application" to be referred to for form and content of a MAP request, including information requirements)
MAP profile	23 June 2021	https://www.oecd.org/tax/dispute/indonesia-dispute-resolution-profile.pdf

Overview of Indonesia's MAP Statistics for 2022

Please refer to https://www.oecd.org/tax/dispute/map-statistics-indonesia.pdf for details with respect to Indonesia's MAP Statistics.

Figure 2. Cases closed in 2022

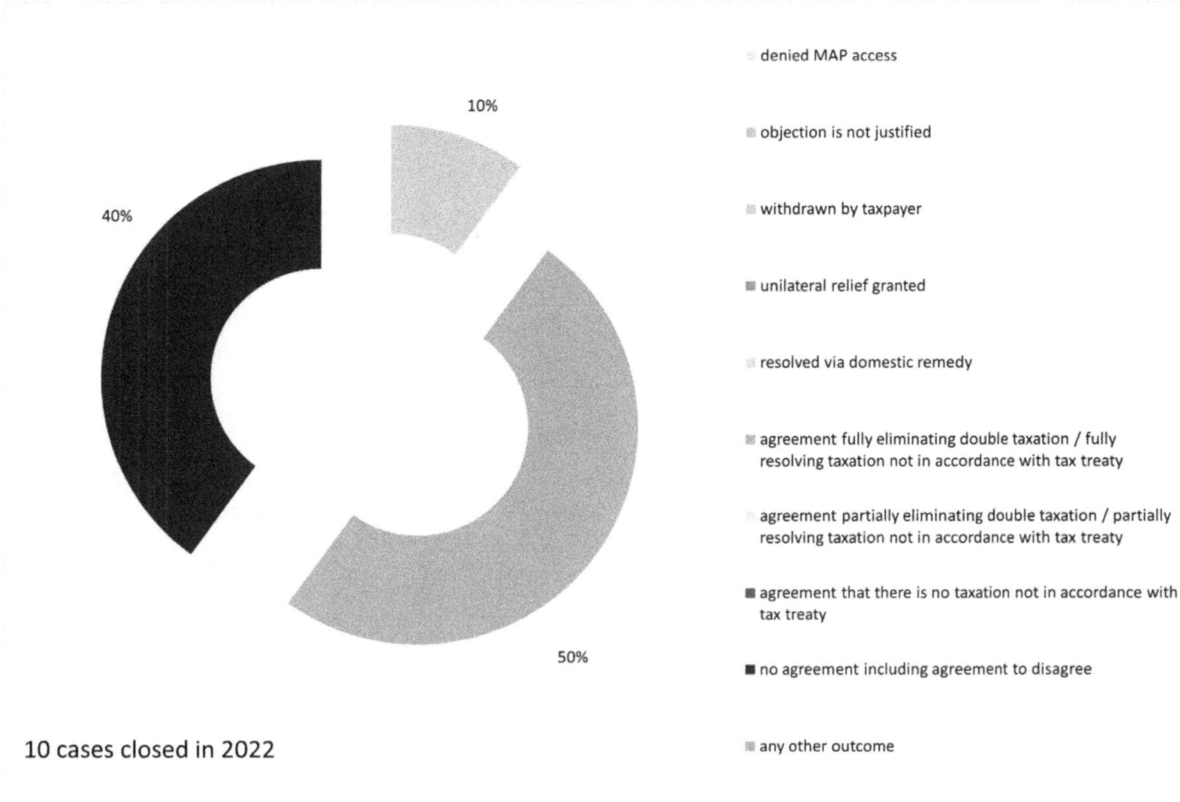

Source: OECD

Figure 3. Evolution of Indonesia's MAP caseload (2016-22)

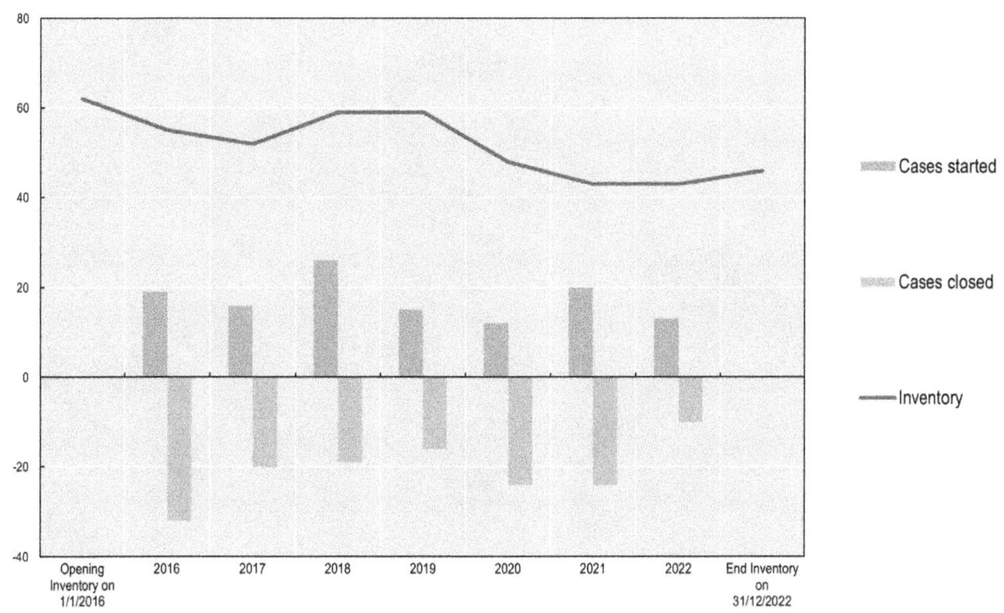

Source: OECD

Table 3. Overview of Indonesia's MAP caseload for 2022

Inventory for year 2022	Opening Inventory 1/1/2022	Cases started	Cases Closed	End Inventory 31/12/2022
Attribution/allocation cases	26	9	6	29
Other cases	17	4	4	17
Total	43	13	10	46

Source: OECD

Table 4. Indonesia's average time to resolve MAP cases in 2022

Cases resolved in year 2022	Pre-2016 cases		Post-2015 cases		All	
	Number of cases	**Average time**	**Number of cases**	**Average time**	**Number of cases**	**Average time**
				Start to End		
Attribution / Allocation cases	2	92.94	4	22.27	6	45.83
Other cases	1	92.94	3	26.92	4	43.43
All cases	3	92.94	7	24.26	10	44.87

Source: OECD

Ireland

Recent developments relating to MAP in Ireland prior to 15 August 2023

Developments relating to MAP in the tax treaty network

- The DTA with Kosovo entered into force on 24 February 2022 and its provisions began to take effect from 1 January 2023.
- A Protocol to the existing limited scope DTA with the Isle of Man entered into force on 19 December 2022. Its provisions began to take effect from 1 January 2023.
- A Protocol to the existing limited scope DTA with Guernsey entered into force on 19 December 2022. Its provisions began to take effect from 1 January 2023.

Other developments relating to MAP

- No developments were reported

Latest Action 14 Peer Review report

15 April 2021 - https://doi.org/10.1787/e0c46317-en

Tax treaty network of Ireland

- 79 treaties, applicable to 79 jurisdictions (covering all treaties signed, although not necessarily in force)
- status of MLI: in force.

Table 1. State of play of Ireland's tax treaty network

Treaties in line with the Action 14 Minimum Standard following MLI impact	Treaties where actions are ongoing to make them in line with the Action 14 Minimum Standard	Following impact/actions, remaining treaties that are not in line with Action 14 Minimum Standard
74	2	3

Source: OECD

Ireland's MAP programme

Organisation of competent authority function

- 26 persons:
  - five head(s) of unit
  - 25 persons working on MAP cases (among which seven persons work on other tasks as well):
    - 20 persons work on attribution/allocation cases and 5 persons work on other cases.
- contact persons for MAP requests:

- for attribution / allocation cases: Director, Transfer Pricing Branch, International Tax Division Office of the Revenue Commissioners, Dublin Castle, D02 F342, Dublin 2, Ireland
  - Tel: +353 1 858 9712 or +353 1 858 9377 / Fax: + 353 1 679 3314
  - Email: transferpricing@revenue.ie.
- for other cases: Director, Tax Treaties Branch, International Tax Division
  - Office of the Revenue Commissioners, Dublin Castle, D02 F342, Dublin 2, Ireland
  - Tel: +353 1 858 9885 or + 353 1 858 9862 / Email: taxtreaties@revenue.ie.

Figure 1. Competent Authority Organisational Structure

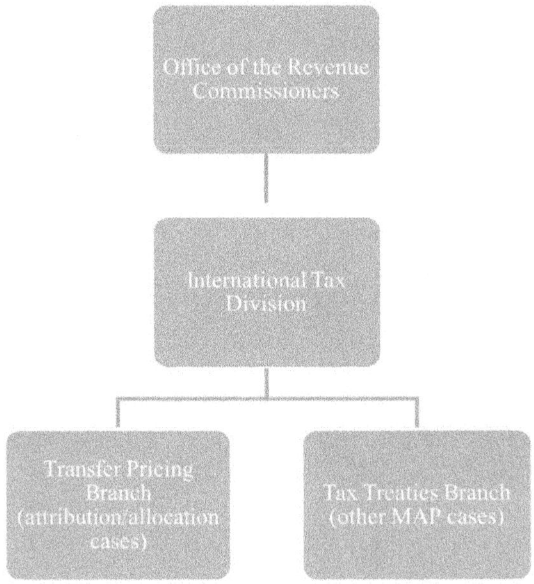

Source: OECD

Table 2. Guidance on the MAP process

MAP guidance	*Guidelines for requesting Mutual Agreement Procedure ("MAP") assistance in Ireland*, December 2021	https://www.revenue.ie/en/tax-professionals/tdm/income-tax-capital-gains-tax-corporation-tax/part-35/35-02-08.pdf (Section 2.1 to be referred to for form and content of a MAP request, including information requirements)
MAP profile	11 September 2018	https://www.oecd.org/tax/dispute/Ireland-Dispute-Resolution-Profile.pdf

Overview of Ireland's MAP Statistics for 2022

Please refer to https://www.oecd.org/tax/dispute/map-statistics-ireland.pdf for details with respect to Ireland's MAP Statistics.

Figure 2. Cases closed in 2022

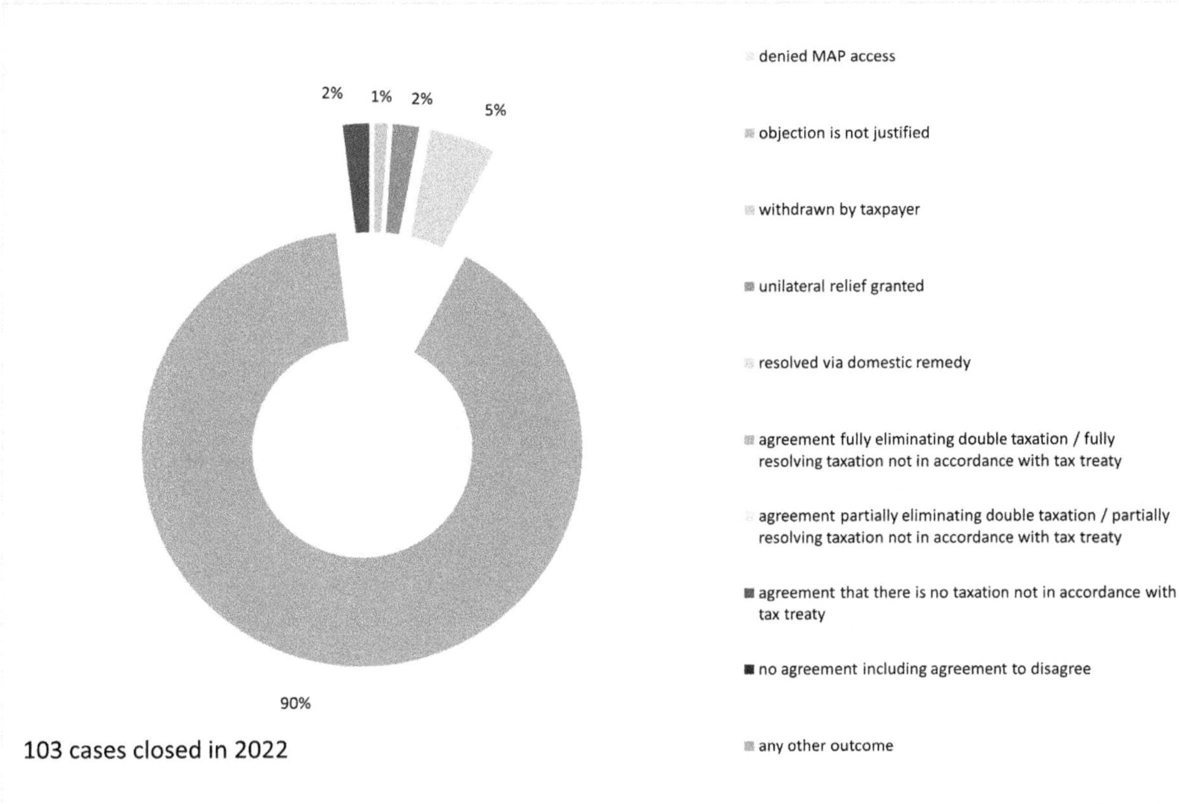

Source: OECD

Figure 3. Evolution of Ireland's MAP caseload (2016-22)

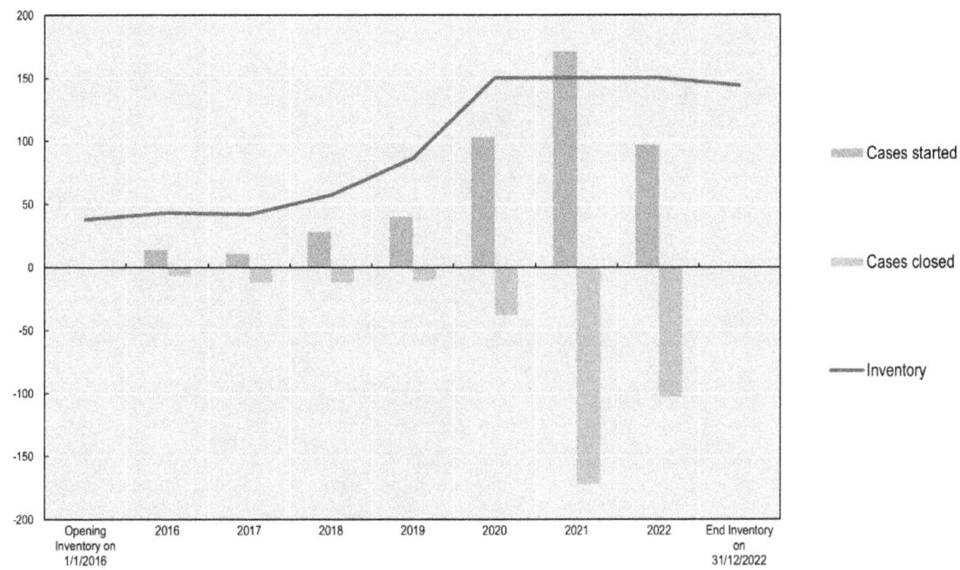

Source: OECD

Table 3. Overview of Ireland's MAP caseload for 2022

Inventory for year 2022	Opening Inventory 1/1/2022	Cases started	Cases Closed	End Inventory 31/12/2022
Attribution/allocation cases	86	28	37	77
Other cases	64	69	66	67
Total	150	97	103	144

Source: OECD

Table 4. Ireland's average time to resolve MAP cases in 2022

Cases resolved in year 2022	Pre-2016 cases		Post-2015 cases		All	
	Number of cases	**Average time**	**Number of cases**	**Average time** **Start to End**	**Number of cases**	**Average time**
Attribution / Allocation cases	1	111.98	36	24.6	37	26.96
Other cases	0	N/A	66	7.60	66	7.60
All cases	1	111.98	102	13.6	103	14.55

Source: OECD

Isle of Man

Recent developments relating to MAP in Isle of Man prior to 15 August 2023

Developments relating to MAP in the tax treaty network

- Isle of Man did not provide the relevant information.

Other developments relating to MAP

- MAP profile updated in 2023.

Latest Action 14 Peer Review report

24 January 2022 - https://doi.org/10.1787/fd56cc8d-en

Tax treaty network of Isle of Man

- 24 treaties, applicable to 24 jurisdictions (covering all treaties signed, although not necessarily in force)
- status of MLI: in force.

Table 1. State of play of Isle of Man's tax treaty network

Treaties in line with the Action 14 Minimum Standard following MLI impact	Treaties where actions are ongoing to make them in line with the Action 14 Minimum Standard	Following impact/actions, remaining treaties that are not in line with Action 14 Minimum Standard
11	No information	No information

Source: OECD

Isle of Man's MAP programme

Organisation of competent authority function

- one person
- contact persons for MAP requests:
    - Mrs Audrey Christian Deputy Assessor, Delegated Competent Authority
      Isle of Man Treasury - Income Tax Division
      Government Offices Bucks Road, Douglas Isle of Man IM1 3TX
      Email: Audrey.Christian@itd.treasury.gov.im
      Tel: +44 (0) 1624 685282 Fax: +44 (0) 1624 685351.

Figure 1. Competent Authority Organisational Structure

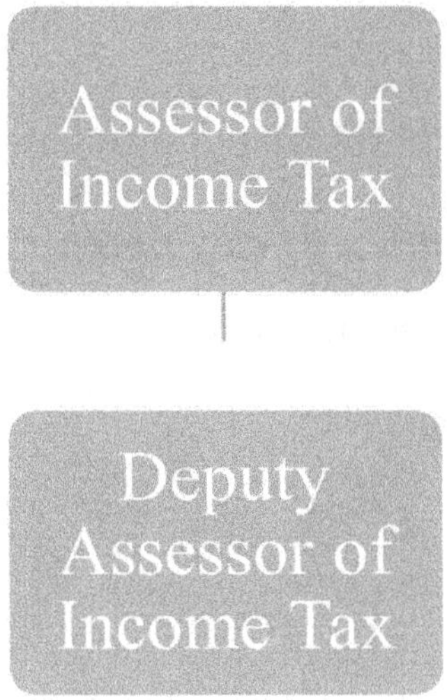

Source: OECD

Table 2. Guidance on the MAP process

MAP guidance	*Mutual Agreement Procedure in the Isle of Man's Double Taxation Agreements Guidance Note – GN 57,* 1 December 2021	https://www.gov.im/media/1364504/gn-57-map-guide-december-2020-update.pdf (Section "What to include in a MAP request" to be referred to for form and content of a MAP request, including information requirements)
MAP profile	10 February 2023	https://www.oecd.org/tax/dispute/isle-of-man-dispute-resolution-profile.pdf

Overview of Isle of Man's MAP Statistics for 2022

Please refer to https://www.oecd.org/tax/dispute/map-statistics-isle-of-man.pdf for details with respect to Isle of Man's MAP Statistics.

Figure 2. Cases closed in 2022

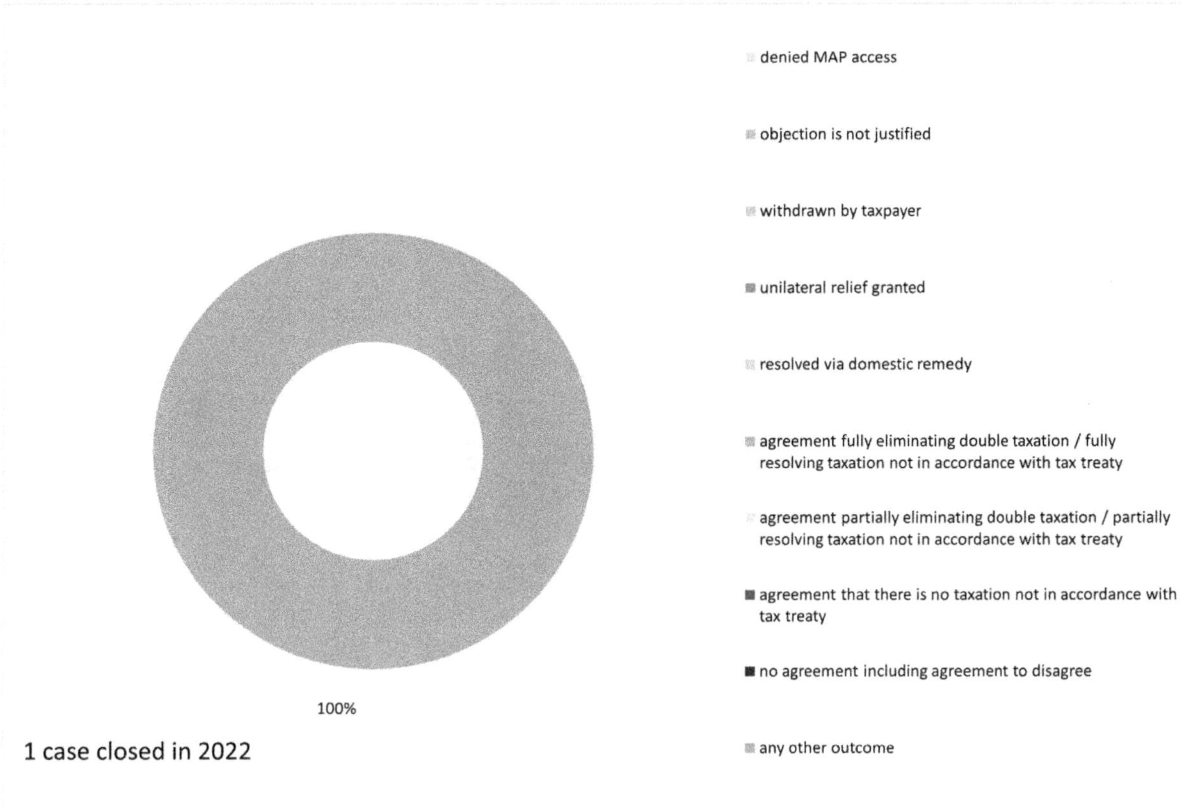

Source: OECD

Figure 3. Evolution of Isle of Man's MAP caseload (2016-22)

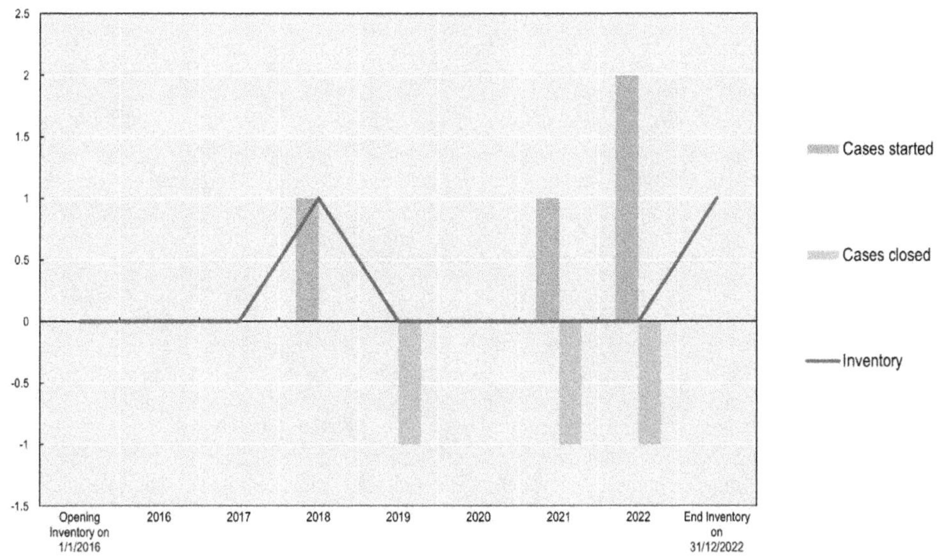

Source: OECD

Table 3. Overview of Isle of Man's MAP caseload for 2022

Inventory for year 2022	Opening Inventory 1/1/2022	Cases started	Cases Closed	End Inventory 31/12/2022
Attribution/allocation cases	0	0	0	0
Other cases	0	2	1	1
Total	0	2	1	1

Source: OECD

Table 4. Isle of Man's average time to resolve MAP cases in 2022

Cases resolved in year 2022	Pre-2016 cases		Post-2015 cases		All	
	Number of cases	**Average time**	**Number of cases**	**Average time** **Start to End**	**Number of cases**	**Average time**
Attribution / Allocation cases	0	N/A	0	N/A	0	N/A
Other cases	0	N/A	1	0.26	1	0.26
All cases	0	N/A	1	0.26	1	0.26

Source: OECD

Israel

Recent developments relating to MAP in Israel prior to 15 August 2023

Developments relating to MAP in the tax treaty network

- New DTT signed with United Arab Emirates on 31.05.2021, entered into force on 01.01.2022.

Other developments relating to MAP

- MAP profile updated in 2023.

Latest Action 14 Peer Review report

15 April 2021 - https://doi.org/10.1787/d6d1fd4e-en

Tax treaty network of Israel

- 60 treaties, applicable to 60 jurisdictions (covering all treaties signed, although not necessarily in force)
- status of MLI: in force.

Table 1. State of play of Israel's tax treaty network

Treaties in line with the Action 14 Minimum Standard following MLI impact	Treaties where actions are ongoing to make them in line with the Action 14 Minimum Standard	Following impact/actions, remaining treaties that are not in line with Action 14 Minimum Standard
51	4	5

Source: OECD

Israel's MAP programme

Organisation of competent authority function

- four persons:
    - one head of unit
    - three persons working on MAP cases (all of which work on other tasks as well).
- contact persons for MAP requests:
    - Israel Tax Authority, International Tax Division
    - Postal Address: P.O. Box 7008, Tel Aviv, 61070 Israel
    - Office Address: 125 Menachem Begin Rd.
    - Tel. +972-74-7613271 / email: MAP@taxes.gov.il
    - Director of International Tax Division: Mr. Michael Asulin / email: MichaelAs@taxes.gov.il
    - Dispute resolution MAP: Ms. Nava Naimer, Senior Advisor / email: NavaNa2@taxes.gov.il.

Figure 1. Competent Authority Organisational Structure

Source: OECD

Table 2. Guidance on the MAP process

MAP guidance	*Income Tax Administrative Circular no. 01/2023,* 16/08/ 2023	https://www.gov.il/he/Departments/policies/professional-directives-01-2023 (Section 5 to be referred to for form and content of a MAP request, including information requirements)
MAP profile	14 February 2023	https://www.oecd.org/tax/dispute/israel-dispute-resolution-profile.pdf

Overview of Israel's MAP Statistics for 2022

Please refer to https://www.oecd.org/tax/dispute/map-statistics-israel.pdf for details with respect to Israel's MAP Statistics.

Figure 2. Cases closed in 2022

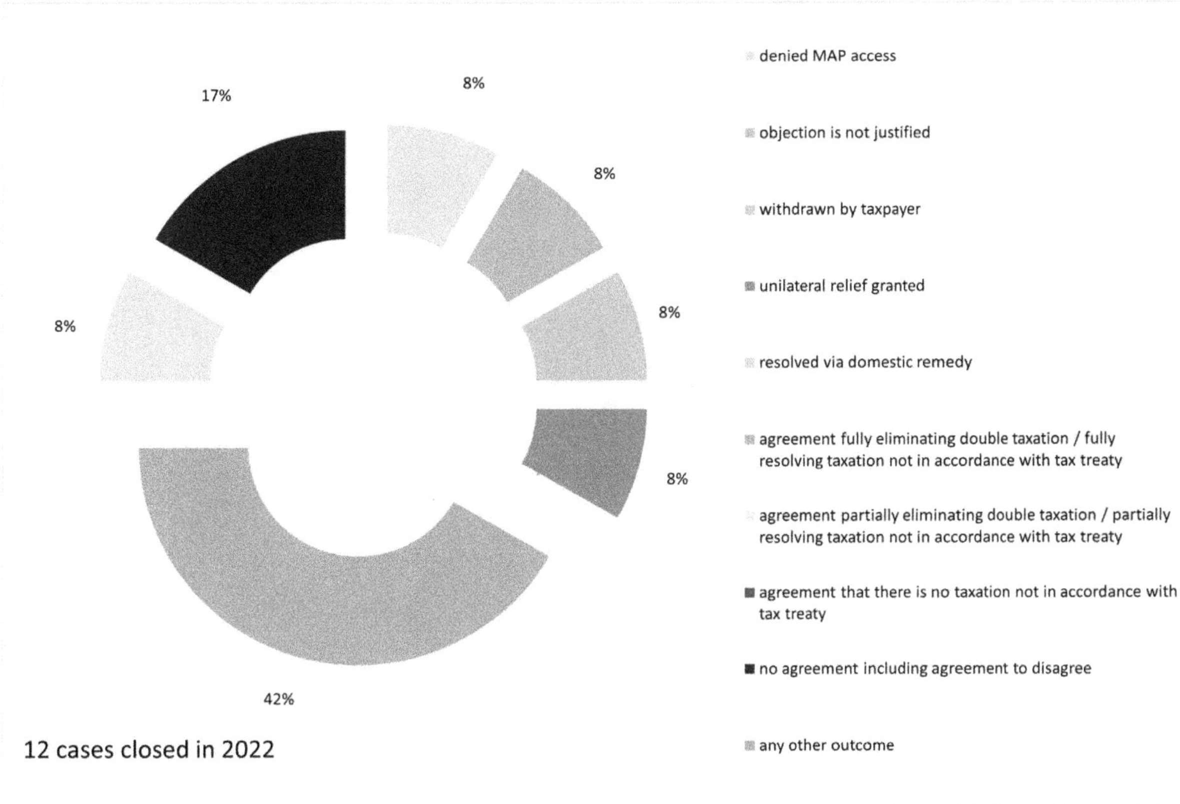

Source: OECD

Figure 3. Evolution of Israel's MAP caseload (2016-22)

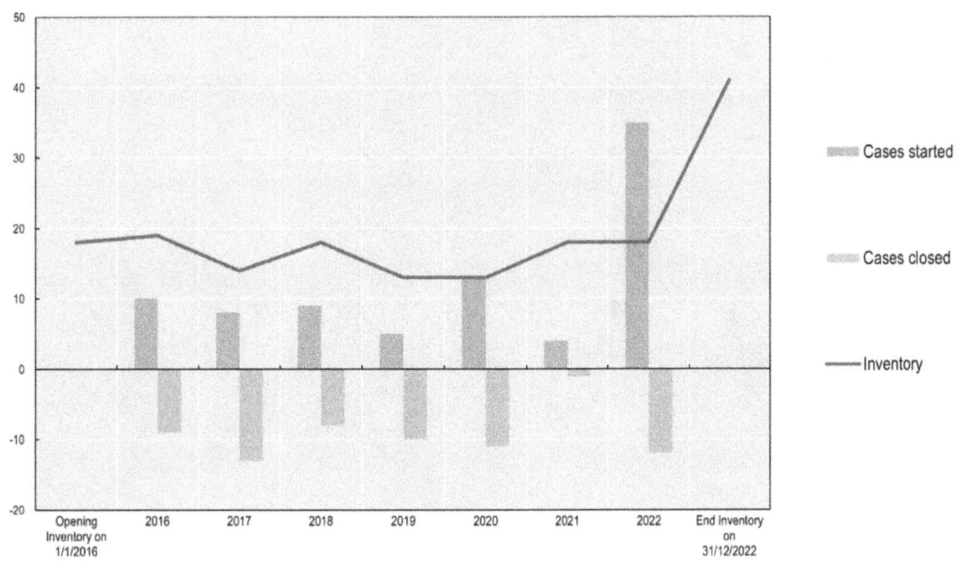

Source: OECD

Table 3. Overview of Israel's MAP caseload for 2022

Inventory for year 2022	Opening Inventory 1/1/2022	Cases started	Cases Closed	End Inventory 31/12/2022
Attribution/allocation cases	7	29	6	30
Other cases	11	6	6	11
Total	18	35	12	41

Source: OECD

Table 4. Israel's average time to resolve MAP cases in 2022

Cases resolved in year 2022	Pre-2016 cases		Post-2015 cases		All	
	Number of cases	**Average time**	**Number of cases**	**Average time** **Start to End**	**Number of cases**	**Average time**
Attribution / Allocation cases	0	N/A	6	17.06	6	17.06
Other cases	0	N/A	6	20.88	6	20.88
All cases	0	N/A	12	18.97	12	18.97

Source: OECD

Italy

Recent developments relating to MAP in Italy prior to 15 August 2023

Developments relating to MAP in the tax treaty network

- Since the approval of its MAP Peer Review Report of Stage 2 (11 December 2019), Italy has signed new tax treaties with Kosovo (June 2021) and Liechtenstein (July 2023), which include provisions on MAP procedure in line with Action 14 Minimum Standard. In addition, the treaty with Liechtenstein provides for an arbitration procedure in line with Part VI of MLI. The treaties signed with Colombia, Jamaica, Mongolia and Uruguay have entered into force.

Other developments relating to MAP

- Italy has implemented the Council Directive (EU) 2017/1852 of 10 October 2017 on tax dispute resolution mechanisms in the European Union in its domestic legislation via Legislative Decree no.49 of 10 June 2020 (entered into force on 25 June 2020, applicable to MAP requests as per 1 July 2019).
- On 16 December 2020 the Italian Revenue Agency issued guidance on modalities and operational procedures for the implementation of provisions of Legislative Decree no.49 of 10 June 2020 transposing the Directive (https://www.agenziaentrate.gov.it/portale/web/guest/-/provvedimento-del-16-12-2020).

Latest Action 14 Peer Review report

9 April 2020 - https://doi.org/10.1787/08a4369e-en

Tax treaty network of Italy

- 106 treaties, applicable to 110 jurisdictions (covering all treaties signed, although not necessarily in force)
- status of MLI: signed.

Table 1. State of play of Italy's tax treaty network

Treaties in line with the Action 14 Minimum Standard following MLI impact	Treaties where actions are ongoing to make them in line with the Action 14 Minimum Standard	Following impact/actions, remaining treaties that are not in line with Action 14 Minimum Standard
12	73	21

Source: OECD

Italy's MAP programme

Organisation of competent authority function

- 24 persons:
  - two heads of unit
  - 22 persons working on MAP cases (among which two persons work on other tasks as well).
- contact persons for MAP requests:
  - for general issues arising from the interpretation of DTT: Ministero dell'Economia e delle Finanze
    - Dipartimento delle Finanze, Direzione rapporti fiscali europei e internazionali
    - Via dei Normanni, 5 – 00184 Roma, e-mail: df.dri.segreteria@finanze.it
  - for all MAP cases concerning specific taxpayers: Agenzia delle entrate, Divisione Contribuenti, Direzione Centrale Grandi Contribuenti e Internazionale, Settore Controllo, Ufficio Risoluzione e prevenzione controversie internazionali
    - Via Giorgione 106 - 00147 Roma
    - e-mail: dc.gci.controversieinternazionali@agenziaentrate.it
    - pec: dc.acc.accordi@pec.agenziaentrate.it.

Figure 1. Competent Authority Organisational Structure

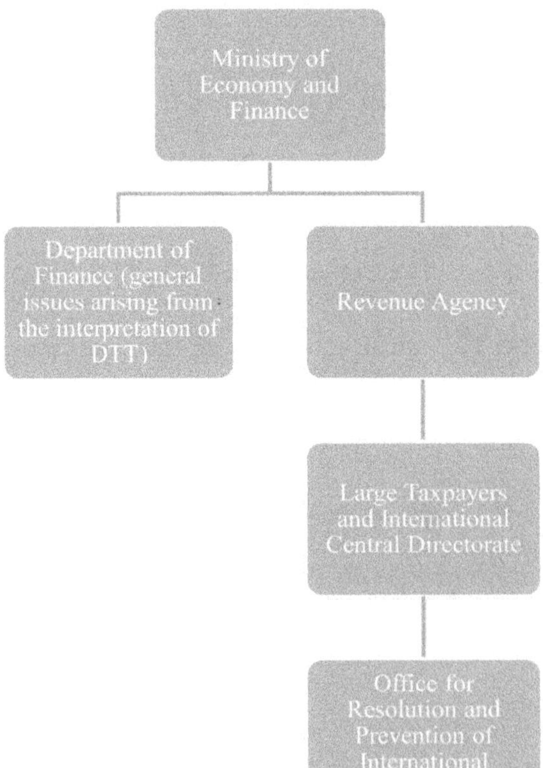

Source: OECD

Table 2. Guidance on the MAP process

MAP guidance	*Settlement of International Tax Disputes. The Mutual Agreement Procedures*, 5 June 2012	https://www.agenziaentrate.gov.it/portale/documents/180690/1186205/Circular+letter+n.+21E+05062012_circularletter21.pdf/02726080-7856-86b4-b530-aa6b6ac775e3 (Section 4.2.4. to be referred to for form and content of a MAP request, including information requirements)
	Web page	https://www.agenziaentrate.gov.it/portale/web/english/nse/business/double-taxation-relief/mutual-agreement-procedure?inheritRedirect=true
MAP profile	14 September 2023	https://www.oecd.org/tax/dispute/Italy-Dispute-Resolution-Profile.pdf

Overview of Italy's MAP Statistics for 2022

Please refer to https://www.oecd.org/tax/dispute/map-statistics-italy.pdf for details with respect to Italy's MAP Statistics.

Figure 2. Cases closed in 2022

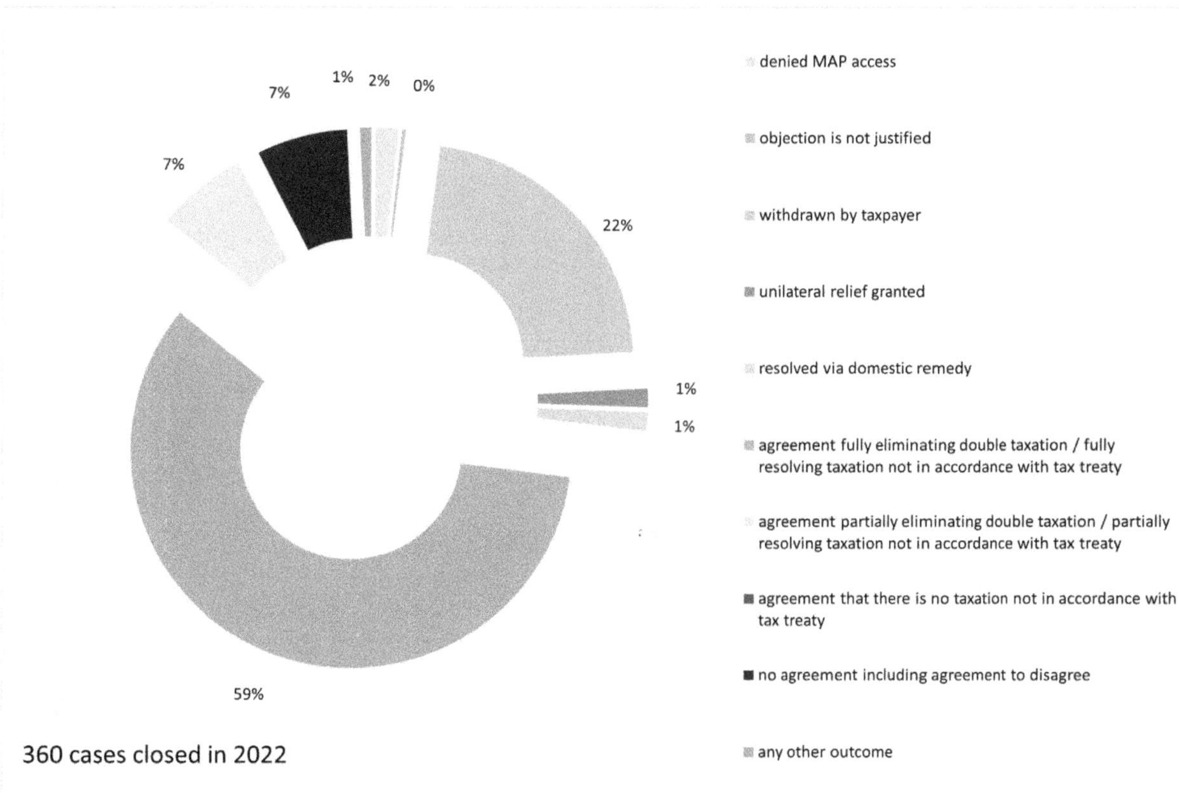

Source: OECD

Figure 3. Evolution of Italy's MAP caseload (2016-22)

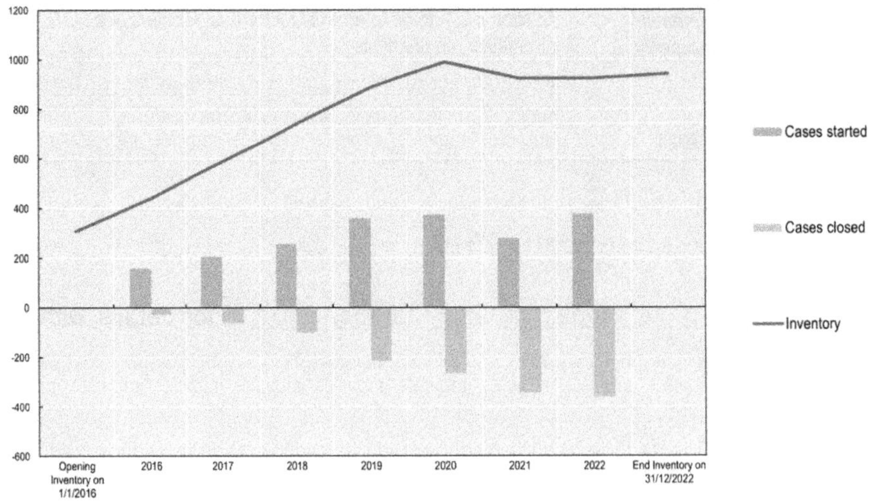

Source: OECD

Table 3. Overview of Italy's MAP caseload for 2022

Inventory for year 2022	Opening Inventory 1/1/2022	Cases started	Cases Closed	End Inventory 31/12/2022
Attribution/allocation cases	668	309	270	707
Other cases	256	69	90	235
Total	924	378	360	942

Source: OECD

Table 4. Italy's average time to resolve MAP cases in 2022

Cases resolved in year 2022	Pre-2016 cases		Post-2015 cases		All	
	Number of cases	**Average time**	**Number of cases**	**Average time** **Start to End**	**Number of cases**	**Average time**
Attribution / Allocation cases	14	94.16	256	25.47	270	29.03
Other cases	21	112.88	69	29.44	90	48.91
All cases	35	105.39	325	26.31	360	34

Source: OECD

Jamaica

Recent developments relating to MAP in Jamaica prior to 15 August 2023

Developments relating to MAP in the tax treaty network

- Jamaica did not provide the relevant information.

Other developments relating to MAP

- Jamaica did not provide the relevant information.

Latest Action 14 Peer Review report

- Stage 1 simplified peer review report forthcoming

Tax treaty network of Jamaica

- 17 treaties, applicable to 26 jurisdictions (covering all treaties signed, although not necessarily in force)
- status of MLI: signed.

Table 1. State of play of Jamaica's tax treaty network

Treaties in line with the Action 14 Minimum Standard following MLI impact	Treaties where actions are ongoing to make them in line with the Action 14 Minimum Standard	Following impact/actions, remaining treaties that are not in line with Action 14 Minimum Standard
11	No information	No information

Source: OECD

Jamaica's MAP programme

Organisation of competent authority function

- six persons (all of which work on other tasks as well)
- contact persons for MAP requests:
    - The Commissioner General, Tax Administration Jamaica, 6th Floor Donald Sangster Building, 116 East Street, Kingston, Jamaica
    - telephone: 876-922-3470-9, Email: disputeresolution@taj.gov.jm.

Figure 1. Competent Authority Organisational Structure

Source: OECD

Table 2. Guidance on the MAP process

MAP guidance	No MAP guidance published	
MAP profile	21 May 2023	https://www.oecd.org/tax/dispute/jamaica-dispute-resolution-profile.pdf

Overview of Jamaica's MAP Statistics for 2022

Please refer to https://www.oecd.org/tax/dispute/map-statistics-jamaica.pdf for details with respect to Jamaica's MAP Statistics.

Cases closed in 2022

No MAP cases were closed by Jamaica in 2022.

Figure 2. Evolution of Jamaica's MAP caseload (2016-22)

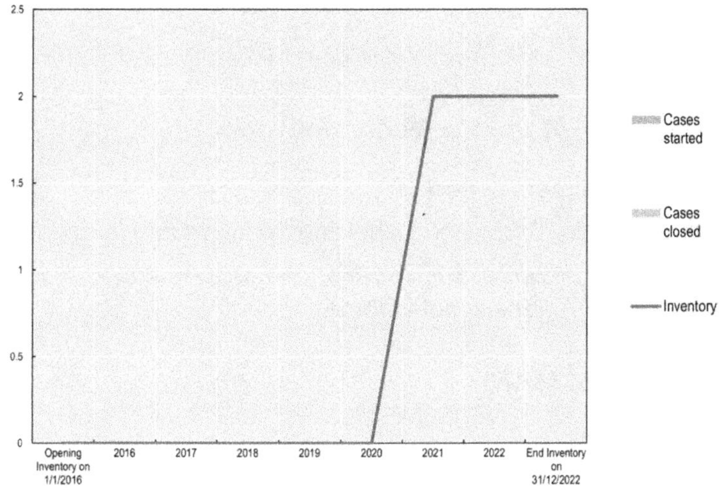

Source: OECD

Table 3. Overview of Jamaica's MAP caseload for 2022

Inventory for year 2022	Opening Inventory 1/1/2022	Cases started	Cases Closed	End Inventory 31/12/2022
Attribution/allocation cases	0	0	0	0
Other cases	2	0	0	2
Total	2	0	0	2

Source: OECD

Table 4. Jamaica's average time to resolve MAP cases in 2022

Cases resolved in year 2022	Pre-2016 cases		Post-2015 cases		All	
	Number of cases	**Average time**	**Number of cases**	**Average time** **Start to End**	**Number of cases**	**Average time**
Attribution / Allocation cases	0	N/A	0	N/A	0	N/A
Other cases	0	N/A	0	N/A	0	N/A
All cases	0	N/A	0	N/A	0	N/A

Source: OECD

Japan

Recent developments relating to MAP in Japan prior to 15 August 2023

Developments relating to MAP in the tax treaty network

- Since the period of the latest peer review:
  - tax treaties with Colombia, Spain and Uzbekistan entered into force; and
  - tax treaties with Algeria, Azerbaijan, Georgia, Jamaica, Morocco, Peru, Serbia and Uruguay were signed (treaty with Algeria is not in force).

Other developments relating to MAP

- No developments were reported

Latest Action 14 Peer Review report

15 April 2021 - https://doi.org/10.1787/e3d454fd-en

Tax treaty network of Japan

- 79 treaties, applicable to 86 jurisdictions (77 treaties of which are in force)
- status of MLI: in force.

Table 1. State of play of Japan's tax treaty network

Treaties in line with the Action 14 Minimum Standard following MLI impact	Treaties where actions are ongoing to make them in line with the Action 14 Minimum Standard	Following impact/actions, remaining treaties that are not in line with Action 14 Minimum Standard
69	0	10

Source: OECD

Japan's MAP programme

Organisation of competent authority function

- 46 persons:
  - four heads of unit
  - 46 persons working on MAP cases (among which three persons work on other tasks as well):
    - all 46 persons can work on any types of MAP cases including attribution/allocation cases and other cases.
- contact persons for MAP requests:
  - Office of Mutual Agreement Procedures ("MAP Office"), National Tax Agency ("NTA")
    Office Address: 3-1-1 Kasumigaseki, Chiyoda-ku, Tokyo 100-8978 JAPAN

Tel: +81-3-3581-5451.

Figure 1. Competent Authority Organisational Structure

Source: OECD

Table 2. Guidance on the MAP process

MAP guidance	*Commissioner's Directive on the Mutual Agreement Procedure*, 14 February 2022	https://www.nta.go.jp/english/00.pdf (Section 6 to be referred to for form and content of a MAP request, including information requirements)
	Ministerial Ordinance of ATT	https://elaws.e-gov.go.jp/document?lawid=344AC0000000046#345
MAP profile	1 August 2019	https://www.oecd.org/tax/dispute/japan-dispute-resolution-profile.pdf

Overview of Japan's MAP Statistics for 2022

Please refer to https://www.oecd.org/tax/dispute/map-statistics-japan.pdf for details with respect to Japan's MAP Statistics.

Figure 2. Cases closed in 2022

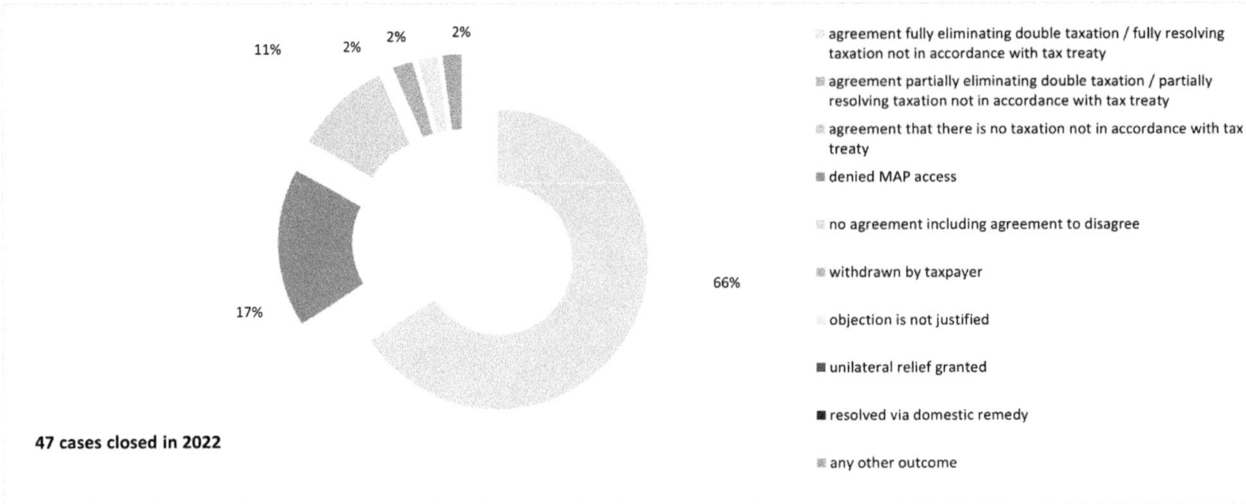

Source: OECD

Figure 3. Evolution of Japan's MAP caseload (2016-22)

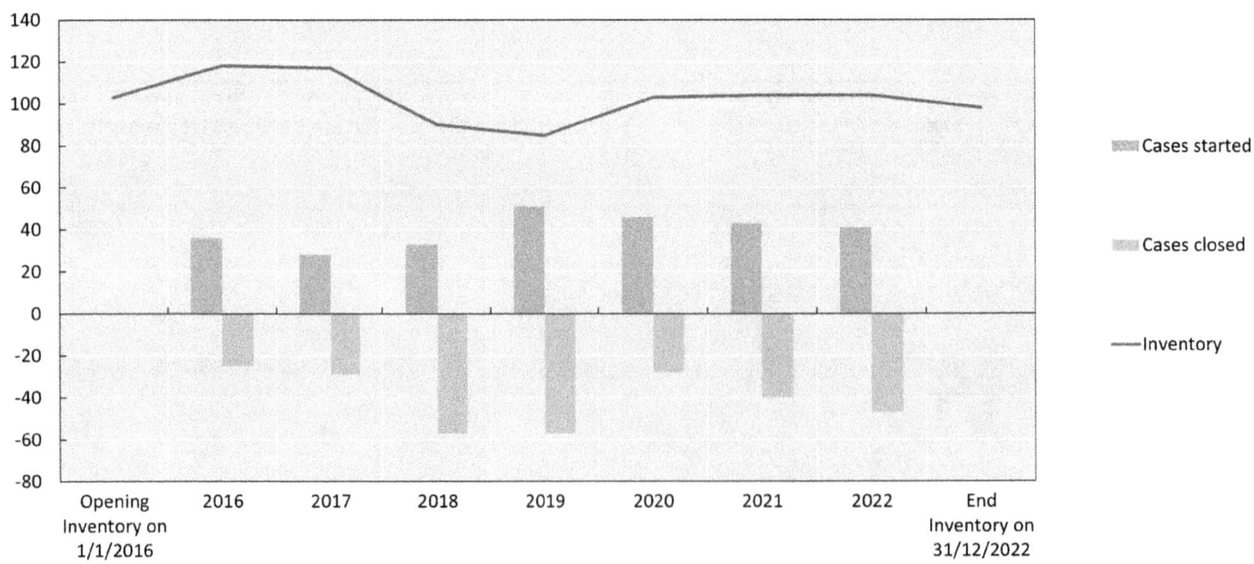

Source: OECD

Table 3. Overview of Japan's MAP caseload for 2022

Inventory for year 2022	Opening Inventory 1/1/2022	Cases started	Cases Closed	End Inventory 31/12/2022
Attribution/allocation cases	88	36	39	85
Other cases	16	5	8	13
Total	104	41	47	98

Source: OECD

Table 4. Japan's average time to resolve MAP cases in 2022

Cases resolved in year 2022	Pre-2016 cases		Post-2015 cases		All	
	Number of cases	**Average time**	**Number of cases**	**Average time** **Start to End**	**Number of cases**	**Average time**
Attribution / Allocation cases	2	88.60	37	27.50	39	30.63
Other cases	0	N/A	8	18.44	8	18.44
All cases	2	88.60	45	25.89	47	28.56

Source: OECD

Jersey (Bailiwick of)

Recent developments relating to MAP in Jersey prior to 15 August 2023

Developments relating to MAP in the tax treaty network

- Jersey did not provide the relevant information.

Other developments relating to MAP

- Jersey did not provide the relevant information.

Latest Action 14 Peer Review report

24 January 2022 - https://doi.org/10.1787/37a6cb02-en

Tax treaty network of Jersey

- 29 treaties, applicable to 29 jurisdictions (covering all treaties signed, although not necessarily in force)
- status of MLI: in force.

Table 1. State of play of Jersey's tax treaty network

Treaties in line with the Action 14 Minimum Standard following MLI impact	Treaties where actions are ongoing to make them in line with the Action 14 Minimum Standard	Following impact/actions, remaining treaties that are not in line with Action 14 Minimum Standard
16	No information	No information

Source: OECD

Jersey's MAP programme

Organisation of competent authority function

- four persons
- contact persons for MAP requests:
  - Richard Summersgill, Comptroller of Taxes Revenue Jersey
    19-21 Broad Street PO Box 56 St Helier Jersey JE2 3RR
    Telephone: + 44 (0) 1534 440305 / r.summersgill@gov.je
  - Paul Eastwood, Deputy Comptroller of Taxes Revenue Jersey
    19-21 Broad Street PO Box 56 St Helier Jersey JE2 3RR
    Telephone: + 44 (0) 1534 440578 / p.eastwood@gov.je

- Niamh Moylan, Director – International Tax Revenue Jersey
  19-21 Broad Street PO Box 56 St Helier Jersey JE2 3RR
  Telephone: + 44 (0) 1534 440415 / n.moylan2@gov.je.

Figure 1. Competent Authority Organisational Structure

Source: OECD

Table 2. Guidance on the MAP process

MAP guidance	*Resolving treaty disputes: The Mutual Agreement Procedure*, April 2019	https://www.gov.je/TaxesMoney/InternationalTaxAgreements/DoubleTaxationProcedure/Pages/TreatyDisputes.aspx%23anchor-1 (Section 2.0 to be referred to for form and content of a MAP request, including information requirements)
MAP profile	24 June 2019	https://www.oecd.org/tax/dispute/jersey-dispute-resolution-profile.pdf

Overview of Jersey's MAP Statistics for 2022

Please refer to https://www.oecd.org/tax/dispute/map-statistics-jersey.pdf for details with respect to Jersey's MAP Statistics.

Cases closed in 2022

No MAP cases were closed by Jersey in 2022.

Figure 2. Evolution of Jersey's MAP caseload (2016-22)

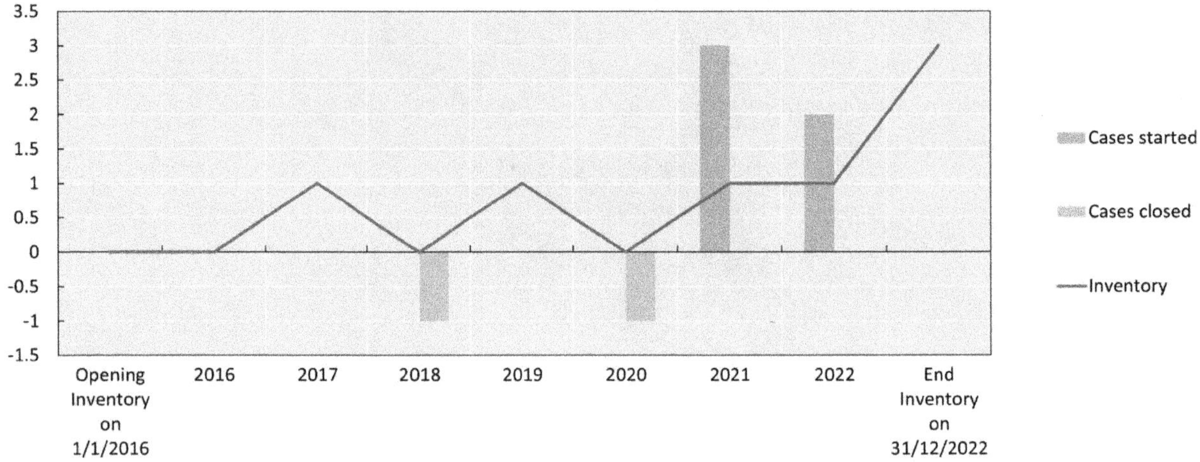

Source: OECD

Table 3. Overview of Jersey's MAP caseload for 2022

Inventory for year 2022	Opening Inventory 1/1/2022	Cases started	Cases Closed	End Inventory 31/12/2022
Attribution/allocation cases	0	0	0	0
Other cases	1	2	0	3
Total	1	2	0	3

Source: OECD

Table 4. Jersey's average time to resolve MAP cases in 2022

Cases resolved in year 2022	Pre-2016 cases		Post-2015 cases		All	
	Number of cases	**Average time**	**Number of cases**	**Average time**	**Number of cases**	**Average time**
				Start to End		
Attribution / Allocation cases	0	N/A	0	N/A	0	N/A
Other cases	0	N/A	0	N/A	0	N/A
All cases	0	N/A	0	N/A	0	N/A

Source: OECD

Jordan

Recent developments relating to MAP in Jordan prior to 15 August 2023

Developments relating to MAP in the tax treaty network

- Jordan did not provide the relevant information.

Other developments relating to MAP

- Jordan did not provide the relevant information.

Latest Action 14 Peer Review report

The stage 1 Simplified Peer Review report of Jordan is expected to be published early 2024.

Tax treaty network of Jordan

- 39 treaties, applicable to 39 jurisdictions (covering all treaties signed, although not necessarily in force)
- status of MLI: in force.

Table 1. State of play of Jordan's tax treaty network

Treaties in line with the Action 14 Minimum Standard following MLI impact	Treaties where actions are ongoing to make them in line with the Action 14 Minimum Standard	Following impact/actions, remaining treaties that are not in line with Action 14 Minimum Standard
33	No information	No information

Source: OECD

Jordan's MAP programme

Organisation of competent authority function

- No competent authority function yet.
- Contact persons for MAP requests: Jordan did not provide the relevant information.

Figure 1. Competent Authority Organisational Structure

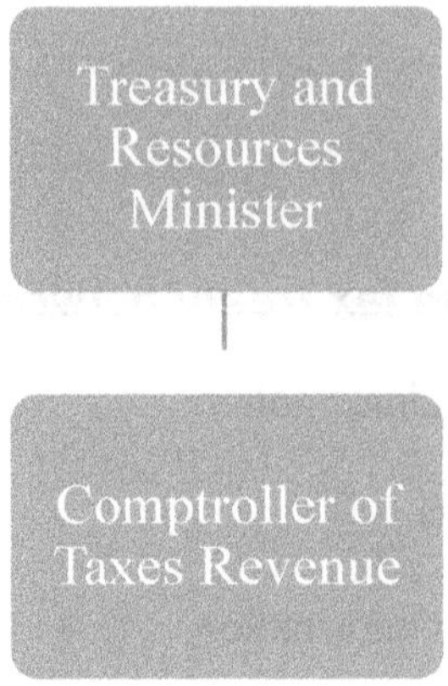

Source: OECD

Table 2. Guidance on the MAP process

MAP guidance	No MAP Guidance published	-
MAP profile	No MAP Profile published	-

Overview of Jordan's MAP Statistics for 2022

Please refer to https://www.oecd.org/tax/dispute/map-statistics-jordan.pdf for details with respect to Jordan's MAP Statistics.

Cases closed in 2022

No MAP cases were closed by Jordan in 2022.

Figure 2. Evolution of Jordan's MAP caseload (2019-22)

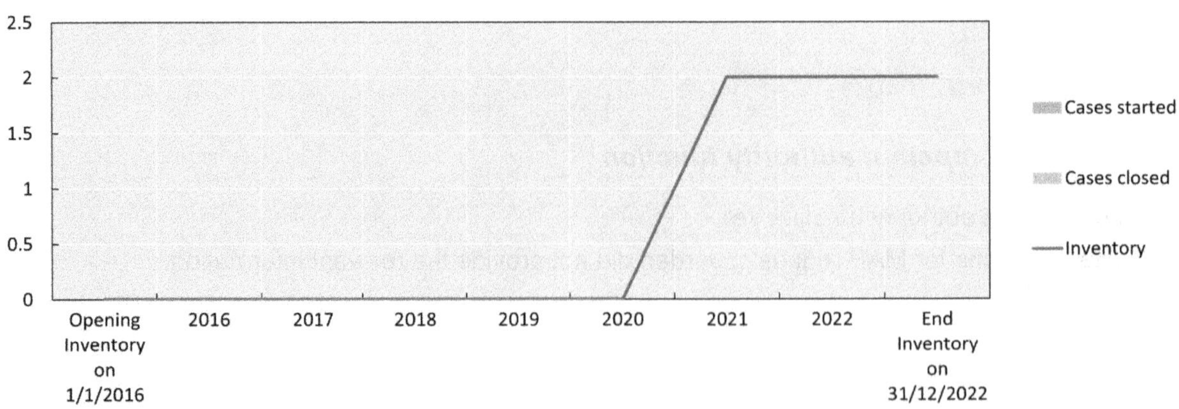

Source: OECD

Table 3. Overview of Jordan's MAP caseload for 2022

Inventory for year 2022	Opening Inventory 1/1/2022	Cases started	Cases Closed	End Inventory 31/12/2022
Attribution/allocation cases	2	0	0	2
Other cases	0	0	0	0
Total	2	0	0	2

Source: OECD

Table 4. Jordan's average time to resolve MAP cases in 2022

Cases resolved in year 2022	Pre-2016 cases		Post-2015 cases		All	
	Number of cases	**Average time**	**Number of cases**	**Average time** **Start to End**	**Number of cases**	**Average time**
Attribution / Allocation cases	0	N/A	0	N/A	0	N/A
Other cases	0	N/A	0	N/A	0	N/A
All cases	0	N/A	0	N/A	0	N/A

Source: OECD

Kazakhstan

Recent developments relating to MAP in Kazakhstan prior to 15 August 2023

Developments relating to MAP in the tax treaty network

- Kazakhstan did not provide the relevant information.

Other developments relating to MAP

- Kazakhstan did not provide the relevant information.

Latest Action 14 Peer Review report

13 September 2022 - https://doi.org/10.1787/34c25884-en

Tax treaty network of Kazakhstan

- 55 treaties, applicable to 55 jurisdictions (covering all treaties signed, although not necessarily in force)
- status of MLI: in force.

Table 1. State of play of Kazakhstan's tax treaty network

Treaties in line with the Action 14 Minimum Standard following MLI impact	Treaties where actions are ongoing to make them in line with the Action 14 Minimum Standard	Following impact/actions, remaining treaties that are not in line with Action 14 Minimum Standard
48	No information	No information

Source: OECD

Kazakhstan's MAP programme

Organisation of competent authority function

- five persons:
  - five persons working on MAP cases (all of which work on other tasks as well).
- contact persons for MAP requests:
  - Non-residents taxation, Department for methodology of taxation
    The State Revenue Committee, Ministry of Finance
    Z10H2B2, 11 Zhenis Avenue, Astana, Kazakhstan
    Tel: +7 (7172) 71 78 91; +7 (7172) 71 77 52.
    Email: a.bagibaev@kgd.gov.kz ; aid.nurpeisov@kgd.gov.kz.

Figure 1. Competent Authority Organisational Structure

Source: OECD

Table 2. Guidance on the MAP process

MAP guidance	No MAP guidance published	-
MAP profile	No MAP profile published	-

Overview of Kazakhstan's MAP Statistics for 2022

Please refer to https://www.oecd.org/tax/dispute/map-statistics-kazakhstan.pdf for details with respect to Kazakhstan's MAP Statistics.

Figure 2. Cases closed in 2022

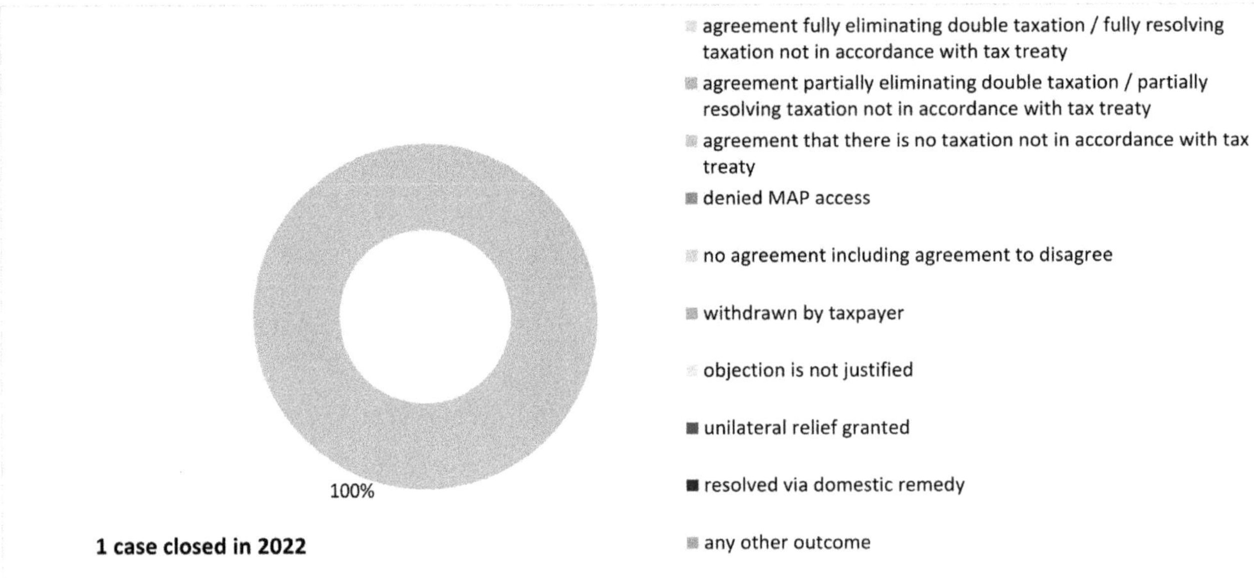

Source: OECD

Figure 3. Evolution of Kazakhstan's MAP caseload (2016-22)

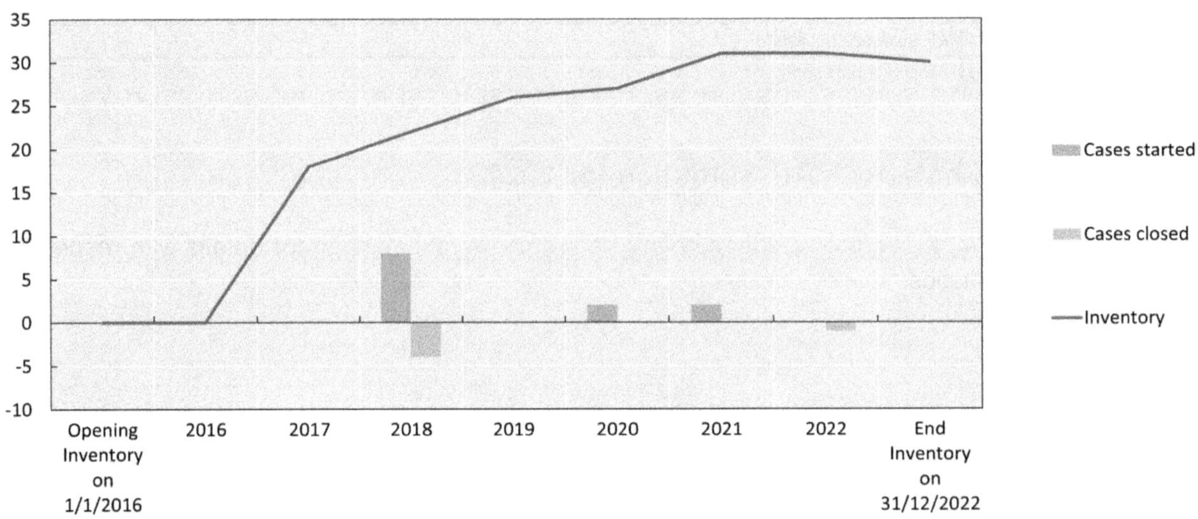

Source: OECD

Table 3. Overview of Kazakhstan's MAP caseload for 2022

Inventory for year 2022	Opening Inventory 1/1/2022	Cases started	Cases Closed	End Inventory 31/12/2022
Attribution/allocation cases	17	0	0	17
Other cases	14	0	1	13
Total	31	0	1	30

Source: OECD

Table 4. Kazakhstan's average time to resolve MAP cases in 2022

Cases resolved in year 2022	Pre-2016 cases		Post-2015 cases		All	
	Number of cases	**Average time**	**Number of cases**	**Average time** **Start to End**	**Number of cases**	**Average time**
Attribution / Allocation cases	0	N/A	0	N/A	0	N/A
Other cases	0	N/A	1	67.63	1	67.63
All cases	0	N/A	1	N/A	1	N/A

Source: OECD

Kenya

Recent developments relating to MAP in Kenya prior to 15 August 2023

Developments relating to MAP in the tax treaty network

- On 21st March 2023, the Kenyan Cabinet approved the ratification of the MLI. The next step is for the MLI to be tabled before Parliament for approval before the instruments of ratification can be deposited.

Other developments relating to MAP

- No developments were reported

Latest Action 14 Peer Review report

Kenya is yet to be peer reviewed under Action 14.

Tax treaty network of Kenya

- 15 treaties, applicable to 15 jurisdictions (covering all treaties signed, although not necessarily in force)
- status of MLI: signed.

Table 1. State of play of Kenya's tax treaty network

Treaties in line with the Action 14 Minimum Standard following MLI impact	Treaties where actions are ongoing to make them in line with the Action 14 Minimum Standard	Following impact/actions, remaining treaties that are not in line with Action 14 Minimum Standard
15	0	0

Source: OECD

Kenya's MAP programme

Organisation of competent authority function

- four persons:
    - one head of unit
    - three persons working on MAP cases (all of which work on other tasks as well).
- contact persons for MAP requests:
    - David K. S. Yego
      Commissioner Intelligence, Strategic Operations, Investigations and Enforcement
      Authorised Competent Authority Representative
      Kenya Revenue Authority

P.O. Box 48240-00100
kenyacompetentauthority@kra.go.ke.

Figure 1. Competent Authority Organisational Structure

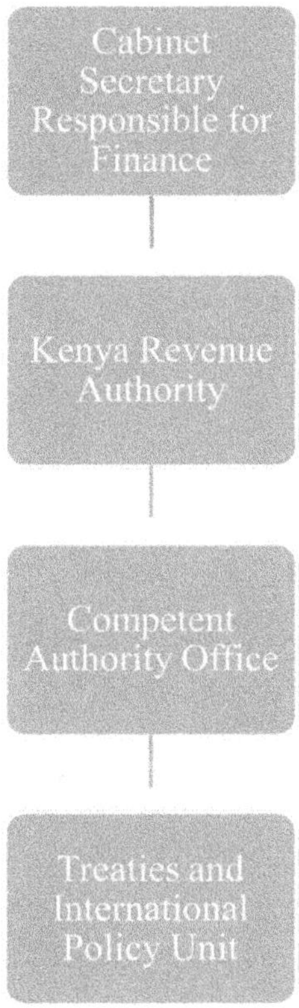

Source: OECD

Table 2. Guidance on the MAP process

MAP guidance	No MAP Guidance published	-
MAP profile	13 June 2022	https://www.oecd.org/tax/dispute/kenya-dispute-resolution-profile.pdf

Overview of Kenya's MAP Statistics for 2022

Please refer to https://www.oecd.org/tax/dispute/map-statistics-kenya.pdf for details with respect to Kenya's MAP Statistics.

Cases closed in 2022

No MAP cases were closed by Kenya in 2022.

Figure 2. Evolution of Kenya's MAP caseload (2017-22)

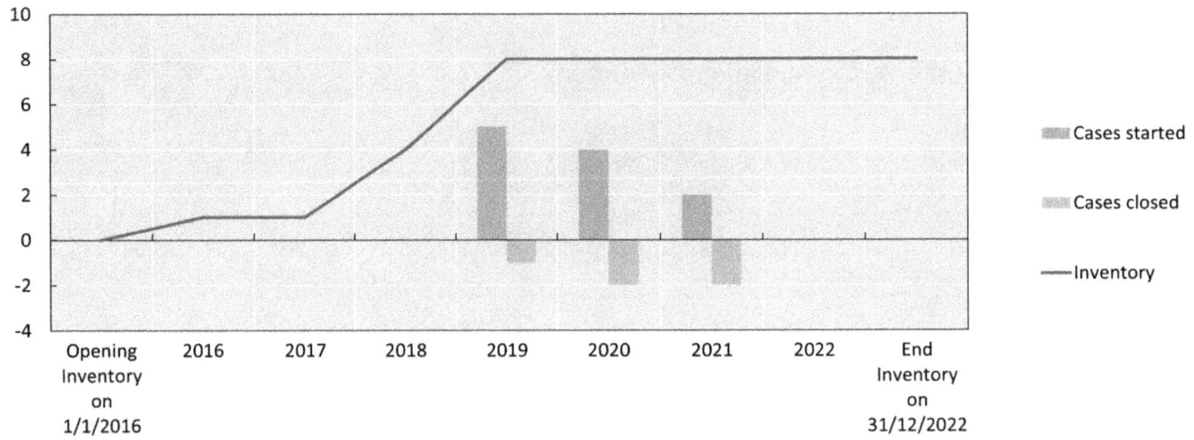

Source: OECD

Table 3. Overview of Kenya's MAP caseload for 2022

Inventory for year 2022	Opening Inventory 1/1/2022	Cases started	Cases Closed	End Inventory 31/12/2022
Attribution/allocation cases	4	0	0	4
Other cases	4	0	0	4
Total	8	0	0	8

Source: OECD

Table 4. Kenya's average time to resolve MAP cases in 2022

Cases resolved in year 2022	Pre-2016 cases		Post-2015 cases		All	
	Number of cases	**Average time**	**Number of cases**	**Average time** **Start to End**	**Number of cases**	**Average time**
Attribution / Allocation cases	0	N/A	0	N/A	0	N/A
Other cases	0	N/A	0	N/A	0	N/A
All cases	0	N/A	0	N/A	0	N/A

Source: OECD

Korea

Recent developments relating to MAP in Korea prior to 15 August 2023

Developments relating to MAP in the tax treaty network

- No developments were reported

Other developments relating to MAP

- No developments were reported

Latest Action 14 Peer Review report

22 October 2020 - https://doi.org/10.1787/a06e58db-en

Tax treaty network of Korea

- 96 treaties, applicable to 96 jurisdictions (covering all treaties signed, although not necessarily in force)
- status of MLI: in force.

Table 1. State of play of Korea's tax treaty network

Treaties in line with the Action 14 Minimum Standard following MLI impact	Treaties where actions are ongoing to make them in line with the Action 14 Minimum Standard	Following impact/actions, remaining treaties that are not in line with Action 14 Minimum Standard
86	10	0

Source: OECD

Korea's MAP programme

Organisation of competent authority function

- 26 persons:
  - two heads of unit
  - 24 persons working on MAP cases.
- contact persons for MAP requests:
  - Mutual Agreement Procedure Division of International Taxation Bureau
    [Email] ntsmap@korea.kr
    [Telephone] +82-44-204-2964, +82-44-204-2966
    [Fax] +82-44-216-6069 (Mutual Agreement Procedure Division)
    [Address] 8-14, Guksecheong-ro, Sejong City, Republic of Korea.

Figure 1. Competent Authority Organisational Structure

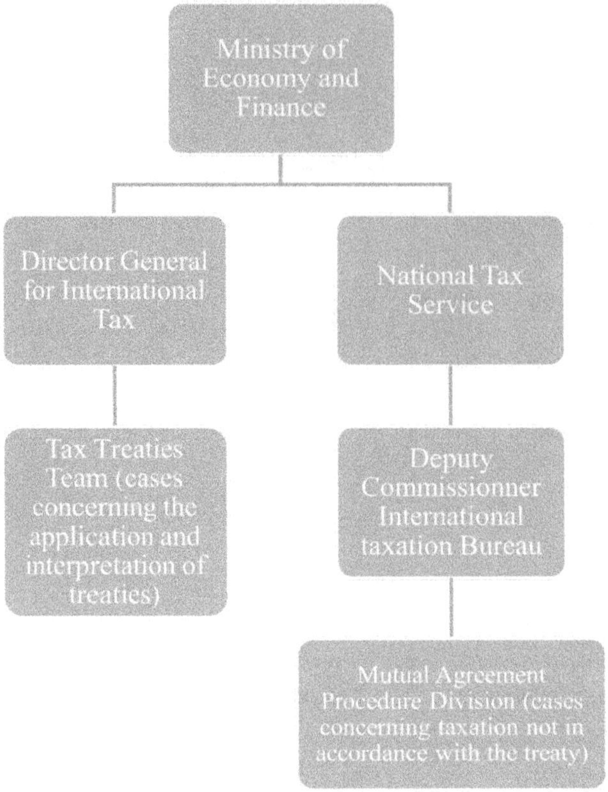

Source: OECD

Table 2. Guidance on the MAP process

MAP guidance	*Guidance on Mutual Agreement Procedure for Taxpayers*, 30 June 2022	https://www.nts.go.kr/english/na/ntt/selectNttInfo.do?mi=10790&nttSn=1306112%20 (Section 2.7 to be referred to for form and content of a MAP request, including information requirements)
MAP profile	25 September 2019	https://www.oecd.org/tax/dispute/korea-dispute-resolution-profile.pdf

Overview of Korea's MAP Statistics for 2022

Please refer to https://www.oecd.org/tax/dispute/map-statistics-korea.pdf for details with respect to Korea's MAP Statistics.

Figure 2. Cases closed in 2022

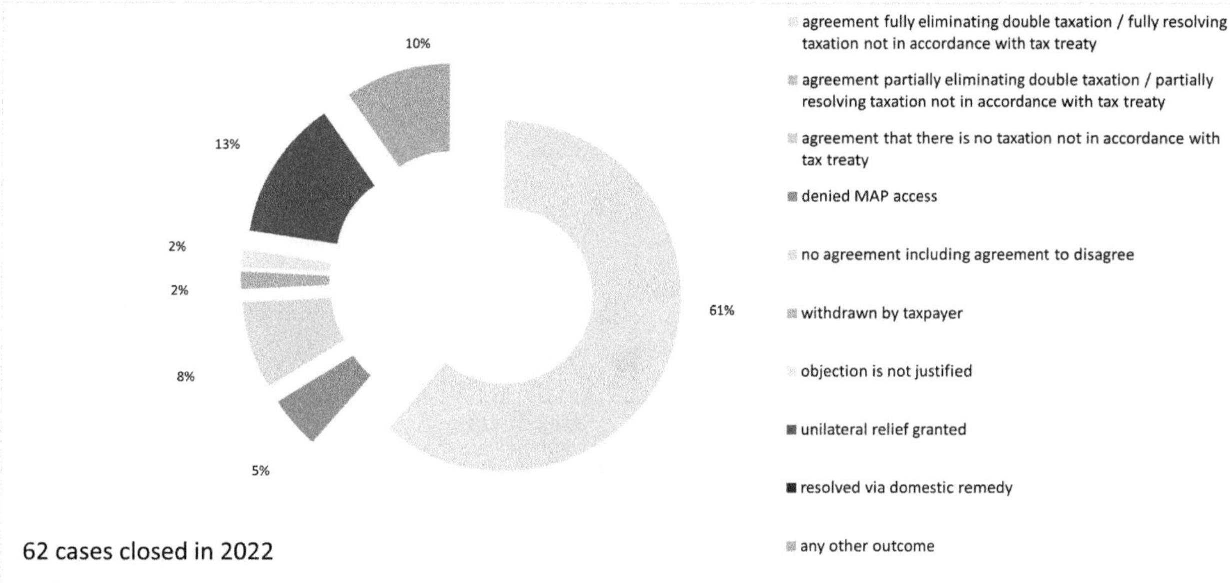

Source: OECD

Figure 3. Evolution of Korea's MAP caseload (2016-22)

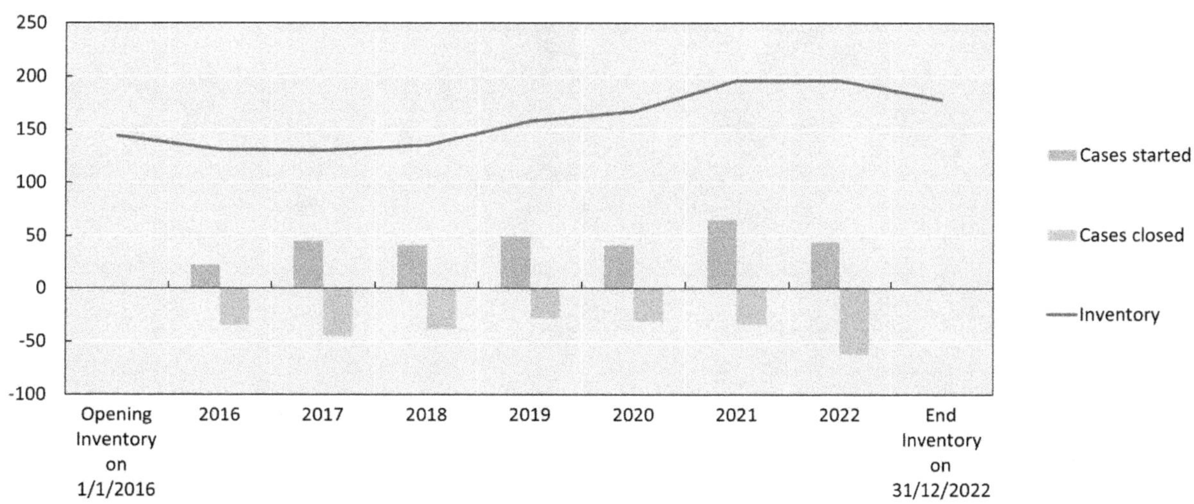

Source: OECD

Table 3. Overview of Korea's MAP caseload for 2022

Inventory for year 2022	Opening Inventory 1/1/2022	Cases started	Cases Closed	End Inventory 31/12/2022
Attribution/allocation cases	133	34	47	120
Other cases	63	10	15	58
Total	196	44	62	178

Source: OECD

Table 4. Korea's average time to resolve MAP cases in 2022

<table>
<tr><th rowspan="3">Cases resolved in year 2022</th><th colspan="2">Pre-2016 cases</th><th colspan="2">Post-2015 cases</th><th colspan="2">All</th></tr>
<tr><th rowspan="2">Number of cases</th><th rowspan="2">Average time</th><th rowspan="2">Number of cases</th><th>Average time</th><th rowspan="2">Number of cases</th><th rowspan="2">Average time</th></tr>
<tr><th>Start to End</th></tr>
<tr><td>Attribution / Allocation cases</td><td>7</td><td>73</td><td>40</td><td>31.03</td><td>47</td><td>37.28</td></tr>
<tr><td>Other cases</td><td>5</td><td>100.31</td><td>10</td><td>33</td><td>15</td><td>55.44</td></tr>
<tr><td>All cases</td><td>12</td><td>84.38</td><td>50</td><td>31.42</td><td>62</td><td>41.67</td></tr>
</table>

Source: OECD

Latvia

Recent developments relating to MAP in Latvia prior to 15 August 2023

Developments relating to MAP in the tax treaty network

- Two new treaties entered into force since last report – Kosovo and Saudi Arabia.

Other developments relating to MAP

- Treaty with Pakistan was signed on 28 April 2023.

Latest Action 14 Peer Review report

26 July 2021 - https://doi.org/10.1787/5fb7733b-en

Tax treaty network of Latvia

- 63 treaties, applicable to 64 jurisdictions (covering all treaties signed, although not necessarily in force)
- status of MLI: in force.

Table 1. State of play of Latvia's tax treaty network

Treaties in line with the Action 14 Minimum Standard following MLI impact	Treaties where actions are ongoing to make them in line with the Action 14 Minimum Standard	Following impact/actions, remaining treaties that are not in line with Action 14 Minimum Standard
60	2	1

Source: OECD

Latvia's MAP programme

Organisation of competent authority function

- 14 persons:
  - four heads of unit
  - ten persons working on MAP cases (all of which work on other tasks as well):
    - of which eight persons work on attribution/allocation cases and six persons work on other cases.
- contact persons for MAP requests:
  - State Revenue Service of the Republic of Latvia
    Via mail to address: Talejas street 1, Riga, Latvia, LV-1978;
    Or via Electronic Declaration System: using the website https://eds.vid.gov.lv

Or via Email: vid@vid.gov.lv signing the documents with a secure electronic signature that conforms to the EU Regulation No 910/2014 of 23 July 2014.

Figure 11. Competent Authority Organisational Structure

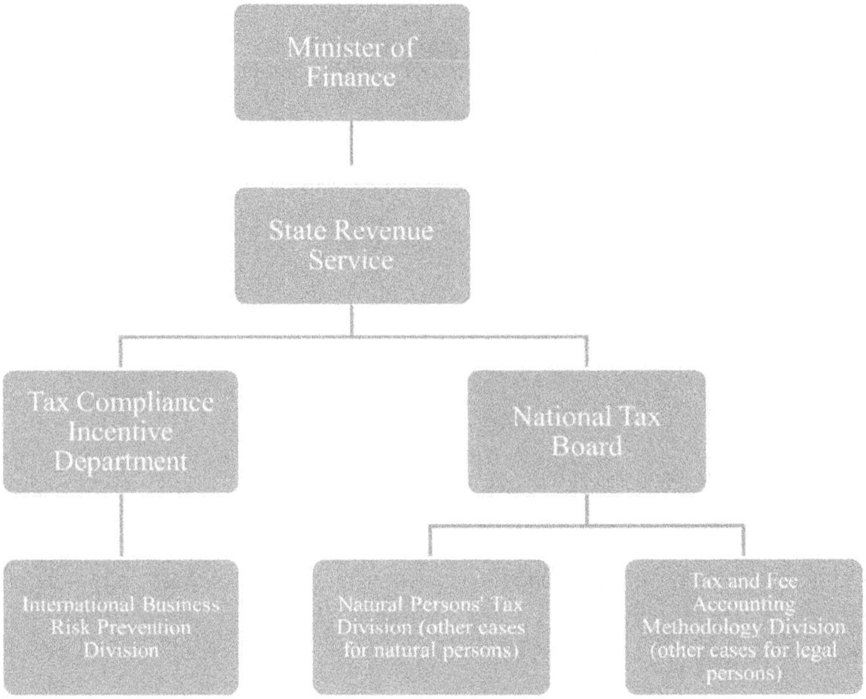

Source: OECD

Table 2. Guidance on the MAP process

MAP guidance	Chapter XV of the law "On Taxes and Duties", 22 October 2019	https://www.vestnesis.lv/op/2019/214.2 (Article 120 to be referred to for form and content of a MAP request, including information requirements)
	Methodological material 25 March 2021	https://www.vid.gov.lv/lv/media/1432/download?attachment
	Methodological material 22 April 2021	https://www.vid.gov.lv/lv/media/1431/download?attachment
MAP profile	16 November 2020	https://www.oecd.org/tax/dispute/latvia-dispute-resolution-profile.pdf

Overview of Latvia's MAP Statistics for 2022

Please refer to https://www.oecd.org/tax/dispute/map-statistics-latvia.pdf for details with respect to Latvia's MAP Statistics.

Figure 2. Cases closed in 2022

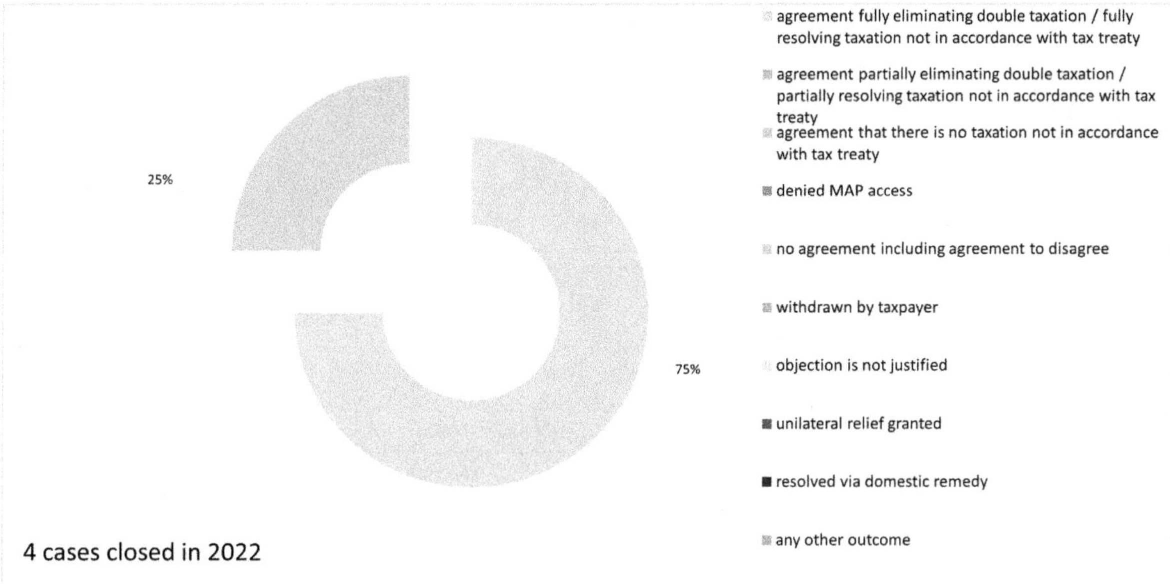

Source: OECD

Figure 3. Evolution of Latvia's MAP caseload (2016-22)

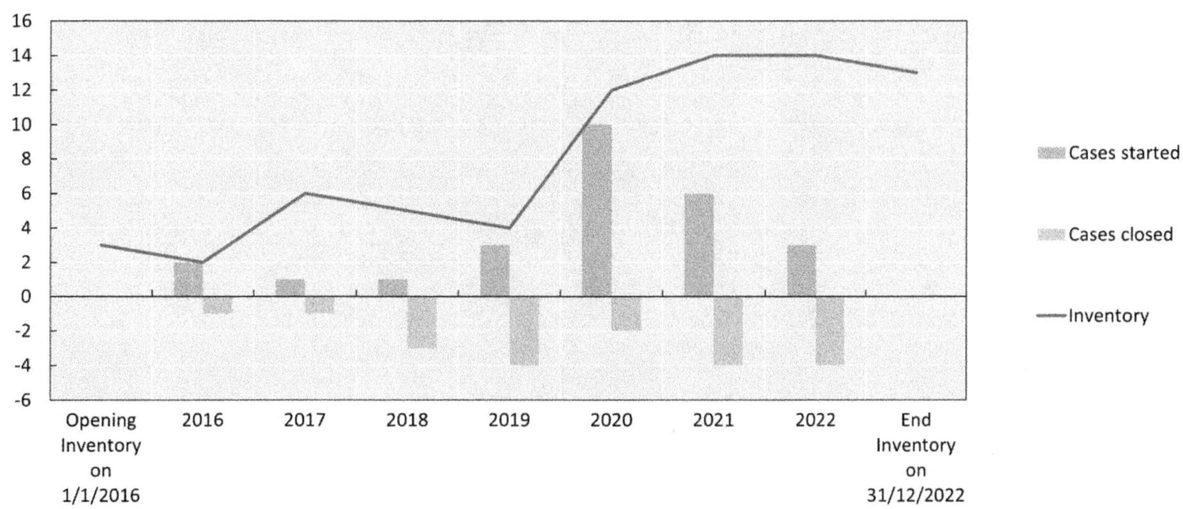

Source: OECD

Table 3. Overview of Latvia's MAP caseload for 2022

Inventory for year 2022	Opening Inventory 1/1/2022	Cases started	Cases Closed	End Inventory 31/12/2022
Attribution/allocation cases	7	2	1	8
Other cases	7	1	3	5
Total	14	3	4	13

Source: OECD

Table 4. Latvia's average time to resolve MAP cases in 2022

Cases resolved in year 2022	Pre-2016 cases		Post-2015 cases		All	
	Number of cases	**Average time**	**Number of cases**	**Average time** **Start to End**	**Number of cases**	**Average time**
Attribution / Allocation cases	0	N/A	1	6.44	1	6.44
Other cases	0	N/A	3	18.52	3	18.52
All cases	0	N/A	4	15.50	4	15.50

Source: OECD

Liberia

Recent developments relating to MAP in Liberia prior to 15 August 2023

Developments relating to MAP in the tax treaty network

- Liberia did not provide the relevant information.

Other developments relating to MAP

- Liberia did not provide the relevant information.

Latest Action 14 Peer Review report

Liberia is yet to be peer reviewed under Action 14.

Tax treaty network of Liberia

- 3 treaties, applicable to 3 jurisdictions (covering all treaties signed, although not necessarily in force).
- status of MLI: not signed.

Table 1. State of play of Liberia's tax treaty network

Treaties in line with the Action 14 Minimum Standard following MLI impact	Treaties where actions are ongoing to make them in line with the Action 14 Minimum Standard	Following impact/actions, remaining treaties that are not in line with Action 14 Minimum Standard
2	No information	No information

Source: OECD

Liberia's MAP programme

Organisation of competent authority function

- Liberia did not provide the relevant information.

Table 2. Guidance on the MAP process

MAP guidance	Liberia did not provide the relevant information.	
MAP profile	No MAP profile published	

Overview of Liberia's MAP Statistics for 2022

Liberia did not declare its MAP Statistics for 2022.

Liechtenstein

Recent developments relating to MAP in Liechtenstein prior to 15 August 2023

Developments relating to MAP in the tax treaty network

- Liechtenstein has signed tax treaties with two new partners: Romania and Italy. Those treaties are not yet in force; they comply with the Action 14 Minimum Standard.

Other developments relating to MAP

- No developments were reported

Latest Action 14 Peer Review report

9 April 2020 - https://doi.org/10.1787/b41a9f75-en

Tax treaty network of Liechtenstein

- 21 treaties, applicable to 21 jurisdictions (covering all treaties signed, although not necessarily in force)
- status of MLI: in force.

Table 1. State of play of Liechtenstein's tax treaty network

Treaties in line with the Action 14 Minimum Standard following MLI impact	Treaties where actions are ongoing to make them in line with the Action 14 Minimum Standard	Following impact/actions, remaining treaties that are not in line with Action 14 Minimum Standard
21	0	0

Source: OECD

Liechtenstein's MAP programme

Organisation of competent authority function

- 2.6 Full Time Equivalents (FTE) :
  - one head of unit
  - 1.6 persons working on MAP cases (all of which work on other tasks as well):
- contact persons for MAP requests:
  - Fiscal Authority of Liechtenstein
    International Division
    Aeulestrasse 38 FL-9490 Vaduz Liechtenstein
    T +423 236 68 17
    dba@llv.li.

Figure 1. Competent Authority Organisational Structure

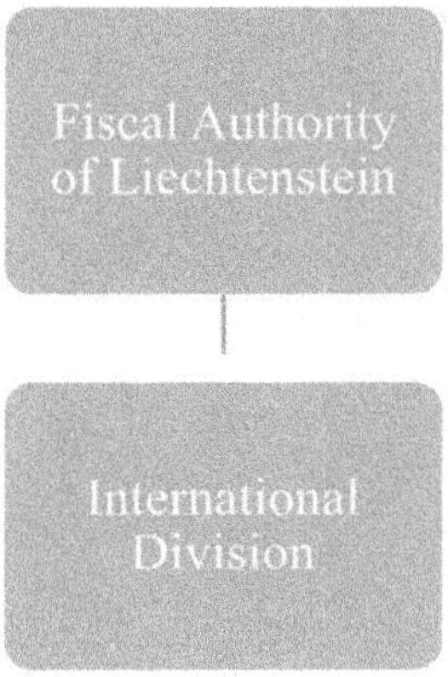

Source: OECD

Table 2. Guidance on the MAP process

MAP guidance	*Fact sheet on international mutual agreement procedures under the double taxation conventions with respect to taxes on income and on capital*, October 2017	https://archiv.llv.li/files/stv/int-mb-mutualagreementprocedure-en.pdf (Section 3.1 to be referred to for form and content of a MAP request, including information requirements)
MAP profile	26 July 2019	https://www.oecd.org/tax/dispute/liechtenstein-dispute-resolution-profile.pdf

Overview of Liechtenstein's MAP Statistics for 2022

Please refer to https://www.oecd.org/tax/dispute/map-statistics-liechtenstein.pdf for details with respect to Liechtenstein's MAP Statistics.

Figure 2. Cases closed in 2022

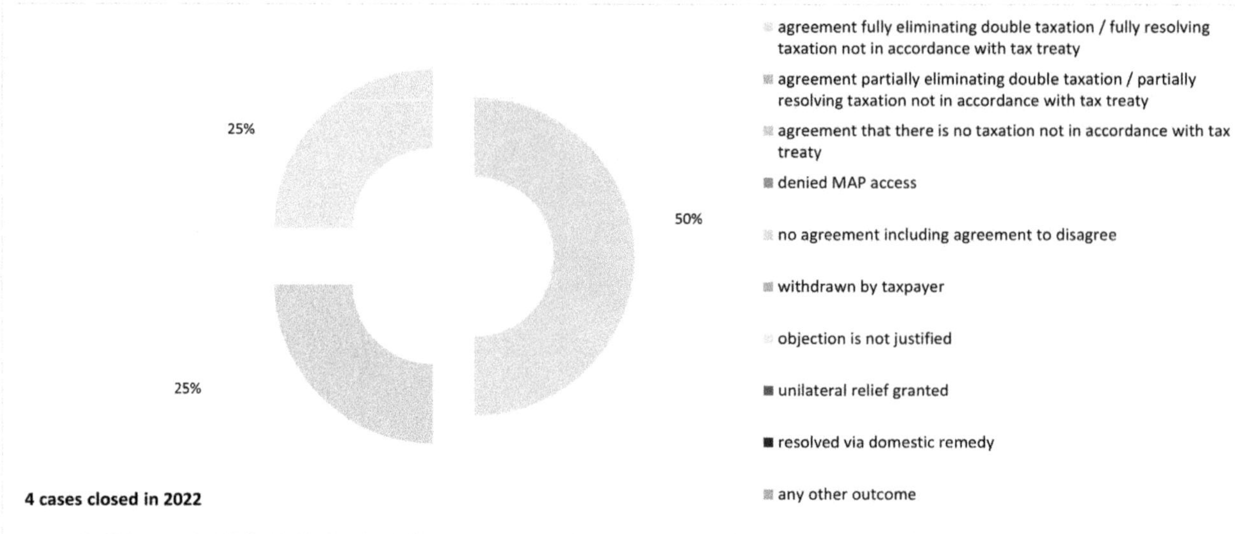

Source: OECD

Figure 3. Evolution of Liechtenstein's MAP caseload (2016-22)

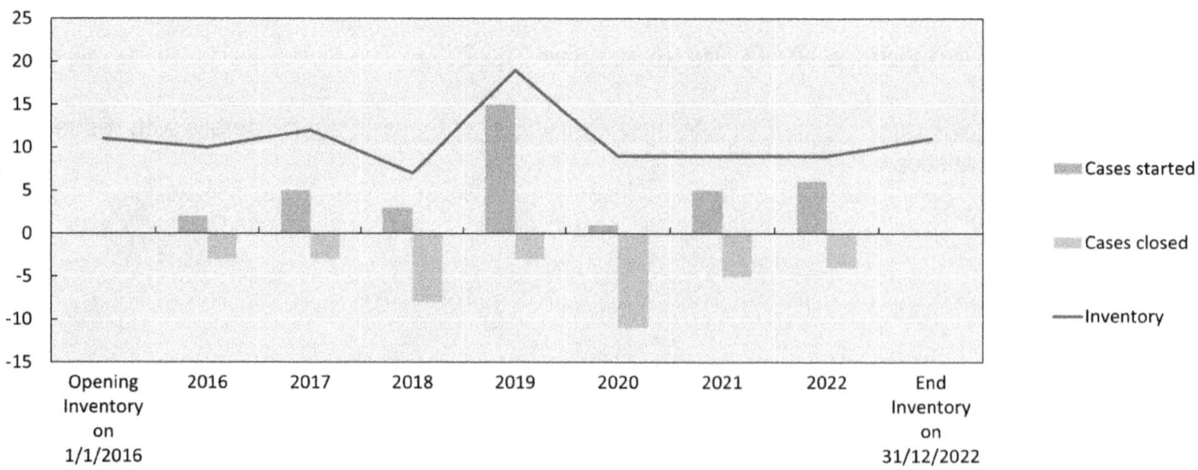

Source: OECD

Table 3. Overview of Liechtenstein's MAP caseload for 2022

Inventory for year 2022	Opening Inventory 1/1/2022	Cases started	Cases Closed	End Inventory 31/12/2022
Attribution/allocation cases	3	1	0	4
Other cases	6	5	4	7
Total	9	6	4	11

Source: OECD

Table 4. Liechtenstein's average time to resolve MAP cases in 2022

Cases resolved in year 2022	Pre-2016 cases		Post-2015 cases		All	
	Number of cases	**Average time**	**Number of cases**	**Average time** **Start to End**	**Number of cases**	**Average time**
Attribution / Allocation cases	0	N/A	0	N/A	0	N/A
Other cases	0	N/A	4	23.88	4	23.88
All cases	0	N/A	4	N/A	4	N/A

Source: OECD

Lithuania

Recent developments relating to MAP in Lithuania prior to 15 August 2023

Developments relating to MAP in the tax treaty network

- Entry into force in 2022 of the tax treaty with Morocco.

Other developments relating to MAP

- No developments were reported

Latest Action 14 Peer Review report

26 July 2021 - https://doi.org/10.1787/692bef12-en

Tax treaty network of Lithuania

- 58 treaties, applicable to 58 jurisdictions (covering all treaties signed, although not necessarily in force)
- status of MLI: in force.

Table 1. State of play of Lithuania's tax treaty network

Treaties in line with the Action 14 Minimum Standard following MLI impact	Treaties where actions are ongoing to make them in line with the Action 14 Minimum Standard	Following impact/actions, remaining treaties that are not in line with Action 14 Minimum Standard
56	0	2

Source: OECD

Lithuania's MAP programme

Organisation of competent authority function

- eight persons:
  - one head of unit
  - seven persons working on MAP cases
  - All members of the unit (working group) work on other tasks as well
- contact persons for MAP requests:
  - State Tax Inspectorate under the Ministry of Finance of the Republic of Lithuania
    Address: Vasario 16-osios str. 14, 01107 Vilnius, Lithuania
    E-mail: MAP@vmi.lt.

Figure 1. Competent Authority Organisational Structure

Source: OECD

Table 2. Guidance on the MAP process

MAP guidance	*The Rules For The Initiation And Execution Of The Mutual Agreement Procedure*, 12 September 2019	https://www.vmi.lt/evmi/documents/20142/704116/MAP_RULES_EN_2020.pdf/a3fb373d-6b4f-6d88-ea5e-54683ebbcef6?t=16026796551551. (Chapter II to be referred to for form and content of a MAP request, including information requirements)
	MAP webpage	https://www.vmi.lt/evmi/en/abipusio-susitarimo-proced%C5%ABra
MAP profile	05 July 2023	https://www.oecd.org/tax/dispute/lithuania-dispute-resolution-profile.pdf

Overview of Lithuania's MAP Statistics for 2022

Please refer to https://www.oecd.org/tax/dispute/map-statistics-lithuania.pdf for details with respect to Lithuania's MAP Statistics.

Figure 2. Cases closed in 2022

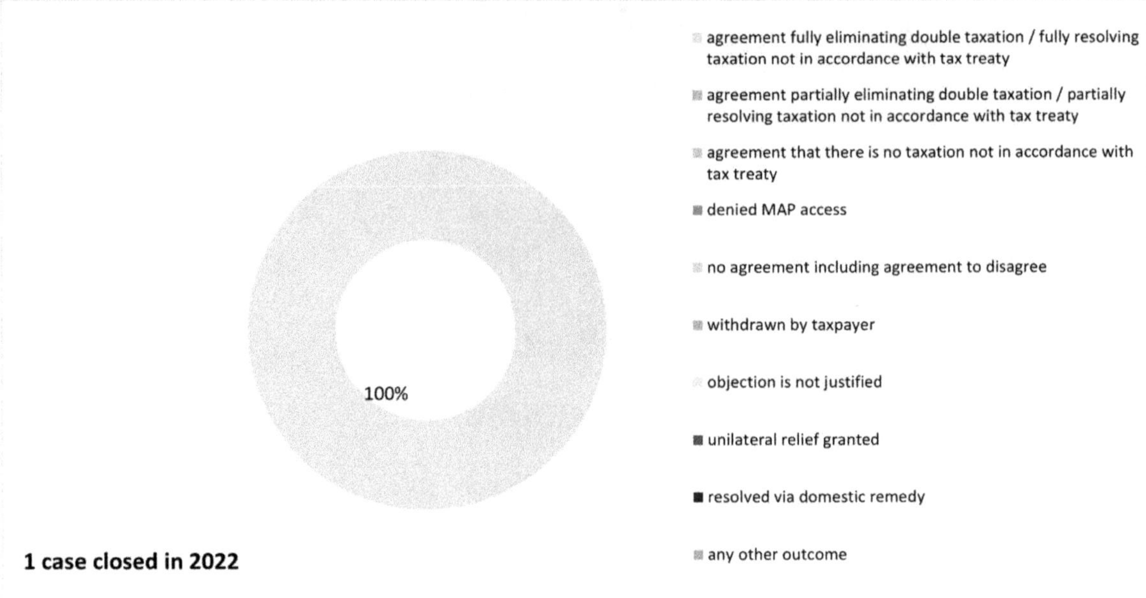

Source: OECD

Figure 3. Evolution of Lithuania's MAP caseload (2016-22)

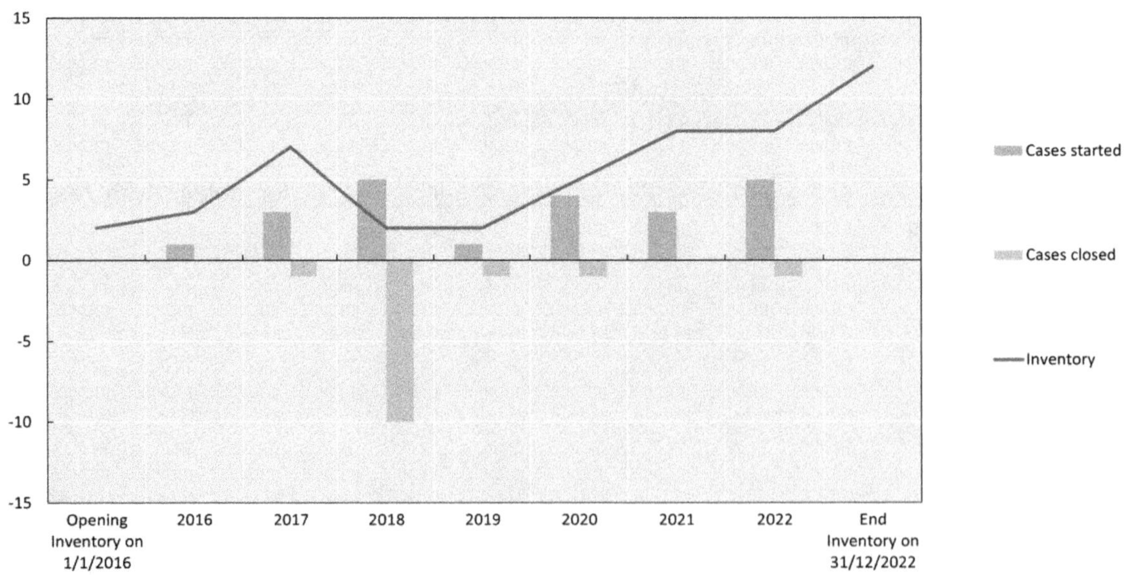

Source: OECD

Table 3. Overview of Lithuania's MAP caseload for 2022

Inventory for year 2022	Opening Inventory 1/1/2022	Cases started	Cases Closed	End Inventory 31/12/2022
Attribution/allocation cases	1	3	1	3
Other cases	7	2	0	9
Total	8	5	1	12

Source: OECD

Table 4. Lithuania's average time to resolve MAP cases in 2022

Cases resolved in year 2022	Pre-2016 cases		Post-2015 cases		All	
	Number of cases	**Average time**	**Number of cases**	**Average time** **Start to End**	**Number of cases**	**Average time**
Attribution / Allocation cases	0	N/A	1	7.00	1	7.00
Other cases	0	N/A	0	N/A	0	N/A
All cases	1	N/A	1	7.00	1	7.00

Source: OECD

Luxembourg

Recent developments relating to MAP in Luxembourg prior to 15 August 2023

Developments relating to MAP in the tax treaty network

- No developments were reported

Other developments relating to MAP

- No developments were reported

Latest Action 14 Peer Review report

9 April 2020 - https://doi.org/10.1787/ffdb81cc-en

Tax treaty network of Luxembourg

- 90 treaties, applicable to 90 jurisdictions (covering all treaties signed, although not necessarily in force)
- status of MLI: in force.

Table 1. State of play of Luxembourg's tax treaty network

Treaties in line with the Action 14 Minimum Standard following MLI impact	Treaties where actions are ongoing to make them in line with the Action 14 Minimum Standard	Following impact/actions, remaining treaties that are not in line with Action 14 Minimum Standard
82	3	5

Source: OECD

Luxembourg's MAP programme

Organisation of competent authority function

- 10 persons:
  - two heads of unit
  - five persons work on “attribution/allocation” MAP cases (among which two persons work on other tasks as well) and five persons work on “other” MAP cases (all of which work on other tasks as well).
- contact persons for MAP requests:
  - **for “attribution/allocation” MAP cases:**
    - Division économique
      Administration des contributions directes – Direction
      Address: 45, boulevard Roosevelt,

L-2450 Luxembourg
Postal address: L-2982 Luxembourg
Fax: +352 247-52441
E-mail: diveco@co.etat.lu.

- **for "other" MAP cases:**
  - Division relations internationales
    Administration des contributions directes – Direction
    Address: 45, boulevard Roosevelt,
    L-2450 Luxembourg
    Postal address: L-2982 Luxembourg
    Fax: +352 247-52441
    E-mail: divrelint@co.etat.lu.

Figure 1. Competent Authority Organisational Structure

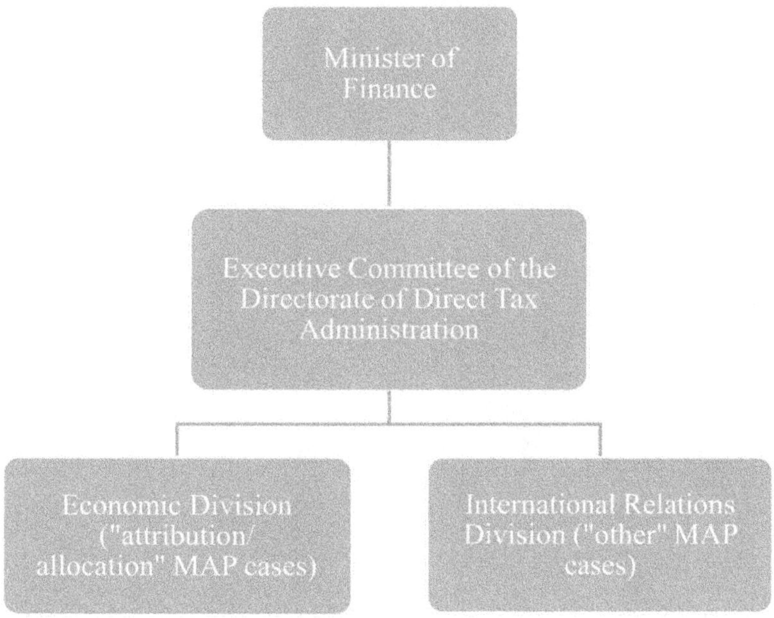

Source: OECD

Table 2. Guidance on the MAP process

MAP guidance	*Modalités de mise en œuvre de la procédure amiable prévue par les conventions fiscales bilatérales conclues par le Luxembourg,* 11 March 2021	https://impotsdirects.public.lu/dam-assets/fr/legislation/legi21/2021-03-11-LG-Conv-DI-60-du-1132021.pdf (Section 2.1 to be referred to for form and content of a MAP request, including information requirements)
	Web page	https://impotsdirects.public.lu/fr/conventions/map.html
MAP profile		https://www.oecd.org/ctp/dispute/luxembourg-dispute-resolution-profile.pdf

Overview of Luxembourg's MAP Statistics for 2022

Please refer to https://www.oecd.org/tax/dispute/map-statistics-luxembourg.pdf for details with respect to Luxembourg's MAP Statistics.

Figure 2. Cases closed in 2022

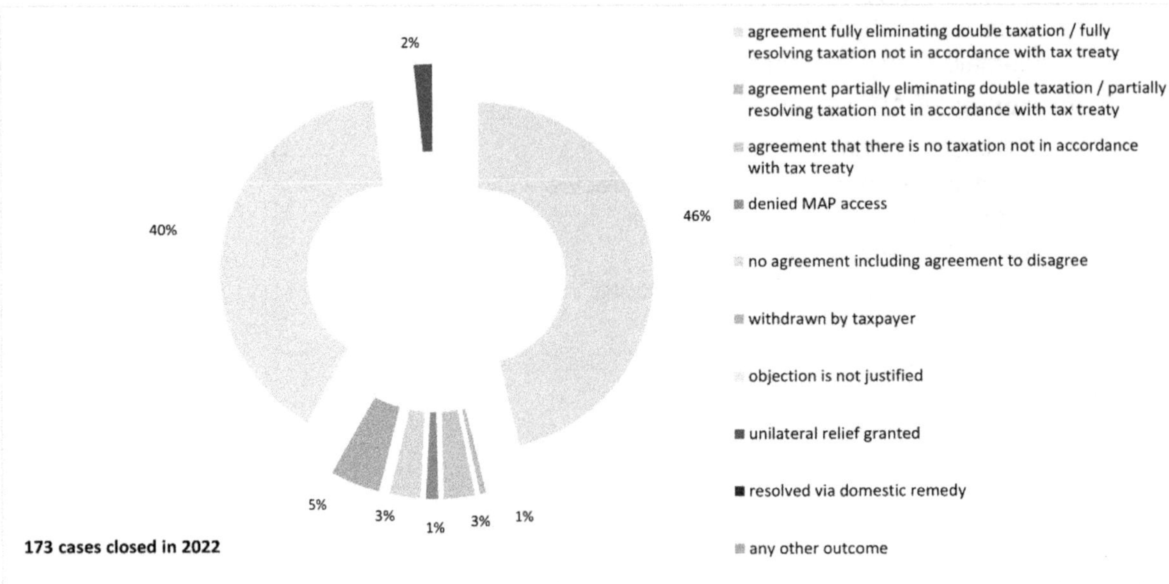

Source: OECD

Figure 3. Evolution of Luxembourg's MAP caseload (2016-22)

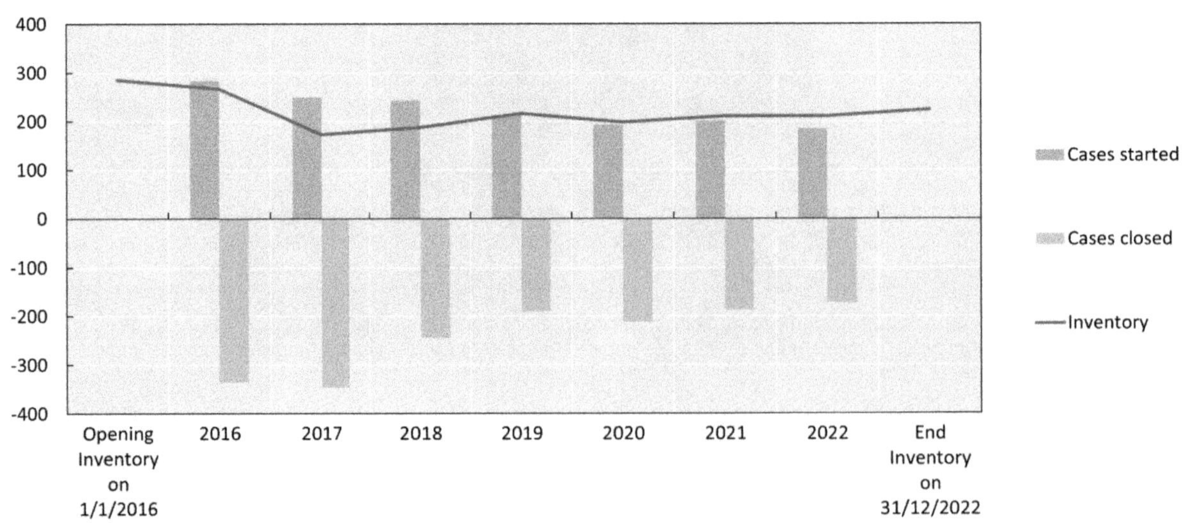

Source: OECD

Table 3. Overview of Luxembourg's MAP caseload for 2022

Inventory for year 2022	Opening Inventory 1/1/2022	Cases started	Cases Closed	End Inventory 31/12/2022
Attribution/allocation cases	52	14	10	56
Other cases	159	172	163	168
Total	211	186	173	224

Source: OECD

Table 4. Luxembourg's average time to resolve MAP cases in 2022

Cases resolved in year 2022	Pre-2016 cases		Post-2015 cases		All	
	Number of cases	**Average time**	**Number of cases**	**Average time** **Start to End**	**Number of cases**	**Average time**
Attribution / Allocation cases	0	N/A	10	34.08	10	34.08
Other cases	7	103.72	156	9.20	163	13.26
All cases	7	103.72	166	10.70	173	14.46

Source: OECD

Macau, China

Recent developments relating to MAP in Macau, China prior to 15 August 2023

Developments relating to MAP in the tax treaty network

- Macau, China did not provide the relevant information.

Other developments relating to MAP

- Macau, China did not provide the relevant information.

Latest Action 14 Peer Review report

14 April 2022 - https://doi.org/10.1787/df263845-en

Tax treaty network of Macau, China

- eight treaties, applicable to eight jurisdictions (covering all treaties signed, although not necessarily in force)
- status of MLI: not signed.

Table 1. State of play of Macau, China's tax treaty network

Treaties in line with the Action 14 Minimum Standard following MLI impact	Treaties where actions are ongoing to make them in line with the Action 14 Minimum Standard	Following impact/actions, remaining treaties that are not in line with Action 14 Minimum Standard
7	No information	No information

Source: OECD

Macau, China's MAP programme

Organisation of competent authority function

- four persons
- contact persons for MAP requests:
  - Iong Kong Leong, Director Financial Services Bureau
    Phone number: +853 2833 6886 | Fax number: +853 2830 0133
    Address: Av. da Praia Grande, Nº 575, 579 e 585, Macau, China.

Figure 1. Competent Authority Organisational Structure

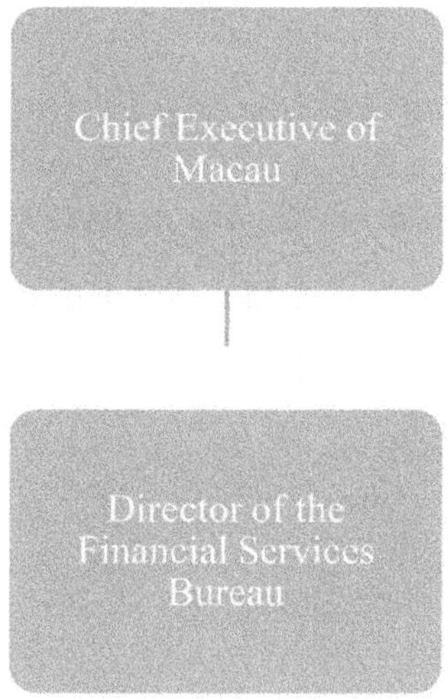

Source: OECD

Table 2. Guidance on the MAP process

MAP guidance	*Mutual Agreement Procedure Guidelines*, June 2021	http://www.dsf.gov.mo/download/tax/E_MAPGuidelines.pdf (Section 4 to be referred to for form and content of a MAP request, including information requirements)
MAP profile	30 June 2021	https://www.oecd.org/tax/dispute/macau-dispute-resolution-profile.pdf

Overview of Macau, China's MAP Statistics for 2022

Macau, China did not report any MAP cases in its 2022 MAP Statistics.

Please refer to https://www.oecd.org/tax/dispute/map-statistics-macau-china.pdf for details with respect to Macau, China's MAP Statistics.

Malaysia

Recent developments relating to MAP in Malaysia prior to 15 August 2023

Developments relating to MAP in the tax treaty network

- Signing of a tax treaty with Maldives in May 2023 that is in line with the Action 14 Minimum Standard.

Other developments relating to MAP

- Publication of a FAQ on MAP in January 2023.
- Final phase of the 2017 Map Guidelines update.

Latest Action 14 Peer Review report

Malaysia is yet to be peer reviewed under Action 14.

Tax treaty network of Malaysia

- 75 treaties, applicable to 75 jurisdictions (covering all treaties signed, although not necessarily in force)
- status of MLI: in force.

Table 1. State of play of Malaysia's tax treaty network

Treaties in line with the Action 14 Minimum Standard following MLI impact	Treaties where actions are ongoing to make them in line with the Action 14 Minimum Standard	Following impact/actions, remaining treaties that are not in line with Action 14 Minimum Standard
62	5	8

Source: OECD

Malaysia's MAP programme

Organisation of competent authority function

- six persons:
  - one head of unit
  - five persons working on MAP cases (among which three persons work on other tasks as well)
- contact persons for MAP requests:
  - The Competent Authority, Tax Division , Ministry of Finance
    6th Floor, Centre Block , Precinct 2, Federal Administration Centre, 62592 Putrajaya, Malaysia

- A copy of the request should be sent to: The Competent Authority, Department of International Taxation, Inland Revenue Board of Malaysia Headquarters Level 12, Menara Hasil, Persiaran Rimba Permai, Cyber 8, 63600 Cyberjaya, Selangor, Malaysia Tel: +603–83138888 / Fax: +603-83137848 or +603-83137849.

Figure 1. Competent Authority Organisational Structure

Source: OECD

Table 2. Guidance on the MAP process

MAP guidance	Mutual Agreement Procedure Guidelines, 19 December 2017	https://www.hasil.gov.my/pdf/pdfam/MAP_Guidelines_2017.pdf (Section 8 to be referred to for form and content of a MAP request, including information requirements)
MAP profile	18 April 2017	https://www.oecd.org/tax/dispute/Malaysia-Dispute-Resolution-Profile.pdf

Overview of Malaysia's MAP Statistics for 2022

Please refer to https://www.oecd.org/tax/dispute/map-statistics-malaysia.pdf for details with respect to Malaysia's MAP Statistics.

Figure 2. Cases closed in 2022

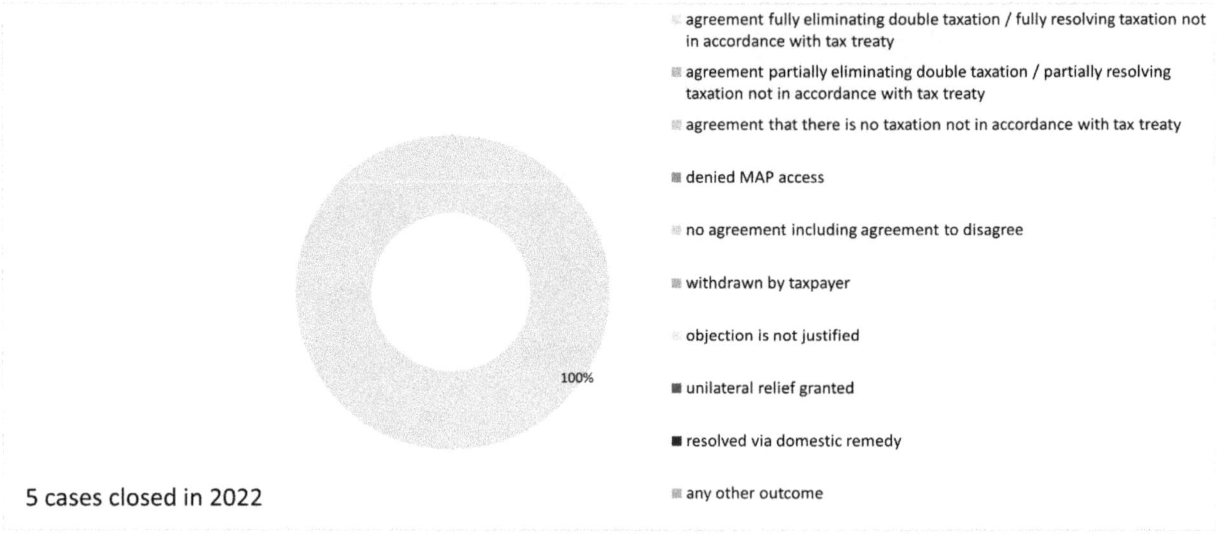

Source: OECD

Figure 3. Evolution of Malaysia's MAP caseload (2017-22)

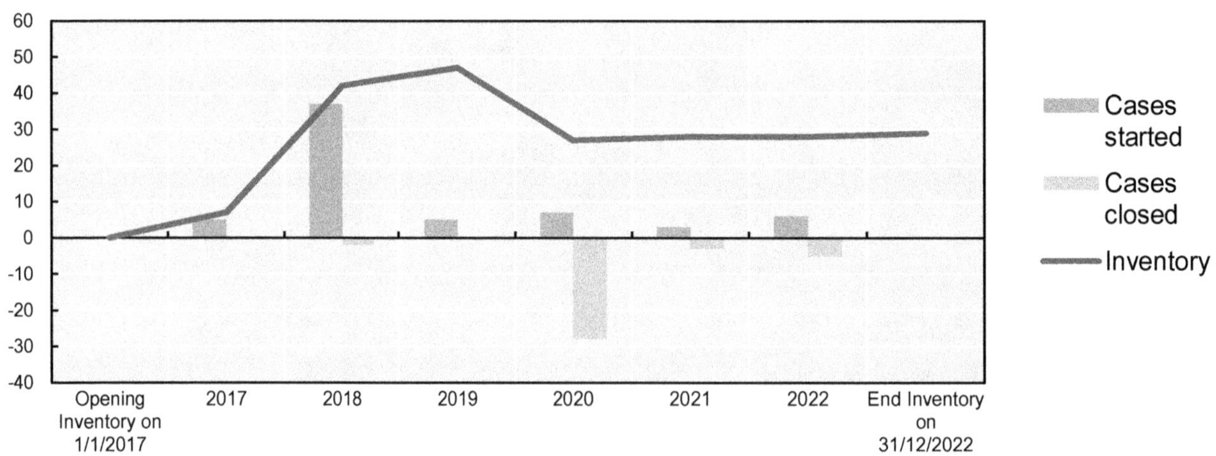

Source: OECD

Table 3. Overview of Malaysia's MAP caseload for 2022

Inventory for year 2022	Opening Inventory 1/1/2022	Cases started	Cases Closed	End Inventory 31/12/2022
Attribution/allocation cases	12	3	5	10
Other cases	16	3	0	19
Total	28	6	5	29

Source: OECD

Table 4. Malaysia's average time to resolve MAP cases in 2022

Cases resolved in year 2022	Pre-2016 cases		Post-2015 cases		All	
	Number of cases	**Average time**	**Number of cases**	**Average time** **Start to End**	**Number of cases**	**Average time**
Attribution / Allocation cases	0	N/A	5	49.16	5	49.16
Other cases	0	N/A	0	N/A	0	N/A
All cases	0	N/A	5	N/A	5	N/A

Source: OECD

Maldives

Recent developments relating to MAP in Maldives prior to 15 August 2023

Developments relating to MAP in the tax treaty network

- Maldives signed a Double Tax Avoidance Agreement with Bangladesh and this treaty covers MAP under article 26.

Other developments relating to MAP

- Maldives published a guide on MAP for the taxpayers. This guide is published in MIRA website.

Latest Action 14 Peer Review report

- Maldives is yet to be peer reviewed under Action 14.

Tax treaty network of Maldives

- three treaties, applicable to eight jurisdictions (covering all treaties signed, although not necessarily in force)
- status of MLI: not signed.

Table 1. State of play of Maldives' tax treaty network

Treaties in line with the Action 14 Minimum Standard following MLI impact	Treaties where actions are ongoing to make them in line with the Action 14 Minimum Standard	Following impact/actions, remaining treaties that are not in line with Action 14 Minimum Standard
2	0	1

Source: OECD

Maldives' MAP programme

Organisation of competent authority function

- three persons:
  - one head of unit
  - two persons working on MAP cases (among which one person works on other tasks as well):
    - of which, one person works on attribution/allocation cases and one person works on other cases.
- Contact persons for MAP requests:
  - Ms. Mariyam Himmath Hassan
  - Deputy Director of International Relations and Cooperation
  - Maldives Inland Revenue Authority

- Ameenee Magu, Male' 20379, Maldives
- Email: himmath.m@mira.gov.mv.

Figure 1. Competent Authority Organisational Structure

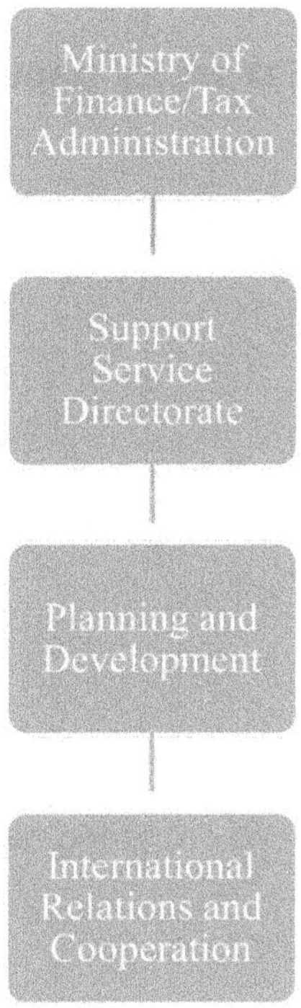

Source: OECD

Table 2. Guidance on the MAP process

MAP guidance	22 June 2023	https://www.mira.gov.mv/Files/GetFile/d2cd5cad-178a-4f88-86e1-a102b9f7f032
MAP profile	14 February 2023	https://www.oecd.org/tax/dispute/maldives-dispute-resolution-profile.pdf

Overview of Maldives' MAP Statistics for 2022

Maldives did not report any MAP cases in its 2022 MAP Statistics.

Please refer to https://www.oecd.org/tax/dispute/map-statistics-maldives.pdf for details with respect to Maldives' MAP Statistics.

Malta

Recent developments relating to MAP in Malta prior to 15 August 2023

Developments relating to MAP in the tax treaty network

- No developments were reported

Other developments relating to MAP

- No developments were reported

Latest Action 14 Peer Review report

15 April 2021 - https://doi.org/10.1787/025e9f0c-en

Tax treaty network of Malta

- 81 treaties, applicable to 81 jurisdictions (covering all treaties signed, although not necessarily in force)
- status of MLI: in force.

Table 1. State of play of Malta's tax treaty network

Treaties in line with the Action 14 Minimum Standard following MLI impact	Treaties where actions are ongoing to make them in line with the Action 14 Minimum Standard	Following impact/actions, remaining treaties that are not in line with Action 14 Minimum Standard
77	No information	No information

Source: OECD

Malta's MAP programme

Organisation of competent authority function

- six persons
- contact persons for MAP requests:
  - Andre' Gialanze Chief Tax Officer, International & Corporate Tax Unit
    AM Business Centre Labour Road Żejtun ZTN 2401 Malta
    Tel. no.: 2258 2264 Email: ca-map.cfr@gov.mt.

Figure 1. Competent Authority Organisational Structure

Source: OECD

Table 2. Guidance on the MAP process

MAP guidance	*Mutual Agreement Procedure, Guidelines* issued under the provisions of Article 96(2) of the Income Tax Act., June 2019	https://cfr.gov.mt/en/inlandrevenue/itu/Documents/MAP Guidelines.pdf (Section "Making a request for MAP" to be referred to for form and content of a MAP request, including information requirements)
MAP profile	28 February 2022	https://www.oecd.org/tax/dispute/malta-dispute-resolution-profile.pdf

Overview of Malta's MAP Statistics for 2022

Please refer to https://www.oecd.org/tax/dispute/map-statistics-malta.pdf for details with respect to Malta's MAP Statistics.

Cases closed in 2022

No MAP cases were closed by Malta in 2022.

Figure 2. Evolution of Malta's MAP caseload (2016-22)

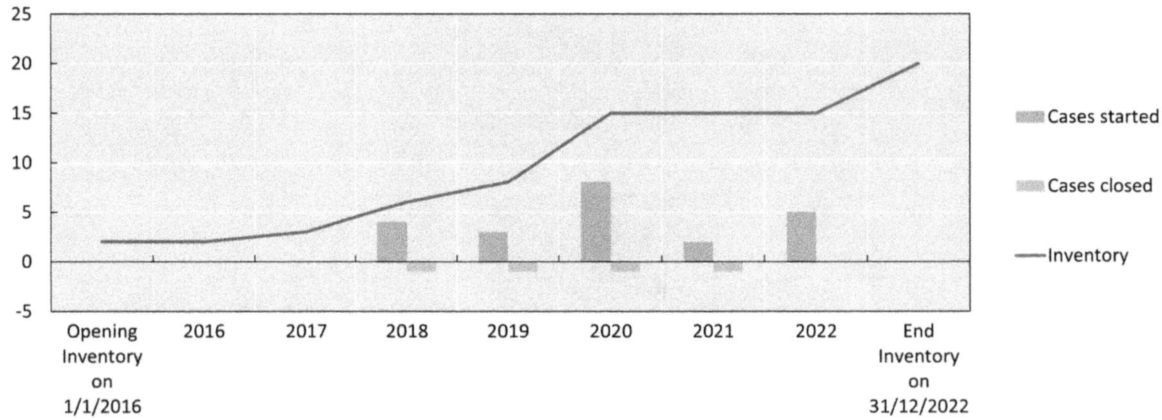

Source: OECD

Table 3. Overview of Malta's MAP caseload for 2022

Inventory for year 2022	Opening Inventory 1/1/2022	Cases started	Cases Closed	End Inventory 31/12/2022
Attribution/allocation cases	13	5	0	18
Other cases	2	0	0	2
Total	15	5	0	20

Source: OECD

Table 4. Malta's average time to resolve MAP cases in 2022

Cases resolved in year 2022	Pre-2016 cases		Post-2015 cases		All	
	Number of cases	**Average time**	**Number of cases**	**Average time** **Start to End**	**Number of cases**	**Average time**
Attribution / Allocation cases	0	N/A	0	N/A	0	N/A
Other cases	0	N/A	0	N/A	0	N/A
All cases	0	N/A	0	N/A	0	N/A

Source: OECD

Mauritania

Recent developments relating to MAP in Mauritania prior to 15 August 2023

Developments relating to MAP in the tax treaty network

- Mauritania did not provide the relevant information.

Other developments relating to MAP

- Mauritania did not provide the relevant information.

Latest Action 14 Peer Review report

Mauritania is yet to be peer reviewed under Action 14.

Tax treaty network of Mauritania

- nine treaties, applicable to 12 jurisdictions (covering all treaties signed, although not necessarily in force).
- status of MLI: not signed.

Table 1. State of play of Mauritania's tax treaty network

Treaties in line with the Action 14 Minimum Standard following MLI impact	Treaties where actions are ongoing to make them in line with the Action 14 Minimum Standard	Following impact/actions, remaining treaties that are not in line with Action 14 Minimum Standard
5	No information	No information

Source: OECD

Mauritania's MAP programme

Organisation of competent authority function

- Mauritania did not provide the relevant information.

Table 2. Guidance on the MAP process

MAP guidance	Mauritania did not provide the relevant information.	
MAP profile	No MAP profile published.	

Overview of Mauritania's MAP Statistics for 2022

Mauritania did not declare its MAP Statistics for 2022.

Mauritius

Recent developments relating to MAP in Mauritius prior to 15 August 2023

Developments relating to MAP in the tax treaty network

- Following the Stage 1 Simplified Peer Review process, Mauritius is engaging with its concerned tax treaty partners by submitting requests for bilateral negotiations and sending reminders in order to make the tax treaties compliant with the minimum standards of BEPS Action 14.

Other developments relating to MAP

- Following the Stage 1 Simplified Peer Review process, Mauritius is currently working to address the recommendations received in respect of its MAP Guidance Notes and its Standard of Procedures.

Latest Action 14 Peer Review report

The stage 1 Simplified Peer Review report of Mauritius is expected to be published early 2024.

Tax treaty network of Mauritius

- 53 treaties, applicable to 53 jurisdictions (covering all treaties signed, although not necessarily in force)
- status of MLI: in force.

Table 1. State of play of Mauritius's tax treaty network

Treaties in line with the Action 14 Minimum Standard following MLI impact	Treaties where actions are ongoing to make them in line with the Action 14 Minimum Standard	Following impact/actions, remaining treaties that are not in line with Action 14 Minimum Standard
37	9	0

Source: OECD

Mauritius's MAP programme

Organisation of competent authority function

- four persons:
  - one head of unit
  - three persons working on MAP cases.
- contact persons for MAP requests:
  - Mr. Mamade Faisal Oozeerally, Director, Faisal.Oozeerally@mra.mu
    Mr. Krishna Rambaksh, Section Head, Krishna.Rambaksh@mra.mu
    Large Taxpayers Department & International Taxation Unit, MRA

Mauritius Revenue Authority
Level 5 Ehram Court Cnr. Sir Virgil Naz & Mgr Gonin Streets Port Louis MAURITIUS.

Figure 1. Competent Authority Organisational Structure

Source: OECD

Table 2. Guidance on the MAP process

MAP guidance	*Mutual Agreement Procedure Guidance Notes*, November 2020	https://www.mra.mu/download/MAPGuidanceNotes.pdf (Chapter 2 to be referred to for form and content of a MAP request, including information requirements)
MAP profile	23 May 2023	https://www.oecd.org/tax/dispute/mauritius-dispute-resolution-profile.pdf

Overview of Mauritius's MAP Statistics for 2022

Please refer to https://www.oecd.org/tax/dispute/map-statistics-mauritius.pdf for details with respect to Mauritius's MAP Statistics.

Figure 2. Cases closed in 2022

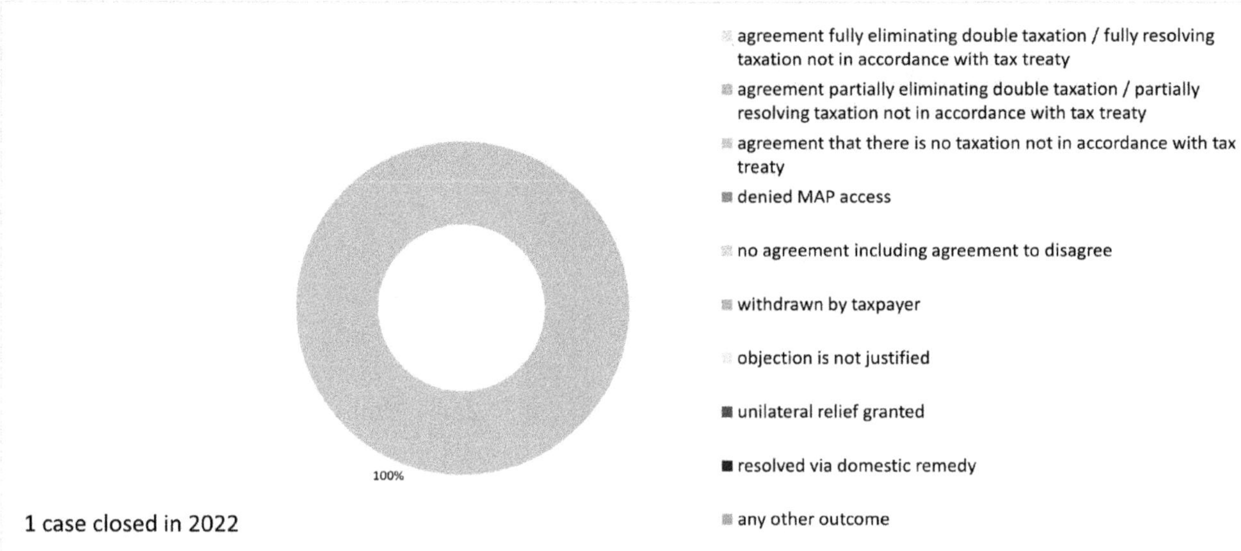

Source: OECD

Figure 3. Evolution of Mauritius's MAP caseload (2016-22)

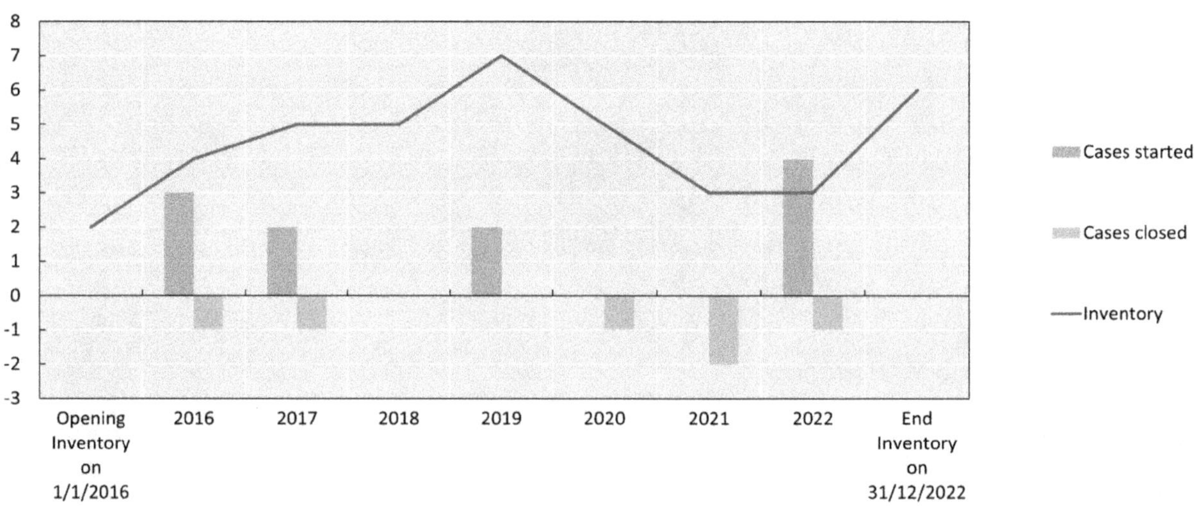

Source: OECD

Table 3. Overview of Mauritius's MAP caseload for 2022

Inventory for year 2022	Opening Inventory 1/1/2022	Cases started	Cases Closed	End Inventory 31/12/2022
Attribution/allocation cases	0	0	0	0
Other cases	3	4	1	6
Total	3	4	1	6

Source: OECD

Table 4. Mauritius's average time to resolve MAP cases in 2022

Cases resolved in year 2022	Pre-2016 cases		Post-2015 cases		All	
	Number of cases	**Average time**	**Number of cases**	**Average time** **Start to End**	**Number of cases**	**Average time**
Attribution / Allocation cases	0	N/A	0	N/A	0	N/A
Other cases	0	N/A	1	1	1	1
All cases	0	N/A	1	N/A	1	N/A

Source: OECD

Mexico

Recent developments relating to MAP in Mexico prior to 15 August 2023

Developments relating to MAP in the tax treaty network

- The Multilateral Instrument entered into force for Mexico on July 1st, 2023.
- As of 4 August 2023, Mexico has 61signed DTT. Of these 61 DTT, 48 are in line with Action 14 Minimum Standard following MLI impact. Out of the remaining 13 DTT, Mexico has taken actions to make 8 of them in line with the Action 14 Minimum Standard: with Germany (Protocol will enter into force on August 6th, 2023), Brazil (communications underway to have a Protocol), Austria (currently negotiating a Protocol), Malta (currently negotiating a Protocol), Indonesia (we have sent them communications in order to make first sentence of paragraph 2 of the MAP Article in line with the minimum standard), Jamaica (we have sent them communications in order to make second sentence of paragraph 2 of the MAP Article in line with the minimum standard), Slovak Republic (we have sent them communications in order to make second sentence of paragraph 2 of the MAP Article in line with the minimum standard) and Italy (communications have taken place to have a Memorandum of Understanding to make the first sentence, of paragraph 1, of the MAP Article in line with the minimum standard). Also, there are 5 remaining DTT that will not be in line with the minimum standard following MLI impact and actions: with Ecuador (not signed the MLI, but we have sent them communications to explore the possibility of updating the MAP Article), Guatemala (not signed the MLI, DTT not yet in force), Philippines (not signed the MLI, but we have sent them communications to explore the possibility of updating the MAP Article), United States (not signed the MLI) and Ukraine (no recent communications).

Other developments relating to MAP

- Update of the MAP profile.
- Update of the MAP Guidance.

Latest Action 14 Peer Review report

15 April 2021 - https://doi.org/10.1787/26bc3948-en

Tax treaty network of Mexico

- 61 treaties, applicable to 61 jurisdictions (covering all treaties signed, although not necessarily in force)
- status of MLI: in force.

Table 1. State of play of Mexico's tax treaty network

Treaties in line with the Action 14 Minimum Standard following MLI impact	Treaties where actions are ongoing to make them in line with the Action 14 Minimum Standard	Following impact/actions, remaining treaties that are not in line with Action 14 Minimum Standard
48	8	5

Source: OECD

Mexico's MAP programme

Organisation of competent authority function

- 26 persons:
  - 2 head(s) of unit
  - 24 persons working on MAP cases (among which 9 persons work on other tasks as well)
    - 15 persons work on attribution/allocation cases and 9 persons work on other cases
- Contact persons for MAP requests:
  - For large taxpayers and taxpayers in the upstream, midstream or downstream Oil & Gas industry (MAP & MAP APA) Mr. Armando Ramírez Sánchez, General Administrator for Large Taxpayers (i.e. Head of the Large Business & International Division) Av. Hidalgo 77, Módulo III, Piso 1, Col. Guerrero, Alcaldía Cuauhtémoc, Ciudad de México, 06300
  - For large taxpayers, not dealing or related to upstream, midstream or downstream Oil & Gas industry (MAP)
  - Central Administration for Legal Support and International Tax Legal Affairs Av. Hidalgo 77, Módulo III, Planta Baja, Col. Guerrero, Alcaldía Cuauhtémoc, Ciudad de México, 06300 t. +52 (55) 5802 2082 / mapsmexico@sat.gob.mx
  - For large taxpayers, not dealing or related to upstream, midstream or downstream Oil & Gas industry (MAP APA) Mr. Carlos Eduardo González Gamero, Central Administrator for Transfer Pricing Audits Av. Hidalgo 77, Módulo III, Piso 1, Col. Guerrero, Alcaldía Cuauhtémoc, Ciudad de México, 06300 t. +52 (55) 5802 2384, 5802 0000 ext. 42384 carlos.gamero@sat.gob.mx / acfpt@sat.gob.mx
  - For taxpayers in the upstream, midstream or downstream Oil & Gas industry (MAP & MAP APA) Central Administration for Tax and Legal Affairs (Hydrocarbons) Av. Hidalgo 77, Módulo III, Piso 1, Col. Guerrero, Alcaldía Cuauhtémoc, Ciudad de México, 06300 t. +52 (55) 5802 2082 / mapsmexico@sat.gob.mx

Figure 1. Competent Authority Organisational Structure

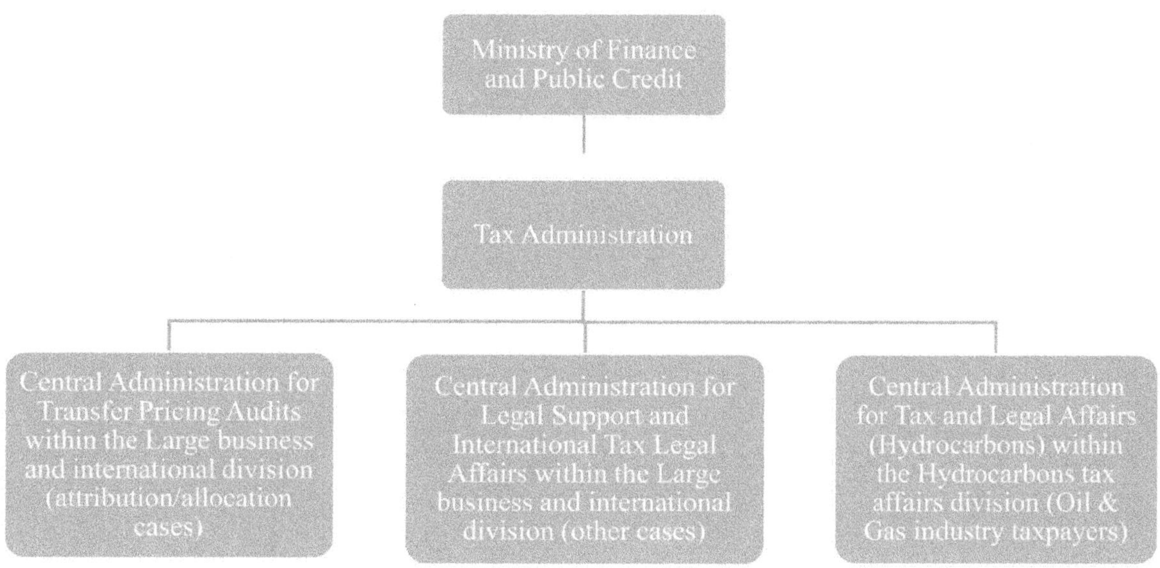

Source: OECD

Table 2. Guidance on the MAP process

MAP guidance	Información relativa a procedimientos amistosos, August 2023	https://www.sat.gob.mx/normatividad/98105/tratados-en-materia-fiscal-y-cuestiones-relacionadastratados-en-materia-fiscal-y-cuestiones-relacionadas (Sections 1. to 6. to be referred to for form and content of a MAP request, including information requirements)
	Administrative rule 2.1.30.	http://omawww.sat.gob.mx/normatividad_RMF_RGCE/Paginas/documentos/rmf/rmf/RMF_2023-27122022.pdf (p. 41)
	Procedure form 244/CFF	http://omawww.sat.gob.mx/normatividad_RMF_RGCE/Paginas/documentos/rmf/anexos/Anexo_1-A-RMF_2023-28122022.pdf (p.384)
MAP profile	29 June 2023	https://www.oecd.org/tax/dispute/mexico-dispute-resolution-profile.pdf

Overview of Mexico's MAP Statistics for 2022

Please refer to https://www.oecd.org/tax/dispute/map-statistics-mexico.pdf for details with respect to Mexico's MAP Statistics.

Figure 2. Cases closed in 2022

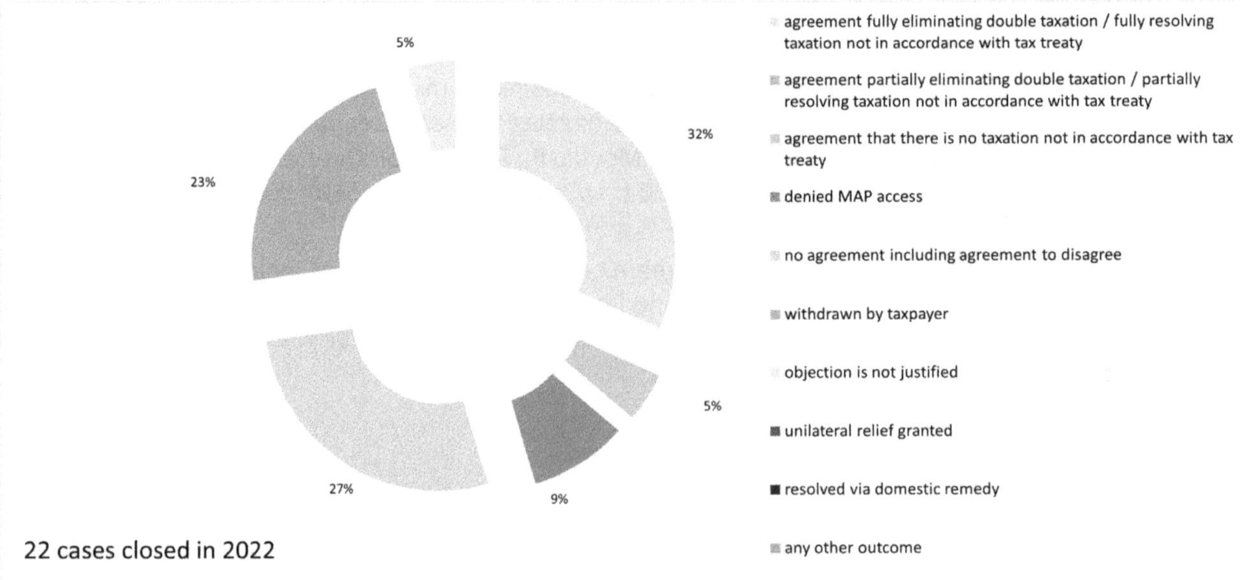

Source: OECD

Figure 3. Evolution of Mexico's MAP caseload (2016-22)

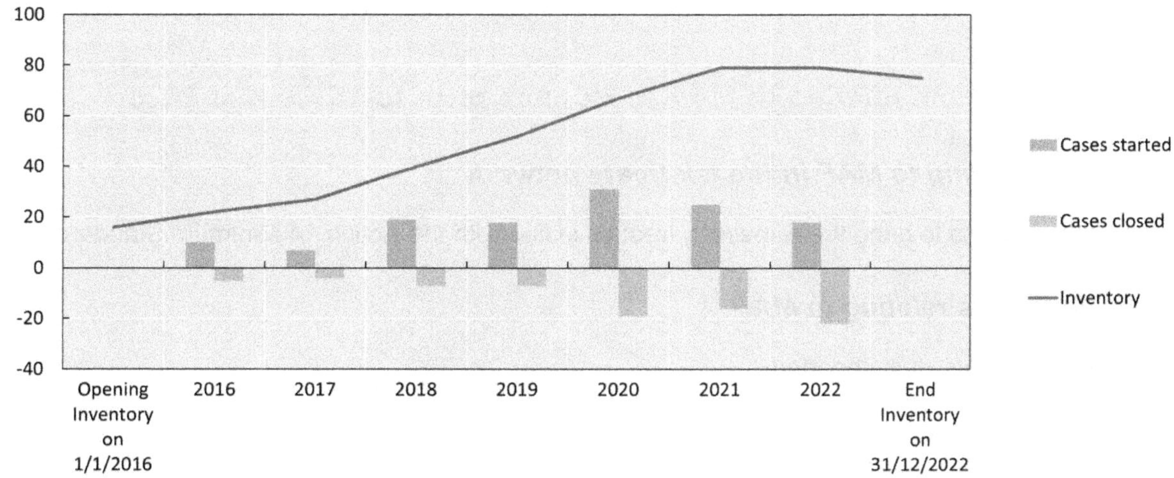

Source: OECD

Table 3. Overview of Mexico's MAP caseload for 2022

Inventory for year 2022	Opening Inventory 1/1/2022	Cases started	Cases Closed	End Inventory 31/12/2022
Attribution/allocation cases	62	17	18	61
Other cases	17	1	4	14
Total	79	18	22	75

Source: OECD

Table 4. Mexico's average time to resolve MAP cases in 2022

Cases resolved in year 2022	Pre-2016 cases		Post-2015 cases		All	
	Number of cases	**Average time**	**Number of cases**	**Average time** **Start to End**	**Number of cases**	**Average time**
Attribution / Allocation cases	1	127.04	17	29.06	18	34.51
Other cases	0	N/A	4	42.64	4	42.64
All cases	1	127.04	21	31.65	22	35.99

Source: OECD

Monaco

Recent developments relating to MAP in Monaco prior to 15 August 2023

Developments relating to MAP in the tax treaty network

- Work in progress to bring the remaining treaties in line with the Action 14 Minimum Standard.

Other developments relating to MAP

- No developments were reported

Latest Action 14 Peer Review report

24 January 2022 - https://doi.org/10.1787/2d772d4f-en

Tax treaty network of Monaco

- 12 treaties, applicable to 12 jurisdictions (covering all treaties signed, although not necessarily in force)
- status of MLI: in force.

Table 1. State of play of Monaco's tax treaty network

Treaties in line with the Action 14 Minimum Standard following MLI impact	Treaties where actions are ongoing to make them in line with the Action 14 Minimum Standard	Following impact/actions, remaining treaties that are not in line with Action 14 Minimum Standard
7	5	0

Source: OECD

Monaco's MAP programme

Organisation of competent authority function

- 10 persons:
  - three heads of unit
  - four persons working on MAP cases (all of which work on other tasks as well).
- contact persons for MAP requests:
  - Département des Finances et de l'Economie
Ministère d'État
Place de la Visitation MC 98000 MONACO
Téléphone : (+377) 98 98 82 56.

Figure 1. Competent Authority Organisational Structure

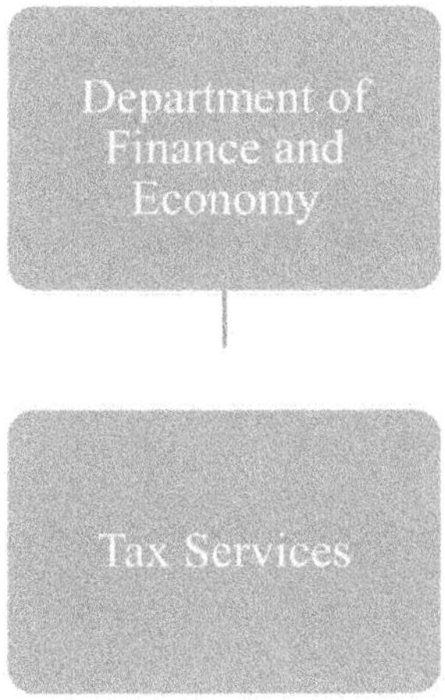

Source: OECD

Table 2. Guidance on the MAP process

MAP guidance	*Notice sur la procédure amiable*, 11 July 2019	https://www.gouv.mc/content/download/464814/5299509/file/2019-07-11%20Notice%20sur%20la%20Proc%C3%A9dure%20Amiable%20v11.pdf (Section VI to be referred to for form and content of a MAP request, including information requirements)
MAP profile	17 May 2019	https://www.oecd.org/tax/dispute/monaco-dispute-resolution-profile.pdf

Overview of Monaco's MAP Statistics for 2022

Monaco did not report any MAP cases in its 2022 MAP Statistics.

Please refer to https://www.oecd.org/tax/dispute/map-statistics-monaco.pdf for details with respect to Monaco's MAP Statistics.

Mongolia

Recent developments relating to MAP in Mongolia prior to 15 August 2023

Developments relating to MAP in the tax treaty network

- No developments were reported

Other developments relating to MAP

- Drafting of an update to the MAP request form and the other additional information form.

Latest Action 14 Peer Review report

Mongolia is yet to be peer reviewed under Action 14.

Tax treaty network of Mongolia

- 26 treaties, applicable to 26 jurisdictions (covering all treaties signed, although not necessarily in force)
- status of MLI: signed.

Table 1. State of play of Mongolia's tax treaty network

Treaties in line with the Action 14 Minimum Standard following MLI impact	Treaties where actions are ongoing to make them in line with the Action 14 Minimum Standard	Following impact/actions, remaining treaties that are not in line with Action 14 Minimum Standard
26	0	0

Source: OECD

Mongolia's MAP programme

Organisation of competent authority function

- two persons:
  - one head of unit
  - one person working on MAP cases who works on other tasks as well).
- contact persons for MAP requests:
  - Mr. Ganbat Jigjid, Secretary of StateMinistry of Finance of Mongolia,
    S.Danzan Street, Government Building II Corp D, Ulaanbaatar 15160, Mongolia
    Tel: +976 11262253; Email: ganbat_j@mof.gov.mn
  - Mr. Telmuun Byambaragchaa, Director of Tax Policy Department
    Ministry of Finance of Mongolia,

S.Danzan Street, Government Building II Corp D, Ulaanbaatar 15160, Mongolia
Tel: +976 11262101; Email: telmuun_b@mof.gov.mn

- Mr. Zayaabal Batjargal, Commissioner of the General Department of Taxation
5/1 United National Street, 4th khoroo, Chingelt District, Ulaanbaatar, Mongolia
Tel: +976 11311137; Email: zayaabal@mta.gov.mn.

Figure 1. Competent Authority Organisational Structure

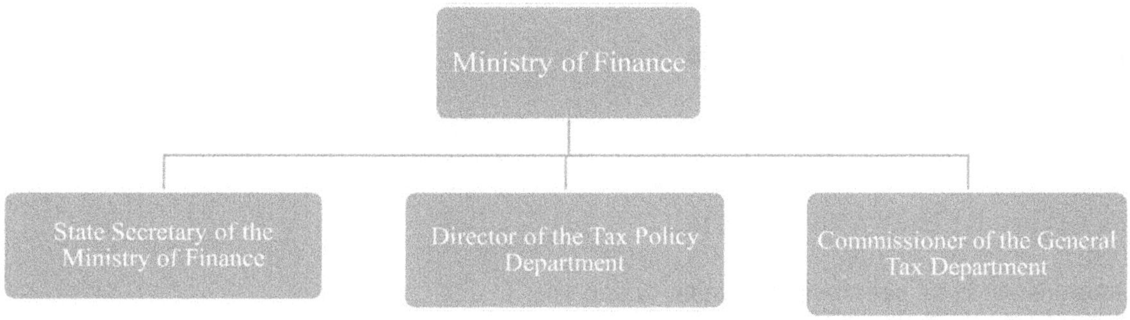

Source: OECD

Table 2. Guidance on the MAP process

MAP guidance	No MAP guidance published	-
MAP profile	No MAP profile published	-

Overview of Mongolia's MAP Statistics for 2022

Mongolia did not report any MAP cases in its 2022 MAP Statistics.

Please refer to https://www.oecd.org/tax/dispute/map-statistics-mongolia.pdf for details with respect to Mongolia's MAP Statistics.

Montenegro

Recent developments relating to MAP in Montenegro prior to 15 August 2023

Developments relating to MAP in the tax treaty network

- No developments were reported

Other developments relating to MAP

- No developments were reported

Latest Action 14 Peer Review report

Montenegro is yet to be peer reviewed under Action 14.

Tax treaty network of Montenegro

- 45 treaties, applicable to 45 jurisdictions (covering all treaties signed, although not necessarily in force).
- status of MLI: not signed.

Table 1. State of play of Montenegro's tax treaty network

Treaties in line with the Action 14 Minimum Standard following MLI impact	Treaties where actions are ongoing to make them in line with the Action 14 Minimum Standard	Following impact/actions, remaining treaties that are not in line with Action 14 Minimum Standard
36	0	9

Source: OECD

Montenegro's MAP programme

Organisation of competent authority function

- Montenegro did not provide the relevant information.

Table 2. Guidance on the MAP process

MAP guidance	Montenegro did not provide the relevant information	
MAP profile	No MAP profile published	

Overview of Montenegro's MAP Statistics for 2022

Montenegro did not declare its MAP Statistics for 2022.

Montserrat

Recent developments relating to MAP in Montserrat prior to 15 August 2023

Developments relating to MAP in the tax treaty network

- Montserrat did not provide the relevant information.

Other developments relating to MAP

- Montserrat did not provide the relevant information.

Latest Action 14 Peer Review report

Montserrat is yet to be peer reviewed under Action 14.

Tax treaty network of Montserrat

- two treaties, applicable to two jurisdictions (covering all treaties signed, although not necessarily in force)
- status of MLI: not signed.

Table 1. State of play of Montserrat's tax treaty network

Treaties in line with the Action 14 Minimum Standard following MLI impact	Treaties where actions are ongoing to make them in line with the Action 14 Minimum Standard	Following impact/actions, remaining treaties that are not in line with Action 14 Minimum Standard
0	No information	No information

Source: OECD

Montserrat's MAP programme

Organisation of competent authority function

- Montserrat did not provide the relevant information.

Table 2. Guidance on the MAP process

MAP guidance	No MAP guidance published	-
MAP profile	No MAP profile published	-

Overview of Montserrat's MAP Statistics for 2022

Montserrat did not report any MAP cases in its 2022 MAP Statistics.

Please refer to https://www.oecd.org/tax/dispute/map-statistics-montserrat.pdf for details with respect to Montserrat's MAP Statistics.

Morocco

Recent developments relating to MAP in Morocco prior to 15 August 2023

Developments relating to MAP in the tax treaty network

- Entry into force of the tax treaty with Benin, Japan, Ghana, Lithuania, Madagascar, Saudi Arabia, Serbia and Slovenia in 2022.
- Signature of a tax treaty with Comoros Islands in 2022.
- Signature of a tax treaty with Cabo Verde in 2023.

Other developments relating to MAP

- No developments were reported

Latest Action 14 Peer Review report

14 April 2022 - https://doi.org/10.1787/f14495d7-en

Tax treaty network of Morocco

- 80 treaties, applicable to 83 jurisdictions (covering all treaties signed, although not necessarily in force)
- status of MLI: signed.

Table 1. State of play of Morocco's tax treaty network

Treaties in line with the Action 14 Minimum Standard following MLI impact	Treaties where actions are ongoing to make them in line with the Action 14 Minimum Standard	Following impact/actions, remaining treaties that are not in line with Action 14 Minimum Standard
68	2	10

Source: OECD

Morocco's MAP programme

Organisation of competent authority function

- eight persons:
  - two heads of unit and two heads of division
  - four persons working on MAP cases (all of which work on other tasks as well)
    - one person works on attribution/allocation cases and three persons work on other cases.

- contact persons for MAP requests:
  - Direction de la Législation, des Etudes et de la Coopération Internationale, Direction Générale des Impôts, Avenue Haj Ahmed Cherkaoui Quartier Administratif Agdal 10090 Rabat
  - TEL : +212 5 37 27 91 88 E-mail : negociationscfi@tax.gov.ma.

Figure 1. Competent Authority Organisational Structure

Source: OECD

Table 2. Guidance on the MAP process

MAP guidance	La Procédure Amiable dans le cadre des conventions de non double imposition, May 2021	https://www.finances.gov.ma/Publication/dgi/2021/Guide_MAP_Final+Version-07-05-21.pdf (Section II. to be referred to for form and content of a MAP request, including information requirements)
MAP profile	02 November 2023	https://www.oecd.org/tax/dispute/morocco-dispute-resolution-profile.pdf

Overview of Morocco's MAP Statistics for 2022

Please refer to https://www.oecd.org/tax/dispute/map-statistics-morocco.pdf for details with respect to Morocco's MAP Statistics.

Figure 2. Cases Closed in 2022

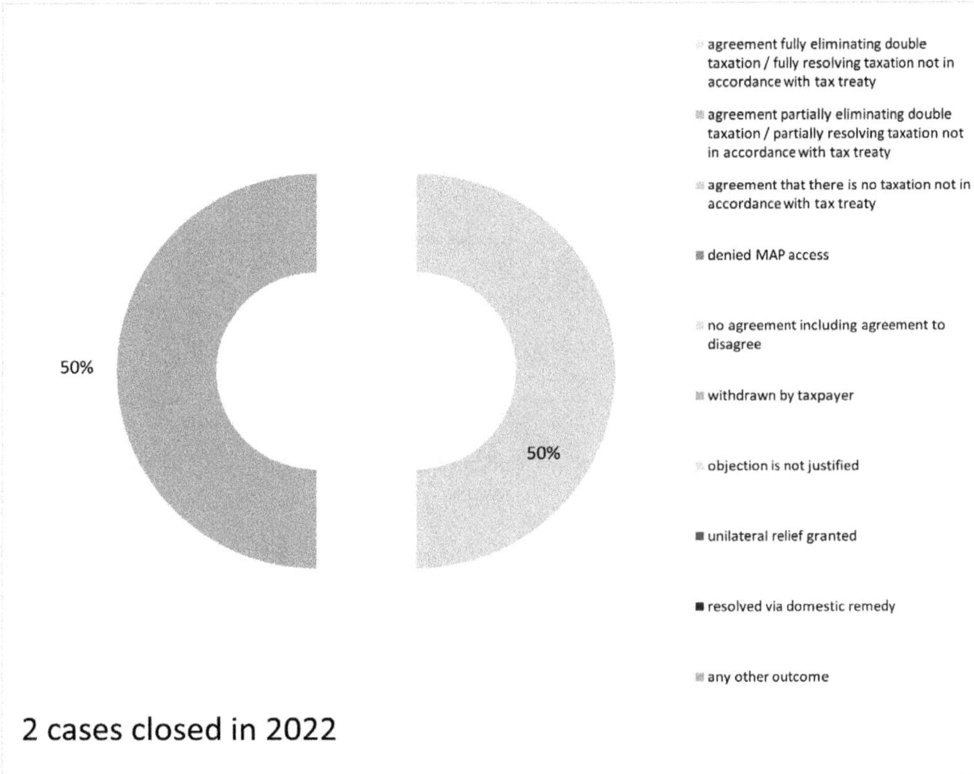

Source: OECD

Figure 3. Evolution of Morocco's MAP caseload (2019-22)

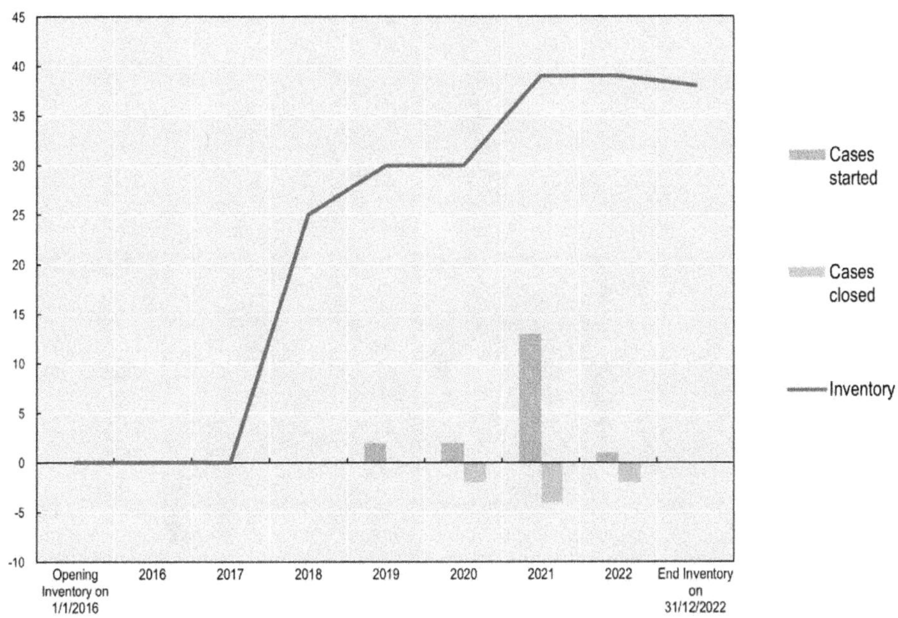

Source: OECD

Table 3. Overview of Morocco's MAP caseload for 2022

Inventory for year 2022	Opening Inventory 1/1/2022	Cases started	Cases Closed	End Inventory 31/12/2022
Attribution/allocation cases	7	0	1	6
Other cases	32	1	1	32
Total	39	1	2	38

Source: OECD

Table 4. Morocco's average time to resolve MAP cases in 2022

Cases resolved in year 2022	Pre-2016 cases		Post-2015 cases		All	
	Number of cases	**Average time**	**Number of cases**	**Average time** **Start to End**	**Number of cases**	**Average time**
Attribution / Allocation cases	0	N/A	1	9.07	1	9.07
Other cases	0	N/A	1	16.31	1	16.31
All cases	0	N/A	2	12.69	2	12.69

Source: OECD

Namibia

Recent developments relating to MAP in Namibia prior to 15 August 2023

Developments relating to MAP in the tax treaty network

- Namibia did not provide the relevant information.

Other developments relating to MAP

- Namibia did not provide the relevant information.

Latest Action 14 Peer Review report

Namibia is yet to be peer reviewed under Action 14.

Tax treaty network of Namibia

- 12 treaties, applicable to 12 jurisdictions (covering all treaties signed, although not necessarily in force)
- status of MLI: signed.

Table 1. State of play of Namibia's tax treaty network

Treaties in line with the Action 14 Minimum Standard following MLI impact	Treaties where actions are ongoing to make them in line with the Action 14 Minimum Standard	Following impact/actions, remaining treaties that are not in line with Action 14 Minimum Standard
11	No information	No information

Source: OECD

Namibia's MAP programme

Organisation of competent authority function

- Namibia did not provide the relevant information.

Table 2. Guidance on the MAP process

MAP guidance	No MAP guidance published	-
MAP profile	No MAP profile published	-

Overview of Namibia's MAP Statistics for 2022

Namibia did not report any MAP cases in its 2022 MAP Statistics.

Please refer to https://www.oecd.org/tax/dispute/map-statistics-namibia.pdf for details with respect to Namibia's MAP Statistics.

Netherlands

Recent developments relating to MAP in Netherlands prior to 15 August 2023

Developments relating to MAP in the tax treaty network

- signature of a new tax treaty with Belgium in June 2023
- advanced treaty negotiations with Spain, Morocco and Thailand
- negotiations intended with Brazil and Surinam.

Other developments relating to MAP

- At the end of 2021, the Ministry of Finance delegated the competence to handle mutual agreement procedures to the Tax Administration. Subsequently, a dedicated MAP-team was set up at the beginning of 2022. This team is responsible for MAP and arbitration cases for individual taxpayers and BAPA/MAPA cases. The Ministry of Finance remains competent to conclude general MAP agreements based on Article 25(3) OECD Model Treaty.

Latest Action 14 Peer Review report

13 August 2019 - https://doi.org/10.1787/cce92832-en

Tax treaty network of Netherlands

- 96 treaties, applicable to 99 jurisdictions (covering all treaties signed, although not necessarily in force)
- status of MLI: in force.

Table 1. State of play of Netherlands' tax treaty network

Treaties in line with the Action 14 Minimum Standard following MLI impact	Treaties where actions are ongoing to make them in line with the Action 14 Minimum Standard	Following impact/actions, remaining treaties that are not in line with Action 14 Minimum Standard
81	5	10

Source: OECD

Netherlands' MAP programme

Organisation of competent authority function

- 22 persons:
  - one head of unit
  - one data manager and one process coordinator

- 19 persons fulltime working on MAP cases (11 persons work on attribution/allocation cases and BAPA/MAPA-cases and eight persons work on other cases).

- contact persons for MAP requests:
  - Netherlands Tax Administration/Large Business, Attn. MAP-team, PO Box 30206, 2500 GE The Hague

    f: +31-88 442 7938 / e: internationalezaken@minfin.nl.

Figure 1. Competent Authority Organisational Structure

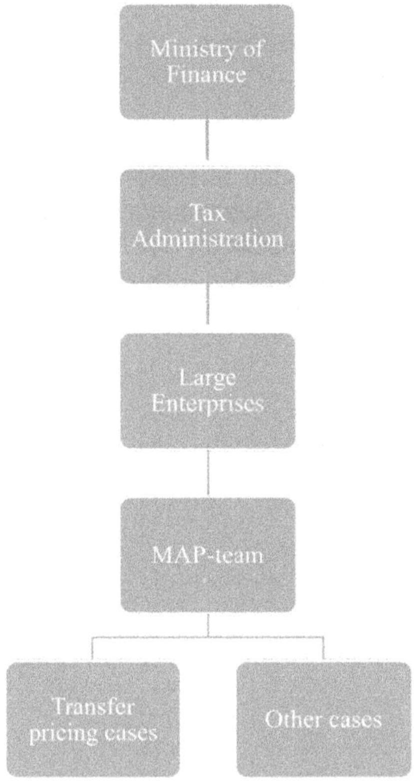

Source: OECD

Table 2. Guidance on the MAP process

MAP guidance	Internationaal Belastingrecht. Besluit Onderlinge overlegprocedures, 22 June 2020	https://zoek.officielebekendmakingen.nl/stcrt-2020-32689.pdf (Section 3.3 and Annex A and B to be referred to for form and content of a MAP request, including information requirements)
MAP profile	17 May 2022	https://www.oecd.org/tax/dispute/the-netherlands-dispute-resolution-profile.pdf

Overview of Netherlands' MAP Statistics for 2022

Please refer to https://www.oecd.org/tax/dispute/map-statistics-netherlands.pdf for details with respect to Netherlands' MAP Statistics.

Figure 2. Cases closed in 2022

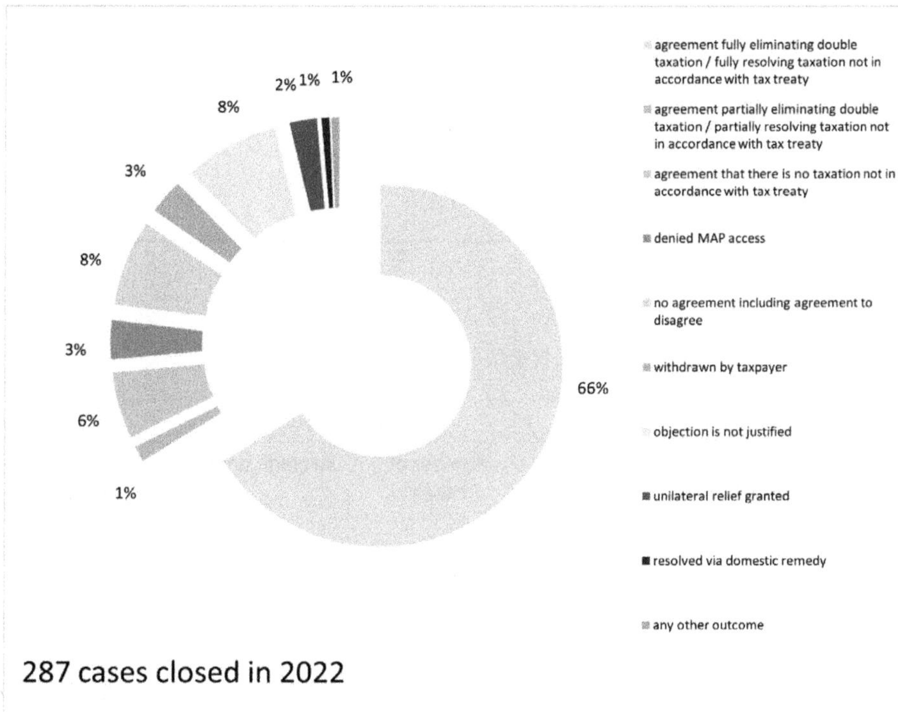

Source: OECD

Figure 3. Evolution of Netherlands' MAP caseload (2016-22)

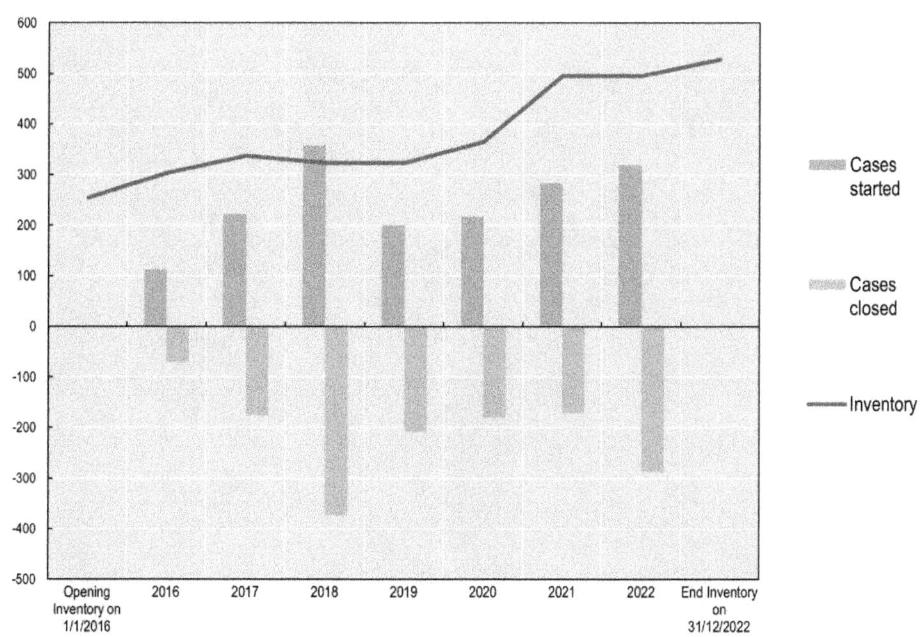

Source: OECD

Table 3. Overview of Netherland's MAP caseload for 2022

Inventory for year 2022	Opening Inventory 1/1/2022	Cases started	Cases Closed	End Inventory 31/12/2022
Attribution/allocation cases	183	76	92	167
Other cases	313	243	195	361
Total	496	319	287	528

Source: OECD

Table 4. Netherland's average time to resolve MAP cases in 2022

Cases resolved in year 2022	Pre-2016 cases		Post-2015 cases		All	
	Number of cases	**Average time**	**Number of cases**	**Average time** **Start to End**	**Number of cases**	**Average time**
Attribution / Allocation cases	1	93	91	18.81	92	19.62
Other cases	4	171	191	14.76	195	17.96
All cases	5	155.4	282	16.06	287	18.49

Source: OECD

New Zealand

Recent developments relating to MAP in New Zealand prior to 15 August 2023

Developments relating to MAP in the tax treaty network

- Amending protocols have been completed with two jurisdictions, and six more are currently under negotiation.
- Two treaty partners have signed but not yet ratified the MLI and we understand that one treaty partner intends to sign the MLI.

Other developments relating to MAP

- MAP guidance and MAP profile updated in 2023
- The suspension of collection procedures has also been clarified recently in our guidance on the public website.

Latest Action 14 Peer Review report

15 April 2021 - https://doi.org/10.1787/794c808c-en

Tax treaty network of New Zealand

- 47 treaties, applicable to 47 jurisdictions (covering all treaties signed, although not necessarily in force)
- status of MLI: in force.

Table 1. State of play of New Zealand's tax treaty network

Treaties in line with the Action 14 Minimum Standard following MLI impact	Treaties where actions are ongoing to make them in line with the Action 14 Minimum Standard	Following impact/actions, remaining treaties that are not in line with Action 14 Minimum Standard
37	6	4

Source: OECD

New Zealand's MAP programme

Organisation of competent authority function

- 21 persons:
  - one head of unit and one strategic advisor
  - on average, four persons working on MAP cases - two persons work on attribution/allocation cases and two persons work on other cases.

- contact persons for MAP requests:
  - For taxpayer specific cases (including TP): Mr John Nash, Strategic Advisor (International), Inland Revenue Department, 55 Featherston Street PO Box 2198 Wellington 6140 New Zealand, Tel 64 4 890 3290 Fax 64 4890 4503 john.nash@ird.govt.nz
  - For treaty interpretation and other treaty issues cases: Ms Carmel Peters, Strategic Policy Advisor, Inland Revenue Department, 55 Featherston Street PO Box 2198 Wellington 6140 New Zealand, Tel 64 4 890 6139 carmel.peters@ird.govt.nz.

Figure 1. Competent Authority Organisational Structure

Source: OECD

Table 2. Guidance on the MAP process

MAP guidance	Mutual agreement procedure (MAP), 20 March 2023	https://www.ird.govt.nz/international-tax/double-tax-agreements/mutual-agreement-procedure (Sections "Filing a MAP request" and "Information required in a MAP request" to be referred to for form and content of a MAP request, including information requirements)
MAP profile	26 January 2023	https://www.oecd.org/tax/dispute/new-zealand-dispute-resolution-profile.pdf

Overview of New Zealand's MAP Statistics for 2022

Please refer to https://www.oecd.org/tax/dispute/map-statistics-new-zealand.pdf for details with respect to New Zealand's MAP Statistics.

Figure 2. Cases closed in 2022

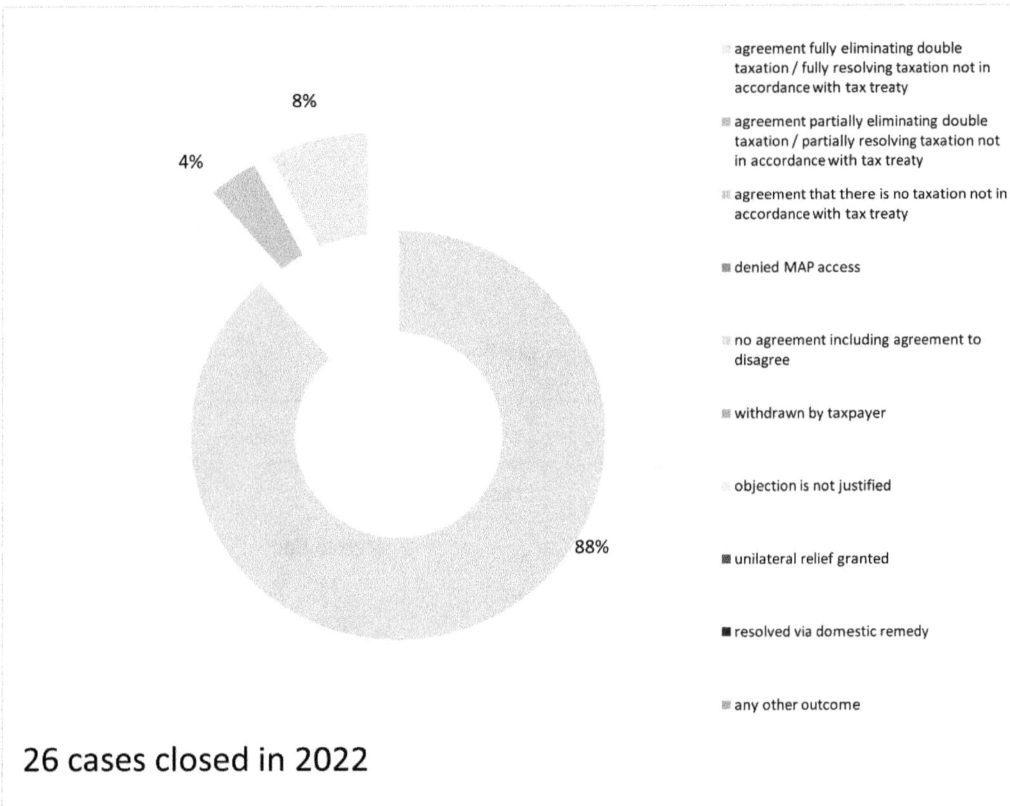

Source: OECD

Figure 3. Evolution of New Zealand's MAP caseload (2016-22)

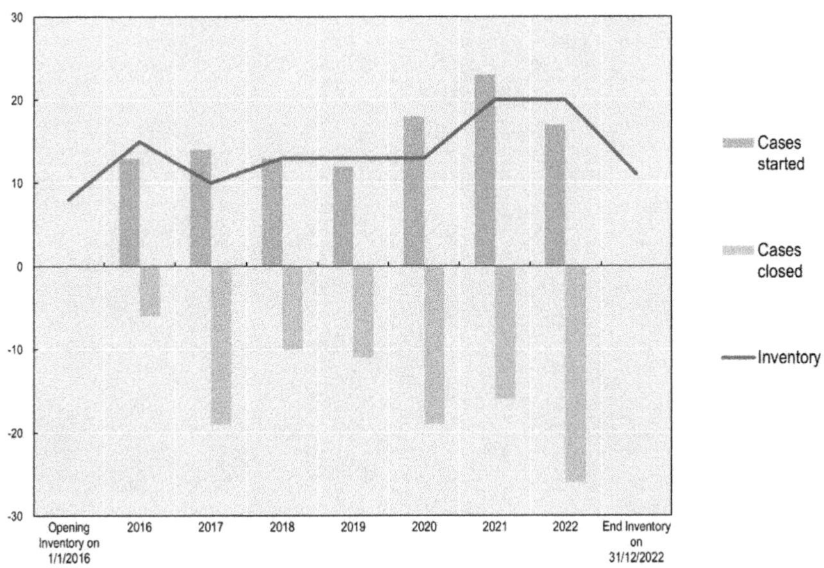

Source: OECD

Table 3. Overview of New Zealand's MAP caseload for 2022

Inventory for year 2022	Opening Inventory 1/1/2022	Cases started	Cases Closed	End Inventory 31/12/2022
Attribution/allocation cases	10	3	4	9
Other cases	10	14	22	2
Total	20	17	26	11

Source: OECD

Table 4. New Zealand's average time to resolve MAP cases in 2022

Cases resolved in year 2022	Pre-2016 cases		Post-2015 cases		All	
	Number of cases	**Average time**	**Number of cases**	**Average time** **Start to End**	**Number of cases**	**Average time**
Attribution / Allocation cases	0	N/A	4	8.53	4	8.53
Other cases	0	N/A	22	6.36	22	6.36
All cases	0	N/A	26	6.70	26	6.70

Source: OECD

Nigeria

Recent developments relating to MAP in Nigeria prior to 15 August 2023

Developments relating to MAP in the tax treaty network

- ECOWAS Supplementary Act undergoing the process of making it to enter into force. When in force, it will activate MAP with 14 member countries with effect from 1st January 2024.
- Signed an Avoidance of Double Taxation Agreement with Turkey on 20th October 2021, which is consistent with Action 14 Minimum Standard. The treaty has not entered into force.

Other developments relating to MAP

- Nigeria updated its MAP Guideline and MAP Profile in 2023.

Latest Action 14 Peer Review report

The stage 1 Simplified Peer Review report of Nigeria is expected to be published early 2024.

Tax treaty network of Nigeria

- 18 treaties, applicable to 31 jurisdictions (covering all treaties signed, although not necessarily in force)
- status of MLI: in force.

Table 1. State of play of Nigeria's tax treaty network

Treaties in line with the Action 14 Minimum Standard following MLI impact	Treaties where actions are ongoing to make them in line with the Action 14 Minimum Standard	Following impact/actions, remaining treaties that are not in line with Action 14 Minimum Standard
16	0	2

Source: OECD

Nigeria's MAP programme

Organisation of competent authority function

- 11 persons assisting the Competent Authority, comprising:
  - five heads of functions and six persons working on MAP cases:
    - out of those 11, six persons work on attribution/allocation cases and five persons work on other cases.
- contact persons for MAP requests:
  - Director, Tax Policy and Advisory Department & Authorized Competent Authority for MAP matters.

- Federal Inland Revenue Service, 3rd Floor, Revenue House Annex, 26 Sokode Crescent, Wuse Zone 5, Abuja, FCT, Nigeria. Email: acatreatiesandmap@firs.gov.ng
- for all MAP cases, please copy requests to: Head, Treaties & International Tax Policy Division, FIRS, 2nd Floor, Revenue House Annex, 26 Sokode Crescent, Wuse Zone 5, Abuja, FCT, Nigeria.
  Phone No: +2348025018750; +2348035512420; Email Address: kajesomo.kehinde@firs.gov.ng
- for specific MAP cases involving transfer pricing, the request should also be copied to: Head, International Tax Department 3rd Floor, FIRS Building 17B, Awolowo Road, Ikoyi, Lagos, Phone Nos: +2349070319922; +2348033093287; Email Address: ab.aliyu@firs.gov.ng.

Figure 1. Competent Authority Organisational Structure

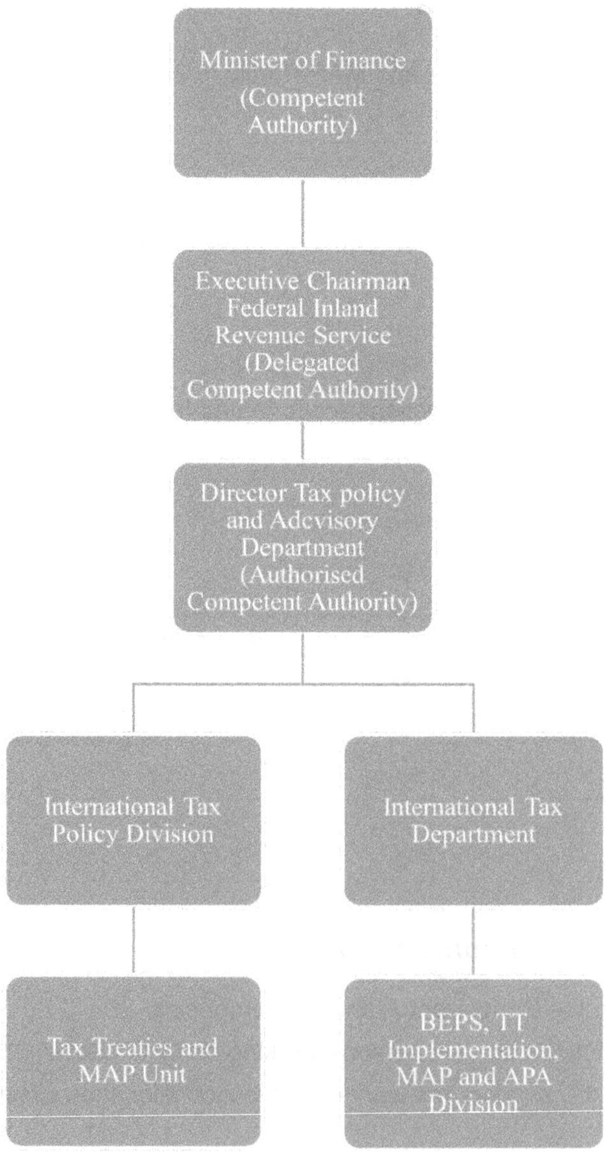

Source: OECD

Table 2. Guidance on the MAP process

MAP guidance	Guidelines on Mutual Administrative Procedure (MAP) in Nigeria, 23 May 2023	https://www.firs.gov.ng/treaty-related-guidelines-and-circulars/ (Section 4.5 to be referred to for form and content of a MAP request, including information requirements)
MAP profile	30 December 2016	https://www.oecd.org/tax/dispute/Nigeria-Dispute-Resolution-Profile.pdf

Overview of Nigeria's MAP Statistics for 2022

Please refer to https://www.oecd.org/tax/dispute/map-statistics-nigeria.pdf for details with respect to Nigeria's MAP Statistics.

Figure 2. Cases closed in 2022

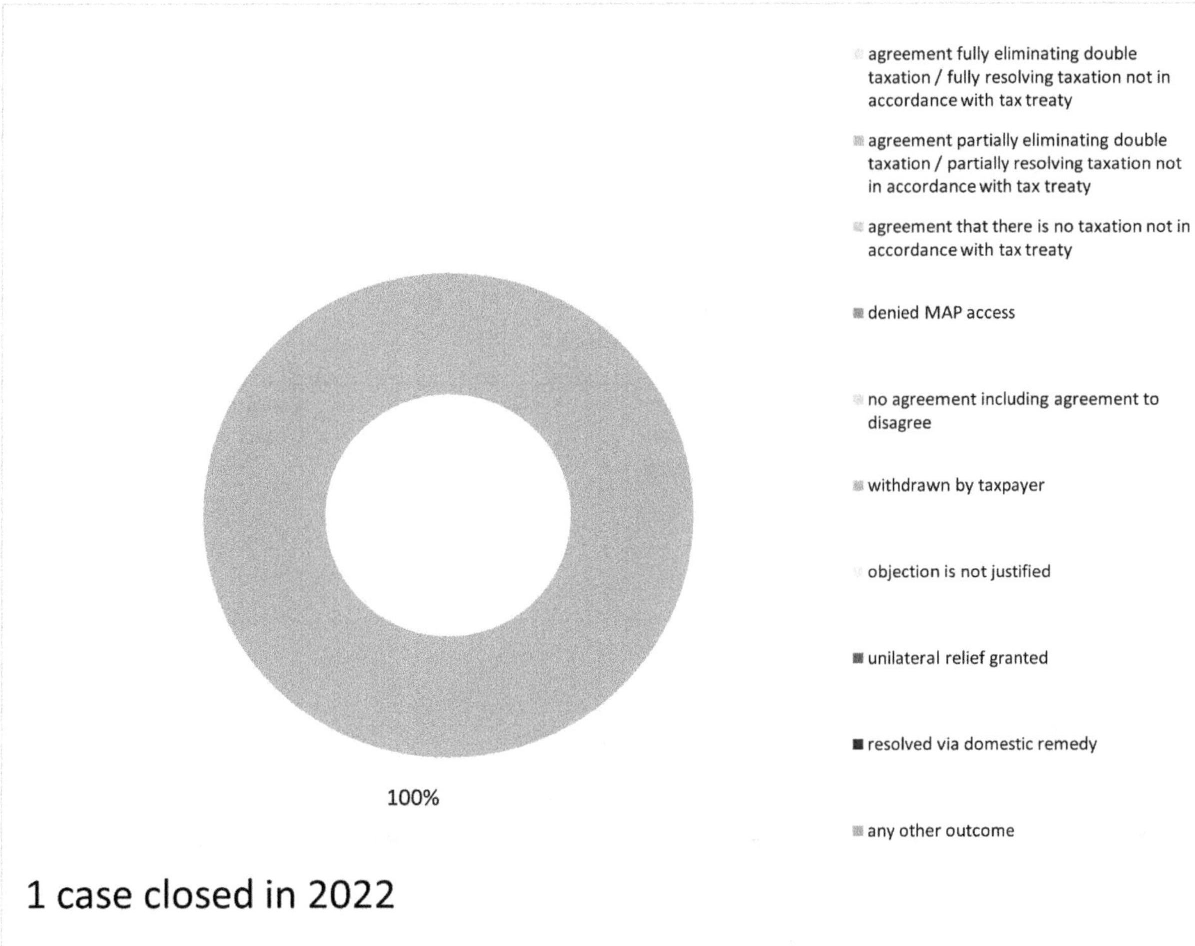

Source: OECD

Figure 3. Evolution of Nigeria's MAP caseload (2016-22)

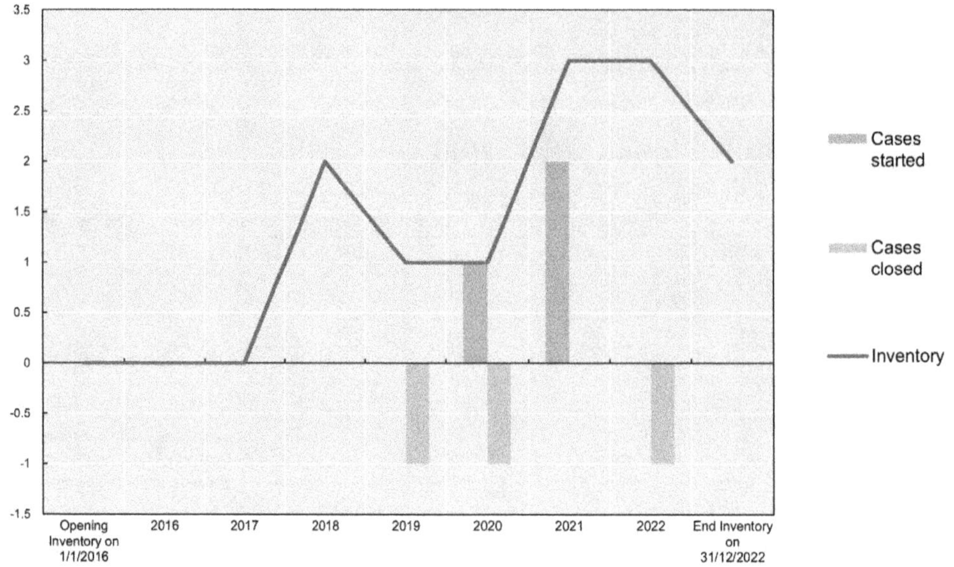

Source: OECD

Table 3. Overview of Nigeria's MAP caseload for 2022

Inventory for year 2022	Opening Inventory 1/1/2022	Cases started	Cases Closed	End Inventory 31/12/2022
Attribution/allocation cases	1	0	0	1
Other cases	2	0	1	1
Total	3	0	1	2

Source: OECD

Table 4. Nigeria's average time to resolve MAP cases in 2022

Cases resolved in year 2022	Pre-2016 cases		Post-2015 cases		All	
	Number of cases	**Average time**	**Number of cases**	**Average time** **Start to End**	**Number of cases**	**Average time**
Attribution / Allocation cases	0	N/A	0	N/A	0	N/A
Other cases	0	N/A	1	18.02	1	18.02
All cases	0	N/A	1	18.02	1	18.02

Source: OECD

North Macedonia (Republic of)

Recent developments relating to MAP in North Macedonia prior to 15 August 2023

Developments relating to MAP in the tax treaty network

- No developments were reported

Other developments relating to MAP

- No developments were reported

Latest Action 14 Peer Review report

The stage 1 Simplified Peer Review report of North Macedonia is expected to be published early 2024.

Tax treaty network of North Macedonia

- 50 treaties, applicable to 50 jurisdictions (covering all treaties signed, although not necessarily in force)
- status of MLI: signed.

Table 1. State of play of North Macedonia's tax treaty network

Treaties in line with the Action 14 Minimum Standard following MLI impact	Treaties where actions are ongoing to make them in line with the Action 14 Minimum Standard	Following impact/actions, remaining treaties that are not in line with Action 14 Minimum Standard
46	0	4

Source: OECD

North Macedonia's MAP programme

Organisation of competent authority function

- six persons:
    - one head of unit
    - four persons working on MAP cases.
- contact persons for MAP requests:
    - Public Revenue Office General Directorate
      Blvd. Kuzman Josifovski Pitu no. 1, 1000 Skopje, Republic of North Macedonia
      Tel: 00389 2 3 299 543 00389 76 445 471 e-mail: map@ujp.gov.mk.

Figure 1. Competent Authority Organisational Structure

Source: OECD

Table 2. Guidance on the MAP process

MAP guidance	No MAP guidance published	
MAP profile	*23 May 2023*	https://www.oecd.org/tax/dispute/north-macedonia-dispute-resolution-profile.pdf

Overview of North Macedonia's MAP Statistics for 2022

Please refer to https://www.oecd.org/tax/dispute/map-statistics-north-macedonia.pdf for details with respect to North Macedonia's MAP Statistics.

Cases closed in 2022

No MAP cases were closed by North Macedonia in 2022.

Figure 2. Evolution of North Macedonia's MAP caseload (2016-22)

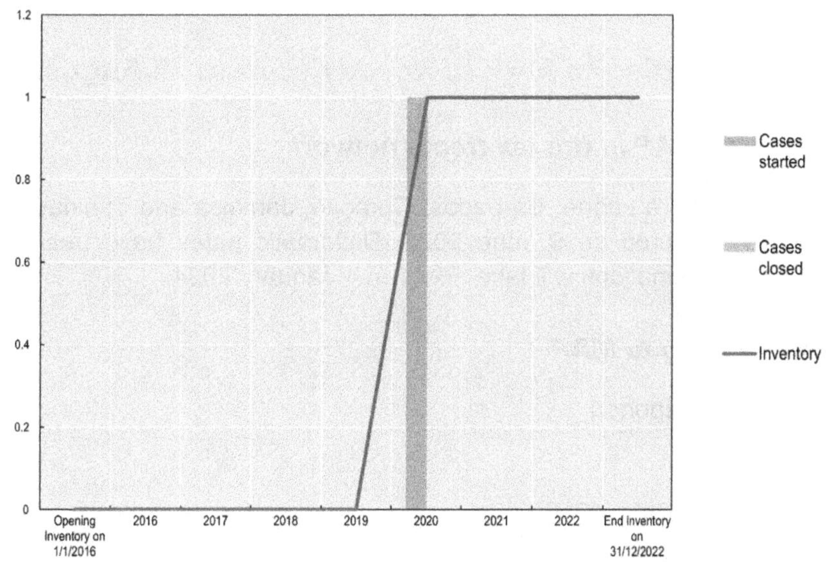

Source: OECD

Table 3. Overview of North Macedonia's MAP caseload for 2022

Inventory for year 2022	Opening Inventory 1/1/2022	Cases started	Cases Closed	End Inventory 31/12/2022
Attribution/allocation cases	0	0	0	0
Other cases	1	0	0	1
Total	1	0	0	1

Source: OECD

Table 4. North Macedonia's average time to resolve MAP cases in 2022

Cases resolved in year 2022	Pre-2016 cases		Post-2015 cases		All	
	Number of cases	**Average time**	**Number of cases**	**Average time** **Start to End**	**Number of cases**	**Average time**
Attribution / Allocation cases	0	N/A	0	N/A	0	N/A
Other cases	0	N/A	0	N/A	0	N/A
All cases	0	N/A	0	N/A	0	N/A

Source: OECD

Norway

Recent developments relating to MAP in Norway prior to 15 August 2023

Developments relating to MAP in the tax treaty network

- The tax treaties with Sierra Leone, Barbados, Curaçao, Jamaica and Trinidad and Tobago were terminated by Royal Decree on 9 June 2023. Diplomatic notes have been sent to all these jurisdictions and the terminations will take effect on 1 January 2024.

Other developments relating to MAP

- No developments were reported

Latest Action 14 Peer Review report

22 October 2020 - https://doi.org/10.1787/48127451-en

Tax treaty network of Norway

- 87 treaties, applicable to 95 jurisdictions (covering all treaties signed, although not necessarily in force)
- status of MLI: in force.

Table 1. State of play of Norway's tax treaty network

Treaties in line with the Action 14 Minimum Standard following MLI impact	Treaties where actions are ongoing to make them in line with the Action 14 Minimum Standard	Following impact/actions, remaining treaties that are not in line with Action 14 Minimum Standard
59	No information	No information

Source: OECD

Norway's MAP programme

Organisation of competent authority function

- 15 persons
- contact persons for MAP requests:
  - for attribution / allocation cases: The Norwegian Tax Administration, Large Business, Section MAP/APA P.O. Box 9200 Grønland | NO - 0134 Oslo
  - for attribution / allocation cases for taxpayers subject to the Norwegian Special Tax on Petroleum Income: Ministry of Finance, Tax Law Department P.O. Box 8008 Dep | NO – 0030 OSLO Tel: +47 22 24 44 31/33 / Email: postmottak@fin.dep.no
  - for other cases: either Ministry of Finance, Tax Law Department P.O. Box 8008 Dep. | NO – 0030 OSLO Tel: +47 22 24 44 31/33 / Email: postmottak@fin.dep.no or Directorate of

Taxes, Legal Department P.O. Box 9200 Grønland | NO – 0134 OSLO Tel.: (+47) 800 80 000 when calling from Norway. (+47) 22 07 70 00 when calling from abroad.

Figure 1. Competent Authority Organisational Structure

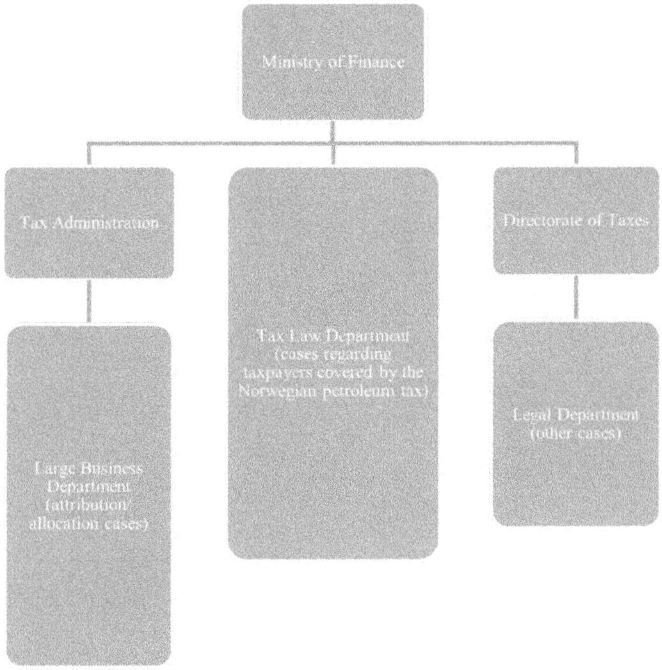

Source: OECD

Table 2. Guidance on the MAP process

MAP guidance	*Guide for the mutual agreement procedure pursuant to tax treaties (MAP),* 20 February 2019	https://www.regjeringen.no/contentassets/a91a5dd41bde46c88ed4dfc2bf724252/guide_for_the_mutual_agreementprocedure.pdf (Sections 3 and 4 to be referred to for form and content of a MAP request, including information requirements)
MAP profile	20 February 2019	https://www.oecd.org/tax/dispute/norway-dispute-resolution-profile.pdf

Overview of Norway's MAP Statistics for 2022

Please refer to https://www.oecd.org/tax/dispute/map-statistics-norway.pdf for details with respect to Norway's MAP Statistics.

Figure 2. Cases closed in 2022

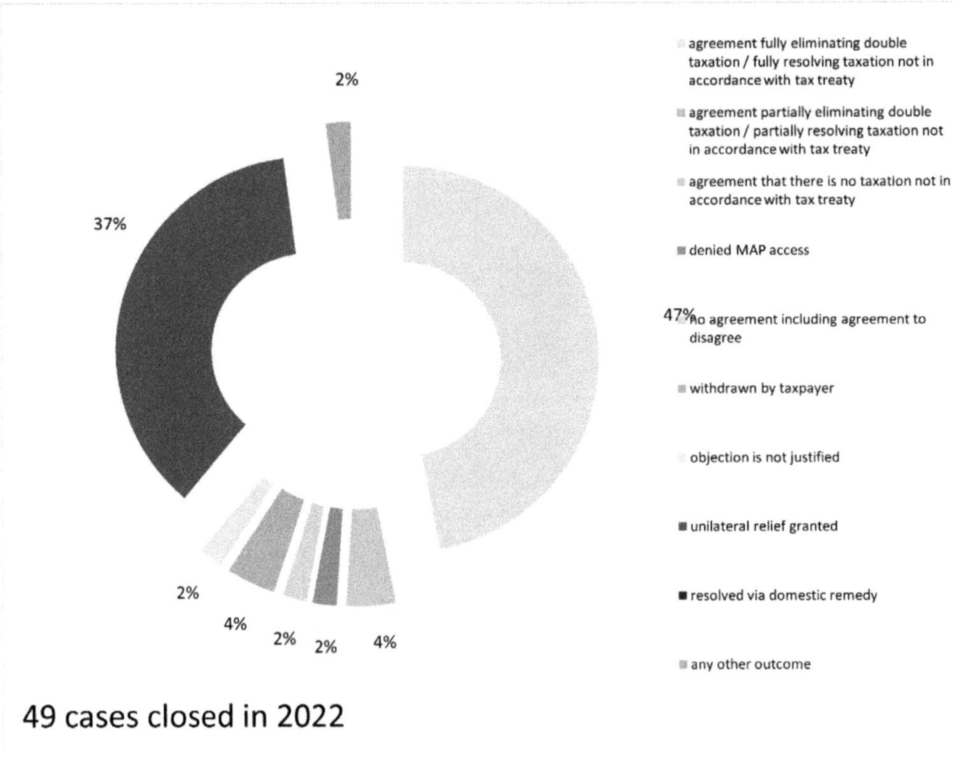

Source: OECD

Figure 3. Evolution of Norway's MAP caseload (2016-22)

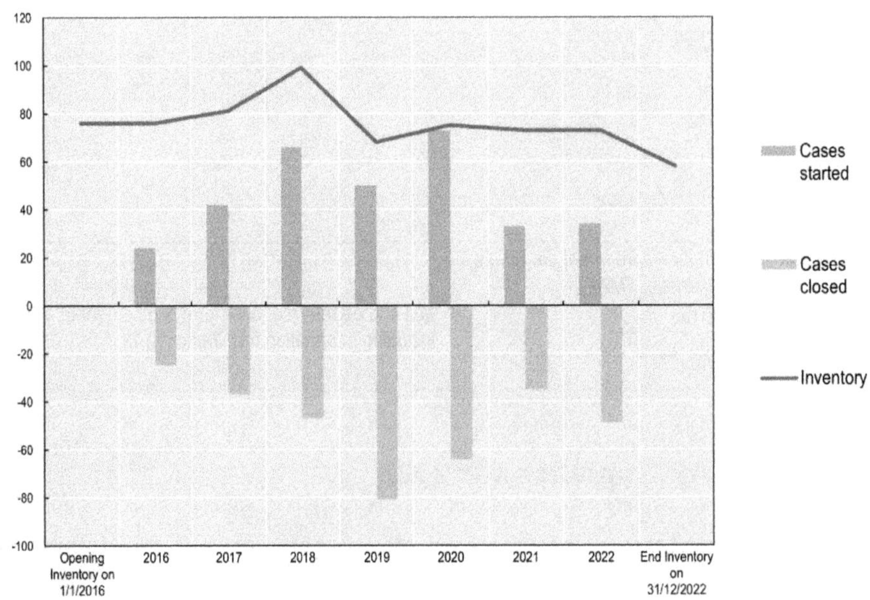

Source: OECD

Table 3. Overview of Norway's MAP caseload for 2022

Inventory for year 2022	Opening Inventory 1/1/2022	Cases started	Cases Closed	End Inventory 31/12/2022
Attribution/allocation cases	28	8	26	10
Other cases	45	26	23	48
Total	73	34	49	58

Source: OECD

Table 4. Norway's average time to resolve MAP cases in 2022

Cases resolved in year 2022	Pre-2016 cases		Post-2015 cases		All	
	Number of cases	**Average time**	**Number of cases**	**Average time** **Start to End**	**Number of cases**	**Average time**
Attribution / Allocation cases	0	N/A	26	20.19	26	20.19
Other cases	1	85.25	22	11.97	23	15.15
All cases	1	85.25	48	16.42	49	17.83

Source: OECD

Oman

Recent developments relating to MAP in Oman prior to 15 August 2023

Developments relating to MAP in the tax treaty network

- Entry into force of the tax treaty with Qatar in 2023.
- Signed tax treaty with Russia in 2023.
- Signed tax treaty with Egypt in 2023.

Other developments relating to MAP

- Oman did not provide the relevant information.

Latest Action 14 Peer Review report

13. September 2022 - https://doi.org/10.1787/30973512-en

Tax treaty network of Oman

- 38 treaties, applicable to 38 jurisdictions (covering all treaties signed, although not necessarily in force)
- status of MLI: in force.

Table 1. State of play of Oman's tax treaty network

Treaties in line with the Action 14 Minimum Standard following MLI impact	Treaties where actions are ongoing to make them in line with the Action 14 Minimum Standard	Following impact/actions, remaining treaties that are not in line with Action 14 Minimum Standard
25	1	12

Source: OECD

Oman's MAP programme

Organisation of competent authority function

- eight persons:
  - one head of unit
  - seven persons working on MAP cases (all of which work on other tasks as well).
- contact persons for MAP requests:
  - Ms. Wisal Al-Abduwani
    Director of international cooperation, Department Tax Authority, Oman, P.O.Box: 285, Postal Code: 100, E: wisal.abduwani@taxoman.gov.om T: +968-24746857.

Figure 1. Competent Authority Organisational Structure

Source: OECD

Table 2. Guidance on the MAP process

MAP guidance	Guidelines on the Mutual Agreement Procedure, 23 February 2022	https://tms.taxoman.gov.om/portal/web/taxportal/manual-guide/-/document_library/jRcw40CZIm2d/view_file/2529383 (Sections "Making a MAP request" and "Minimum information required for a MAP request" to be referred to for form and content of a MAP request, including information requirements)
MAP profile	28 February 2022	https://www.oecd.org/tax/dispute/oman-dispute-resolution-profile.pdf

Overview of Oman's MAP Statistics for 2022

Please refer to https://www.oecd.org/tax/dispute/map-statistics-oman.pdf for details with respect to Oman's MAP Statistics.

Cases closed in 2022

No MAP cases were closed by Oman in 2022.

Figure 2. Evolution of Oman's MAP caseload (2017-22)

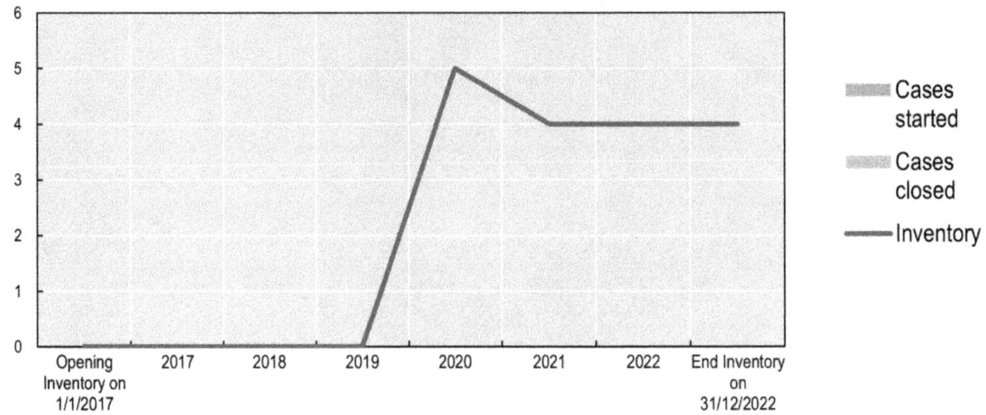

Source: OECD

Table 3. Overview of Oman's MAP caseload for 2022

Inventory for year 2022	Opening Inventory 1/1/2022	Cases started	Cases Closed	End Inventory 31/12/2022
Attribution/allocation cases	4	0	0	4
Other cases	0	0	0	0
Total	4	0	0	4

Source: OECD

Table 4. Oman's average time to resolve MAP cases in 2022

Cases resolved in year 2022	Pre-2016 cases		Post-2015 cases		All	
	Number of cases	**Average time**	**Number of cases**	**Average time** **Start to End**	**Number of cases**	**Average time**
Attribution / Allocation cases	0	N/A	0	N/A	0	N/A
Other cases	0	N/A	0	N/A	0	N/A
All cases	0	N/A	0	N/A	0	N/A

Source: OECD

Pakistan

Recent developments relating to MAP in Pakistan prior to 15 August 2023

Developments relating to MAP in the tax treaty network

- Pakistan did not provide the relevant information.

Other developments relating to MAP

- Pakistan did not provide the relevant information.

Latest Action 14 Peer Review report

The stage 1 Simplified Peer Review report of Pakistan is expected to be published early 2024.

Tax treaty network of Pakistan

- 66 treaties, applicable to 66 jurisdictions (covering all treaties signed, although not necessarily in force)
- status of MLI: in force.

Table 1. State of play of Pakistan's tax treaty network

Treaties in line with the Action 14 Minimum Standard following MLI impact	Treaties where actions are ongoing to make them in line with the Action 14 Minimum Standard	Following impact/actions, remaining treaties that are not in line with Action 14 Minimum Standard
54	No information	No information

Source: OECD

Pakistan's MAP programme

Organisation of competent authority function

- two persons (both of which on other tasks as well)
- contact persons for MAP requests:
  - Mr. Sajidullah Siddiqui, Director General (International Tax Operations)
    FBR House, Constitution Avenue, G-5, Islamabad-44000, Pakistan.
    Tel. No. +92-51-9202771 Fax No. +92-51-9219558 ittaxes@fbr.gov.pk.

Figure 1. Competent Authority Organisational Structure

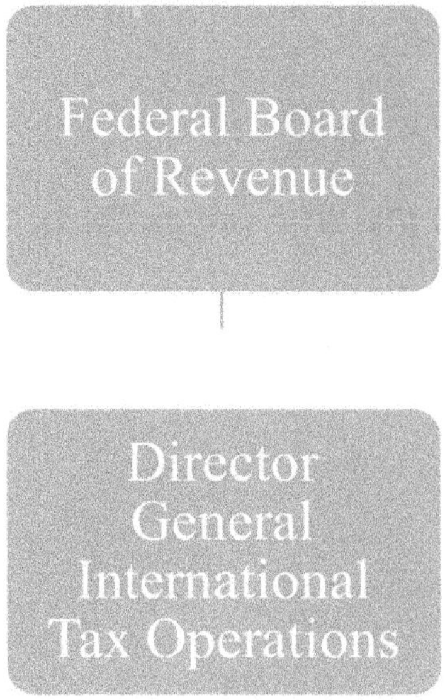

Source: OECD

Table 2. Guidance on the MAP process

MAP guidance	*RULE 19D: APPLICATION FOR INITIATION OF MUTUAL AGREEMENT PROCEDURE (MAP),* 2002	https://www.fbr.gov.pk/m-a-p/132245/132255 (Section "RULE 19F: FORM OF APPLICATION FOR INITIATION OF MAP PROCEEDINGS" to be referred to for form and content of a MAP request, including information requirements)
MAP profile	23 February 2023	https://www.oecd.org/tax/dispute/pakistan-dispute-resolution-profile.pdf

Overview of Pakistan's MAP Statistics for 2022

Please refer to https://www.oecd.org/tax/dispute/map-statistics-pakistan.pdf for details with respect to Pakistan's MAP Statistics.

Cases closed in 2022

No MAP cases were closed by Pakistan in 2022.

Figure 2. Evolution of Pakistan's MAP caseload (2016-22)

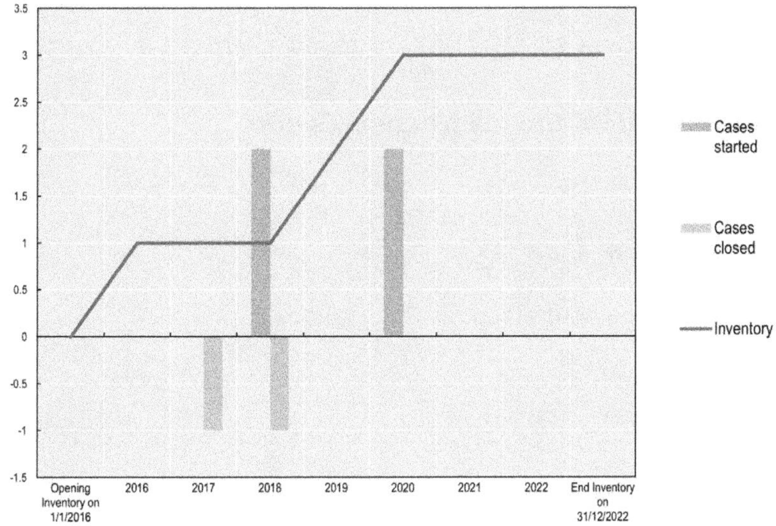

Source: OECD

Table 3. Overview of Pakistan's MAP caseload for 2022

Inventory for year 2022	Opening Inventory 1/1/2022	Cases started	Cases Closed	End Inventory 31/12/2022
Attribution/allocation cases	1	0	0	1
Other cases	2	0	0	2
Total	3	0	0	3

Source: OECD

Table 4. Pakistan's average time to resolve MAP cases in 2022

Cases resolved in year 2022	Pre-2016 cases		Post-2015 cases		All	
	Number of cases	**Average time**	**Number of cases**	**Average time** **Start to End**	**Number of cases**	**Average time**
Attribution / Allocation cases	0	N/A	0	N/A	0	N/A
Other cases	0	N/A	0	N/A	0	N/A
All cases	0	N/A	0	N/A	0	N/A

Source: OECD

Panama

Recent developments relating to MAP in Panama prior to 15 August 2023

Developments relating to MAP in the tax treaty network

- No developments were reported

Other developments relating to MAP

- Panama is currently working on drafting MAP guidance.

Latest Action 14 Peer Review report

Panama is yet to be peer reviewed under Action 14.

Tax treaty network of Panama

- 17 treaties, applicable to 17 jurisdictions (covering all treaties signed, although not necessarily in force)
- status of MLI: in force.

Table 1. State of play of Panama's tax treaty network

Treaties in line with the Action 14 Minimum Standard following MLI impact	Treaties where actions are ongoing to make them in line with the Action 14 Minimum Standard	Following impact/actions, remaining treaties that are not in line with Action 14 Minimum Standard
16	0	1

Source: OECD

Panama's MAP programme

Organisation of competent authority function

- four persons (all of whom work on other tasks as well)
- contact persons for MAP requests:
  - dgimap@mef.gob.pa.

Figure 1. Competent Authority Organisational Structure

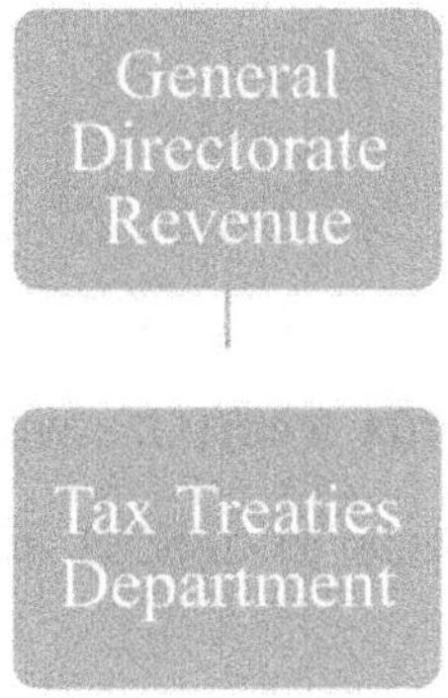

Source: OECD

Table 2. Guidance on the MAP process

MAP guidance	No MAP guidance published	-
MAP profile	30 January 2017	https://www.oecd.org/tax/dispute/panama-dispute-resolution-profile.pdf

Overview of Panama's MAP Statistics for 2022

Panama did not report any MAP cases in its 2022 MAP Statistics.

Please refer to https://www.oecd.org/tax/dispute/map-statistics-panama.pdf for details with respect to Panama's MAP Statistics.

Papua New Guinea

Recent developments relating to MAP in Papua New Guinea prior to 15 August 2023

Developments relating to MAP in the tax treaty network

- Papua New Guinea (PNG) anticipates to deposit instrument of ratification for the MAAC by 31/8/2023.

Other developments relating to MAP

- PNG MAP Guidance finalised. Guidance will be available on Internal Revenue Commission (IRC) website by 31/8/2023.

Latest Action 14 Peer Review report

Papua New Guinea is yet to be peer reviewed under Action 14.

Tax treaty network of Papua New Guinea

- 10 treaties, applicable to 10 jurisdictions (covering all treaties signed, although not necessarily in force)
- Status of MLI: signed

Table 1. State of play of Papua New Guinea's tax treaty network

Treaties in line with the Action 14 Minimum Standard following MLI impact	Treaties where actions are ongoing to make them in line with the Action 14 Minimum Standard	Following impact/actions, remaining treaties that are not in line with Action 14 Minimum Standard
5	No Information	No Information

Source: OECD

Papua New Guinea's MAP programme

Organisation of competent authority function

- Two persons:
  - one head of unit
  - one person working on MAP cases (among which that same person works on other tasks as well). The same person works on attribution/allocation cases as well as other cases.
- Contact persons for MAP requests:
  - Mr Elijah Titus, Assistant Commissioner
    Legal Services Division, Internal Revenue Commission

9th Floor, Revenue Haus, Downtown Port Moresby National Capital District, Papua New Guinea
Phone: (+675) 322 6874 | Fax: (+675) 321 7962 | Email: tituse@irc.gov.pg

Figure 1. Competent Authority Organisational Structure

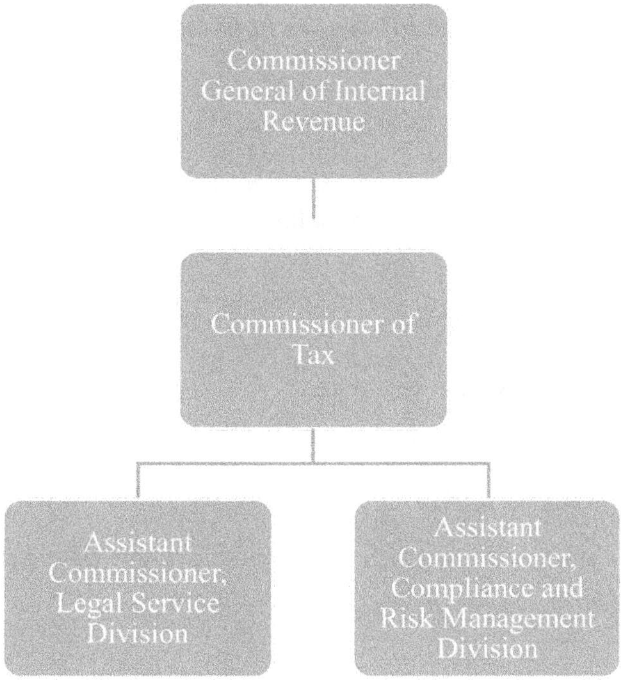

Source: OECD

Table 2. Guidance on the MAP process

MAP guidance	Finalised. Guidance will be posted on IRC website soon.	-
MAP profile	16 October 2017	https://www.oecd.org/tax/dispute/papua-new-guinea-dispute-resolution-profile.pdf

Overview of Papua New Guinea's MAP Statistics for 2022

Papua New Guinea did not report any MAP cases in its 2022 MAP Statistics.

Please refer to https://www.oecd.org/tax/dispute/map-statistics-papua-new-guinea.pdf for details with respect to Papua New Guinea's MAP Statistics.

Paraguay

Recent developments relating to MAP in Paraguay prior to 15 August 2023

Developments relating to MAP in the tax treaty network

- Paraguay did not provide the relevant information.

Other developments relating to MAP

- Paraguay did not provide the relevant information.

Latest Action 14 Peer Review report

Paraguay is yet to be peer reviewed under Action 14.

Tax treaty network of Paraguay

- seven treaties, applicable to seven jurisdictions (covering all treaties signed, although not necessarily in force).
- status of MLI: not signed.

Table 1. State of play of Paraguay's tax treaty network

Treaties in line with the Action 14 Minimum Standard following MLI impact	Treaties where actions are ongoing to make them in line with the Action 14 Minimum Standard	Following impact/actions, remaining treaties that are not in line with Action 14 Minimum Standard
2	No information	No information

Source: OECD

Paraguay's MAP programme

Organisation of competent authority function

- contact persons for MAP requests:
  - Ministerio de Hacienda, Chile 252, Asuncion – Paraguay.

Competent Authority Organisational Structure

Paraguay did not provide the relevant information.

Table 2. Guidance on the MAP process

MAP guidance	Paraguay did not provide the relevant information.	
MAP profile	27 June 2017	https://www.oecd.org/tax/dispute/Paraguay-Dispute-Resolution-Profile.pdf

Overview of Paraguay's MAP Statistics for 2022

Paraguay did not declare its MAP Statistics for 2022.

Peru

Recent developments relating to MAP in Peru prior to 15 August 2023

Developments relating to MAP in the tax treaty network

- Peru and Colombia have signed a new tax treaty (Annex I of the Convention to Standardize the Tax Treatment established in Conventions for the Avoidance of Double Taxation signed between the States that are Parties to the Framework Agreement of the Pacific Alliance). It entered into force on 2nd, July, 2023 and will has effect from January 1st, 2024. It has a limited scope of application (certain items of income obtained by recognised pension funds).

Other developments relating to MAP

- No developments were reported

Latest Action 14 Peer Review report

Peru is yet to be peer reviewed under Action 14.

Tax treaty network of Peru

- 10 treaties, applicable to 11 jurisdictions (covering all treaties signed, although not necessarily in force)
- status of MLI: signed.

Table 1. State of play of Peru's tax treaty network

Treaties in line with the Action 14 Minimum Standard following MLI impact	Treaties where actions are ongoing to make them in line with the Action 14 Minimum Standard	Following impact/actions, remaining treaties that are not in line with Action 14 Minimum Standard
6	3	1

Source: OECD

Peru's MAP programme

Organisation of competent authority function

- five persons:
  - one head of unit
  - four persons working on MAP cases (all of which work on other tasks as well).
- contact persons for MAP requests:
  - Peruvian competent authority: Mr. Luis Enrique Vera Castillo, National Superintendent of the National Superintendence of Customs and Tax Administration (SUNAT)

E-mail: map-peru@sunat.gob.pe

- Point of contact at SUNAT: Mr. Carlos Rojas Chávez, Strategies Supervisor

  E-mail: map-peru@sunat.gob.pe; crojas4@sunat.gob.pe

  Phone number: +511 6343300 – Ext: 23436.

Figure 1. Competent Authority Organisational Structure

Source: OECD

Table 2. Guidance on the MAP process

MAP guidance	No MAP guidance published	-
MAP profile	13 January 2022	https://www.oecd.org/tax/dispute/peru-dispute-resolution-profile.pdf

Overview of Peru's MAP Statistics for 2022

Please refer to https://www.oecd.org/tax/dispute/map-statistics-peru.pdf for details with respect to Peru's MAP Statistics.

Cases closed in 2022

No MAP cases were closed by Peru in 2022.

Figure 2. Evolution of Peru's MAP caseload (2017-22)

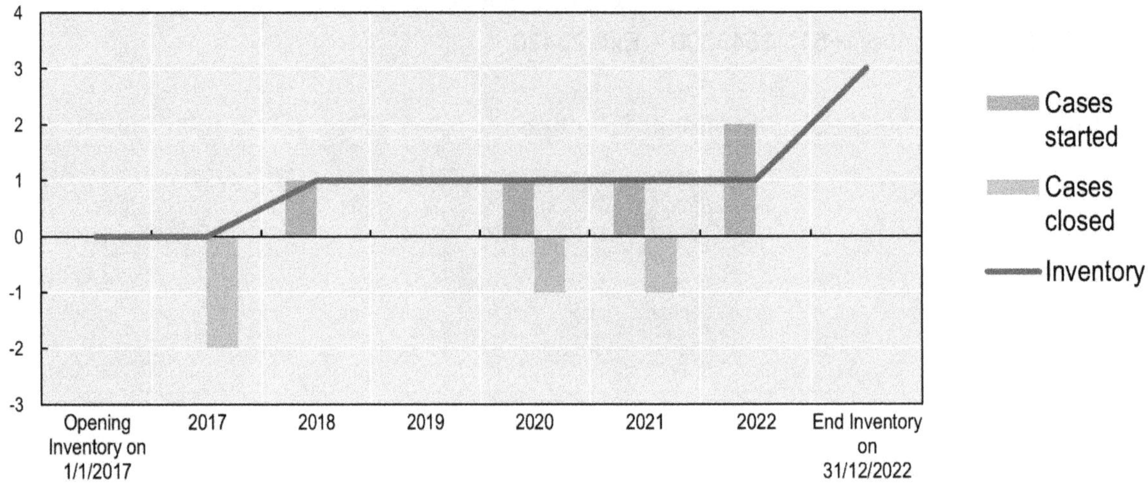

Source: OECD

Table 3. Overview of Peru's MAP caseload for 2022

Inventory for year 2022	Opening Inventory 1/1/2022	Cases started	Cases Closed	End Inventory 31/12/2022
Attribution/allocation cases	0	2	0	2
Other cases	1	0	0	1
Total	1	2	0	3

Source: OECD

Table 4. Peru's average time to resolve MAP cases in 2022

Cases resolved in year 2022	Pre-2016 cases		Post-2015 cases		All	
	Number of cases	**Average time**	**Number of cases**	Average time Start to End	Number of cases	**Average time**
Attribution / Allocation cases	0	N/A	0	N/A	0	N/A
Other cases	0	N/A	0	N/A	0	N/A
All cases	0	N/A	0	N/A	0	N/A

Source: OECD

Poland

Recent developments relating to MAP in Poland prior to 15 August 2023

Developments relating to MAP in the tax treaty network

- Entry into force of the new tax treaties with Georgia and Malaysia in 2023 (effective in 2024).

Other developments relating to MAP

- MAP guidance updated in 2023.

Latest Action 14 Peer Review report

22 October 2020 - https://doi.org/10.1787/ea220bff-en

Tax treaty network of Poland

- 86 treaties, applicable to 87 jurisdictions (covering all treaties signed, although not necessarily in force)
- status of MLI: in force.

Table 1. State of play of Poland's tax treaty network

Treaties in line with the Action 14 Minimum Standard following MLI impact	Treaties where actions are ongoing to make them in line with the Action 14 Minimum Standard	Following impact/actions, remaining treaties that are not in line with Action 14 Minimum Standard
66	3	18

Source: OECD

Poland's MAP programme

Organisation of competent authority function

- 14 persons:
  - two heads of unit
  - 12 persons working on MAP cases (among which four persons work on other tasks as well):
    - Eight persons work on attribution/allocation cases and four persons work on other cases.
- contact persons for MAP requests:
  - MINISTRY OF FINANCE ul. Świętokrzyska 12 00-916 Warsaw Poland
  - for attribution / allocation cases: Mr Konrad Szpadzik

    Deputy Director of Department for Large Business National Revenue Administration

    tel.: +48 22 694 48 87 fax: + 48 22 694 49 87 e-mail: konrad.szpadzik@mf.gov.pl

- for other cases: Income Taxes Department

  tel.: +48 22 694 33 26 fax: +48 22 694 33 31 e-mail: sekretariat.dd@mf.gov.pl

- for MAP under art. 25(3) of DTC: Ms Joanna Węgrzyn, Deputy Director of Tax Policy Department

  tel.: + 48 22 694 54 05, e-mail: joanna.wegrzyn@mf.gov.pl

  Mr Marcin Lachowicz, Director of Tax Policy Department

  tel.: +48 22 694 38 86, e-mail: marcin.lachowicz@mf.gov.pl

  Mr Artur Soboń, Secretary of State

  tel.: +48 22 694 32 02, e-mail: sekretariat.sekretarzastanu4@mf.gov.pl.

Figure 1. Competent Authority Organisational Structure

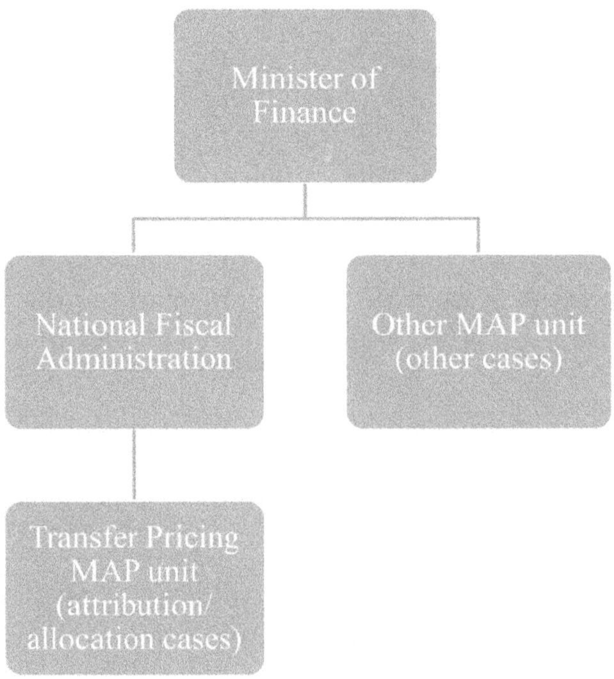

Source: OECD

Table 2. Guidance on the MAP process

MAP guidance	For attribution / allocation cases: Procedura wzajemnego porozumiewania się (MAP); 13 July 2023 For other cases: Procedury rozstrzygania sporów dotyczących podwójnego opodatkowania w sprawach indywidualnych (MAP i DRM); 13 July 2023	https://www.podatki.gov.pl/ceny-transferowe/procedury-map-i-apa-statystyki/procedura-wzajemnego-porozumiewania-sie-map/ (Section II. to be referred to for form and content of a MAP request, including information requirements) https://www.podatki.gov.pl/podatkowa-wspolpraca-miedzynarodowa/procedury-rozstrzygania-sporow-dotyczacych-podwojnego-opodatkowania-w-sprawach-indywidualnych/ (Section I to be referred to for form and content of a MAP request, including information requirements).
MAP profile	27 July 2023	https://www.oecd.org/tax/dispute/Poland-Dispute-Resolution-Profile.pdf

Overview of Poland's MAP Statistics for 2022

Please refer to https://www.oecd.org/tax/dispute/map-statistics-poland.pdf for details with respect to Poland's MAP Statistics.

Figure 2. Cases closed in 2022

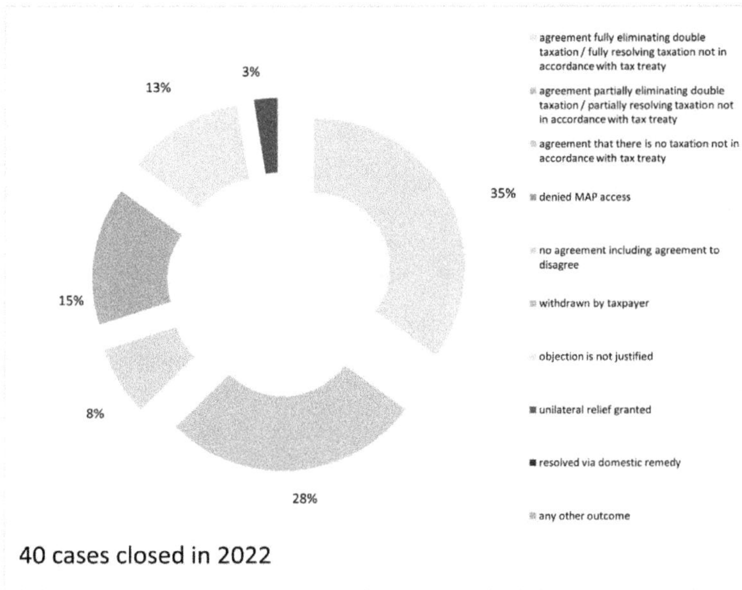

Source: OECD

Figure 3. Evolution of Poland's MAP caseload (2016-22)

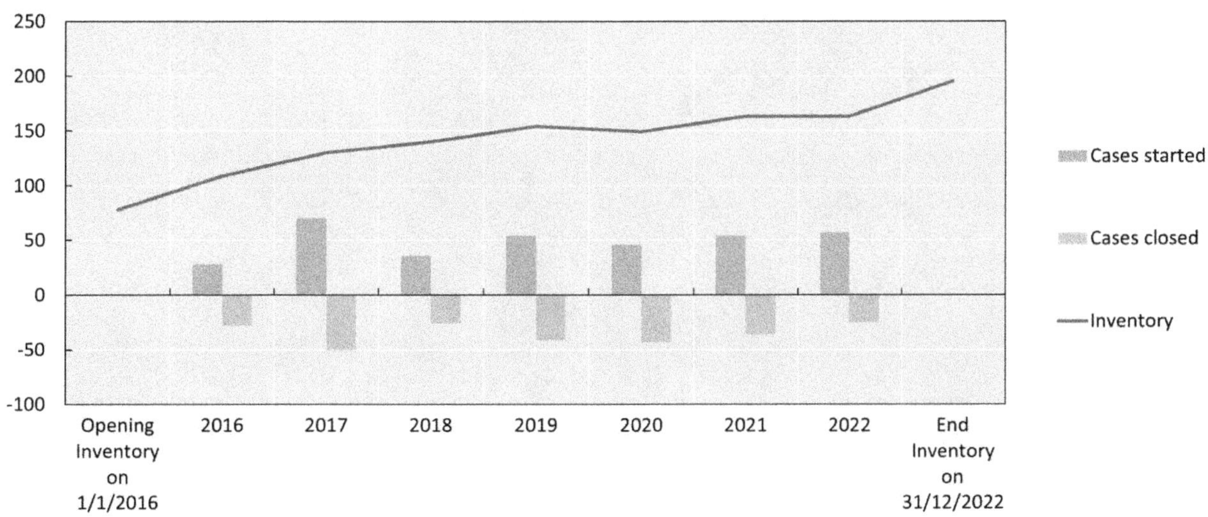

Source: OECD

Table 3. Overview of Poland's MAP caseload for 2022

Inventory for year 2022	Opening Inventory 1/1/2022	Cases started	Cases Closed	End Inventory 31/12/2022
Attribution/allocation cases	80	17	11	86
Other cases	83	40	14	109
Total	163	57	25	195

Source: OECD

Table 4. Poland's average time to resolve MAP cases in 2022

Cases resolved in year 2022	Pre-2016 cases		Post-2015 cases		All	
	Number of cases	**Average time**	**Number of cases**	**Average time** **Start to End**	**Number of cases**	**Average time**
Attribution / Allocation cases	1	3.55	10	31.9	11	29.32
Other cases	2	112.09	12	19.81	14	32.99
All cases	3	75.91	22	25.3	25	31.38

Source: OECD

Portugal

Recent developments relating to MAP in Portugal prior to 15 August 2023

Developments relating to MAP in the tax treaty network

- Entry into force of the tax treaty with Timor Leste on 12 October 2022.

Other developments relating to MAP

- No developments were reported

Latest Action 14 Peer Review report

15 April 2021 - https://doi.org/10.1787/b7f3e217-en

Tax treaty network of Portugal

- 81 treaties, applicable to 81 jurisdictions (covering all treaties signed, although not necessarily in force)
- status of MLI: in force.

Table 1. State of play of Portugal's tax treaty network

Treaties in line with the Action 14 Minimum Standard following MLI impact	Treaties where actions are ongoing to make them in line with the Action 14 Minimum Standard	Following impact/actions, remaining treaties that are not in line with Action 14 Minimum Standard
63	16	1

Source: OECD

Portugal's MAP programme

Organisation of competent authority function

- nine persons:
  - one Head of Department
  - one head of unit
  - seven persons working on MAP:
    - of which, five persons work on attribution/allocation cases and two persons work on other cases.
- contact persons for MAP requests:
  - Ministro das Finanças / Diretora Geral da Autoridade Tributária e Aduaneira
    Direção de Serviços de Relações Internacionais (DSRI)

Address: Av. Eng. Duarte Pacheco, nº 28- 4º andar, 1099-013 Lisboa
Phone: (+351) 213834426 Fax: (+351) 213834414/ Email address: dsri@at.gov.pt.

Figure 1. Competent Authority Organisational Structure

Source: OECD

Table 2. Guidance on the MAP process

MAP guidance	*Mutual Agreement Procedure Guidelines*, December 2017	https://info.portaldasfinancas.gov.pt/pt/docs/Conteudos_1pagina/Documents/Mutual_Agreement_Procedure.pdf (Section 4 to be referred to for form and content of a MAP request, including information requirements)
MAP profile	06 April 2018	https://www.oecd.org/tax/dispute/portugal-dispute-resolution-profile.pdf

Overview of Portugal's MAP Statistics for 2022

Please refer to https://www.oecd.org/tax/dispute/map-statistics-portugal.pdf for details with respect to Portugal's MAP Statistics.

Figure 2. Cases closed in 2022

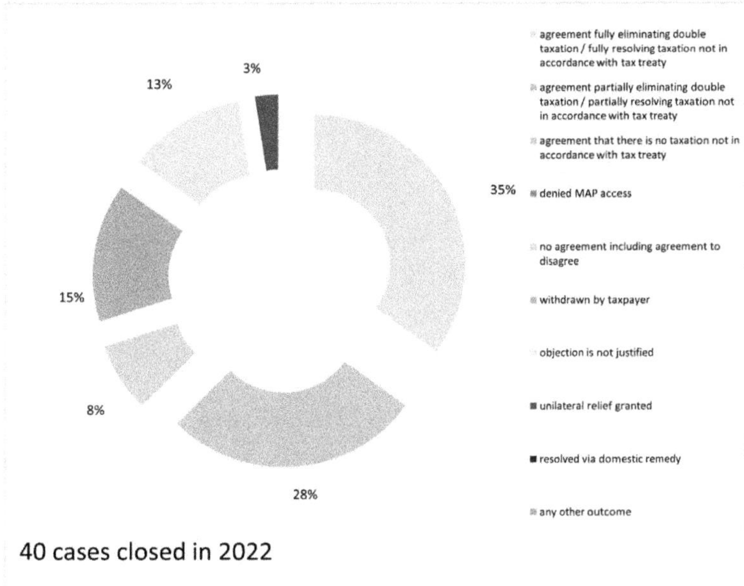

Source: OECD

Figure 3. Evolution of Portugal's MAP caseload (2016-22)

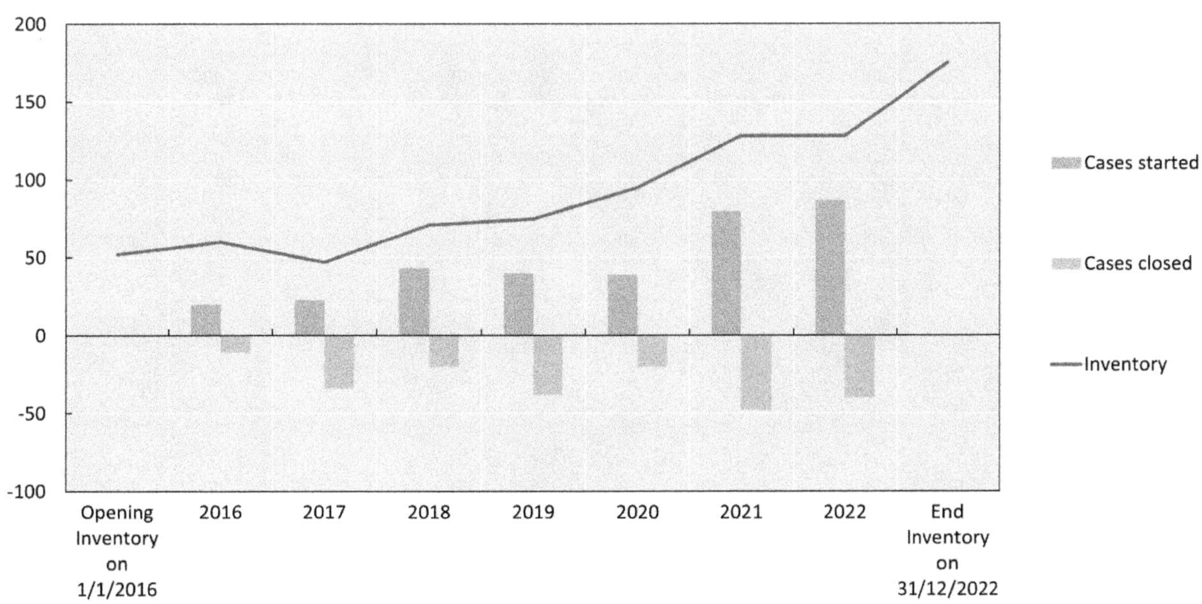

Source: OECD

Table 3. Overview of Portugal's MAP caseload for 2022

Inventory for year 2022	Opening Inventory 1/1/2022	Cases started	Cases Closed	End Inventory 31/12/2022
Attribution/allocation cases	65	28	5	88
Other cases	63	59	35	87
Total	128	87	40	175

Source: OECD

Table 4. Portugal's average time to resolve MAP cases in 2022

Cases resolved in year 2022	Pre-2016 cases		Post-2015 cases		All	
	Number of cases	**Average time**	**Number of cases**	**Average time** **Start to End**	**Number of cases**	**Average time**
Attribution / Allocation cases	0	N/A	5	29.02	5	29.02
Other cases	0	N/A	35	11.42	35	11.42
All cases	0	N/A	40	13.62	40	13.62

Source: OECD

Qatar

Recent developments relating to MAP in Qatar prior to 15 August 2023

Developments relating to MAP in the tax treaty network

- In 2023, the tax conventions between Qatar and Egypt and between Qatar and Uzbekistan have been signed.

Other developments relating to MAP

- Qatar will publish a manual on bilateral advance pricing arrangement, based on OECD (2022), Bilateral Advance Pricing Arrangement Manual. OECD Publishing, Paris.

Latest Action 14 Peer Review report

13 September 2023 - https://doi.org/10.1787/0e20fb46-en

Tax treaty network of Qatar

- 91 treaties, applicable to 91 jurisdictions (covering all treaties signed, although not necessarily in force)
- status of MLI: in force.

Table 1. State of play of Qatar's tax treaty network

Treaties in line with the Action 14 Minimum Standard following MLI impact	Treaties where actions are ongoing to make them in line with the Action 14 Minimum Standard	Following impact/actions, remaining treaties that are not in line with Action 14 Minimum Standard
69	13	9

Source: OECD

Qatar's MAP programme

Organisation of competent authority function

- 11 persons:
  - 1 Director – 1 Deputy Director - 1 head of Unit
  - 8 persons working on MAP cases
    - Where applicable,3 persons work on attribution/allocation cases and 5 persons work on other cases
- contact persons for MAP requests:
  - Primary contact: Mrs. Bodour Yousef Al Baker,
    Director of the Tax Treaty and International Cooperation (TTIC) Department,

General Tax Authority of the State of Qatar,
email: b.albakeri@gta.gov.qa and TTIC@gta.gov.qa

- Secondary contact: Mr. Yousuf Buhaddoud, Deputy Director of the TTIC Department, email: y.albuhadoud@gta.gov.qa

  Mr. Abdulla Al'Sulaiti, Head of Unit (MAP cases, BAPAs programs, MAP statistics), email: aaalsulaiti@gta.gov.qa

  Mrs. Fatima Al'Taweel, Tax Specialist (MAP cases, BAPAs programs, MAP statistics), email: f.altweel@gta.gov.qa

Figure 1. Competent Authority Organisational Structure

Source: OECD

Table 2. Guidance on the MAP process

MAP guidance	Manual on Mutual Agreement Procedures, January 2021	https://gta.gov.qa/MANUAL-ON-MUTUAL-AGREEMENT-PROCEDURE (Section 7.1 to be referred to for form and content of a MAP request, including information requirements)
	Web page	https://www.gta.gov.qa/en/mutual-agreement-procedure/
MAP profile	8 November 2021	https://www.oecd.org/tax/dispute/qatar-dispute-resolution-profile.pdf

Overview of Qatar's MAP Statistics for 2022

Please refer to https://www.oecd.org/tax/dispute/map-statistics-qatar.pdf for details with respect to Qatar's MAP Statistics.

Cases closed in 2022

No MAP cases were closed by Qatar in 2022.

Figure 2. Evolution of Qatar's MAP caseload (2017-22)

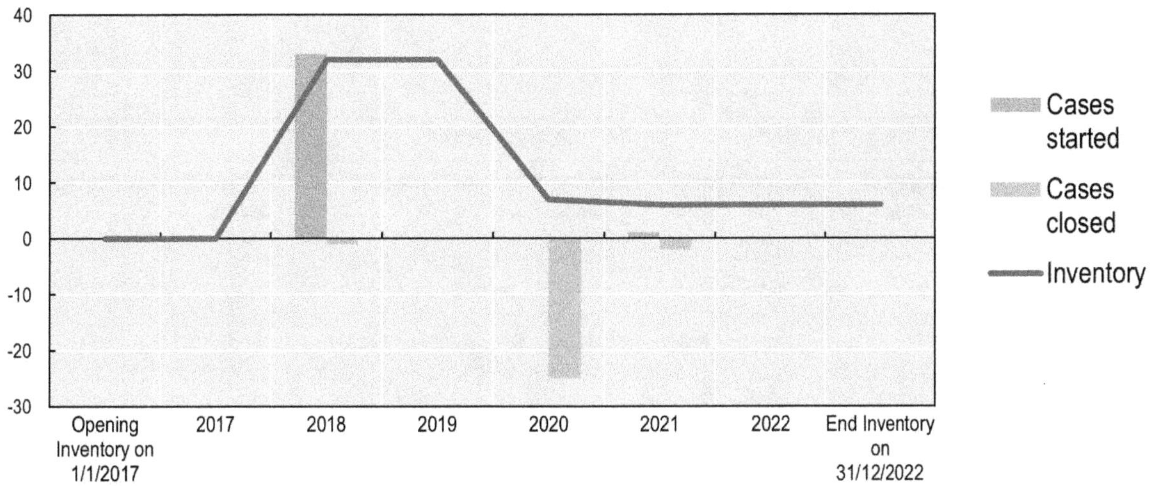

Source: OECD

Table 3. Overview of Qatar's MAP caseload for 2022

Inventory for year 2022	Opening Inventory 1/1/2022	Cases started	Cases Closed	End Inventory 31/12/2022
Attribution/allocation cases	0	0	0	0
Other cases	6	0	0	6
Total	6	0	0	6

Source: OECD

Table 4. Qatar's average time to resolve MAP cases in 2022

<table>
<tr><th rowspan="3">Cases resolved in year 2022</th><th colspan="2">Pre-2016 cases</th><th colspan="2">Post-2015 cases</th><th colspan="2">All</th></tr>
<tr><th rowspan="2">Number of cases</th><th rowspan="2">Average time</th><th rowspan="2">Number of cases</th><th>Average time</th><th rowspan="2">Number of cases</th><th rowspan="2">Average time</th></tr>
<tr><th>Start to End</th></tr>
<tr><td>Attribution / Allocation cases</td><td>0</td><td>N/A</td><td>0</td><td>N/A</td><td>0</td><td>N/A</td></tr>
<tr><td>Other cases</td><td>0</td><td>N/A</td><td>0</td><td>N/A</td><td>0</td><td>N/A</td></tr>
<tr><td>All cases</td><td>0</td><td>N/A</td><td>0</td><td>N/A</td><td>0</td><td>N/A</td></tr>
</table>

Source: OECD

Romania

Recent developments relating to MAP in Romania prior to 15 August 2023

Developments relating to MAP in the tax treaty network

- Romania has in force 88 tax treaties ratified by law, covering 89 jurisdictions. Romania has transposed in its law some of the commentaries to the Model Tax Convention (Law no. 227/2015 on the Fiscal Code).Based on the analysis of its existing tax treaties, Romania launches negotiations and aligns its tax treaties with the instrument and with present-day needs. Romania aims to conclude tax treaties with the remaining OECD member countries.

Other developments relating to MAP

- As an overall practice rule in this area, Romanian authorities apply entirely the provisions of its tax treaties. The Romanian Tax Administration follows also the Commentaries on the Articles of the Model Tax Convention, as modified from time to time, when applying and interpreting the provisions of the bilateral tax conventions that are based on these Articles. This is being applied without prejudice for the national legal framework or for the provisions included in the bilateral treaties.

Latest Action 14 Peer Review report

25 May 2021 - https://doi.org/10.1787/800bcae2-en

Tax treaty network of Romania

- 88 treaties, applicable to 89 jurisdictions (covering all treaties signed, although not necessarily in force)
- status of MLI: in force.

Table 1. State of play of Romania's tax treaty network

Treaties in line with the Action 14 Minimum Standard following MLI impact	Treaties where actions are ongoing to make them in line with the Action 14 Minimum Standard	Following impact/actions, remaining treaties that are not in line with Action 14 Minimum Standard
69	19	0

Source: OECD

Romania's MAP programme

Organisation of competent authority function

- 14 persons:
  - one head of unit

    - 13 persons working on MAP cases (among which three persons work on other tasks as well).
- contact persons for MAP requests:
    - Daniela Teodoru - General Director
      Sia Nicoleta Jiru - Director
      General Directorate for Fiscal Control Coordination
      Romanian National Agency for Fiscal Administration
      17 Apolodor street, District 5, Bucharest, Romania
      Tel: + 021 327 06 28
      email: secretariat.dgcif@anaf.ro ; daniela.teodoru@anaf.ro; sia.jiru@anaf.ro.

Figure 1. Competent Authority Organisational Structure

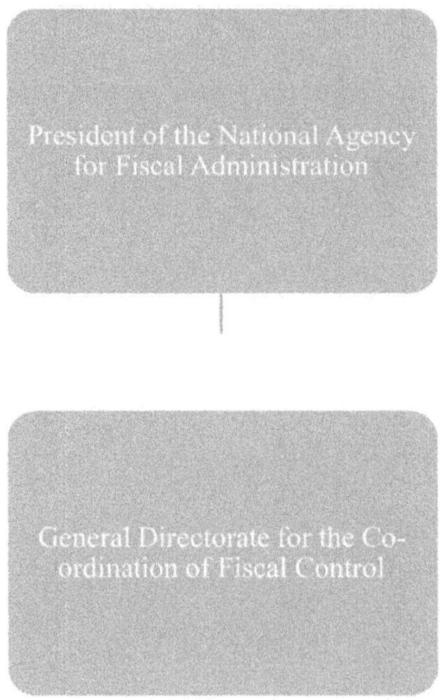

Source: OECD

Table 2. Guidance on the MAP process

MAP guidance	Guide on the avoidance/elimination of double taxation, August 2020	https://static.anaf.ro/static/10/Anaf/Prezentare_R/GUIDE_eliminating_double_taxation20082020.pdf (Section "Steps in the conduct of avoidance the double taxation procedure" to be referred to for form and content of a MAP request, including information requirements)
MAP profile	3 December 2020	https://www.oecd.org/tax/dispute/Romania-Dispute-Resolution-Profile.pdf

Overview of Romania's MAP Statistics for 2022

Please refer to https://www.oecd.org/tax/dispute/map-statistics-romania.pdf for details with respect to Romania's MAP Statistics.

Figure 2. Cases closed in 2022

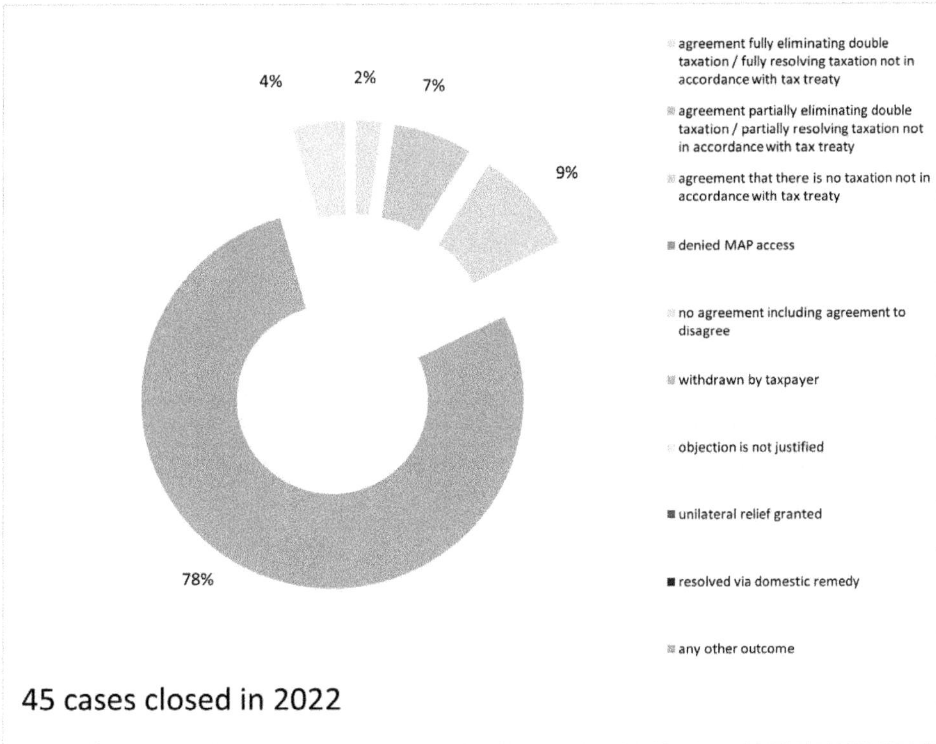

Source: OECD

Figure 3. Evolution of Romania's MAP caseload (2016-22)

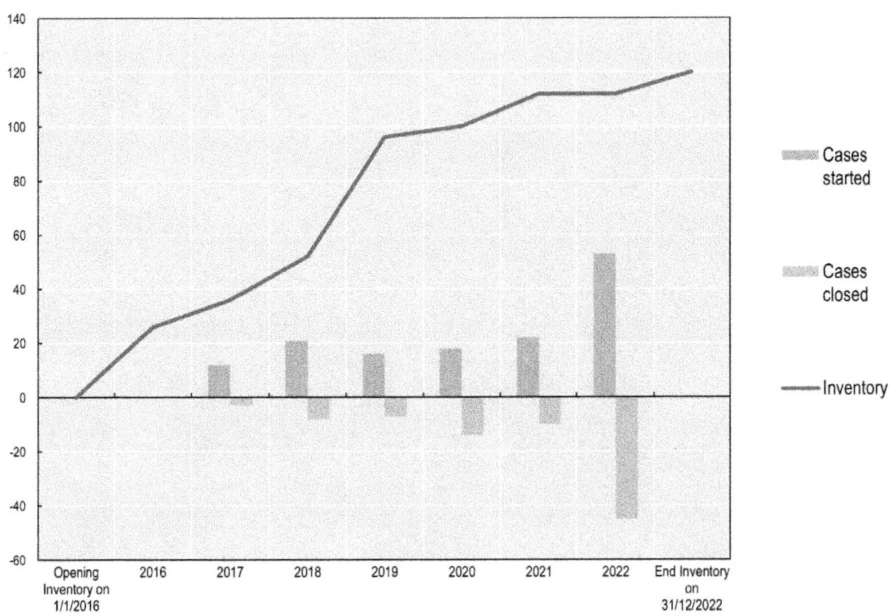

Source: OECD

Table 3. Overview of Romania' MAP caseload for 2022

Inventory for year 2022	Opening Inventory 1/1/2022	Cases started	Cases Closed	End Inventory 31/12/2022
Attribution/allocation cases	73	46	37	82
Other cases	39	7	8	38
Total	112	53	45	120

Source: OECD

Table 4. Romania's average time to resolve MAP cases in 2022

Cases resolved in year 2022	Pre-2016 cases		Post-2015 cases		All	
	Number of cases	**Average time**	**Number of cases**	**Average time** **Start to End**	**Number of cases**	**Average time**
Attribution / Allocation cases	1	N/A	36	N/A	37	N/A
Other cases	2	N/A	6	N/A	8	N/A
All cases	3	N/A	42	N/A	45	N/A

Source: OECD

Saint Kitts and Nevis

Recent developments relating to MAP in Saint Kitts and Nevis prior to 15 August 2023

Developments relating to MAP in the tax treaty network

- Meetings have been facilitated by the Caricom Secretariat to update the Caricom DTA. Work is currently ongoing and expected to be completed by the end of 2023.

Other developments relating to MAP

- No developments were reported

Latest Action 14 Peer Review report

13 September 2022 - https://doi.org/10.1787/32b8feb8-en

Tax treaty network of Saint Kitts and Nevis

- seven treaties, applicable to 16 jurisdictions (covering all treaties signed, although not necessarily in force)
- status of MLI: not signed.

Table 1. State of play of Saint Kitts and Nevis' tax treaty network

Treaties in line with the Action 14 Minimum Standard following MLI impact	Treaties where actions are ongoing to make them in line with the Action 14 Minimum Standard	Following impact/actions, remaining treaties that are not in line with Action 14 Minimum Standard
2	1	4

Source: OECD

Saint Kitts and Nevis' MAP programme

Organisation of competent authority function

- seven persons:
  - one head of unit
  - four persons working on MAP cases (all of which work on other tasks as well).
- contact persons for MAP requests:
  - Name: Mr. Edward Gift
    Designation: Competent Authority
    Organisation: Inland Revenue Department

Email: competentauthority@ird.gov.kn and edward.gift@ird.gov.kn
Telephone: 869-465-8485 ext. 3555

- Name: Mrs. Velda Irish-Browne
  Designation: Competent Authority Designate
  Organisation: Inland Revenue Department
  Email: competentauthority@ird.gov.kn and velda.irish-browne@ird.gov.kn
  Telephone: 869-465-8485 ext. 3541.

Figure 1. Competent Authority Organisational Structure

Source: OECD

Table 2. Guidance on the MAP process

MAP guidance	Mutual Agreement Procedure (MAP) Guidelines, January 2020	https://www.sknird.com/wp-content/uploads/2020/09/Mutual_Agreement_Procedures_guidelines.pdf (Section 6 to be referred to for form and content of a MAP request, including information requirements)
MAP profile	24 January 2020	https://www.oecd.org/tax/dispute/st.kitts-and-nevis-dispute-resolution-profile.pdf

Overview of Saint Kitts and Nevis' MAP Statistics for 2022

Saint Kitts and Nevis did not report any MAP cases in its 2022 MAP Statistics.

Please refer to https://www.oecd.org/tax/dispute/map-statistics-saint-kitts-and-nevis.pdf for details with respect to Saint Kitts and Nevis' MAP Statistics.

.

Saint Lucia

Recent developments relating to MAP in Saint Lucia prior to 15 August 2023

Developments relating to MAP in the tax treaty network

- Preparation of MAP Profile (expected to be completed in the last quarter of 2023).
- Drafting of MAP Guidelines (expected to be completed in the last quarter of 2023).

Other developments relating to MAP

- No developments were reported

Latest Action 14 Peer Review report

Saint Lucia is currently undergoing its first peer review under Action 14.

Tax treaty network of Saint Lucia

- two treaties, applicable to 11 jurisdictions (covering all treaties signed, although not necessarily in force)
- status of MLI: not signed.

Table 1. State of play of Saint Lucia's tax treaty network

Treaties in line with the Action 14 Minimum Standard following MLI impact	Treaties where actions are ongoing to make them in line with the Action 14 Minimum Standard	Following impact/actions, remaining treaties that are not in line with Action 14 Minimum Standard
0	0	2

Source: OECD

Saint Lucia's MAP programme

Organisation of competent authority function

- three persons:
  - comptroller
  - two persons working on MAP cases (all of which work on other tasks as well)

- contact persons for MAP requests:
  - Comptroller of Inland Revenue Department/Competent Authority (Delegate), Inland Revenue Department, Waterfront, Castries.

Figure 1. Competent Authority Organisational Structure

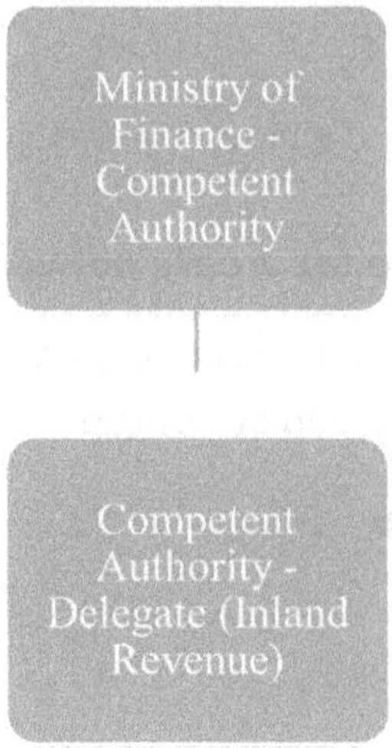

Source: OECD

Table 2. Guidance on the MAP process

MAP guidance	Saint Lucia did not provide the relevant information	-
MAP profile	No MAP profile published	-

Overview of Saint Lucia's MAP Statistics for 2022

Saint Lucia did not report any MAP cases in its 2022 MAP Statistics.

Please refer to https://www.oecd.org/tax/dispute/map-statistics-saint-lucia.pdf or details with respect to Saint Lucia's MAP Statistics.

Saint Vincent and the Grenadines

Recent developments relating to MAP in Saint Vincent and the Grenadines prior to 15 August 2023

Developments relating to MAP in the tax treaty network

- Saint Vincent and the Grenadines did not provide the relevant information.

Other developments relating to MAP

- Saint Vincent and the Grenadines did not provide the relevant information.

Latest Action 14 Peer Review report

Saint Vincent and the Grenadines is yet to be peer reviewed under Action 14.

Tax treaty network of Saint Vincent and the Grenadines

- three treaties, applicable to 12 jurisdictions (covering all treaties signed, although not necessarily in force)
- status of MLI: in force.

Table 1. State of play of Saint Vincent and the Grenadines' tax treaty network

Treaties in line with the Action 14 Minimum Standard following MLI impact	Treaties where actions are ongoing to make them in line with the Action 14 Minimum Standard	Following impact/actions, remaining treaties that are not in line with Action 14 Minimum Standard
1	No information	No information

Source: OECD

Saint Vincent and the Grenadines' MAP programme

Organisation of competent authority function

- Saint Vincent and the Grenadines did not provide the relevant information.

Table 2. Guidance on the MAP process

MAP guidance	Saint Vincent and the Grenadines did not provide the relevant information.	-
MAP profile	No MAP profile published	-

Overview of Saint Vincent and the Grenadines' MAP Statistics for 2022

Saint Vincent and the Grenadines did not report any MAP cases in its 2022 MAP Statistics.

Please refer to https://www.oecd.org/tax/dispute/map-statistics-saint-vincent-and-the-grenadines.pdf for details with respect to Saint Vincent and the Grenadines' MAP Statistics.

Samoa

Recent developments relating to MAP in Samoa prior to 15 August 2023

Developments relating to MAP in the tax treaty network

- No developments were reported

Other developments relating to MAP

- MAP Guidelines were approved by the authorised competent authority in May 2023 and will soon be published on the Ministry of Customs and Revenue's website.

Latest Action 14 Peer Review report

- Samoa is yet to be peer reviewed under Action 14.

Tax treaty network of Samoa

- one treaty, applicable to one jurisdiction (covering all treaties signed, although not necessarily in force)
- status of MLI: not signed.

Table 1. State of play of Samoa's tax treaty network

Treaties in line with the Action 14 Minimum Standard following MLI impact	Treaties where actions are ongoing to make them in line with the Action 14 Minimum Standard	Following impact/actions, remaining treaties that are not in line with Action 14 Minimum Standard
1	0	0

Source: OECD

Samoa's MAP programme

Organisation of competent authority function

- three persons:
  - one head of unit
  - two persons working on MAP cases
- contact persons for MAP requests:

  Fonoti Talaitupu Lia Taefu

  Competent Authority

  Chief Executive Officer/Commissioner

  Ministry of Customs and Revenue

Level 4, DBS Building Apia SAMOA.

Figure 1. Competent Authority Organisational Structure

Source: OECD

Table 2. Guidance on the MAP process

MAP guidance	No MAP guidance published	To be published soon
MAP profile	17 May 2021	https://www.oecd.org/tax/dispute/samoa-dispute-resolution-profile.pdf

Overview of Samoa's MAP Statistics for 2022

Samoa did not report any MAP cases in its 2022 MAP Statistics.

Please refer to https://www.oecd.org/tax/dispute/map-statistics-samoa.pdf for details with respect to Samoa's MAP Statistics.

San Marino

Recent developments relating to MAP in San Marino prior to 15 August 2023

Developments relating to MAP in the tax treaty network

- Entry into force of the tax treaty with Czechia in 2023.

Other developments relating to MAP

- No developments were reported

Latest Action 14 Peer Review report

24 January 2022 - https://doi.org/10.1787/22b43680-en

Tax treaty network of San Marino

- 25 treaties, applicable to 25 jurisdictions (covering all treaties signed, although not necessarily in force)
- status of MLI: in force.

Table 1. State of play of San Marino's tax treaty network

Treaties in line with the Action 14 Minimum Standard following MLI impact	Treaties where actions are ongoing to make them in line with the Action 14 Minimum Standard	Following impact/actions, remaining treaties that are not in line with Action 14 Minimum Standard
16	3	6

Source: OECD

San Marino's MAP programme

Organisation of competent authority function

- three persons:
  - three persons working on MAP cases (all of which work on other tasks as well).
- contact persons for MAP requests:
  - Segreteria di Stato per le Finanze e il Bilancio (Ministry of Finance and Budget), Contrada Omerelli, 31 47890 – San Marino Repubblica di San Marino
  - Email: info.finanze@gov.sm
  - Tel. (+378) 0549 – 882661 / (+378) 0549 – 882242 fax. (+378) 0549 – 882244.

Figure 1. Competent Authority Organisational Structure

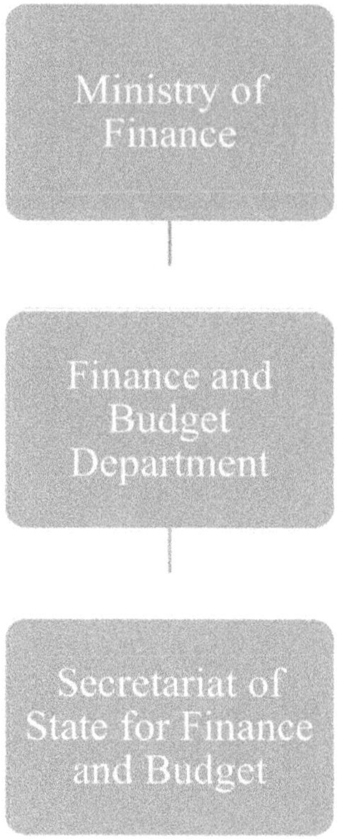

Source: OECD

Table 2. Guidance on the MAP process

MAP guidance	Mutual agreement procedures for the resolution of international tax disputes, Guideline, 3 December 2020	http://www.finanze.sm/on-line/home/aree-tematiche/fiscalita-internazionale/documento24121327.html (Section 4.2.4. to be referred to for form and content of a MAP request, including information requirements)
	Web page	http://www.finanze.sm/on-line/home/aree-tematiche/fiscalita-internazionale/articolo24013526.html
MAP profile	6 July 2021	https://www.oecd.org/tax/dispute/san-marino-dispute-resolution-profile.pdf

Overview of San Marino's MAP Statistics for 2022

Please refer to https://www.oecd.org/tax/dispute/map-statistics-san-marino.pdf for details with respect to San Marino's MAP Statistics.

Cases closed in 2022

No MAP cases were closed by San Marino in 2022.

Figure 2. Evolution of San Marino's MAP caseload (2016-22)

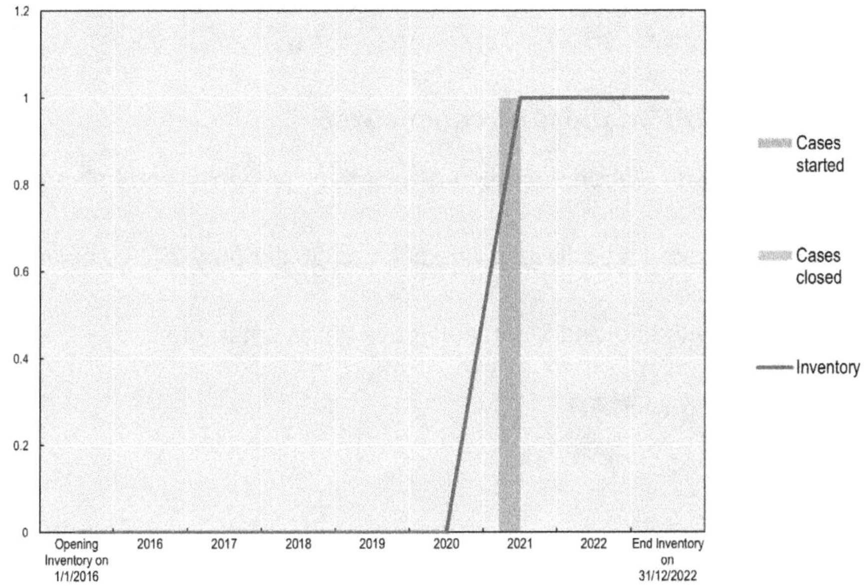

Source: OECD

Table 3. Overview of San Marino's MAP caseload for 2022

Inventory for year 2022	Opening Inventory 1/1/2022	Cases started	Cases Closed	End Inventory 31/12/2022
Attribution/allocation cases	0	0	0	0
Other cases	1	0	0	1
Total	1	0	0	1

Source: OECD

Table 4. San Marino's average time to resolve MAP cases in 2022

Cases resolved in year 2022	Pre-2016 cases		Post-2015 cases		All	
	Number of cases	**Average time**	**Number of cases**	**Average time** **Start to End**	**Number of cases**	**Average time**
Attribution / Allocation cases	0	N/A	0	N/A	0	N/A
Other cases	0	N/A	0	N/A	0	N/A
All cases	0	N/A	0	N/A	0	N/A

Source: OECD

Saudi Arabia

Recent developments relating to MAP in Saudi Arabia prior to 15 August 2023

Developments relating to MAP in the tax treaty network

- Saudi Arabia's treaties with Gabon, Morocco, Switzerland, Albania, and Latvia have entered into force.
- Saudi Arabia has also signed a treaty with Sri Lanka on 26 January 2023, however, the treaty has yet to enter into force.
- Saudi Arabia's treaties with Iraq and Mauritania have yet to enter into force.

Other developments relating to MAP

- MAP profile updated in 2023.

Latest Action 14 Peer Review report

18 October 2021 - https://doi.org/10.1787/c12a071c-en

Tax treaty network of Saudi Arabia

- 56 treaties, applicable to 56 jurisdictions (covering all treaties signed, although not necessarily in force)
- three treaties signed but not in force, applicable to three Jurisdictions
- status of MLI: in force.

Table 1. State of play of Saudi Arabia's tax treaty network

Treaties in line with the Action 14 Minimum Standard following MLI impact	Treaties where actions are ongoing to make them in line with the Action 14 Minimum Standard	Following impact/actions, remaining treaties that are not in line with Action 14 Minimum Standard
31	24	1 (4 including the treaties that have yet to enter into force)

Source: OECD

Saudi Arabia's MAP programme

Organisation of competent authority function

- MAP committee:
  - the MAP committee consists of 9 members, this committee is chaired by the Vice Governor and comprises experts in tax administration and International /domestic tax laws.
- contact /Authorized persons for MAP requests:

- Abdullah A. Alfuntukh, Vice Governor Strategy and Development, Zakat, Tax and Customs Authority (ZATCA) ; MAP@zatca.gov.sa; Phone: +966112893149 2.
- Wassal M. Almalki, International Relations & Treaties General Manager, ZATCA; walmalki@zatca.gov.sa, Phone: +966114342774 3.
- Osama Alzuhymeel, International Treaties Director, ZATCA; zuhymeeloa@zatca.gov.sa; Phone: +966114349364.
- Address: Zakat, Tax and Customs Authority, Headquarters Prince Abdulrahman bin Abdul Aziz Street - Al Murabba City: Riyadh. P.O.Box : 6898 Postal Code : 11187.

Figure 1. Competent Authority Organisational Structure

Source: OECD

Table 2. Guidance on the MAP process

MAP guidance	Request for Mutual Agreement Procedure, Taxpayer guidance	https://zatca.gov.sa/en/HelpCenter/guidelines/Documents/Request%20for%20Mutual%20Agreement%20Procedure%20%E2%80%93%20Taxpayer%20guidance%5B3%5D%5B1%5D.pdf (Section 4. to be referred to for form and content of a MAP request, including information requirements)
	Web page to request a MAP	https://zatca.gov.sa/en/eServices/Pages/eServices_93.aspx
MAP profile	8 March 2023	https://www.oecd.org/tax/dispute/saudi-arabia-dispute-resolution-profile.pdf

Overview of Saudi Arabia's MAP Statistics for 2022

Please refer to https://www.oecd.org/tax/dispute/map-statistics-saudi-arabia.pdf for details with respect to Saudi Arabia's MAP Statistics.

Figure 2. Cases Closed in 2022

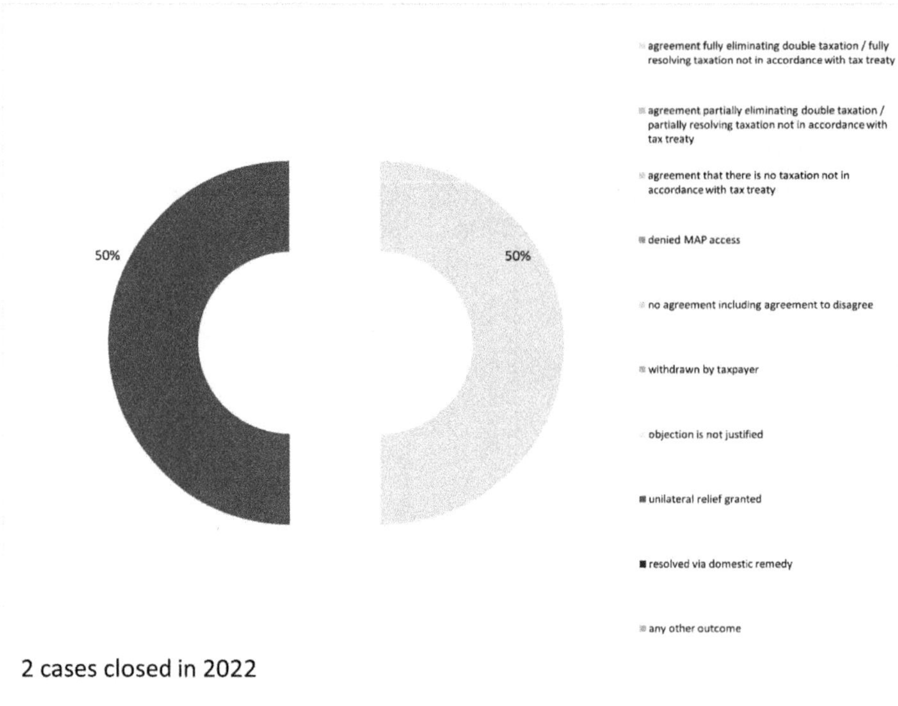

Source: OECD

Figure 3. Evolution of Saudi Arabia's MAP caseload (2016-22)

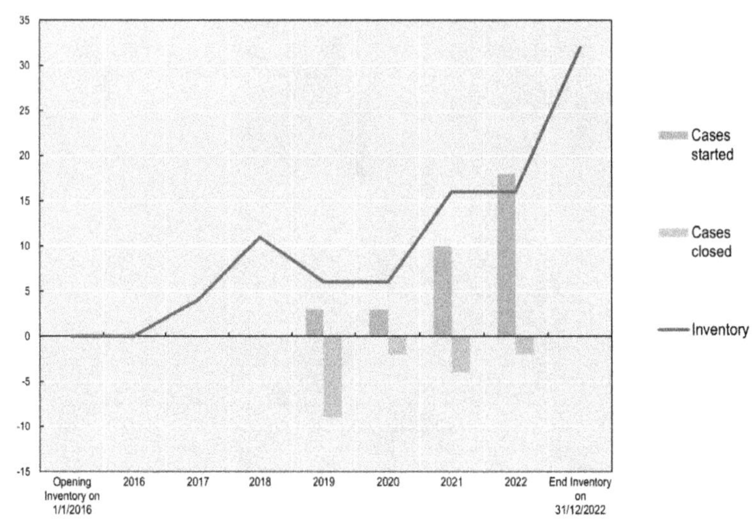

Source: OECD

Table 3. Overview of Saudi Arabia's MAP caseload for 2022

Inventory for year 2022	Opening Inventory 1/1/2022	Cases started	Cases Closed	End Inventory 31/12/2022
Attribution/allocation cases	14	9	1	22
Other cases	2	9	1	10
Total	16	18	2	32

Source: OECD

Table 4. Saudi Arabia's average time to resolve MAP cases in 2022

Cases resolved in year 2022	Pre-2016 cases		Post-2015 cases		All	
	Number of cases	**Average time**	**Number of cases**	**Average time** **Start to End**	**Number of cases**	**Average time**
Attribution / Allocation cases	0	N/A	1	19.33	1	19.33
Other cases	0	N/A	1	2.93	1	2.93
All cases	0	N/A	2	11.13	2	11.13

Source: OECD

Senegal

Recent developments relating to MAP in Senegal prior to 15 August 2023

Developments relating to MAP in the tax treaty network

- Senegal did not provide the relevant information.

Other developments relating to MAP

- Senegal did not provide the relevant information.

Latest Action 14 Peer Review report

Senegal is yet to be peer reviewed under Action 14.

Tax treaty network of Senegal

- 22 treaties, applicable to 28 jurisdictions (covering all treaties signed, although not necessarily in force)
- status of MLI: in force.

Table 1. State of play of Senegal's tax treaty network

Treaties in line with the Action 14 Minimum Standard following MLI impact	Treaties where actions are ongoing to make them in line with the Action 14 Minimum Standard	Following impact/actions, remaining treaties that are not in line with Action 14 Minimum Standard
11	No Information	No Information

Source: OECD

Senegal's MAP programme

Organisation of competent authority function

- contact persons for MAP requests:
  - Directeur général des Impôts et des Domaines, Rue de Thiong x Vincens – Dakar
  - Téléphone : +221 33 889 20 02 | Fax : +221 33 823 21 29 | Boîte postale : 1561 Dakar.

Table 2. Guidance on the MAP process

MAP guidance	Senegal did not provide the relevant information.	-
MAP profile	31 March 2017	https://www.oecd.org/tax/dispute/senegal-dispute-resolution-profile-fr.pdf

Overview of Senegal's MAP Statistics for 2022

Senegal did not report any MAP cases in its 2022 MAP Statistics.

Please refer to https://www.oecd.org/tax/dispute/map-statistics-senegal.pdf for details with respect to Senegal's MAP Statistics.

Serbia

Recent developments relating to MAP in Serbia prior to 15 August 2023

Developments relating to MAP in the tax treaty network

- Serbia did not provide the relevant information.

Other developments relating to MAP

- Serbia did not provide the relevant information.

Latest Action 14 Peer Review report

24 January 2022 - https://doi.org/10.1787/577cb1f7-en

Tax treaty network of Serbia

- 64 treaties, applicable to 64 jurisdictions (covering all treaties signed, although not necessarily in force)
- status of MLI: in force.

Table 1. State of play of Serbia's tax treaty network

Treaties in line with the Action 14 Minimum Standard following MLI impact	Treaties where actions are ongoing to make them in line with the Action 14 Minimum Standard	Following impact/actions, remaining treaties that are not in line with Action 14 Minimum Standard
60	No Information	No Information

Source: OECD

Serbia's MAP programme

Organisation of competent authority function

- one person
- contact persons for MAP requests:
  - Ministry of Finance, Fiscal System Department, 20, Kneza Milosa str. 11000 Belgrade
  - Phone: +381 11 3642 851 Email: fiskalni.sektor@mfin.gov.rs.

Figure 1. Competent Authority Organisational Structure

Source: OECD

Table 2. Guidance on the MAP process

MAP guidance	*Explanation on the mutual agreement procedure under international treaties for the avoidance of double taxation*, April 2019	https://www.mfin.gov.rs/upload/media/mG1Tn9_618b93a089ec1.pdf (Section 2.1 to be referred to for form and content of a MAP request, including information requirements)
MAP profile	25 May 2021	https://www.oecd.org/tax/dispute/serbia-dispute-resolution-profile.pdf

Overview of Serbia's MAP Statistics for 2022

Please refer to https://www.oecd.org/tax/dispute/map-statistics-serbia.pdf for details with respect to Serbia's MAP Statistics.

Figure 2. Cases Closed in 2022

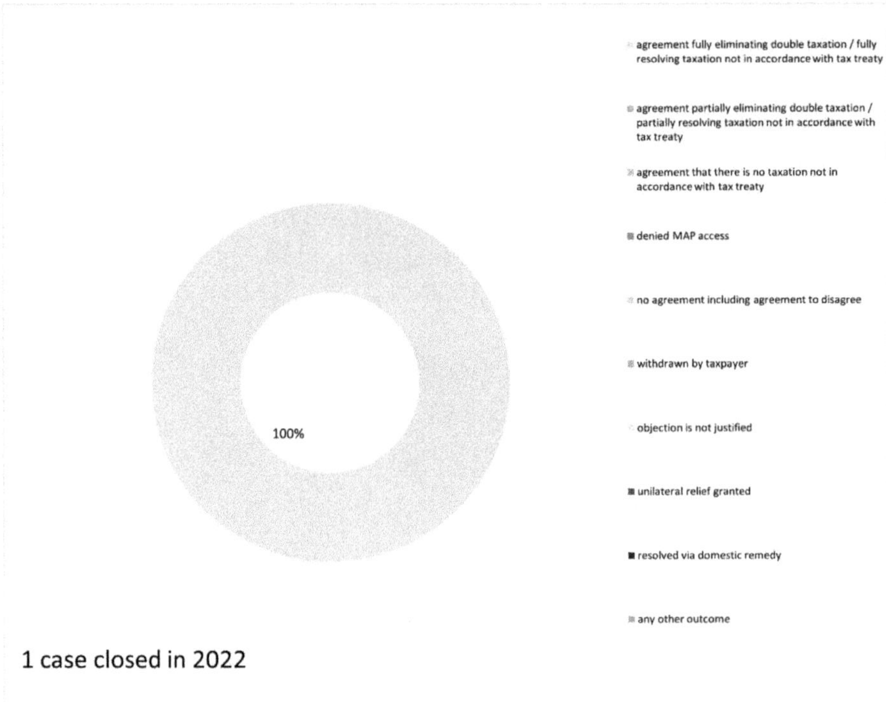

Source: OECD

Figure 3. Evolution of Serbia's MAP caseload (2018-22)

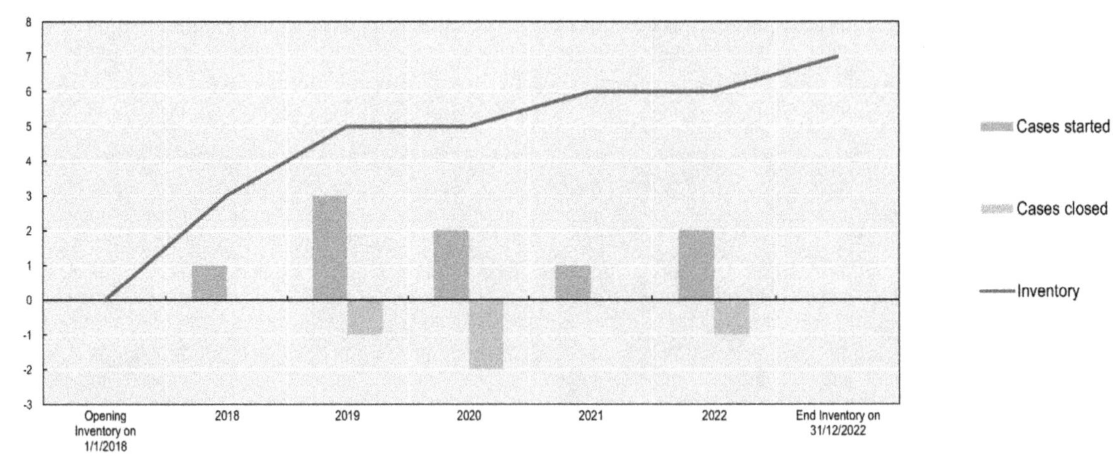

Source: OECD

Table 3. Overview of Serbia's MAP caseload for 2022

Inventory for year 2022	Opening	Cases started	Cases	End

	Inventory 1/1/2022		Closed	Inventory 31/12/2022
Attribution/allocation cases	4	2	1	5
Other cases	2	0	0	2
Total	6	2	1	7

Source: OECD

Table 4. Serbia's average time to resolve MAP cases in 2022

Cases resolved in year 2022	Pre-2018 cases		Post-2017 cases		All	
	Number of cases	**Average time**	**Number of cases**	**Average time** **Start o End**	**Number of cases**	**Average time**
Attribution / Allocation cases	0	N/A	1	6.53	1	6.53
Other cases	0	N/A	0	N/A	0	N/A
All cases	0	N/A	1	N/A	1	N/A

Source: OECD

Seychelles

Recent developments relating to MAP in Seychelles prior to 15 August 2023

Developments relating to MAP in the tax treaty network

- No developments were reported

Other developments relating to MAP

- A MAP guidance document is currently in the process of being drafted and will be subsequently published.

Latest Action 14 Peer Review report

The stage 1 Simplified Peer Review report of Seychelles is expected to be published early 2024.

Tax treaty network of Seychelles

- 33 treaties, applicable to 33 jurisdictions (covering all treaties signed, although not necessarily in force)
- status of MLI: in force.

Table 1. State of play of Seychelles' tax treaty network

Treaties in line with the Action 14 Minimum Standard following MLI impact	Treaties where actions are ongoing to make them in line with the Action 14 Minimum Standard	Following impact/actions, remaining treaties that are not in line with Action 14 Minimum Standard
27	0	6

Source: OECD

Seychelles' MAP programme

Organisation of competent authority function

- six persons in the unit:
  - one head of unit
  - two persons working on MAP cases (both of which work on other tasks as well)
- contact persons for MAP requests:
  - Mr. Fred Morel, Seychelles Revenue Commissioner, 2nd Floor, Maison Collet, Palm Street, P.O Box 50, Victoria, Mahé
  - +2484294921
  - commissioner@src.gov.sc.

Figure 1. Competent Authority Organisational Structure

Source: OECD

Table 2. Guidance on the MAP process

MAP guidance	No MAP guidance published	-
MAP profile	28 December 2016	https://www.oecd.org/tax/dispute/Seychelles-Dispute-Resolution-Profile.pdf

Overview of Seychelles' MAP Statistics for 2022

Seychelles did not report any MAP cases in its 2022 MAP Statistics.

Please refer to https://www.oecd.org/tax/dispute/map-statistics-seychelles.pdf for details with respect to Seychelles' MAP Statistics.

Sierra Leone

Recent developments relating to MAP in Sierra Leone prior to 15 August 2023

Developments relating to MAP in the tax treaty network

- Sierra Leone did not provide the relevant information.

Other developments relating to MAP

- Sierra Leone did not provide the relevant information.

Latest Action 14 Peer Review report

Sierra Leone is yet to be peer reviewed under Action 14.

Tax treaty network of Sierra Leone

- four treaties, applicable to four jurisdictions (covering all treaties signed, although not necessarily in force).
- status of MLI: not signed.

Table 1. State of play of Sierra Leone's tax treaty network

Treaties in line with the Action 14 Minimum Standard following MLI impact	Treaties where actions are ongoing to make them in line with the Action 14 Minimum Standard	Following impact/actions, remaining treaties that are not in line with Action 14 Minimum Standard
1	No information	No information

Source: OECD

Sierra Leone's MAP programme

Organisation of competent authority function

- Sierra Leone did not provide the relevant information.

Table 2. Guidance on the MAP process

MAP guidance	Sierra Leone did not provide the relevant information.	-
MAP profile	No MAP profile published	-

Overview of Sierra Leone's MAP Statistics for 2022

Sierra Leone did not declare its MAP Statistics for 2022.

Singapore

Recent developments relating to MAP in Singapore prior to 15 August 2023

Developments relating to MAP in the tax treaty network

- As reported in Singapore's stage 2 peer review report published in October 2020, Singapore had 93 tax treaties of which 87 were in force and 6 (Armenia, Brazil, Gabon, Greece, Kenya and Turkmenistan) not yet in force. Of the 93 tax treaties, 83 contained a MAP provision that is in line with or will be modified by the Multilateral Instrument to be in line the Action 14 Minimum Standard.
- As of 15 August 2023, Singapore has 96 tax treaties of which 93 are in force and 3 (Gabon, Kenya, and Cabo Verde) not yet in force. Of the 96 tax treaties, 88 contained a MAP provision that is in line with or will be modified by the Multilateral Instrument to be in line with the Action 14 Minimum Standard. Singapore has already initiated negotiations or is in contact with the treaty partners of the remaining 8 tax treaties to initiate renegotiation of the tax treaties to be in line with the Action 14 Minimum Standard.

Other developments relating to MAP

- In October 2021, Singapore updated its e-Tax Guide on Avoidance of Double Taxation Agreements (https://www.iras.gov.sg/media/docs/) to provide guidance on arbitration provisions found in Singapore's tax treaties.

Latest Action 14 Peer Review report

22 October 2020 - https://doi.org/10.1787/3d152880-en

Tax treaty network of Singapore

- 96 treaties, applicable to 96 jurisdictions (covering all treaties signed, although not necessarily in force)
- status of MLI: in force.

Table 1. State of play of Singapore's tax treaty network

Treaties in line with the Action 14 Minimum Standard following MLI impact	Treaties where actions are ongoing to make them in line with the Action 14 Minimum Standard	Following impact/actions, remaining treaties that are not in line with Action 14 Minimum Standard
88	8	0

Source: OECD

Singapore's MAP programme

Organisation of competent authority function

- 21 persons:
  - four Competent Authorities for MAP
  - 11 staff handling attribution/allocation MAP cases (and other areas relating to cross border transfer pricing matters)
  - six staff handling other MAP cases (and other areas relating to tax treaty matters).
- contact persons for MAP requests:
  - please refer to https://www.iras.gov.sg/taxes/international-tax
  - the MAP application may also be submitted electronically via: https://mytax.iras.gov.sg.

Figure 1. Competent Authority Organisational Structure

Source: OECD

Table 2. Guidance on the MAP process

MAP guidance	Transfer Pricing Guidelines (Sixth Edition), 10 August 2021	https://www.iras.gov.sg/media/docs/default-source/e-tax/etaxguide_cit_transfer-pricing-guidelines_6th.pdf?sfvrsn=26bfb1a6_9%20 (For attribution/allocation cases - Section 11 and Annexes B1 and B2 to be referred to for form and content of a MAP request, including information requirements)
	Avoidance of DTAs (Third Edition), 23 October 2021	https://www.iras.gov.sg/media/docs/default-source/e-tax/etaxguide_income-tax_avoidance-of-double-taxation-agreements-(dtas)_3rd-edition.pdf?sfvrsn=5b9f3b30_17 (For other cases cases - Section 7 and Annexes A and B to be referred to for form and content of a MAP request, including information requirements)
	Web page	https://www.iras.gov.sg/taxes/international-tax/dispute-prevention-and-resolution/mutual-agreement-procedure-(map)-and-arbitration
MAP profile	27 June 2019	https://www.oecd.org/tax/dispute/Singapore-Dispute-Resolution-Profile.pdf

Overview of Singapore's MAP Statistics for 2022

Please refer to https://www.oecd.org/tax/dispute/map-statistics-singapore.pdf for details with respect to Singapore's MAP Statistics.

Figure 2. Cases Closed in 2022

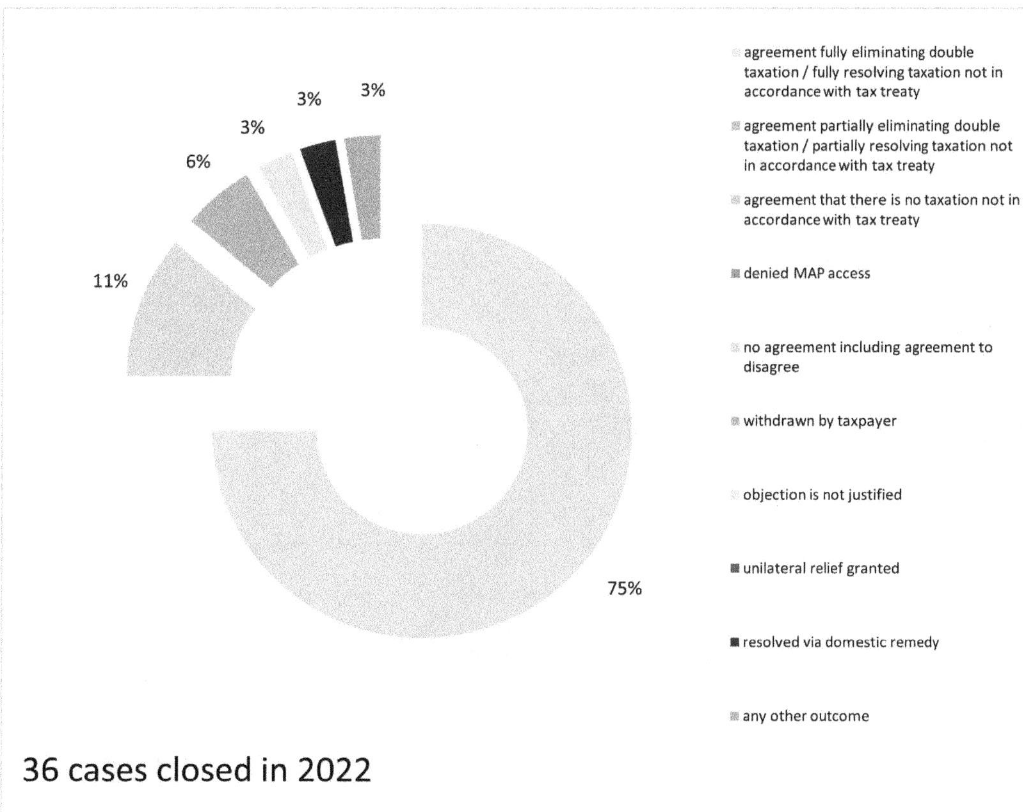

Source: OECD

Figure 3. Evolution of Singapore's MAP caseload (2016-22)

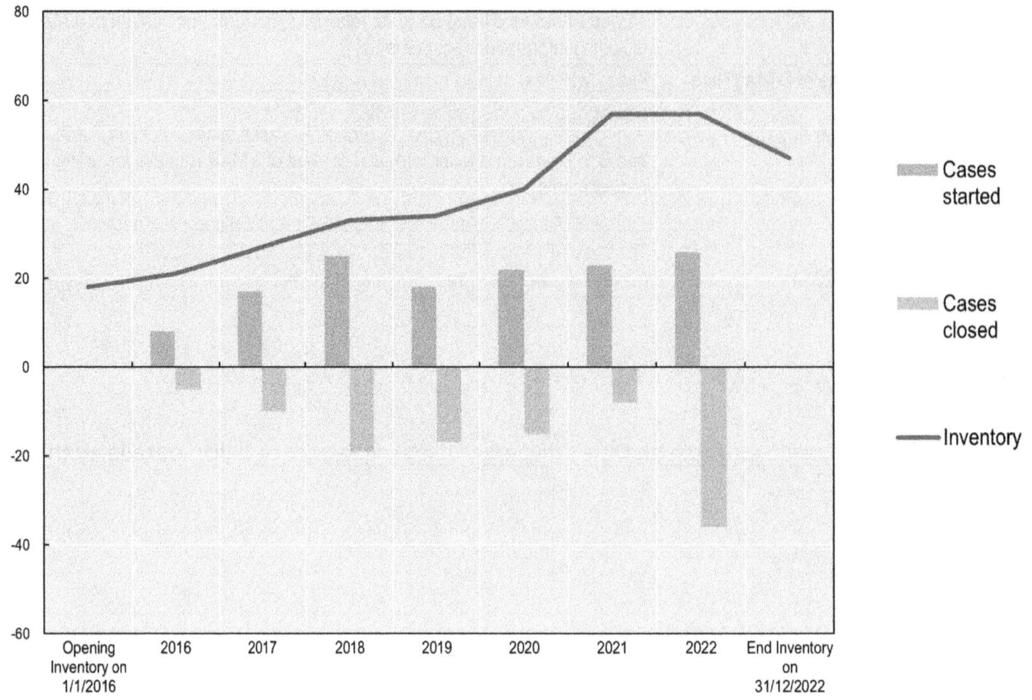

Source: OECD

Table 3. Overview of Singapore's MAP caseload for 2022

Inventory for year 2022	Opening Inventory 1/1/2022	Cases started	Cases Closed	End Inventory 31/12/2022
Attribution/allocation cases	35	13	25	23
Other cases	22	13	11	24
Total	57	26	36	47

Source: OECD

Table 4. Singapore's average time to resolve MAP cases in 2022

Cases resolved in year 2022	Pre-2016 cases		Post-2015 cases		All	
	Number of cases	**Average time**	**Number of cases**	**Average time** **Start to End**	**Number of cases**	**Average time**
Attribution / Allocation cases	0	N/A	25	21.20	25	21.20
Other cases	1	103.07	10	14.17	11	22.25
All cases	1	103.07	35	19.20	36	21.53

Source: OECD

Slovak Republic

Recent developments relating to MAP in Slovak Republic prior to 15 August 2023

Developments relating to MAP in the tax treaty network

- Due to the MLI taking effect on an increasing number of treaties, more treaties are aligning with the Action 14 minimum standard.

Other developments relating to MAP

- No significant developments since the publication of the latest Action 14 peer review report.

Latest Action 14 Peer Review report

25 May 2021 - https://doi.org/10.1787/df4ca02e-en

Tax treaty network of Slovak Republic

- 71 treaties, applicable to 72 jurisdictions (covering all treaties signed, although not necessarily in force)
- status of MLI: in force.

Table 1. State of play of Slovak Republic's tax treaty network

Treaties in line with the Action 14 Minimum Standard following MLI impact	Treaties where actions are ongoing to make them in line with the Action 14 Minimum Standard	Following impact/actions, remaining treaties that are not in line with Action 14 Minimum Standard
53*	9	10*

* The tax treaty covering two jurisdictions has been brought in line by the MLI for only one of the two jurisdictions
Source: OECD

Slovak Republic's MAP programme

Organisation of competent authority function

- Director General of the Tax and Customs Section (general supervision and sign-off)
- Director of the Department of Direct Taxes (general supervision and sign-off)
- nine persons in the International Tax Relations Unit:
  - one head of unit
  - eight persons working on MAP cases (all of which work on other tasks as well)
  - generally, three persons work on attribution/allocation cases and five persons work on other cases.

- contact persons for MAP requests:
  - Ministerstvo financií SR, Štefanovičova 5, 872 82 Bratislava
  - Email: podatelna@mfsr.sk.

Figure 1. Competent Authority Organisational Structure

Source: OECD

Table 2. Guidance on the MAP process

MAP guidance	Act No. 11/2019 Coll. of 5 December 2018, 16 January 2019	https://www.mfsr.sk/files/archiv/59/Actonthetaxdisputeresolutionrules_190701.pdf (Article 3 to be referred to for form and content of a MAP request, including information requirements)
	Metodické usmernenie Ministerstva financií Slovenskej republiky č. MF/020525/2017-724 k postupom v rámci procedúry vzájomnej dohody	https://www.mfsr.sk/files/archiv/financny-spravodajca/4577/42/Metodicke-usmernenie-Ministerstva-financii-Slovenskej-republiky.pdf
MAP profile	7 August 2020	https://www.oecd.org/tax/dispute/Slovak-Republic-Dispute-Resolution-Profile.pdf

Overview of Slovak Republic's MAP Statistics for 2022

Please refer to https://www.oecd.org/tax/dispute/map-statistics-slovak-republic.pdf for details with respect to Slovak Republic's MAP Statistics.

Figure 2. Cases Closed in 2022

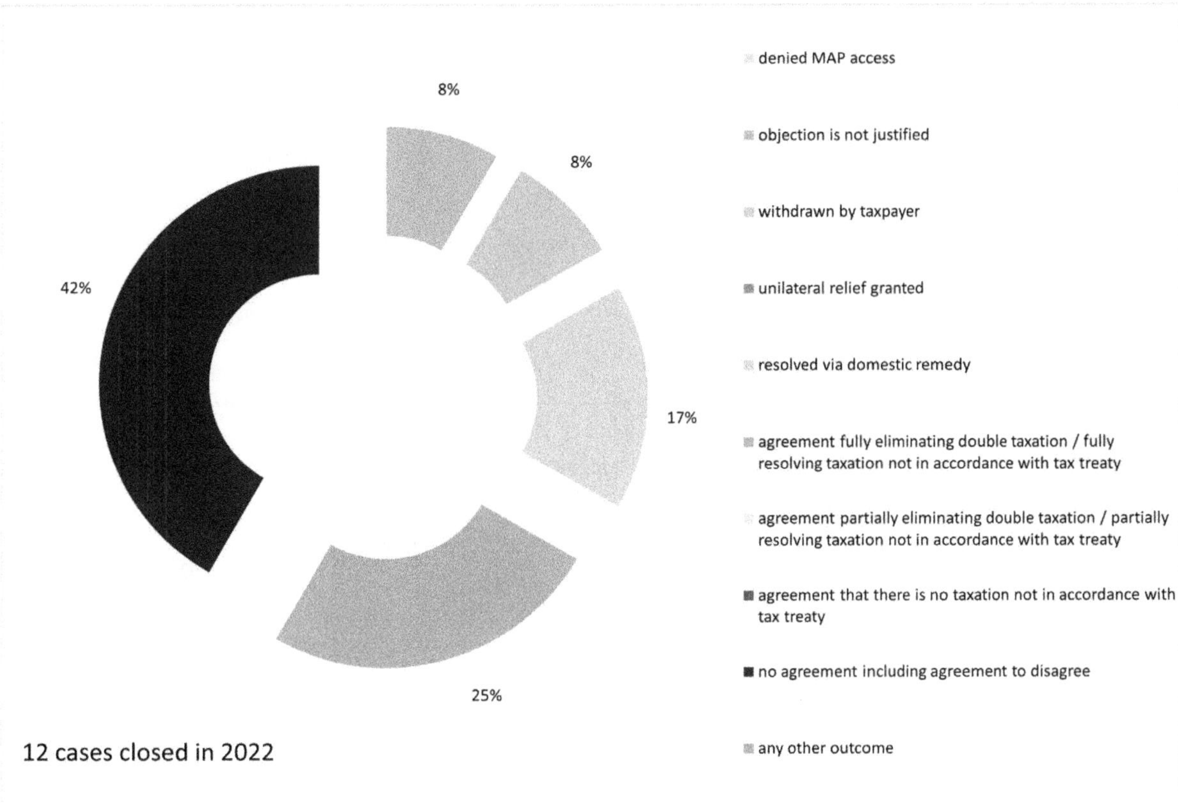

Source: OECD

Figure 3. Evolution of Slovak Republic's MAP caseload (2016-22)

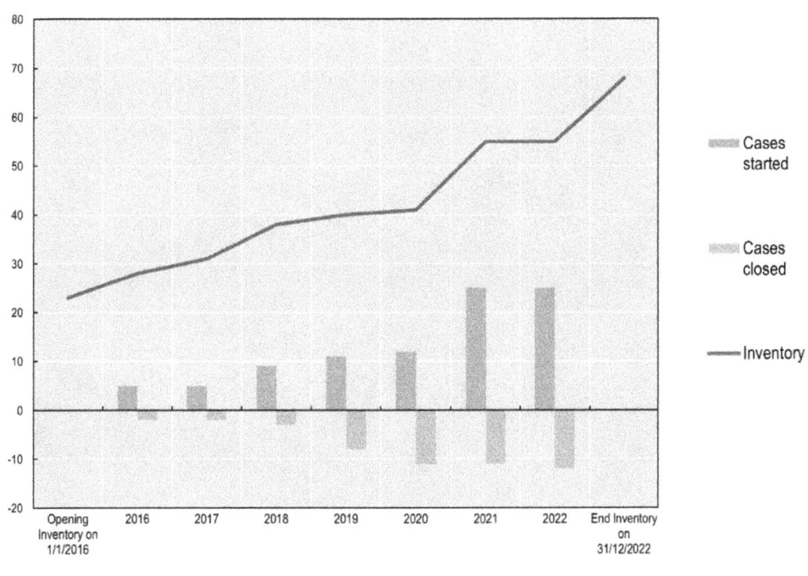

Source: OECD

Table 3. Overview of Slovak Republic's MAP caseload for 2022

Inventory for year 2022	Opening Inventory 1/1/2022	Cases started	Cases Closed	End Inventory 31/12/2022
Attribution/allocation cases	34	24	5	53
Other cases	21	1	7	15
Total	55	25	12	68

Source: OECD

Table 4. Slovak Republic's average time to resolve MAP cases in 2022

Cases resolved in year 2022	Pre-2016 cases		Post-2015 cases		All	
	Number of cases	**Average time**	**Number of cases**	**Average time** **Start to End**	**Number of cases**	**Average time**
Attribution / Allocation cases	1	111.78	4	13.85	5	33.43
Other cases	3	96.42	4	47.25	7	68.32
All cases	4	100.26	8	30.55	12	53.78

Source: OECD

Slovenia

Recent developments relating to MAP in Slovenia prior to 15 August 2023

Developments relating to MAP in the tax treaty network

- Since the publication of the latest Action 14 Peer Review Report Slovenia has made efforts to make the following two tax Treaties in line with the Action 14 Minimum Standard: tax treaty between Slovenia and Thailand (entry into force of the MLI for the tax treaty) and tax treaty between Slovenia and Sweden (entry into force of the new tax treaty replacing the existing tax treaty). Furthermore, additional action is currently ongoing to make the tax treaty between Slovenia and Switzerland (signature of the protocol to the tax treaty on 30 May 2023) in line with the Action 14 Minimum Standard.

Other developments relating to MAP

- Since the publication of the latest Action 14 Peer Review Report an amendment to the provisions of the Tax Procedure Act relating to MAP was adopted in 2022 (available in Slovenian only: Zakon o spremembah in dopolnitvah Zakona o davčnem postopku - ZDavP-2N).

Latest Action 14 Peer Review report

25 May 2021 - https://doi.org/10.1787/27a608bc-en

Tax treaty network of Slovenia

- 61 treaties (60 of which are in force), applicable to 62 jurisdictions (covering all treaties signed, although not necessarily in force)
- status of MLI: in force.

Table 1. State of play of Slovenia's tax treaty network

Treaties in line with the Action 14 Minimum Standard following MLI impact	Treaties where actions are ongoing to make them in line with the Action 14 Minimum Standard	Following impact/actions, remaining treaties that are not in line with Action 14 Minimum Standard
59	1	1

Source: OECD

Slovenia's MAP programme

Organisation of competent authority function

- Ministry of Finance of the Republic of Slovenia (competent authority for all cases apart from attribution/allocation cases):
  - o three persons:
    - one head of unit

- two persons working on MAP cases (all of which work on other tasks as well).

- The Financial Administration of the Republic of Slovenia (competent authority for attribution/allocation cases):
  - four persons:
    - one head of unit
    - three persons working on MAP cases (among which two persons work on other tasks as well).
- contacts for MAP requests:
  - competent authority for all cases apart from attribution/allocation cases:
    - Ministry of Finance of the Republic of Slovenia, Tax, Customs and Other Public Revenue Systems Directorate, Income and Property Taxation System Division, Župančičeva 3, 1001 Ljubljana, Slovenia
    - Phone: (+386) 1/369 6710 | Fax: (+386) 1/369 6719 | E-mail: gp.mf@gov.si.
  - competent authority for attribution/allocation cases:
    - Financial Administration of the Republic of Slovenia, General Financial Office - Tax Department, Division for International Taxation and Exchange of Information, Šmartinska cesta 55, 1000 Ljubljana, Slovenia
    - Phone: +386 1/478 38 00 | E-mail: gfu.fu@gov.si.

Figure 1. Competent Authority Organisational Structure

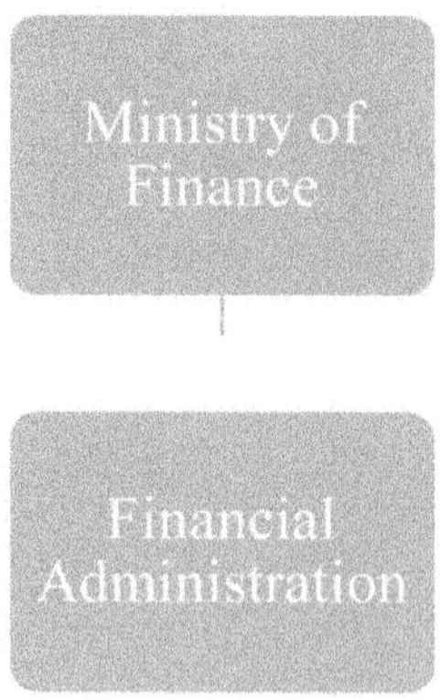

Source: OECD

Table 2. Guidance on the MAP process

MAP guidance	Postopek skupnega dogovarjanja po mednarodnih pogodbah o izogibanju dvojnega obdavčevanja, April 2018	https://www.gov.si/assets/ministrstva/MF/Davcni-direktorat/DOKUMENTI/Postopek-skupnega-dogovarjanja-po-mednarodnih-pogodbah-o-izogibanju-dvojnega-obdavcevanja.pdf (Section 2.1.6. to be referred to for form and content of a MAP request, including information requirements)
MAP profile	5 November 2020	https://www.oecd.org/tax/dispute/slovenia-dispute-resolution-profile.pdf

Overview of Slovenia's MAP Statistics for 2022

Please refer to https://www.oecd.org/tax/dispute/map-statistics-slovenia.pdf for details with respect to Slovenia's MAP Statistics.

Figure 2. Cases Closed in 2022

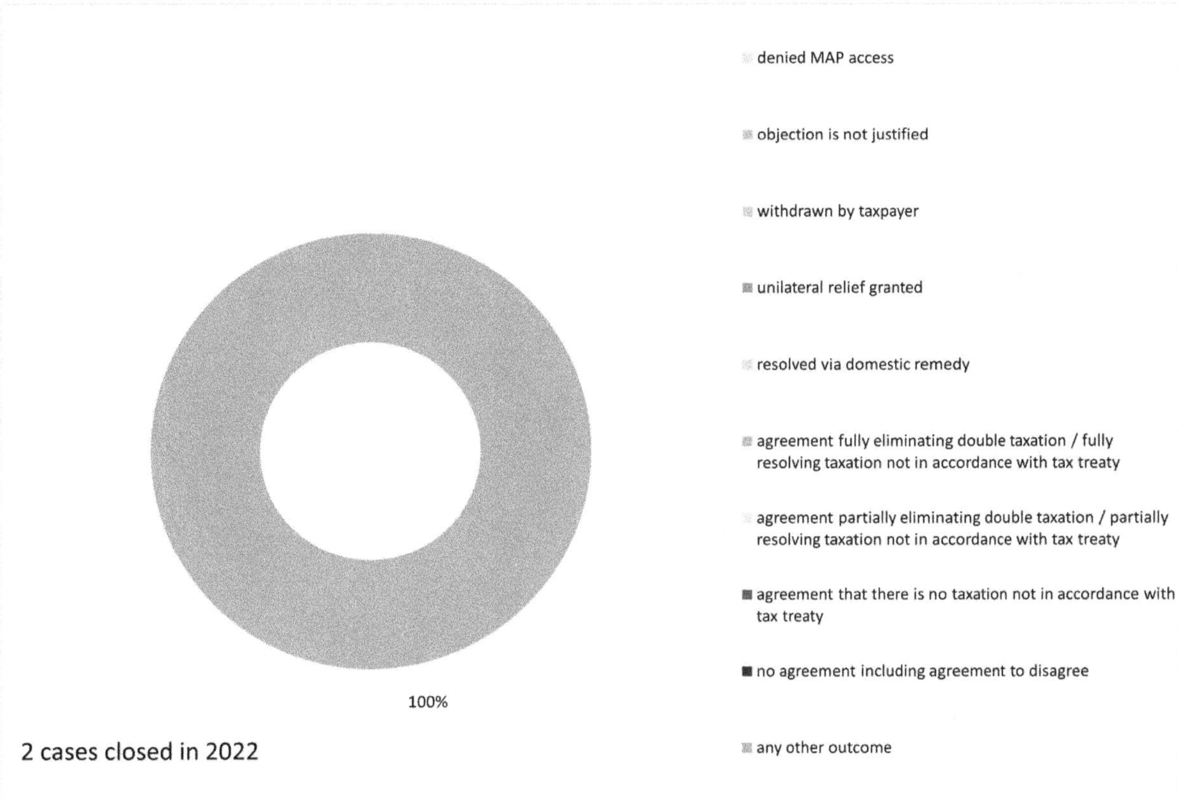

Source: OECD

Figure 3. Evolution of Slovenia's MAP caseload (2016-22)

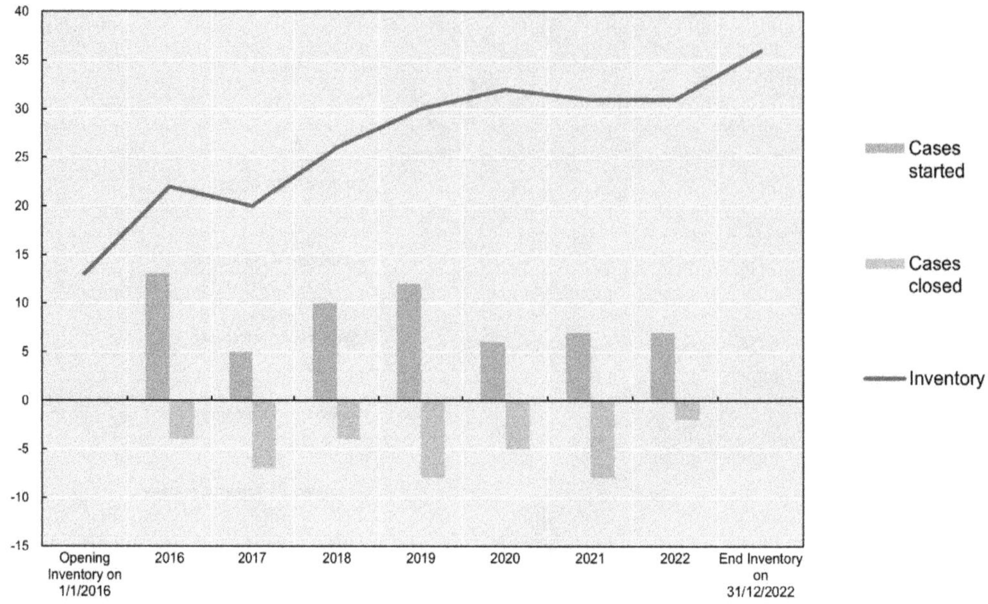

Source: OECD

Table 3. Overview of Slovenia's MAP caseload for 2022

Inventory for year 2022	Opening Inventory 1/1/2022	Cases started	Cases Closed	End Inventory 31/12/2022
Attribution/allocation cases	11	4	2	13
Other cases	20	3	0	23
Total	31	7	2	36

Source: OECD

Table 4. Slovenia's average time to resolve MAP cases in 2022

Cases resolved in year 2022	Pre-2016 cases		Post-2015 cases		All	
	Number of cases	**Average time**	**Number of cases**	**Average time** **Start to End**	**Number of cases**	**Average time**
Attribution / Allocation cases	0	N/A	2	63.06	2	63.06
Other cases	0	N/A	0	N/A	0	N/A
All cases	0	N/A	2	63.06	2	63.06

Source: OECD

South Africa

Recent developments relating to MAP in South Africa prior to 15 August 2023

Developments relating to MAP in the tax treaty network

- The stage 2 report noted that South Africa was conducting tax treaty negotiations with several jurisdictions. This situation has remained the same. Further, the stage 2 report noted that South Africa had signed a new treaty with Germany, which have not yet entered into force since the treaty partner had not yet ratified it. This situation has remained the same as well. South Africa and Germany have also negotiated an Amending Protocol to the DTA which has not yet been signed. South Africa ratified the BEPS MLI on 30 September 2022, which entered into force from 1 January 2023.

Other developments relating to MAP

- South Africa is in the process of introducing an Advanced Pricing Agreement (APA) programme in its legislation. Draft legislation with regards to APAs has been included in South Africa's Draft Tax Administration Laws Amendment Bill, 2023, (the draft Bill) that will insert it as a new Part IA in Chapter III in the Income Tax Act, 1962. The draft Bill was released for public comment on 30 July 2023 after which the normal legislative process will follow. It is expected that the legislation will be promulgated by the President during December this year or January 2024, following which it will be brought into force by the Minister of Finance. As the APA programme will require scarce resources, it is envisaged that the programme will commence with a pilot shortly after the legislative framework has been put in place.

Latest Action 14 Peer Review report

26 July 2021 - https://doi.org/10.1787/bdae3e57-en

Tax treaty network of South Africa

- 78 treaties, applicable to 79 jurisdictions (covering all treaties signed, although not necessarily in force)
- status of MLI: in force.

Table 1. State of play of South Africa's tax treaty network

Treaties in line with the Action 14 Minimum Standard following MLI impact	Treaties where actions are ongoing to make them in line with the Action 14 Minimum Standard	Following impact/actions, remaining treaties that are not in line with Action 14 Minimum Standard
66	5	8

Source: OECD

South Africa's MAP programme

Organisation of competent authority function

- five persons:
    - one head of unit
    - four persons working on MAP cases (all of which work on other tasks as well):
        - one person works on attribution/allocation cases and three persons work on other cases.
- contact persons for MAP requests:
    - South African Revenue Service, Legislative Policy Tax, Customs and Excise, Private Bag X923, Pretoria, 0001, Tel: +27 12 422 4000
    - for attribution / allocation cases: Mr Franz Tomasek, Head: Legislative Policy Tax, Customs and Excise, South African Revenue Service, Email: TransferPricingMAP@sars.gov.za.
    - for other cases:
        - Mr Morne Van Niekerk, Manager: International Development and Treaties, South African Revenue Service, Ms Celeste van der Lith, Manager: International Development and Treaties, South African Revenue Service
        - Ms Zandile Magaqa, Specialist: International Development and Treaties, South African Revenue Service, Email: SARSMAP@sars.gov.za.

Figure 1. Competent Authority Organisational Structure

Source: OECD

Table 2. Guidance on the MAP process

MAP guidance	Guide on Mutual Agreement Procedures, 20 March 2020	https://www.sars.gov.za/wp-content/uploads/Ops/Guides/LAPD-IT-G24-Guide-on-Mutual-Agreement-Procedures.pdf (Section 4. to be referred to for form and content of a MAP request, including information requirements)
	Web page	https://www.sars.gov.za/legal-counsel/international-treaties-agreements/double-taxation-agreements-protocols/mutual-agreement-procedure-map/
	Minimum information requirements	https://www.sars.gov.za/wp-content/uploads/Legal/Agreements/LAPD-IntA-DTA-2015-03-Minimum-Information-Requirements-for-MAPs.pdf
MAP profile	14 December 2021	https://www.oecd.org/tax/dispute/south-africa-dispute-resolution-profile.pdf

Overview of South Africa's MAP Statistics for 2022

Please refer to https://www.oecd.org/tax/dispute/map-statistics-south-africa.pdf for details with respect to South Africa's MAP Statistics.

Figure 2. Cases Closed in 2022

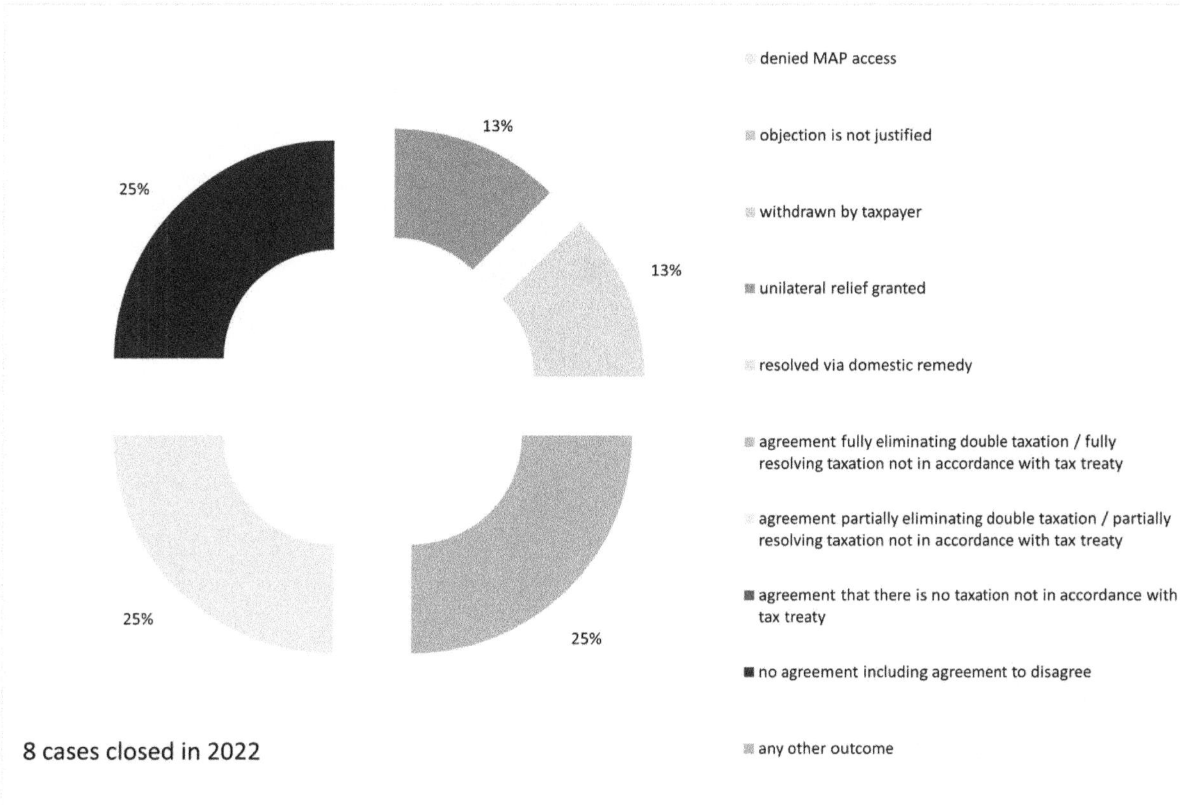

Source: OECD

Figure 3. Evolution of South Africa's MAP caseload (2016-22)

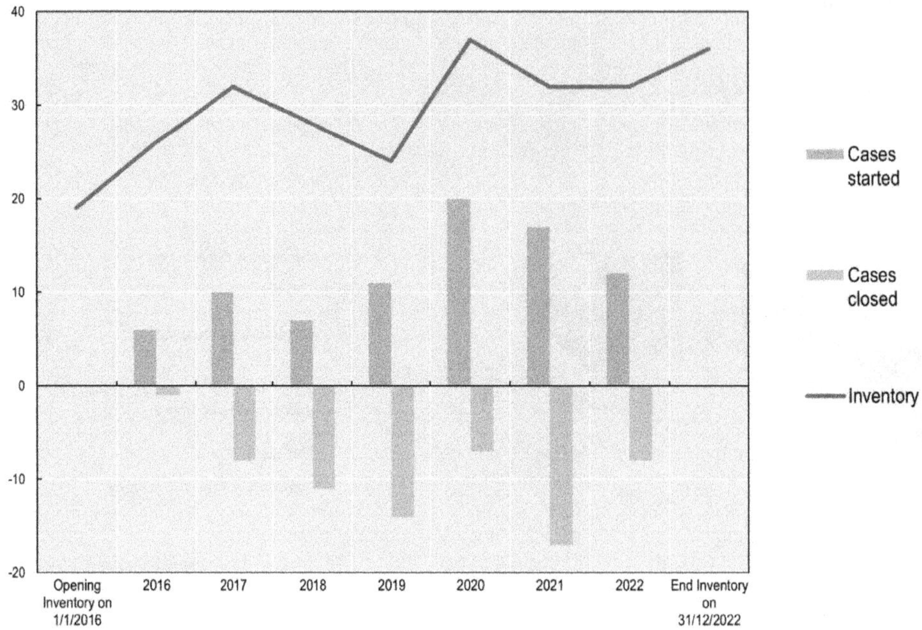

Source: OECD

Table 3. Overview of South Africa's MAP caseload for 2022

Inventory for year 2022	Opening Inventory 1/1/2022	Cases started	Cases Closed	End Inventory 31/12/2022
Attribution/allocation cases	13	8	0	21
Other cases	19	4	8	15
Total	32	12	8	36

Source: OECD

Table 4. South Africa's average time to resolve MAP cases in 2022

Cases resolved in year 2022	Pre-2016 cases		Post-2015 cases		All	
	Number of cases	**Average time**	**Number of cases**	**Average time** **Start to End**	**Number of cases**	**Average time**
Attribution / Allocation cases	0	N/A	0	N/A	0	N/A
Other cases	0	N/A	8	26.07	8	26.07
All cases	0	N/A	8	26.07	8	26.07

Source: OECD

Spain

Recent developments relating to MAP in Spain prior to 15 August 2023

Developments relating to MAP in the tax treaty network

- No developments were reported

Other developments relating to MAP

- Under the MLI BEPS, signed on June 7, 2017, ratified on September 28, 2021, and entered into force on January 1, 2022, Spain has made 3 notifications, one on June 1, 2022, which covered 50 agreements, another on November 30, 2022, which covered 3 agreements and recently on June, 1, 2023, which covered 2 jurisdictions.

Latest Action 14 Peer Review report

22 October 2020 - https://doi.org/10.1787/8f4792bc-en

Tax treaty network of Spain

- 91 treaties, applicable to 93 jurisdictions (covering all treaties signed, although not necessarily in force)
- status of MLI: in force.

Table 1. State of play of Spain's tax treaty network

Treaties in line with the Action 14 Minimum Standard following MLI impact	Treaties where actions are ongoing to make them in line with the Action 14 Minimum Standard	Following impact/actions, remaining treaties that are not in line with Action 14 Minimum Standard
81	12	0

Source: OECD

Spain's MAP programme

Organisation of competent authority function

- 34 persons:
  - two heads of unit: one Attribution/Allocation Cases CA and one Other Cases CA.
  - 20 persons working on MAP cases (among which 11 persons work on other tasks as well):
    - nine persons work on attribution/allocation cases and 11 persons work on other cases.
- contact persons for MAP requests:

- for attribution / allocation cases: Mr. Luis Jones Rodríguez, Head of International Taxation Office. Spanish Tax Agency (AEAT), Address: Paseo de la Castellana 147. 28046 Madrid. Tel: +34 917498666 Fax: +34 917498685 Email: onfi.map@correo.aeat.es.
- for other cases: Ms. Elena de las Morenas Ferrándiz, Deputy Director General for International Taxation, General Directorate for Taxation, Ministry of Finance and Civil Service. Address: C/ Alcalá.5. 28014 Madrid Tel: +34 915958055 Fax: +34 915958003 Email: fiscalidad.internacional@tributos.hacienda.gob.es.

Figure 1. Competent Authority Organisational Structure

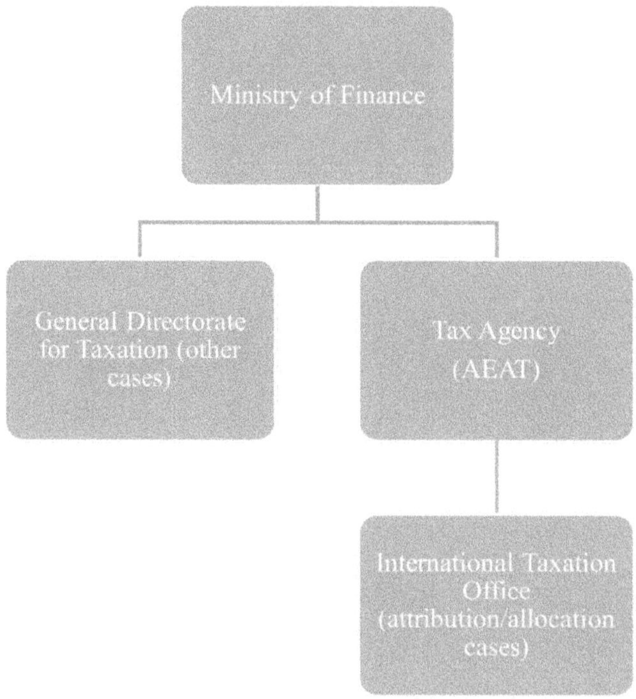

Source: OECD

Table 2. Guidance on the MAP process

MAP guidance	Guide to mutual agreement procedures	https://sede.agenciatributaria.gob.es/Sede/en_gb/ayuda/manuales-videos-folletos/manuales-practicos/guia-procedimientos-amistosos.html (Section I.2. to be referred to for form and content of a MAP request, including information requirements)
	REAL DECRETO 1794/2008, 18 November 2008	https://www.boe.es/eli/es/rd/2008/11/03/1794/con https://www.hacienda.gob.es/Documentacion/Publico/NormativaDoctrina/Tributaria/Impuesto%20sobre%20la%20Renta%20de%20no%20Residentes/MAP-Regulation-Spain.pdf (Article 6 to be referred to for form and content of a MAP request, including information requirements)
MAP profile	14 June 2023	https://www.oecd.org/tax/dispute/spain-dispute-resolution-profile.pdf

Overview of Spain's MAP Statistics for 2022

Please refer to https://www.oecd.org/tax/dispute/map-statistics-spain.pdf for details with respect to Spain's MAP Statistics.

Figure 2. Cases Closed in 2022

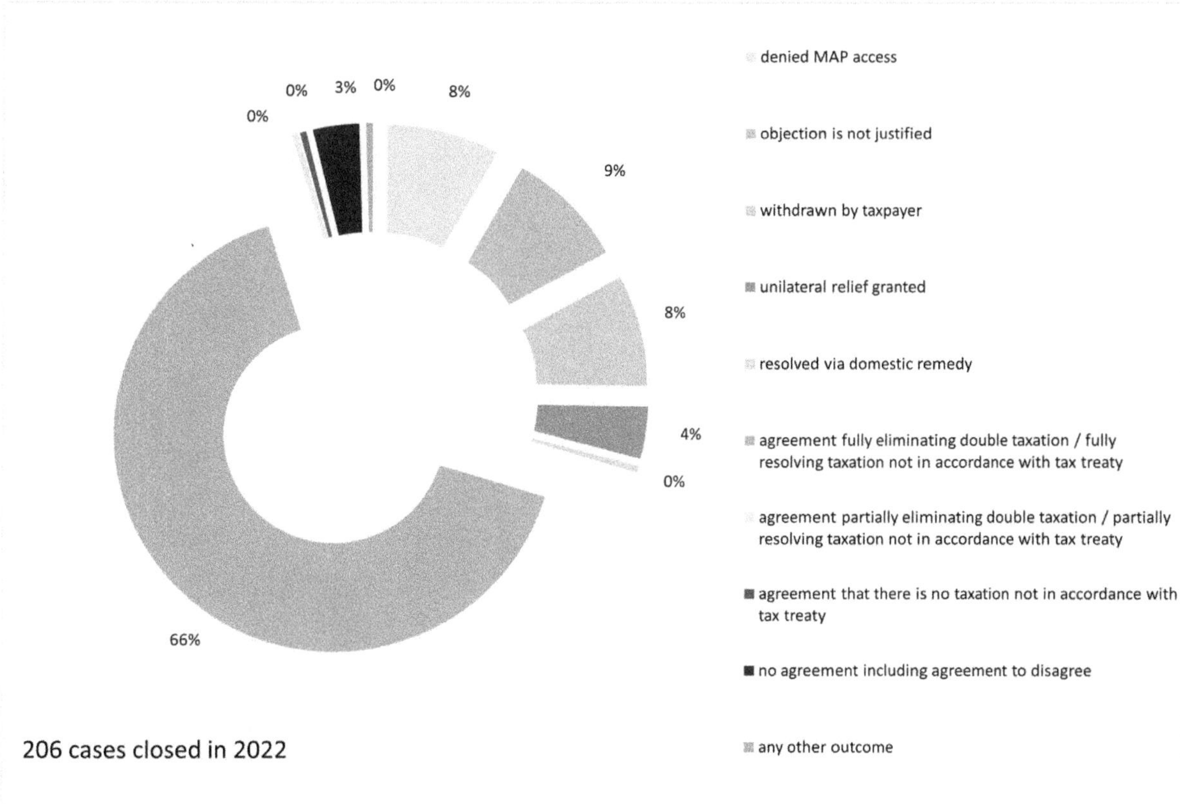

Source: OECD

Figure 3. Evolution of Spain's MAP caseload (2016-22)

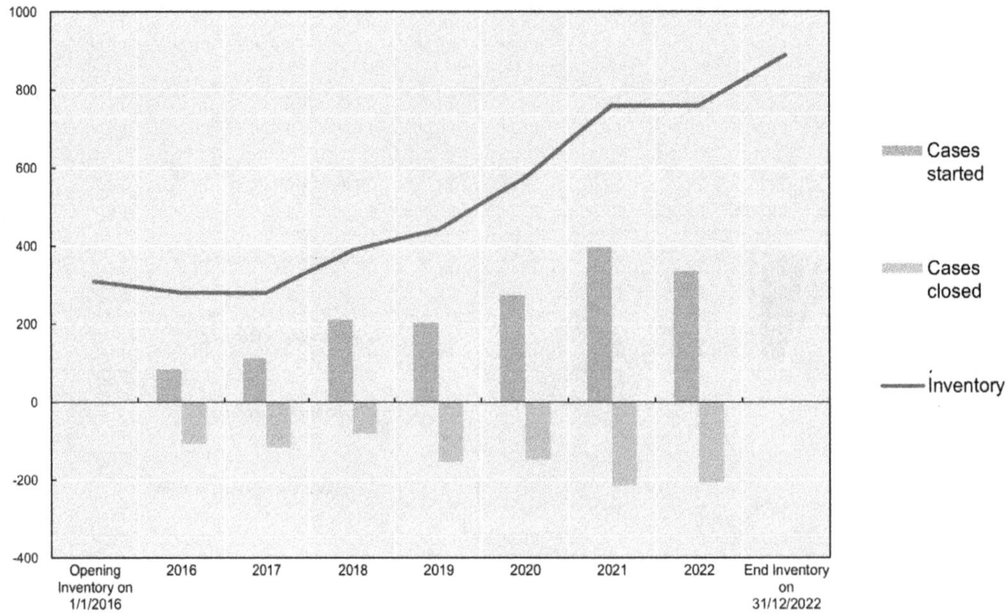

Source: OECD

Table 3. Overview of Spain's MAP caseload for 2022

Inventory for year 2022	Opening Inventory 1/1/2022	Cases started	Cases Closed	End Inventory 31/12/2022
Attribution/allocation cases	442	201	149	494
Other cases	318	134	57	395
Total	760	335	206	889

Source: OECD

Table 4. Spain's average time to resolve MAP cases in 2022

Cases resolved in year 2022	Pre-2016 cases		Post-2015 cases		All	
	Number of cases	**Average time**	**Number of cases**	**Average time** **Start to End**	**Number of cases**	**Average time**
Attribution / Allocation cases	0	N/A	149	25.85	149	25.85
Other cases	2	102.43	55	14.14	57	17.24
All cases	2	102.43	204	22.69	206	23.47

Source: OECD

Sri Lanka

Recent developments relating to MAP in Sri Lanka prior to 15 August 2023

Developments relating to MAP in the tax treaty network

- Sri Lanka did not provide the relevant information.

Other developments relating to MAP

- Sri Lanka did not provide the relevant information.

Latest Action 14 Peer Review report

Sri Lanka did not provide the relevant information.

Tax treaty network of Sri Lanka

- 44 treaties, applicable to 44 jurisdictions (covering all treaties signed, although not necessarily in force)
- status of MLI: not signed.

Table 1. State of play of Sri Lanka's tax treaty network

Treaties in line with the Action 14 Minimum Standard following MLI impact	Treaties where actions are ongoing to make them in line with the Action 14 Minimum Standard	Following impact/actions, remaining treaties that are not in line with Action 14 Minimum Standard
18	0	26

Source: OECD

Sri Lanka's MAP programme

Organisation of competent authority function

- three persons (all of whom also work on other tasks as well)
- contact persons for MAP requests:
    - Mr D. R. S. Hapuarachchi Deputy Commissioner General of Inland Revenue (Tax Policy & International Tax Policy) Inland Revenue Department, Colombo 02, Sri Lanka, hapuarachchi.drs@ird.gov.lk , +94 11 21354300 & +94 718572108
    - or Mr N.M.M.Mifly Senior Commissioner of Inland Revenue (Tax Policy & International Tax Policy) Inland Revenue Department, Colombo 02, Sri Lanka, mifly.nmm@ird.gov.lk, +94 11 2135410 & +94 77 2246262
    - or Ms S O A C R Niwunhella Commissioner of Inland Revenue (International Tax Policy) Inland Revenue Department, Colombo 02, Sri Lanka, niwunhella.soacr@ird.gov.lk, +94 11 2135413 & +94 71 8317186.

Figure 1. Competent Authority Organisational Structure

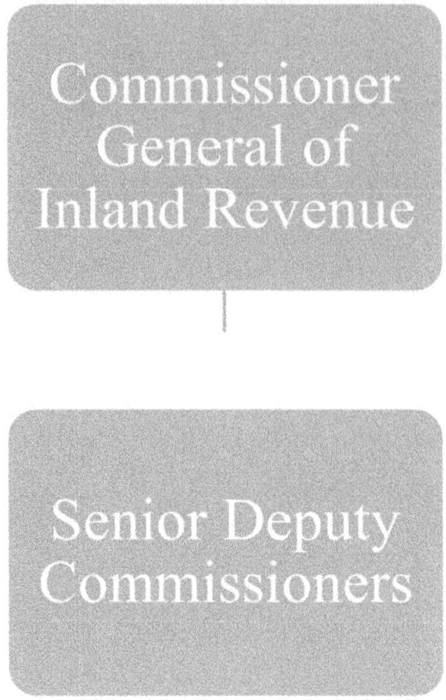

Source: OECD

Table 2. Guidance on the MAP process

MAP guidance	Mutual Agreement Procedure (MAP) Guidelines, 2023	http://www.ird.gov.lk/en/publications/International/IRDSL_MAP_Guideline.pdf (Section 2.5 to be referred to for form and content of a MAP request, including information requirements)
MAP profile	10 March 2021	https://www.oecd.org/tax/dispute/sri-lanka-dispute-resolution-profile.pdf

Overview of Sri Lanka's MAP Statistics for 2022

Please refer to https://www.oecd.org/tax/dispute/map-statistics-sri-lanka.pdf for details with respect to Sri Lanka's MAP Statistics.

Cases closed in 2022

No MAP cases were closed by Sri Lanka in 2022.

Figure 2. Evolution of Sri Lanka's MAP caseload (2016-22)

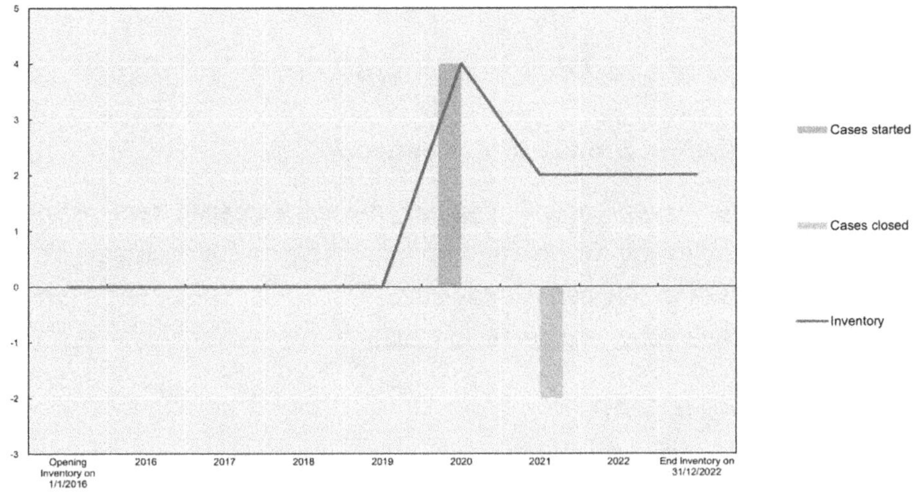

Source: OECD

Table 3. Overview of Sri Lanka's MAP caseload for 2022

Inventory for year 2022	Opening Inventory 1/1/2022	Cases started	Cases Closed	End Inventory 31/12/2022
Attribution/allocation cases	0	0	0	0
Other cases	2	0	0	2
Total	2	0	0	2

Source: OECD

Table 4. Sri Lanka's average time to resolve MAP cases in 2022

Cases resolved in year 2022	Pre-2016 cases		Post-2015 cases		All	
	Number of cases	**Average time**	**Number of cases**	**Average time** **Start to End**	**Number of cases**	**Average time**
Attribution / Allocation cases	0	N/A	0	N/A	0	N/A
Other cases	0	N/A	0	N/A	0	N/A
All cases	0	N/A	0	N/A	0	N/A

Source: OECD

Sweden

Recent developments relating to MAP in Sweden prior to 15 August 2023

Developments relating to MAP in the tax treaty network

- new tax treaty with Slovenia (applicable 01/01/2022, replacing existing treaty with Yugoslavia)
- termination of the tax treaties with Greece and Portugal (treaties not applicable since 01/01/2022)
- amending protocol with France (signed 22 May 2023)
- amending protocol with Germany (signed 18 Jan 2023).

Other developments relating to MAP

- No developments were reported

Latest Action 14 Peer Review report

9 April 2020 - https://doi.org/10.1787/7b3b1492-en

Tax treaty network of Sweden

- 80 treaties, applicable to 84 jurisdictions (covering all treaties signed, although not necessarily in force)
- status of MLI: in force.

Table 1. State of play of Sweden's tax treaty network

Treaties in line with the Action 14 Minimum Standard following MLI impact	Treaties where actions are ongoing to make them in line with the Action 14 Minimum Standard	Following impact/actions, remaining treaties that are not in line with Action 14 Minimum Standard
60	2	13

Source: OECD

Sweden's MAP programme

Organisation of competent authority function

- 15 persons:
    - one head of unit
    - 14 persons working on MAP cases:
        - nine persons work on attribution/allocation cases and five persons work on other cases.
- contact persons for MAP requests:

- Skatteverket, Enheten för internationell samverkan, Behörig myndighet MAP/APA, 205 30 MALMÖ The Swedish Tax Agency, Unit for International Cooperation, Competent Authority MAP/APA, 205 30 Malmö, Sweden.
- e-mail to the Office of the Competent Authority: oca@skatteverket.se.

Figure 1. Competent Authority Organisational Structure

Source: OECD

Table 2. Guidance on the MAP process

MAP guidance	*Ansökan om undanröjande av internationell dubbelbeskattning*	https://www.skatteverket.se/privat/skatter/arbeteinkomst/internationellainkomster/dubbelbeskattningavrakning/undanrojandeavdubbelbeskattning.4.69ef368911e1304a625800011554.html (Section "Ansökan" to be referred to for form and content of a MAP request, including information requirements)
MAP profile	3 June 2022	https://www.oecd.org/tax/dispute/sweden-dispute-resolution-profile.pdf

Overview of Sweden's MAP Statistics for 2022

Please refer to https://www.oecd.org/tax/dispute/map-statistics-sweden.pdf for details with respect to Sweden's MAP Statistics.

Figure 2. Cases Closed in 2022

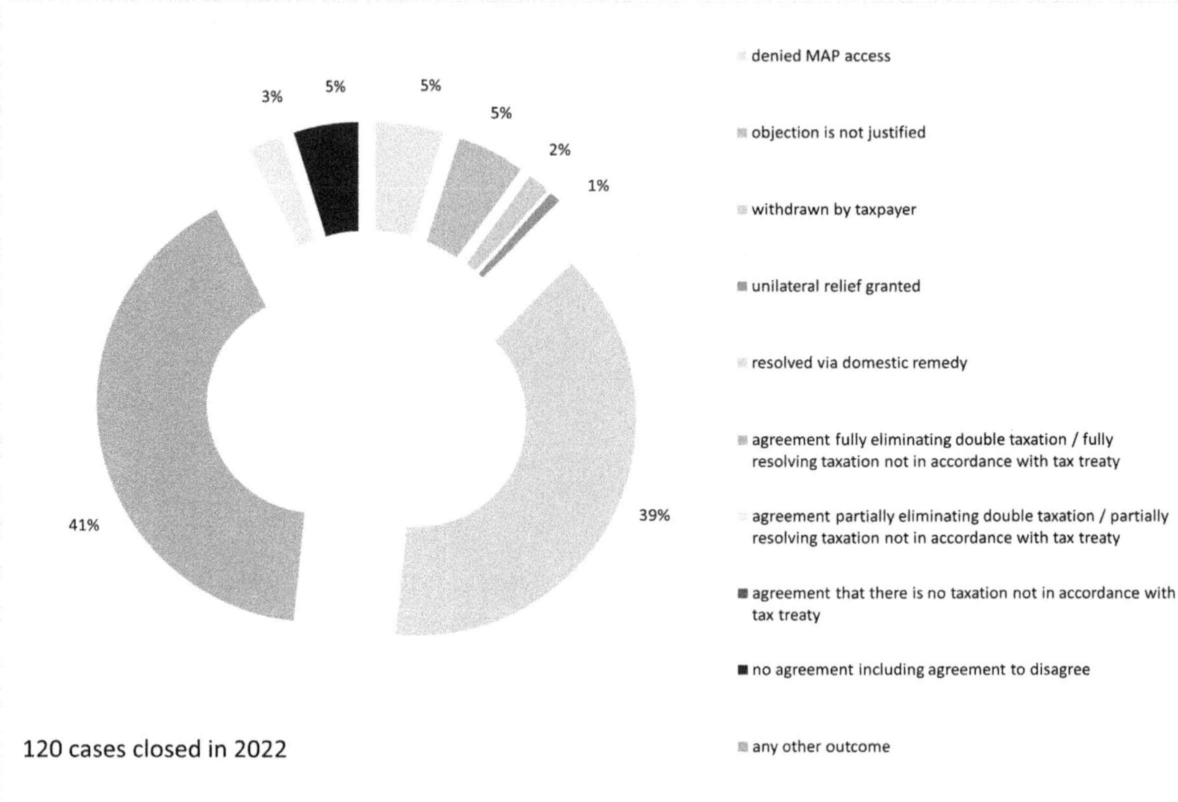

Source: OECD

Figure 3. Evolution of Sweden's MAP caseload (2016-22)

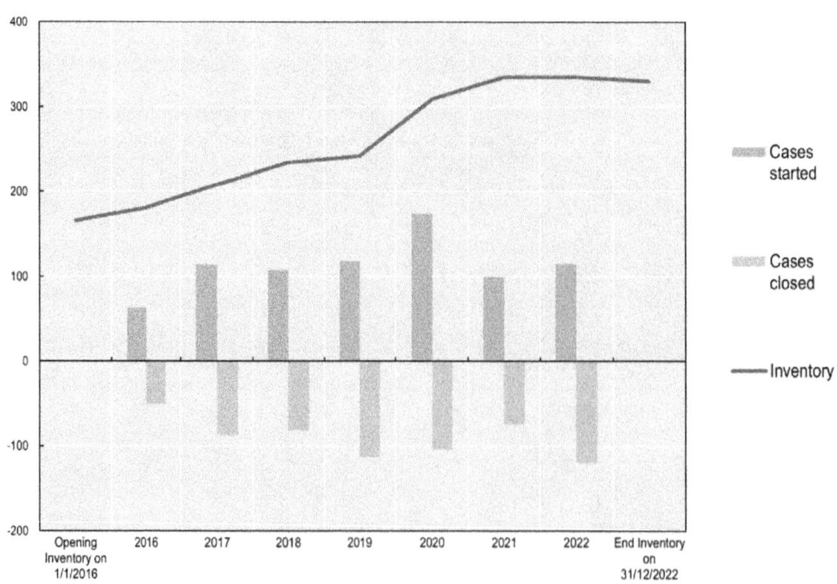

Source: OECD

Table 3. Overview of Sweden's MAP caseload for 2022

Inventory for year 2022	Opening Inventory 1/1/2022	Cases started	Cases Closed	End Inventory 31/12/2022
Attribution/allocation cases	195	34	87	142
Other cases	140	81	33	188
Total	335	115	120	330

Source: OECD

Table 4. Sweden's average time to resolve MAP cases in 2022

Cases resolved in year 2022	Pre-2016 cases		Post-2015 cases		All	
	Number of cases	**Average time**	**Number of cases**	**Average time** **Start to End**	**Number of cases**	**Average time**
Attribution / Allocation cases	4	97.55	83	25.5	87	28.82
Other cases	0	N/A	33	14.32	33	14.32
All cases	4	97.55	116	22.32	120	24.83

Source: OECD

Switzerland

Recent developments relating to MAP in Switzerland prior to 15 August 2023

Developments relating to MAP in the tax treaty network

- In 2023, two amending protocols (with Armenia and Iran) implementing the Action 14 Minimum Standard entered into force.

Other developments relating to MAP

- No developments were reported

Latest Action 14 Peer Review report

13 August 2019 - https://doi.org/10.1787/77ab98a6-en

Tax treaty network of Switzerland

- 97 treaties, applicable to 108 jurisdictions (covering all treaties signed, although not necessarily in force)
- status of MLI: in force.

Table 1. State of play of Switzerland's tax treaty network

Treaties in line with the Action 14 Minimum Standard following MLI impact	Treaties where actions are ongoing to make them in line with the Action 14 Minimum Standard	Following impact/actions, remaining treaties that are not in line with Action 14 Minimum Standard
35	53	20

Source: OECD

Switzerland's MAP programme

Organisation of competent authority function

- 15 persons:
  - one head of unit
  - 14 persons working on MAP cases (among which seven persons work on other tasks as well):
    - seven persons work on attribution/allocation cases and seven persons work on other cases.
- contact persons for MAP requests:
  - for attribution / allocation cases: Federal Department of Finance, State Secretariat for International Finance (SIF), Tax Division Section VP, Bundesgasse 3 CH-3003 Bern | Email: transferpricing@sif.admin.ch

- for other cases: Federal Department of Finance, State Secretariat for International Finance (SIF), Tax Division Section BS, Bundesgasse 3 CH-3003 Bern | Email: dba@sif.admin.ch

Figure 1. Competent Authority Organisational Structure

Source: OECD

Table 2. Guidance on the MAP process

MAP guidance	*Factsheet on the mutual agreement procedure*, January 2023	https://www.sif.admin.ch/dam/sif/en/dokumente/Internationale-Steuerpolitik/Doppelbesteuerung/Merkblatt%20Verst%C3%A4ndigungsverfahren.pdf.download.pdf/20230112%20-%20MAP%20Guidance%20-%20e.pdf https://www.sif.admin.ch/dam/sif/en/dokumente/Internationale-Steuerpolitik/Doppelbesteuerung/Merkblatt Verst%C3%A4ndigungsverfahren.pdf.download.pdf/20230112 - MAP Guidance - e.pdf (Section 4. to be referred to for form and content of a MAP request, including information requirements)
	Web page	https://www.sif.admin.ch/sif/en/home/bilateral-relations/tax-agreements/double-taxation-agreements/mutual-agreement-procedure.html
MAP profile	9 November 2018	https://www.oecd.org/tax/dispute/switzerland-dispute-resolution-profile.pdf

Overview of Switzerland's MAP Statistics for 2022

Please refer to https://www.oecd.org/tax/dispute/map-statistics-switzerland.pdf for details with respect to Switzerland's MAP Statistics.

Figure 2. Cases Closed in 2022

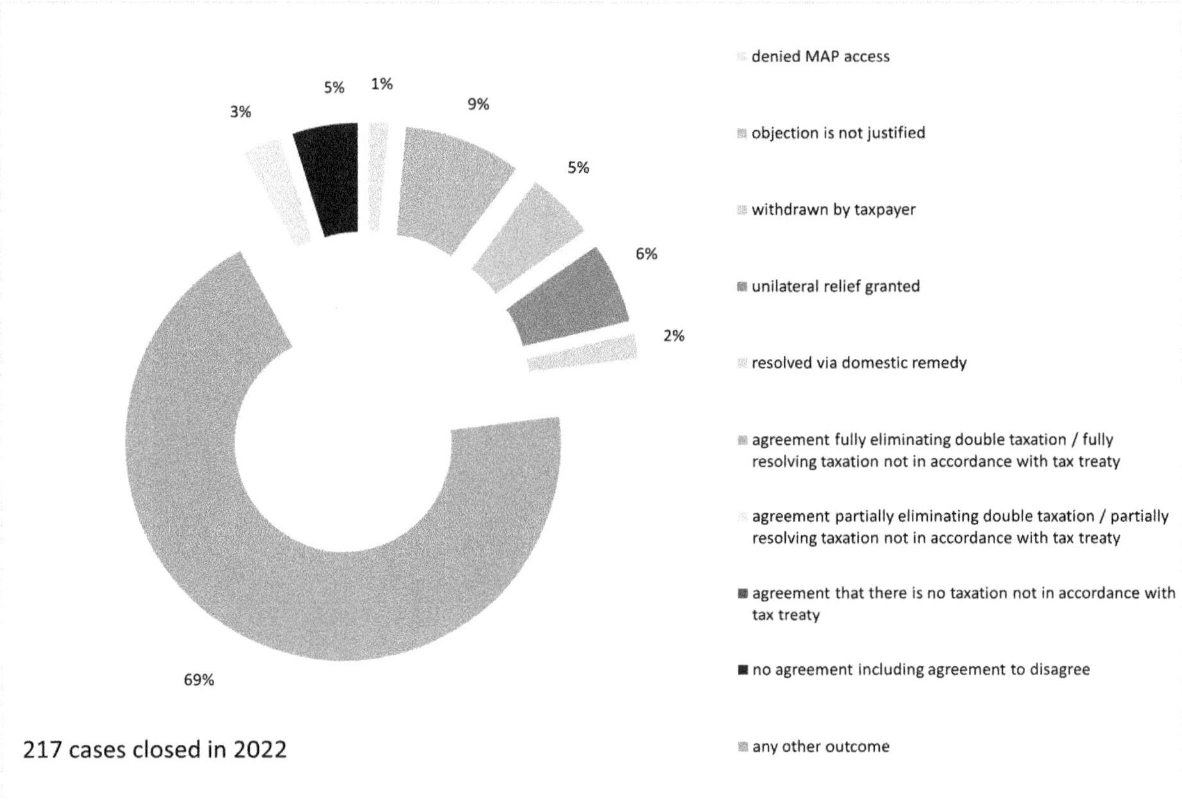

Source: OECD

Figure 3. Evolution of Switzerland's MAP caseload (2016-22)

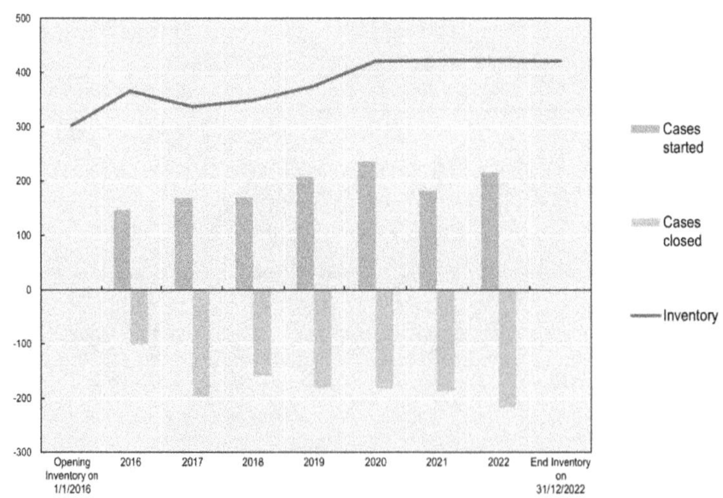

Source: OECD

Table 3. Overview of Switzerland's MAP caseload for 2022

Inventory for year 2022	Opening Inventory 1/1/2022	Cases started	Cases Closed	End Inventory 31/12/2022
Attribution/allocation cases	202	81	57	226
Other cases	220	135	160	195
Total	422	216	217	421

Source: OECD

Table 4. Switzerland's average time to resolve MAP cases in 2022

Cases resolved in year 2022	Pre-2016 cases		Post-2015 cases		All	
	Number of cases	**Average time**	**Number of cases**	**Average time** **Start to End**	**Number of cases**	**Average time**
Attribution / Allocation cases	0	N/A	57	21.34	57	21.34
Other cases	6	100.53	154	16.74	160	19.88
All cases	6	100.53	211	17.98	217	20.27

Source: OECD

Thailand

Recent developments relating to MAP in Thailand prior to 15 August 2023

Developments relating to MAP in the tax treaty network

- Thailand signed and ratified the Multilateral Instrument (MLI) to modify existing tax treaties to contain the equivalent of Article 25 of the OECD Model Tax Convention (OECD, 2017). Tax treaties have been modified to fulfil the requirements under the Action 14 Minimum Standard.

Other developments relating to MAP

- Thailand has published the Map Guideline on 2021 and the Guideline on APA process on 2022 which include roll-backs.

Latest Action 14 Peer Review report

13 September 2022 - https://doi.org/10.1787/18aa2039-en

Tax treaty network of Thailand

- 61 treaties, applicable to 61 jurisdictions (covering all treaties signed, although not necessarily in force)
- status of MLI: in force.

Table 1. State of play of Thailand's tax treaty network

Treaties in line with the Action 14 Minimum Standard following MLI impact	Treaties where actions are ongoing to make them in line with the Action 14 Minimum Standard	Following impact/actions, remaining treaties that are not in line with Action 14 Minimum Standard
39	3	19

Source: OECD

Thailand's MAP programme

Organisation of competent authority function

- five persons:
  - one head of unit
  - four persons working on MAP cases (all of which also work on other tasks as well).
- contact persons for MAP requests:
  - Mr.Lavaron Sangsnit, Director-General, The Revenue Department of Thailand, 90 Soi Phaholyothin 7, Phaholyothin Road, Phayathai, Bangkok 10400
  - Tel. (+66) (2) 272 8639 E-mail address: MAPThailand@rd.go.th

Figure 1. Competent Authority Organisational Structure

Source: OECD

Table 2. Guidance on the MAP process

MAP guidance	*Mutual Agreement Procedure Guideline*, 2021	https://www.rd.go.th/final_MAPmanualEN.pdf (Section 6 to be referred to for form and content of a MAP request, including information requirements)
MAP profile	8 April 2022	https://www.oecd.org/ctp/dispute/thailand-dispute-resolution-profile.pdf

Overview of Thailand's MAP Statistics for 2022

Please refer to https://www.oecd.org/tax/dispute/map-statistics-thailand.pdf for details with respect to Thailand's MAP Statistics.

Figure 2. Cases Closed in 2022

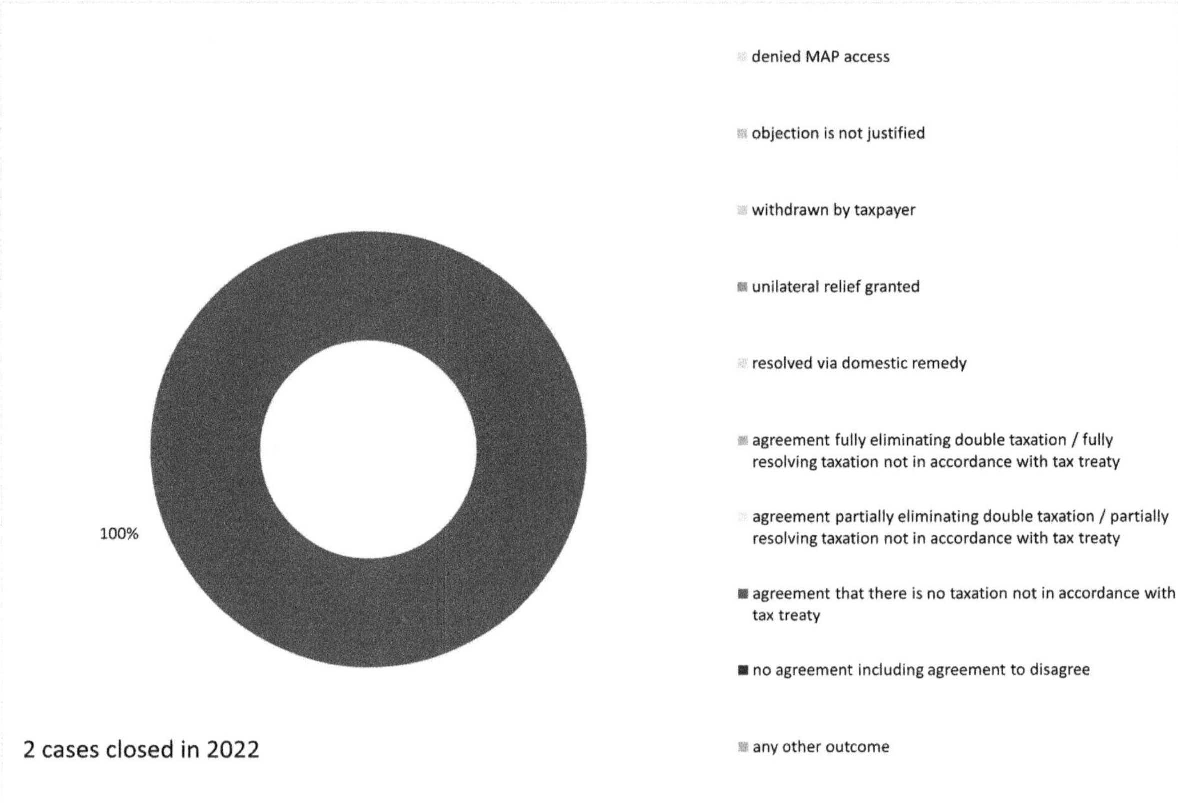

Source: OECD

Figure 3. Evolution of Thailand's MAP caseload (2017-22)

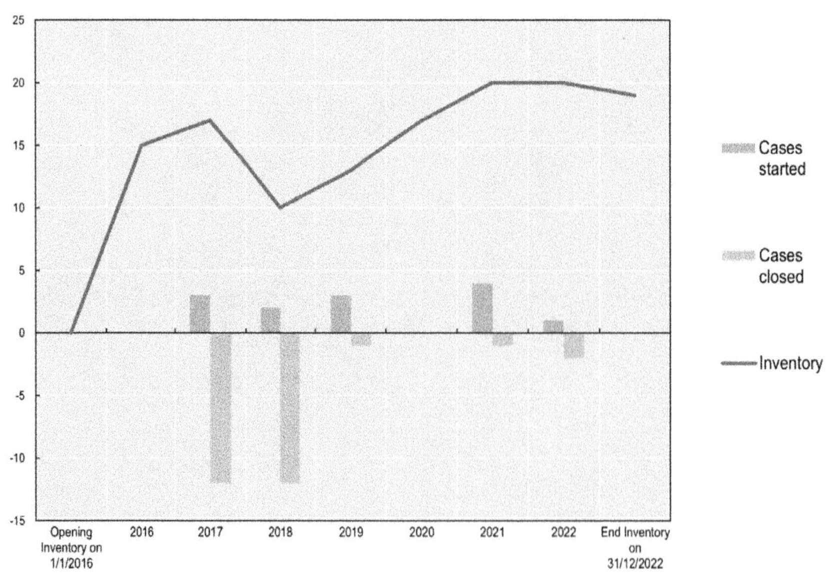

Source: OECD

Table 3. Overview of Thailand's MAP caseload for 2022

Inventory for year 2022	Opening Inventory 1/1/2022	Cases started	Cases Closed	End Inventory 31/12/2022
Attribution/allocation cases	0	0	0	0
Other cases	20	1	2	19
Total	20	1	2	19

Source: OECD

Table 4. Thailand's average time to resolve MAP cases in 2022

Cases resolved in year 2022	Pre-2016 cases		Post-2015 cases		All	
	Number of cases	**Average time**	**Number of cases**	**Average time** **Start to End**	**Number of cases**	**Average time**
Attribution / Allocation cases	0	N/A	0	N/A	0	N/A
Other cases	1	77.00	1	39	2	58.00
All cases	1	77.00	1	N/A	2	58.00

Source: OECD

Togo

Recent developments relating to MAP in Togo prior to 15 August 2023

Developments relating to MAP in the tax treaty network

- Togo did not provide the relevant information.

Other developments relating to MAP

- Togo did not provide the relevant information.

Latest Action 14 Peer Review report

Togo is yet to be peer reviewed under Action 14.

Tax treaty network of Togo

- three treaties, applicable to eight jurisdictions (covering all treaties signed, although not necessarily in force)
- status of MLI: not signed.

Table 1. State of play of Togo's tax treaty network

Treaties in line with the Action 14 Minimum Standard following MLI impact	Treaties where actions are ongoing to make them in line with the Action 14 Minimum Standard	Following impact/actions, remaining treaties that are not in line with Action 14 Minimum Standard
0	0	3

Source: OECD

Togo's MAP programme

Organisation of competent authority function

- contact persons for MAP requests:
  - Le Commissaire général de l'Office Togolais des Recettes (OTR)
  - Monsieur Philippe Kokou B. TCHODIE
  - tél : +228 22 53 14 02, email : ptchodie@otr.tg, otr@otr.tg
  - 41 Rue des Impôts-02 BP : 20823 Lomé-TOGO.

Figure 1. Competent Authority Organisational Structure

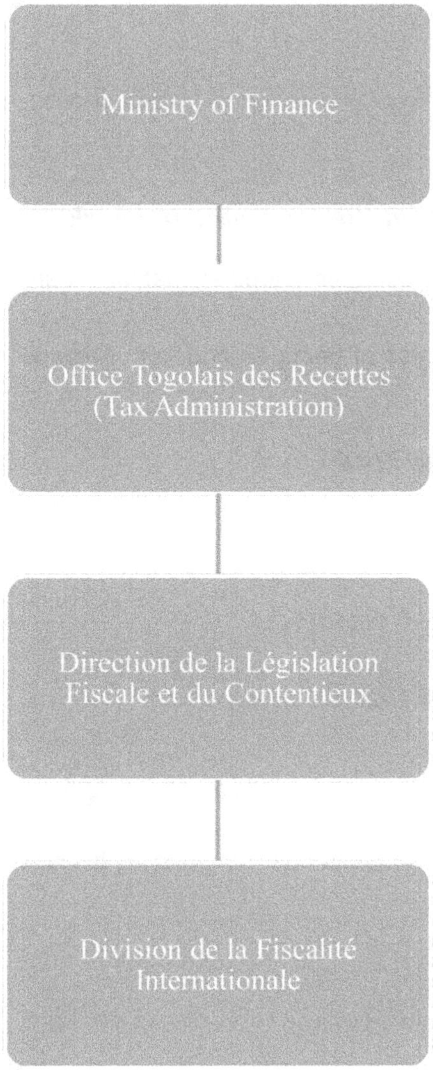

Source : OECD

Table 2. Guidance on the MAP process

MAP guidance	Togo did not provide the relevant information.	-
MAP profile	No MAP profile published	-

Overview of Togo's MAP Statistics for 2022

Togo did not report any MAP cases in its 2022 MAP Statistics.

Please refer to https://www.oecd.org/tax/dispute/map-statistics-togo.pdf for details with respect to Togo's MAP Statistics.

Trinidad and Tobago

Recent developments relating to MAP in Trinidad and Tobago prior to 15 August 2023

Developments relating to MAP in the tax treaty network

- CARICOM treaty is currently being amended so that MAP can be initiated in any (affected) Member state.
- Ten treaties are in the process of being amended to become in line with the Action 14 Minimum Standard.

Other developments relating to MAP

- MAP profile updated in 2023.

Latest Action 14 Peer Review report

13 September 2022 - https://doi.org/10.1787/b4daac65-en

Tax treaty network of Trinidad and Tobago

- 16 treaties, applicable to 25 jurisdictions (covering all treaties signed, although not necessarily in force)
- status of MLI: not signed.

Table 1. State of play of Trinidad and Tobago's tax treaty network

Treaties in line with the Action 14 Minimum Standard following MLI impact	Treaties where actions are ongoing to make them in line with the Action 14 Minimum Standard	Following impact/actions, remaining treaties that are not in line with Action 14 Minimum Standard
7	4	5

Source: OECD

Trinidad and Tobago's MAP programme

Organisation of competent authority function

- seven persons
- contact persons for MAP requests:
  - Sharon Boodoosingh, Commissioner of Inland Revenue and Chairman of the Board, Inland Revenue Division, LEVEL 22, IRD TOWER, #2 - 4 AJAX STREET
  - POS EMAIL: birchair@ird.gov.tt
  - Telephone: 1-868-623-4921 (DIRECT) 1-868-800-8299 Ext. 12290/ 12213/ 12212 (PBX)

- Fax: 1-868-627-7967.

Figure 1. Competent Authority Organisational Structure

Source: OECD

Table 2. Guidance on the MAP process

MAP guidance	*Guidelines for Mutual Agreement Procedure*, 2023	https://www.ird.gov.tt//law-policy/map-guidelines (Sections "Making a MAP request" and "Information required for submitting a valid MAP request" to be referred to for form and content of a MAP request, including information requirements)
MAP profile	31 January 2023	https://www.oecd.org/tax/dispute/trinidad-and-tobago-dispute-resolution-profile.pdf

Overview of Trinidad and Tobago's MAP Statistics for 2022

Please refer to https://www.oecd.org/tax/dispute/map-statistics-trinidad-and-tobago.pdf for details with respect to Trinidad and Tobago's MAP Statistics.

Cases closed in 2022

No MAP cases were closed by Trinidad and Tobago in 2022.

Figure 2. Evolution of Trinidad and Tobago's MAP caseload (2017-22)

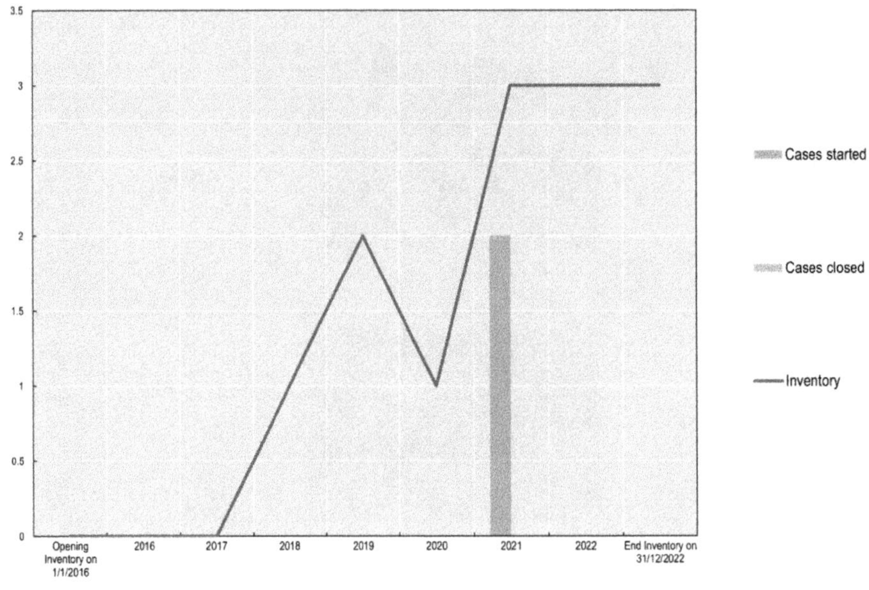

Source: OECD

Table 3. Overview of Trinidad and Tobago's MAP caseload for 2022

Inventory for year 2022	Opening Inventory 1/1/2022	Cases started	Cases Closed	End Inventory 31/12/2022
Attribution/allocation cases	1	0	0	1
Other cases	2	0	0	2
Total	3	0	0	3

Source: OECD

Table 4. Trinidad and Tobago's average time to resolve MAP cases in 2022

Cases resolved in year 2022	Pre-2016 cases		Post-2015 cases		All	
	Number of cases	**Average time**	**Number of cases**	**Average time** **Start to End**	**Number of cases**	**Average time**
Attribution / Allocation cases	0	N/A	0	N/A	0	N/A
Other cases	0	N/A	0	N/A	0	N/A
All cases	0	N/A	0	N/A	0	N/A

Source: OECD

Tunisia

Recent developments relating to MAP in Tunisia prior to 15 August 2023

Developments relating to MAP in the tax treaty network

- Tunisia did not provide the relevant information.

Other developments relating to MAP

- Tunisia did not provide the relevant information.

Latest Action 14 Peer Review report

14 April 2022 - https://doi.org/10.1787/5e8a9cac-en

Tax treaty network of Tunisia

- 52 treaties, applicable to 55 jurisdictions (covering all treaties signed, although not necessarily in force)
- status of MLI: in force.

Table 1. State of play of Tunisia's tax treaty network

Treaties in line with the Action 14 Minimum Standard following MLI impact	Treaties where actions are ongoing to make them in line with the Action 14 Minimum Standard	Following impact/actions, remaining treaties that are not in line with Action 14 Minimum Standard
28	No information	No information

Source: OECD

Tunisia's MAP programme

Organisation of competent authority function

- three persons
- contact persons for MAP requests:
  - Sihem Nemsia Directeur Général des Etudes et de la Législation Fiscales, Ministère des Finances, Place du Gouvernement – La Kasbah, 1000
  - Tel : (+216) 71 783 786 Fax : (+216) 71 790 550
  - e-mail address: dg.dgelf@finances.tn.

Figure 1. Competent Authority Organisational Structure

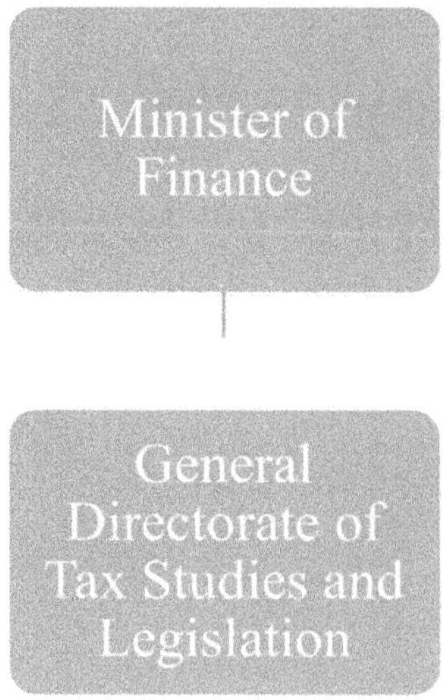

Source: OECD

Table 2. Guidance on the MAP process

MAP guidance	*Note Commune n°23/2019*, 12 September 2019	https://doc-fiscale.finances.gov.tn/cimf-internet/page/doc-portal/fr/#path=%2FNotes%20communes%2F2019&currentPage=1 (Section V. to be referred to for form and content of a MAP request, including information requirements)
MAP profile	26 September 2019	https://www.oecd.org/tax/dispute/Tunisia-Dispute-Resolution-Profile.pdf

Overview of Tunisia's MAP Statistics for 2022

Please refer to https://www.oecd.org/tax/dispute/map-statistics-tunisia.pdf for details with respect to Tunisia's MAP Statistics.

Cases closed in 2022

No MAP cases were closed by Tunisia in 2022.

Figure 2. Evolution of Tunisia's MAP caseload (2017-22)

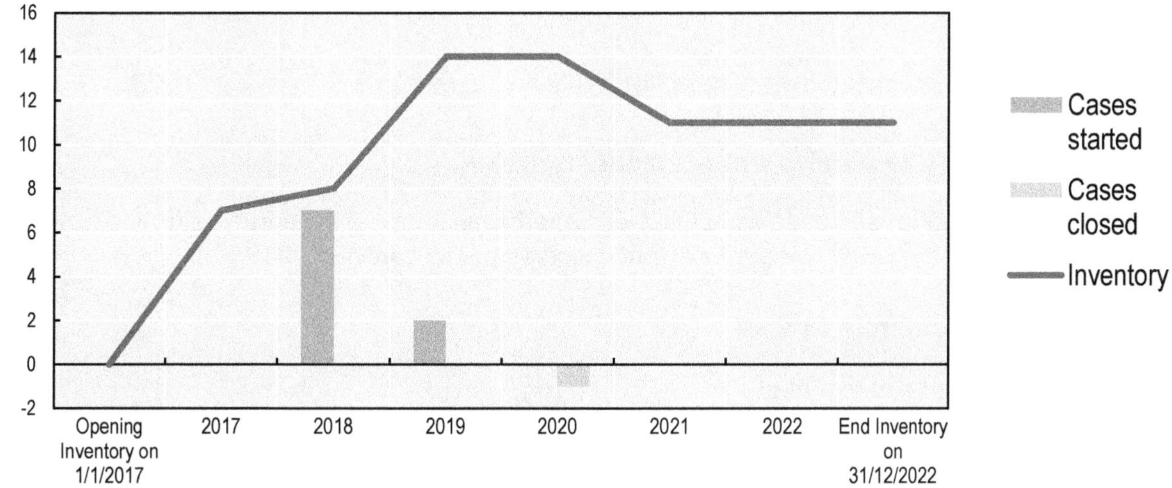

Source: OECD

Table 3. Overview of Tunisia's MAP caseload for 2022

Inventory for year 2022	Opening Inventory 1/1/2022	Cases started	Cases Closed	End Inventory 31/12/2022
Attribution/allocation cases	3	0	0	3
Other cases	11	0	0	11
Total	14	0	0	14

Source: OECD

Table 4. Tunisia's average time to resolve MAP cases in 2022

Cases resolved in year 2022	Pre-2017 cases		Post-2016 cases		All	
	Number of cases	**Average time**	**Number of cases**	**Average time** **Start to End**	**Number of cases**	**Average time**
Attribution / Allocation cases	0	N/A	0	N/A	0	N/A
Other cases	0	N/A	0	N/A	0	N/A
All cases	0	N/A	0	N/A	0	N/A

Source: OECD

Türkiye

Recent developments relating to MAP in Türkiye prior to 15 August 2023

Developments relating to MAP in the tax treaty network

- Bilateral negotiations have been completed with Azerbaijan to revise the agreement which contains Article 25(1-3) of the OECD Model Tax Convention as per its version of 2017.

Other developments relating to MAP

- No developments were reported

Latest Action 14 Peer Review report

25 May 2021 - https://doi.org/10.1787/6dd47527-en

Tax treaty network of Türkiye

- 100 treaties, applicable to 101 jurisdictions (covering all treaties signed, although not necessarily in force)
- status of MLI: signed.

Table 1. State of play of Türkiye's tax treaty network

Treaties in line with the Action 14 Minimum Standard following MLI impact	Treaties where actions are ongoing to make them in line with the Action 14 Minimum Standard	Following impact/actions, remaining treaties that are not in line with Action 14 Minimum Standard
67	1	32

Source: OECD

Türkiye's MAP programme

Organisation of competent authority function

- 31 persons:
  - six heads of unit
  - nine persons working on MAP cases (all of which work on other tasks as well):
    - three persons work on attribution/allocation cases and six persons work on other cases.
- contact persons for MAP requests:
  - Mr. Bekir BAYRAKDAR Commissioner/Turkish Revenue Administration/Ministry of Treasury and Finance Full Address: Devlet Mahallesi, Merasim Caddesi No: 9/1 06450 Çankaya-Ankara/TÜRKİYE Tel: +90 312 415 30 17-18; Fax:+90 312 415 28 21-22

- Mr. Mehmet ARABACI Deputy Commissioner/Turkish Revenue Administration/Ministry of Treasury and Finance Full Address: Devlet Mahallesi, Merasim Caddesi No:9/1 06450 Çankaya-Ankara/TÜRKİYE Tel: +90 312 415 36 26; Fax:+90 312 415 28 21-22
- Mr. Ahmet YILDIRIM Head of Department/European Union and International Relations Department/Turkish Revenue Administration /Ministry of Treasury and Finance Full Address: Devlet Mahallesi, Merasim Caddesi No:9/1 06450 Çankaya-Ankara/TÜRKİYE Tel: +90 312 415 34 60; Fax: +90 312 415 28 21-22; e-mail: ahmet.yildirim@gelirler.gov.tr
- Mr. Mustafa Cemil KARA Head of Group/European Union and International Relations Department/Turkish Revenue Administration /Ministry of Treasury and Finance Full Address: Devlet Mahallesi, Merasim Caddesi No:9/1 06450 Çankaya-Ankara/TÜRKİYE Tel: +90 312 415 34 51; Fax: +90 312 415 28 21-22; e-mail: mustafa.cemil.kara@gelirler.gov.tr
- Mrs. Gülru İSKENDER KAYA Head of Group/European Union and International Relations Department/Turkish Revenue Administration/Ministry of Treasury and Finance Full Address: Devlet Mahallesi, Merasim Caddesi No:9/1 06450 Çankaya-Ankara/TÜRKİYE Tel: +90 312 415 36 79; Fax: +90 312 415 28 21-22; e-mail: gkaya@gelirler.gov.tr.

Figure 1. Competent Authority Organisational Structure

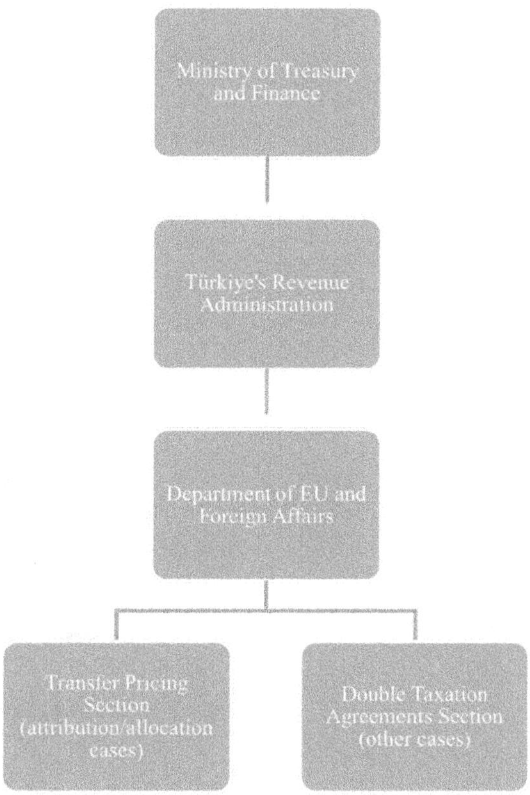

Source: OECD

Table 2. Guidance on the MAP process

MAP guidance	*Guideline on the mutual agreement procedure for the elimination of double taxation agreements*, October 2019	https://www.gib.gov.tr/sites/default/files/fileadmin/CifteVergilendirme/MAP_Guidelines2019.pdf (Section 10 to be referred to for form and content of a MAP request, including information requirements)
MAP profile	24 March 2023	https://www.oecd.org/tax/dispute/turkiye-dispute-resolution-profile.pdf

Overview of Türkiye's MAP Statistics for 2022

Please refer to https://www.oecd.org/tax/dispute/map-statistics-turkiye.pdf for details with respect to Türkiye's MAP Statistics.

Figure 2. Cases Closed in 2022

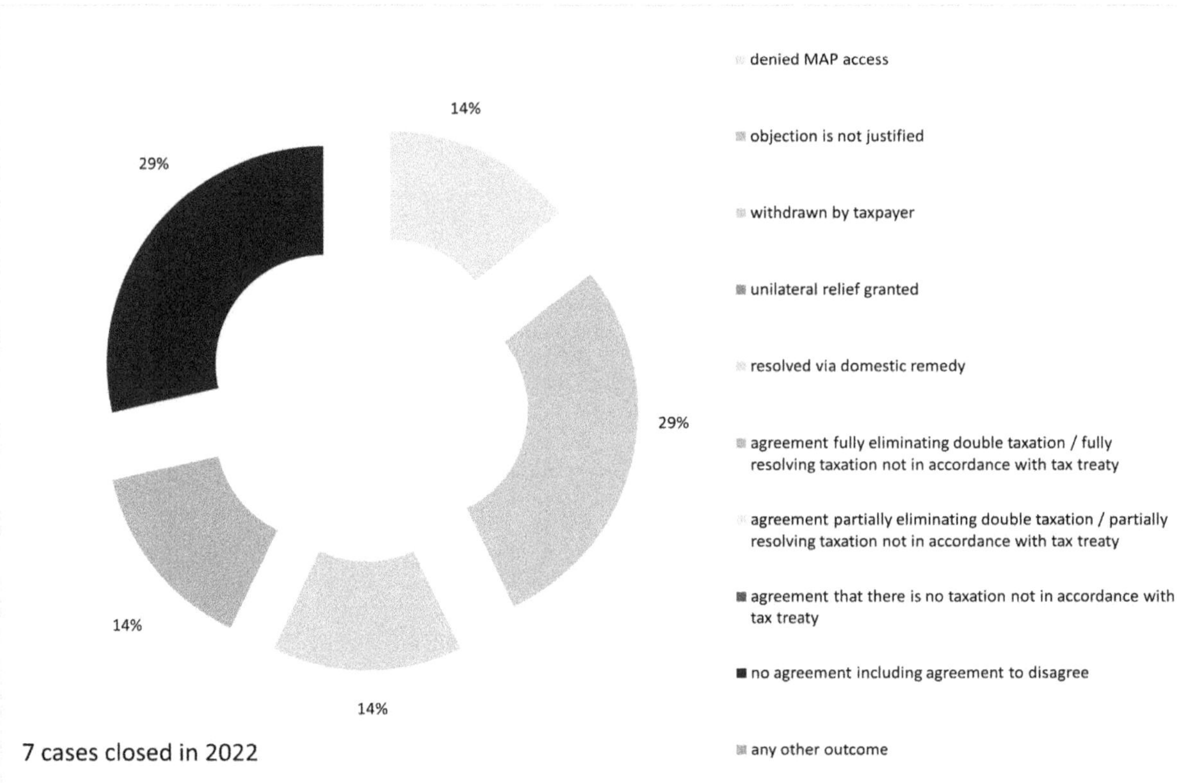

Source: OECD

Figure 3. Evolution of Türkiye's MAP caseload (2016-22)

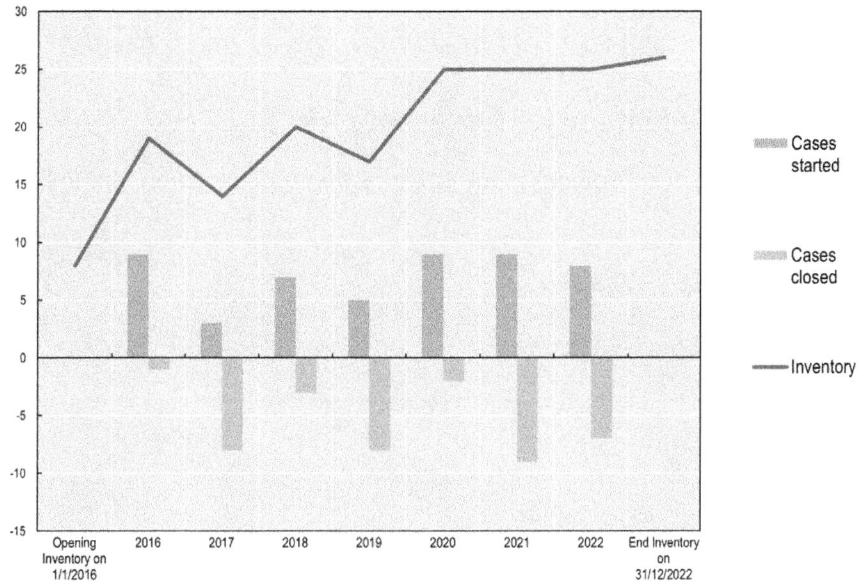

Source: OECD

Table 3. Overview of Türkiye's MAP caseload for 2022

Inventory for year 2022	Opening Inventory 1/1/2022	Cases started	Cases Closed	End Inventory 31/12/2022
Attribution/allocation cases	10	2	2	10
Other cases	15	6	5	16
Total	25	8	7	26

Source: OECD

Table 4. Türkiye's average time to resolve MAP cases in 2022

Cases resolved in year 2022	Pre-2016 cases		Post-2015 cases		All	
	Number of cases	**Average time**	**Number of cases**	**Average time** **Start to End**	**Number of cases**	**Average time**
Attribution / Allocation cases	0	N/A	2	17.51	2	17.51
Other cases	2	80.83	3	17.98	5	43.12
All cases	2	80.83	5	17.79	7	35.80

Source: OECD

Ukraine

Recent developments relating to MAP in Ukraine prior to 15 August 2023

Developments relating to MAP in the tax treaty network

- Ratification in April 2023 of a Protocol to the tax treaty with Qatar to bring it in line with the Action 14 Minimum Standard

Other developments relating to MAP

- Update in March 2023 of the MAP profile.

Latest Action 14 Peer Review report

Ukraine is yet to be peer reviewed under Action 14.

Tax treaty network of Ukraine

- 71 treaties, applicable to 72 jurisdictions (covering all treaties signed, although not necessarily in force)
- Status of MLI: in force

Table 1. State of play of Ukraine's tax treaty network

Treaties in line with the Action 14 Minimum Standard following MLI impact	Treaties where actions are ongoing to make them in line with the Action 14 Minimum Standard	Following impact/actions, remaining treaties that are not in line with Action 14 Minimum Standard
26	35	10

Source: OECD

Ukraine's MAP programme

Organisation of competent authority function

- Five persons work on MAP cases in the Ministry of Finance including three in the dedicated MAP unit.
- Due to the absence of cases under the tax treaties where the State Tax Service acts as the competent authority there is no dedicated MAP staff.
- contact persons for MAP requests:
  - Ministry of Finance of Ukraine 11 Mezhigirska str., 04071 Kyiv, Ukraine, Tel: +38 (044) 277 56 27 E-mail: infomf@minfin.gov.ua
  - Ms Liudmyla Palamar Director of the International Taxation Department, Tel: +38 (044) 277 53 69 E-mail: palamar@minfin.gov.ua

- Ms Nadiia Gorieva Deputy Director of the International Taxation Department - Head of the Unit for Implementation of International Agreements and Mutual Agreement Procedures, Tel: +38 (044) 201 56 84 E-mail: nhorieva@minfin.gov.ua
- Ms Lesia Kuchmuk Head of the International Tax Treaties and Exchange of Information Unit International Taxation Department, Tel: +38 (044) 206 59 35 E-mail: lkuchmuk@minfin.gov.ua
- State Tax Service of Ukraine 6-8 Lvivska Square, 04053 Kyiv, Ukraine, Tel: +38 (044) 272 62 55 E-mail: post@tax.gov.ua
- Ms Olena Mykytenko Acting Director of the International Cooperation Department, Tel: +38 (044) 590 48 50 E-mail: omykytenko@tax.gov.ua
- Ms Kateryna Ryzhenkova Director of the Transfer Pricing Department, Tel: +38 (044) 481 48 78 E-mail: irebko@tax.gov.ua.

Figure 1. Competent Authority Organisational Structure

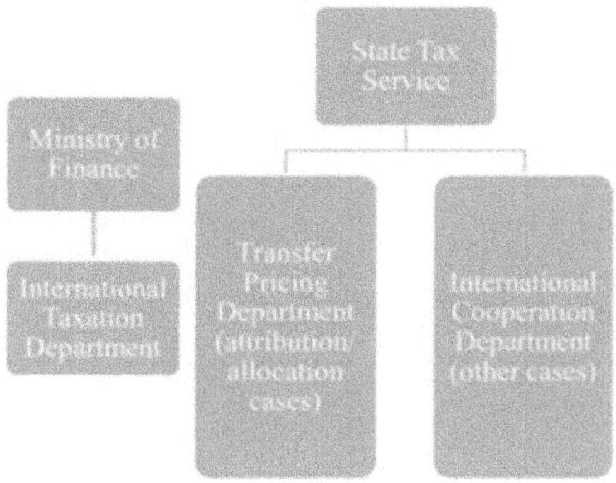

Source: OECD

Table 2. Guidance on the MAP process

MAP guidance	Tax code of Ukraine, Article 108-1,	https://zakon.rada.gov.ua/laws/show/2755-17#Text (Section XX to be referred to for form and content of a MAP request, including information requirements)
	Order of the Ministry of Finance of Ukraine №820 of 30 December 2020	https://zakon.rada.gov.ua/laws/show/z0305-21#Text
MAP profile	29 March 2023	https://www.oecd.org/tax/dispute/ukraine-dispute-resolution-profile.pdf

Overview of Ukraine's MAP Statistics for 2022

Please refer to https://www.oecd.org/tax/dispute/map-statistics-ukraine.pdf for details with respect to Ukraine's MAP Statistics.

Cases closed in 2022

No MAP cases were closed by Ukraine in 2022.

Figure 2. Evolution of Ukraine's MAP caseload (2017-22)

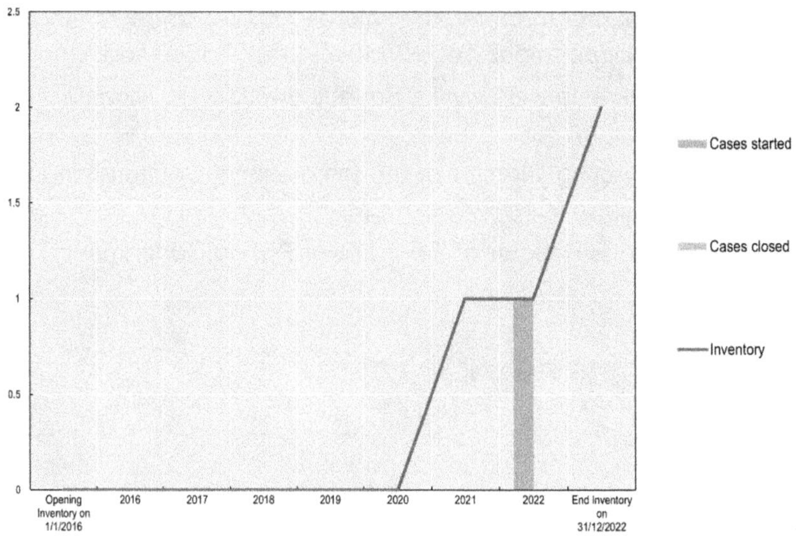

Source: OECD

Table 3. Overview of Ukraine's MAP caseload for 2022

Inventory for year 2022	Opening Inventory 1/1/2022	Cases started	Cases Closed	End Inventory 31/12/2022
Attribution/allocation cases	0	0	0	0
Other cases	1	1	0	2
Total	1	1	0	2

Source: OECD

Table 4. Ukraine's average time to resolve MAP cases in 2022

Cases resolved in year 2022	Pre-2016 cases		Post-2015 cases		All	
	Number of cases	**Average time**	**Number of cases**	**Average time** **Start to End**	**Number of cases**	**Average time**
Attribution / Allocation cases	0	N/A	0	N/A	0	N/A
Other cases	0	N/A	0	N/A	0	N/A
All cases	0	N/A	0	N/A	0	N/A

Source: OECD

United Arab Emirates

Recent developments relating to MAP in United Arab Emirates prior to 15 August 2023

Developments relating to MAP in the tax treaty network

- No developments were reported

Other developments relating to MAP

- No developments were reported

Latest Action 14 Peer Review report

13 September 2022 - https://doi.org/10.1787/d4e40420-en

Tax treaty network of United Arab Emirates

- 141 treaties, applicable to 134 jurisdictions (covering all treaties signed, although not necessarily in force)
- status of MLI: in force.

Table 1. State of play of United Arab Emirates' tax treaty network

Treaties in line with the Action 14 Minimum Standard following MLI impact	Treaties where actions are ongoing to make them in line with the Action 14 Minimum Standard	Following impact/actions, remaining treaties that are not in line with Action 14 Minimum Standard
125	16	0

Source: OECD

United Arab Emirates' MAP programme

Organisation of competent authority function

- eight persons:
  - two heads of unit
  - six persons working on MAP cases.
- contact persons for MAP requests:
  - Ms. Thuraiya Hamid Alhashmi, Director of International Tax Department, Ministry of Finance, E: aaalobaidli@mof.gov.ae
  - Mrs. Shabana Begum, Executive Director - Tax Policy Sector, E: sbegum@mof.gov.ae
  - Dr. Hamed Nasr, Economic Expert, Ministry of Finance, E: hamidnassr57@hotmail.com

- Ms Asma Al Zarooni, EOI Unit, Ministry of Finance, E: amalzarooni@mof.gov.ae; Taxinfo@mof.gov.ae
- Mr. Mohamed Abdulmonem, Tax Agreements Section, Ministry of Finance, E: mabdulahmed@mof.gov.ae, E: taxinfo@mof.gov.ae
- Mr. Christopher Searing, Tax Policies and Legislations Expert, E: cjsearing@mof.gov.ae
- Mrs. Anika Goel, International Tax Policy Specialist, E: agashok@mof.gov.ae.

Figure 1. Competent Authority Organisational Structure

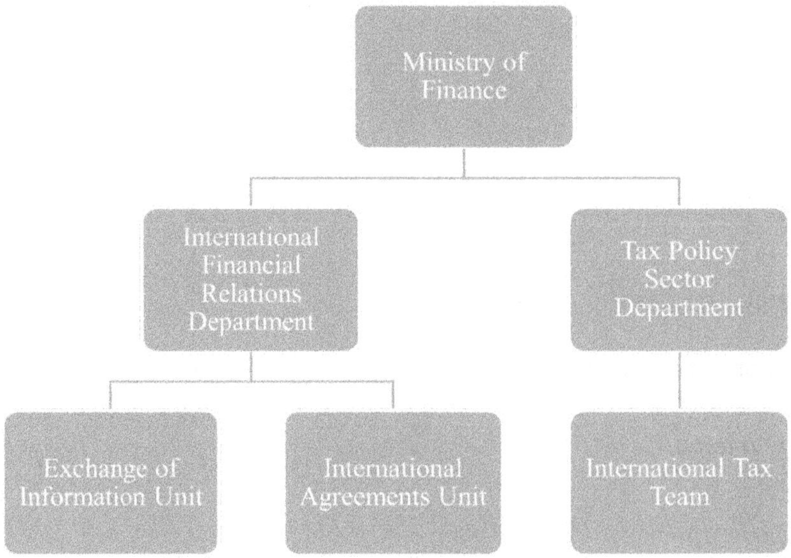

Source: OECD

Table 2. Guidance on the MAP process

MAP guidance	The link is currently inactive and will be reinstated	-
MAP profile	27 May 2020	https://www.oecd.org/tax/dispute/united-arab-emirates-dispute-resolution-profile.pdf

Overview of United Arab Emirates' MAP Statistics for 2022

United Arab Emirates did not report any MAP cases in its 2022 MAP Statistics.

Please refer to https://www.oecd.org/tax/dispute/map-statistics-united-arab-emirates.pdf for details with respect to United Arab Emirates' MAP Statistics.

United Kingdom

Recent developments relating to MAP in United Kingdom prior to 15 August 2023

Developments relating to MAP in the tax treaty network

- The UK signed a new treaty with San Marino on 17 May 2023. It has not yet entered into force.

Other developments relating to MAP

- No developments were reported

Latest Action 14 Peer Review report

13 August 2019 - https://doi.org/10.1787/33e2bf3d-en

Tax treaty network of United Kingdom

- 128 treaties, applicable to 132 jurisdictions (covering all treaties signed, although not necessarily in force)
- status of MLI: in force.

Table 1. State of play of United Kingdom's tax treaty network

Treaties in line with the Action 14 Minimum Standard following MLI impact	Treaties where actions are ongoing to make them in line with the Action 14 Minimum Standard	Following impact/actions, remaining treaties that are not in line with Action 14 Minimum Standard
84	44	0

Source: OECD

United Kingdom's MAP programme

Organisation of competent authority function

- 49 persons:
  - three heads of unit
  - 49 persons working on MAP cases (among which 15 persons work on other tasks as well). 38 persons work on attribution/allocation cases and 11 persons work on other cases.
- contact persons for MAP requests:
  - Transfer pricing and permanent establishment: Ahmed Dar, Dev Singh, Shane Booth, Ciaran Macken, MAP mailbox: map.mailbox@hmrc.gov.uk, APA mailbox: apa.mailbox@hmrc.gov.uk
  - Corporate residence, withholding tax and general questions of treaty interpretation: David Price, Email: david.e.price@hmrc.gov.uk
  - Personal tax: Kelly Grisdale, Email: ukmap.individuals@hmrc.gov.uk.

Figure 1. Competent Authority Organisational Structure

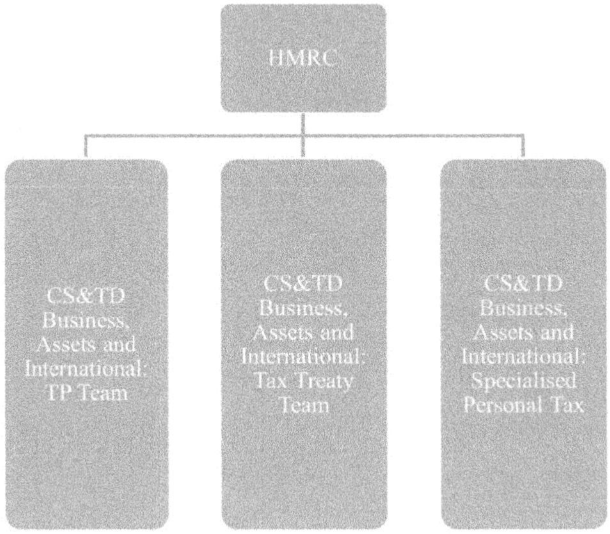

Source: OECD

Table 2. Guidance on the MAP process

MAP guidance	Statement of Practice 1 (2018) – Mutual Agreement Procedure, 20 February 2018	https://www.gov.uk/government/publications/statement-of-practice-1-2018/statement-of-practice-1-2018 (Section "How to make a MAP request" to be referred to for form and content of a MAP request, including information requirements)
	INTM423130, 17 April 2023	https://www.gov.uk/hmrc-internal-manuals/international-manual/intm423130
MAP profile	13 April 2022	https://www.oecd.org/tax/dispute/united-kingdom-dispute-resolution-profile.pdf

Overview of United Kingdom's MAP Statistics for 2022

Please refer to https://www.oecd.org/tax/dispute/map-statistics-united-kingdom.pdf for details with respect to United Kingdom's MAP Statistics.

Figure 2. Cases Closed in 2022

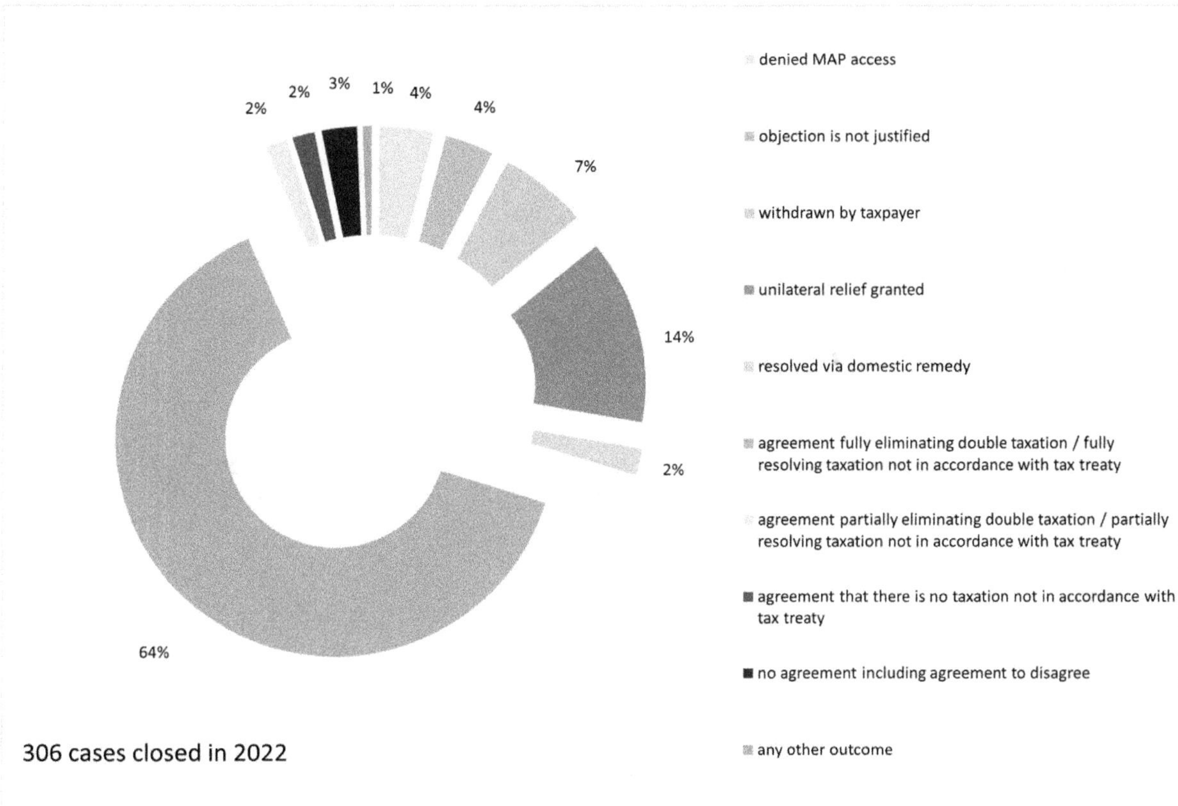

Source: OECD

Figure 3. Evolution of the United Kingdom's MAP caseload (2016-22)

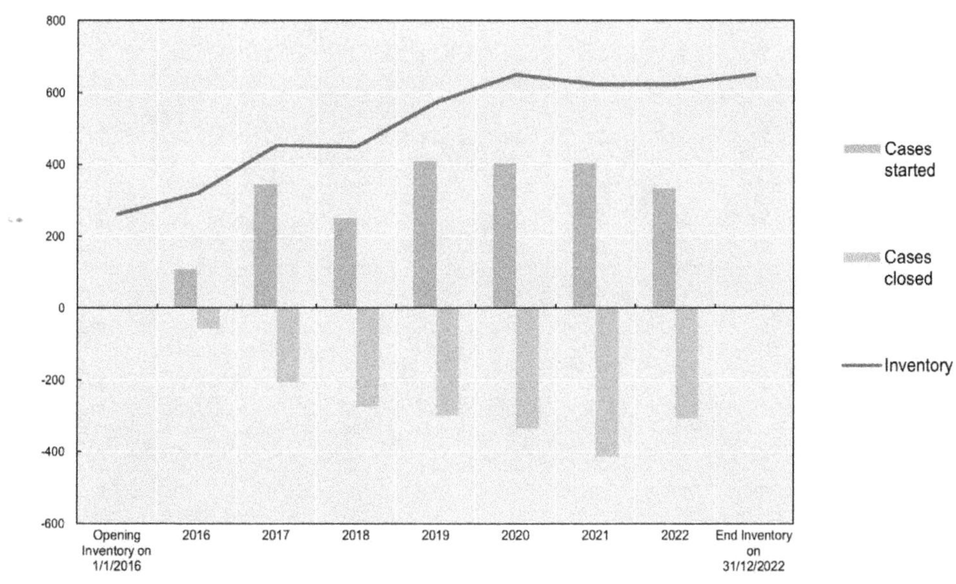

Source: OECD

Table 3. Overview of the United Kingdom's MAP caseload for 2022

Inventory for year 2022	Opening Inventory 1/1/2022	Cases started	Cases Closed	End Inventory 31/12/2022
Attribution/allocation cases	303	120	126	297
Other cases	320	213	180	353
Total	623	333	306	650

Source: OECD

Table 4. United Kingdom's average time to resolve MAP cases in 2022

Cases resolved in year 2022	Pre-2016 cases		Post-2015 cases		All	
	Number of cases	**Average time**	**Number of cases**	**Average time** **Start to End**	**Number of cases**	**Average time**
Attribution / Allocation cases	9	93.22	117	26.96	126	31.69
Other cases	1	100.64	179	11.18	180	11.68
All cases	10	93.96	296	17.42	306	19.92

Source: OECD

United States

Recent developments relating to MAP in United States prior to 15 August 2023

Developments relating to MAP in the tax treaty network

- The United States signed a new treaty with Croatia, and the United States Senate has approved the Chilean treaty for ratification. Neither treaty has entered into force.
- Amending protocols entered into with Japan, Spain, and Switzerland, which incorporate mandatory and binding arbitration provisions to resolve MAP disputes under those treaties, are now in force.

Other developments relating to MAP

- No developments were reported

Latest Action 14 Peer Review report

13 August 2019 - https://doi.org/10.1787/305147e9-en

Tax treaty network of United States

- 62 treaties, applicable to 70 jurisdictions (covering all treaties signed, although not necessarily in force)
- status of MLI: not signed.

Table 1. State of play of United States' tax treaty network

Treaties in line with the Action 14 Minimum Standard following MLI impact	Treaties where actions are ongoing to make them in line with the Action 14 Minimum Standard	Following impact/actions, remaining treaties that are not in line with Action 14 Minimum Standard
35	--	27

Source: OECD

United States' MAP programme

Organisation of competent authority function

- 114 persons:
  - one head of unit, leading four groups
  - 109 persons working on MAP cases:
    - 97 persons work on attribution/allocation MAP/APA cases and 12 persons work on other MAP cases.
- contact persons for MAP requests:

- for attribution / allocation cases: Commissioner, Large Business and International Division, Internal Revenue Service, 1111 Constitution Avenue, N.W., Washington, DC 20224, SE:LB:TTPO:APMA:K (Attention: APMA)
- for other cases: Commissioner, Large Business and International Division, Internal Revenue Service, 1111 Constitution Avenue, N.W., Washington, DC 20224, SE:LB:TTPO:APMA:TAIT:K (Attention: TAIT).

Figure 1. Competent Authority Organisational Structure

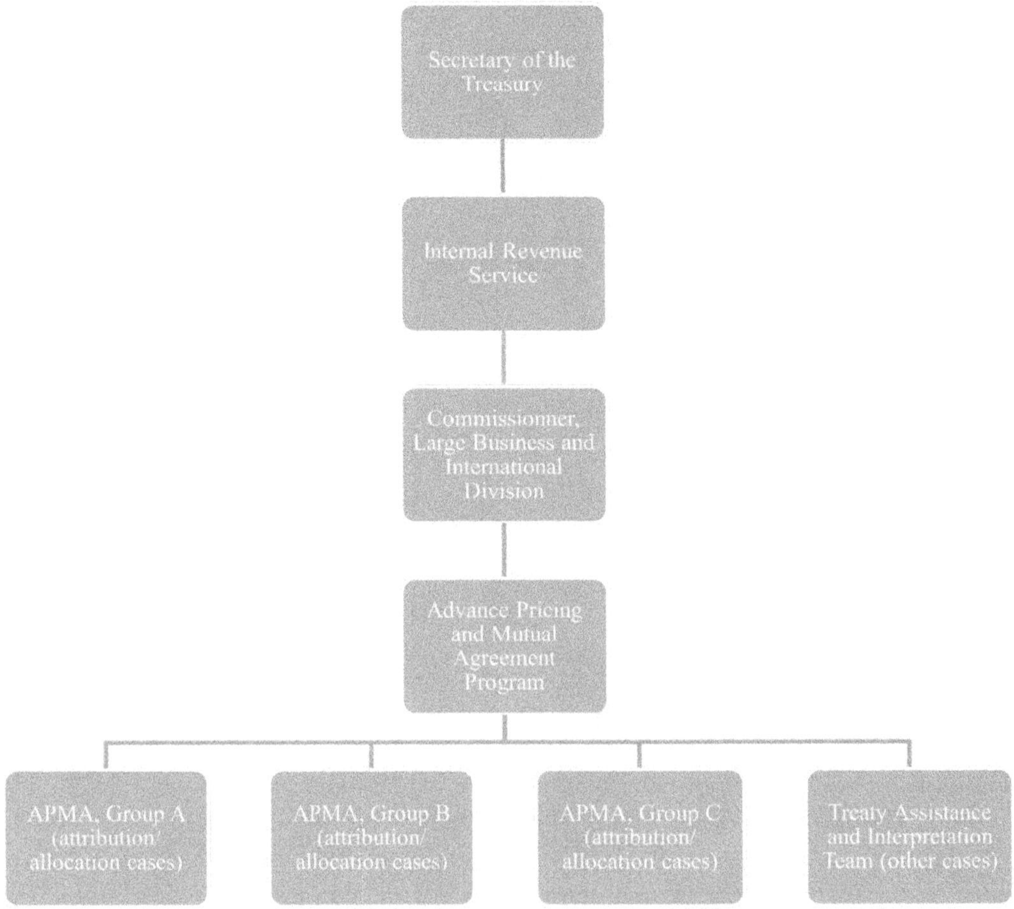

Source: OECD

Table 2. Guidance on the MAP process

MAP guidance	Rev. Proc. 2015-40, section 3 and the Appendix	https://www.irs.gov/pub/irs-drop/rp-15-40.pdf (Section 2 to be referred to for form and content of a MAP request, including information requirements)
	Web page	https://www.irs.gov/businesses/overview-of-the-map-process
MAP profile	14 October 2022	https://www.oecd.org/tax/dispute/united-states-dispute-resolution-profile.pdf

Overview of United States' MAP Statistics for 2022

Please refer to https://www.oecd.org/tax/dispute/map-statistics-united-states.pdf for details with respect to United States' MAP Statistics.

Figure 2. Cases Closed in 2022

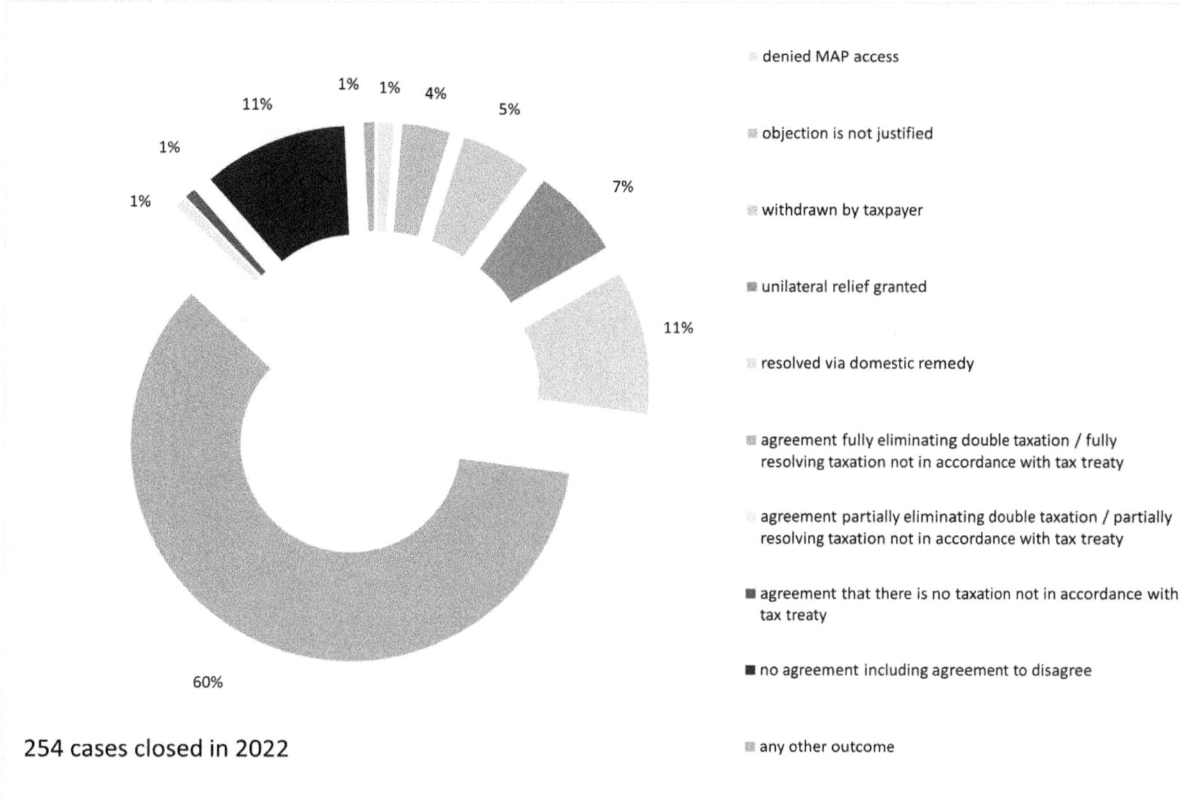

Source: OECD

Figure 3. Evolution of the United States' MAP caseload (2016-22)

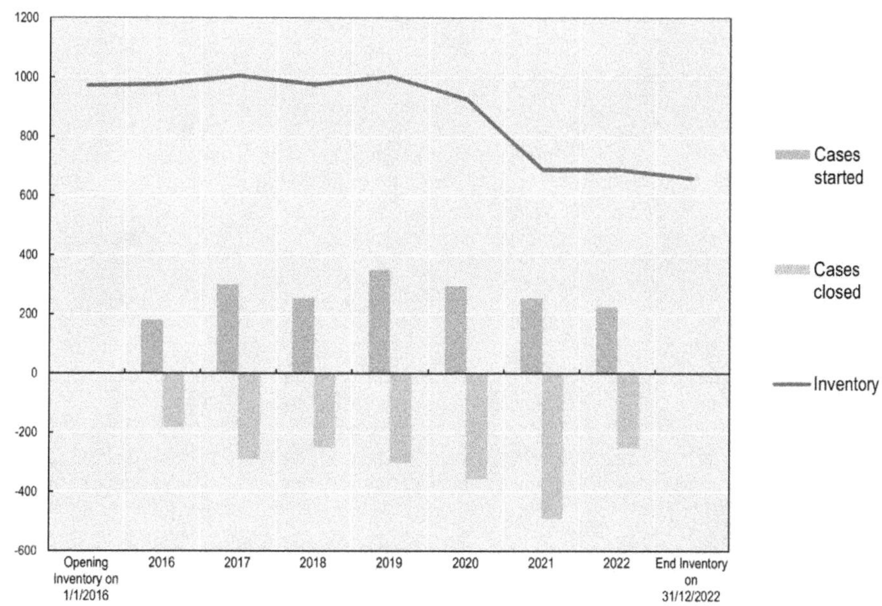

Source: OECD

Table 3. Overview of the United States' MAP caseload for 2022

Inventory for year 2022	Opening Inventory 1/1/2022	Cases started	Cases Closed	End Inventory 31/12/2022
Attribution/allocation cases	424	145	129	440
Other cases	263	80	125	218
Total	687	225	254	658

Source: OECD

Table 4. United States' average time to resolve MAP cases in 2022

Cases resolved in year 2022	Pre-2016 cases		Post-2015 cases		All	
	Number of cases	**Average time**	**Number of cases**	**Average time** **Start to End**	**Number of cases**	**Average time**
Attribution / Allocation cases	23	97.37	106	31.06	129	42.88
Other cases	24	103.55	101	22.31	125	37.91
All cases	47	100.53	207	26.79	254	40.43

Source: OECD

Uruguay

Recent developments relating to MAP in Uruguay prior to 15 August 2023

Developments relating to MAP in the tax treaty network

- No developments were reported

Other developments relating to MAP

- MAP guidance and MAP framework decree are under elaboration.

Latest Action 14 Peer Review report

Uruguay is yet to be peer reviewed under Action 14.

Tax treaty network of Uruguay

- 26 treaties, applicable to 26 jurisdictions (covering all treaties signed, although not necessarily in force)
- status of MLI: in force.

Table 1. State of play of Uruguay's tax treaty network

Treaties in line with the Action 14 Minimum Standard following MLI impact	Treaties where actions are ongoing to make them in line with the Action 14 Minimum Standard	Following impact/actions, remaining treaties that are not in line with Action 14 Minimum Standard
22	0	4

Source: OECD

Uruguay's MAP programme

Organisation of competent authority function

- 11 persons:
  - one head of unit
  - two persons working on MAP cases both of which work on other tasks as well).
- contact persons for MAP requests:
  - Ministerio de Economía y Finanzas- Asesoría Tributaria
  - Tel: +598217122789 | Fax: +598217122710
  - Email address: asesoria.tributaria@mef.gub.uy
  - Office Address: Colonia 1089, Piso 3.

Figure 1. Competent Authority Organisational Structure

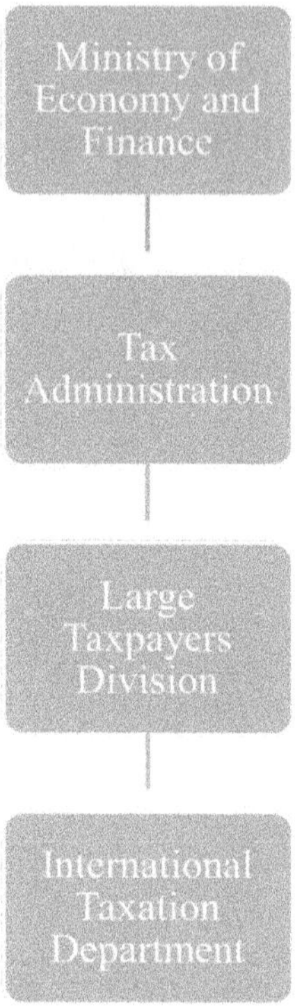

Source: OECD

Table 2. Guidance on the MAP process

MAP guidance	Uruguay did not provide the relevant information.	-
MAP profile	29 December 2016	https://www.oecd.org/tax/dispute/uruguay-dispute-resolution-profile.pdf

Overview of Uruguay's MAP Statistics for 2022

Uruguay did not report any MAP cases in its 2022 MAP Statistics.

Please refer to https://www.oecd.org/tax/dispute/map-statistics-uruguay.pdf for details with respect to Uruguay's MAP Statistics.

Uzbekistan

Recent developments relating to MAP in Uzbekistan prior to 15 August 2023

Developments relating to MAP in the tax treaty network

- Treaty with Qatar signed and ratified in 2023

Other developments relating to MAP

- No developments were reported

Latest Action 14 Peer Review report

- Uzbekistan is yet to be peer reviewed under Action 14

Tax treaty network of Uzbekistan

- 54 treaties, applicable to 54 jurisdictions (covering all treaties signed, although not necessarily in force)
- Status of MLI: not signed

Table 1. State of play of Uzbekistan's tax treaty network

Treaties in line with the Action 14 Minimum Standard following MLI impact	Treaties where actions are ongoing to make them in line with the Action 14 Minimum Standard	Following impact/actions, remaining treaties that are not in line with Action 14 Minimum Standard
42	No information	No information

Source: OECD

Uzbekistan's MAP programme

Organisation of competent authority function

- two persons (both of which work on other tasks as well)
- contact persons for MAP requests:
    - International Tax Relations Division
    - Tax Committee under the Cabinet of Ministers
    - Address: 100011, 13A Abdulla Kadiri str., Shaykhontohur District, Tashkent, Uzbekistan
    - Ms Nafisa Sadullaeva
    - Deputy Head of Division
    - Tel.: +998(71) 244 98 64
    - Email: map.apa.tc@soliq.uz.

Figure 1. Competent Authority Organisational Structure

Source: OECD

Table 2. Guidance on the MAP process

MAP guidance	No MAP guidance published	-
MAP profile	No MAP profile published	-

Source: OECD

Overview of Uzbekistan's MAP Statistics for 2022

Uzbekistan joined the Inclusive Framework after the deadline for reporting 2022 MAP statistics.

Viet Nam

Recent developments relating to MAP in Viet Nam prior to 15 August 2023

Developments relating to MAP in the tax treaty network

- Viet Nam did not provide the relevant information.

Other developments relating to MAP

- Viet Nam did not provide the relevant information.

Latest Action 14 Peer Review report

13 September 2022 - https://doi.org/10.1787/89ec62ed-en

Tax treaty network of Viet Nam

- 78 treaties, applicable to 78 jurisdictions (covering all treaties signed, although not necessarily in force)
- status of MLI: signed.

Table 1. State of play of Viet Nam's tax treaty network

Treaties in line with the Action 14 Minimum Standard following MLI impact	Treaties where actions are ongoing to make them in line with the Action 14 Minimum Standard	Following impact/actions, remaining treaties that are not in line with Action 14 Minimum Standard
60	No information	No information

Source: OECD

Viet Nam's MAP programme

Organisation of competent authority function

- 10 persons:
  - two heads of unit
  - eight persons working on MAP cases.
- contact persons for MAP requests:
  - Mr. CAO ANH TUAN, Competent Authority Director General, General Department of Taxation of Viet Nam, Tel: +84.024.3971.2555 Fax: +84.024.3971.2288. Office address: 123 Lo Duc, Hai Ba Trung, Ha Noi, Viet Nam
  - or Mr. Vu Chi Hung, Competent Authority Director of International Taxation Department General Department of Taxation of Viet Nam, Email: vchung@gdt.gov.vn 2 Tel: (84-24)

3971.2555 Fax: (84-24) 3971.2288. Office address: 123 Lo Duc, Hai Ba Trung, Ha Noi, Viet Nam

- or Ms. TRAN THI THANH BINH International Taxation Department, General Department of Taxation Director, Email: tttbinh@gdt.gov.vn Tel: +84.024.3971.2555 Fax: +84.024.3971.2288.

Figure 1. Competent Authority Organisational Structure

Source: OECD

Table 2. Guidance on the MAP process

MAP guidance	Article 7, Circular 205/2013/TT-BTC, 24 December 2013	https://www.gdt.gov.vn/wps/portal
MAP profile	17 February 2020	https://www.oecd.org/tax/dispute/vietnam-dispute-resolution-profile.pdf

Overview of Viet Nam's MAP Statistics for 2022

Please refer to https://www.oecd.org/tax/dispute/map-statistics-viet-nam.pdf for details with respect to Viet Nam's MAP Statistics.

Figure 2. Cases Closed in 2022

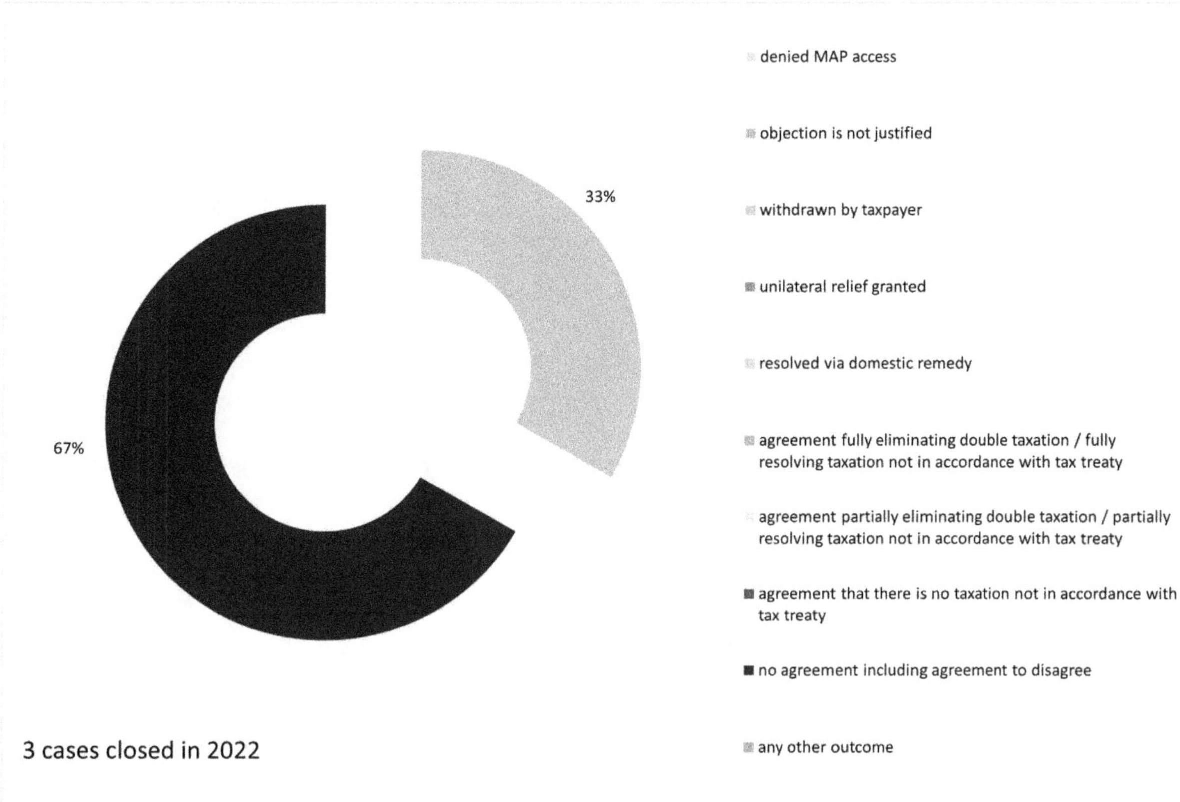

Source: OECD

Figure 3. Evolution of Viet Nam's MAP caseload (2017-22)

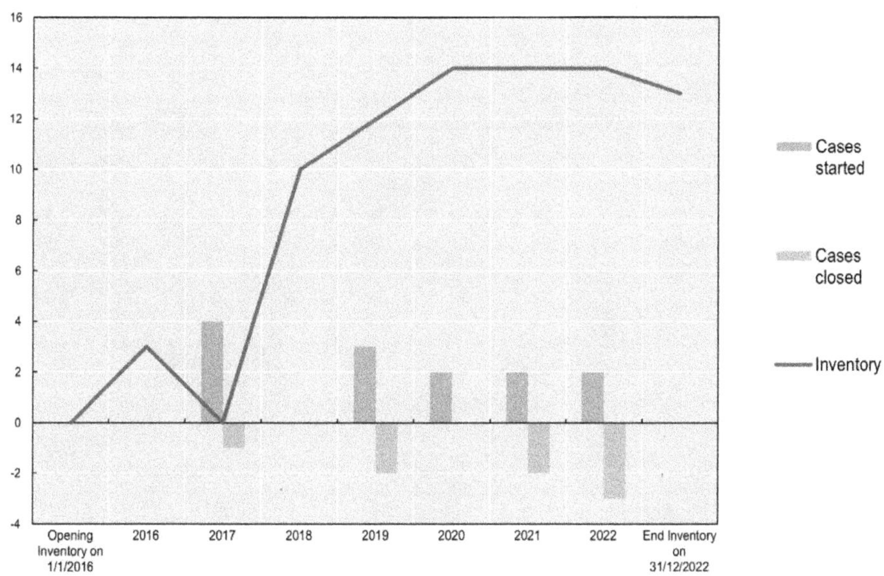

Source: OECD

Table 3. Overview of Viet Nam's MAP caseload for 2022

Inventory for year 2022	Opening Inventory 1/1/2022	Cases started	Cases Closed	End Inventory 31/12/2022
Attribution/allocation cases	10	1	3	8
Other cases	4	1	0	5
Total	14	2	3	13

Source: OECD

Table 4. Viet Nam's average time to resolve MAP cases in 2022

Cases resolved in year 2022	Pre-2016 cases		Post-2015 cases		All	
	Number of cases	**Average time**	**Number of cases**	**Average time** **Start to End**	**Number of cases**	**Average time**
Attribution / Allocation cases	2	73.58	1	28.54	3	58.57
Other cases	0	N/A	0	N/A	0	N/A
All cases	2	73.58	1	28.54	3	58.57

Source: OECD

Zambia

Recent developments relating to MAP in Zambia prior to 15 August 2023

Developments relating to MAP in the tax treaty network

- Zambia did not provide the relevant information.

Other developments relating to MAP

- Zambia did not provide the relevant information.

Latest Action 14 Peer Review report

The stage 1 Simplified Peer Review report of Zambia is expected to be published early 2024.

Tax treaty network of Zambia

- 24 treaties, applicable to 24 jurisdictions (covering all treaties signed, although not necessarily in force)
- status of MLI: not signed.

Table 1. State of play of Zambia's tax treaty network

Treaties in line with the Action 14 Minimum Standard following MLI impact	Treaties where actions are ongoing to make them in line with the Action 14 Minimum Standard	Following impact/actions, remaining treaties that are not in line with Action 14 Minimum Standard
13	No Information	No Information

Source: OECD

Zambia's MAP programme

Organisation of competent authority function

- four persons (all of whom work on other tasks as well)
- contact persons for MAP requests:
  - Competent Authority Mr. Dingani Banda Commissioner-General Zambia Revenue Authority P.O Box 35710 Lusaka, Zambia. Phone: +260211382900 E mail: BANDADI@zra.org.zm
  - Authorised Signatories Mr. Joseph Nonde Commissioner- Direct Taxes Zambia Revenue Authority P.O Box 35710 Lusaka, Zambia. Phone: +260211382908 Email: NONDEJ@zra.org.zm
  - Authorised Contact Persons for Exchange of Information and Mutual Agreement Procedure Mr. Richard Kapasa Director: Design, Monitoring & International Relations Zambia Revenue Authority: P.O Box 35710 Lusaka, Zambia. Phone: +260211382500 Email: KapasaR@zra.org.zm

- Mr. Felix Ntalasha Assistant Director: Policy & Legislation Zambia Revenue Authority P.O Box 35710 Lusaka, Zambia. Phone:+260 211 383038 Email: NtalashF@zra.org.zm.

Figure 1. Competent Authority Organisational Structure

Source: OECD

Table 2. Guidance on the MAP process

MAP guidance	*Mutual Agreement Procedure, Practice Note No. 3/2022*, July 2022	https://www.zra.org.zm/wp-content/uploads/2022/07/Practice-Note-No.-3-of-2022-Mutual-Agreement-Procedure.pdf (Section 5.0 to be referred to for form and content of a MAP request, including information requirements)
MAP profile	6 March 2023	https://www.oecd.org/tax/dispute/zambia-dispute-resolution-profile.pdf

Overview of Zambia's MAP Statistics for 2022

Please refer to https://www.oecd.org/tax/dispute/map-statistics-zambia.pdf for details with respect to Zambia's MAP Statistics.

Cases closed in 2022

No MAP cases were closed by Zambia in 2022.

Figure 3. Evolution of Zambia's MAP caseload (2017-22)

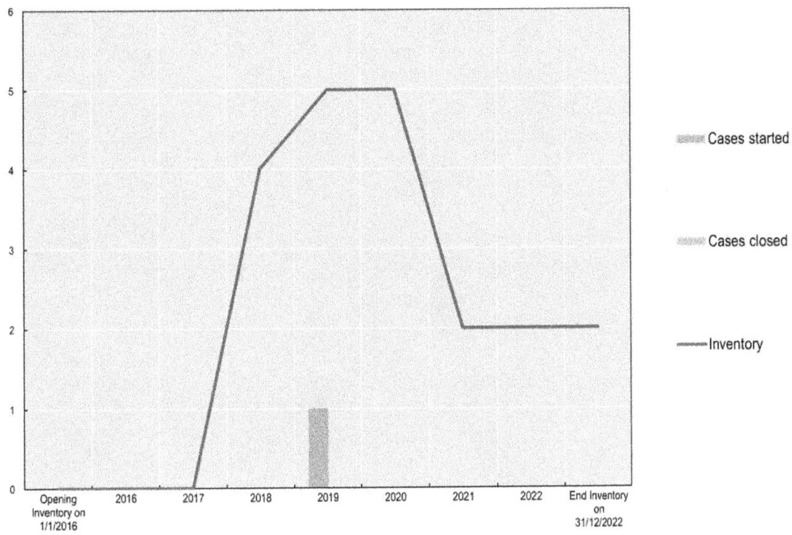

Source: OECD

Table 3. Overview of Zambia's MAP caseload for 2022

Inventory for year 2022	Opening Inventory 1/1/2022	Cases started	Cases Closed	End Inventory 31/12/2022
Attribution/allocation cases	2	0	0	2
Other cases	0	0	0	0
Total	2	0	0	2

Source: OECD

Table 4. Zambia's average time to resolve MAP cases in 2022

Cases resolved in year 2022	Pre-2016 cases		Post-2015 cases		All	
	Number of cases	**Average time**	**Number of cases**	**Average time** **Start to End**	**Number of cases**	**Average time**
Attribution / Allocation cases	0	N/A	0	N/A	0	N/A
Other cases	0	N/A	0	N/A	0	N/A
All cases	0	N/A	0	N/A	0	N/A

Source: OECD

www.ingramcontent.com/pod-product-compliance
Lightning Source LLC
Chambersburg PA
CBHW061153240926
51846CB00006B/1007
9789264641006